EQUALITY ACT 201

Related titles from Law Society Publishing:

Discrimination in Employment
General Editor: Jenny Mulvaney

Drafting Employment Contracts (2nd edn)
Gillian Howard

Employment Law Handbook (4th edn)
Henry Scrope and Daniel Barnett

Employment Tribunals (2nd edn)
Isabel Manley and Elaine Heslop

Titles from Law Society Publishing can be ordered from all good bookshops or direct (telephone 0870 850 1422, email **lawsociety@prolog.uk.com** or visit our online bookshop at **www.lawsociety.org.uk/bookshop**).

EQUALITY ACT 2010

A Guide to the New Law

General Editor: Michael Duggan

The Law Society

ISBN-13: 978-1-85328-759-6

Crown copyright material is reproduced here with the permission of the Controller of HMSO.

Published in 2010 by the Law Society
113 Chancery Lane, London WC2A 1PL

Typeset by Columns Design Ltd, Reading
Printed by Hobbs the Printers Ltd, Totton, Hants

The paper used for the text pages of this book is FSC certified. FSC (the Forest Stewardship Council) is an international network to promote responsible management of the world's forests.

FSC
Mixed Sources
Product group from well-managed
forests and other controlled sources

Cert no. SGS-COC-2482
www.fsc.org
© 1996 Forest Stewardship Council

CONTENTS

ABOUT THE CONTRIBUTORS

The commentary on this Act has been prepared by a specialist employment team at Littleton Chambers that was the 'Chambers Employment Set of 2009'. The authors have contributed individually and collectively to the chapters and are all specialist employment lawyers in their own right. The team, in alphabetical order, consisted of:

- Katherine Apps

- Niran de Silva

- Michael Duggan

- Martin Fodder

- David Reade QC

- Alexander Robson

- Joanne Sefton

- James Wynne

TABLE OF CASES

TABLE OF STATUTES

TABLE OF STATUTORY INSTRUMENTS

TABLE OF EUROPEAN LEGISLATION

ABBREVIATIONS

BIS	Department for Business Innovation & Skills
DDA 1995	Disability Discrimination Act 1995
DDA 2005	Disability Discrimination Act 2005
DTI	Department for Trade and Industry
ECHR	European Convention on Human Rights
ECJ	Court of Justice of the European Communities
ECtHR	European Court of Human Rights
EHRC	Equality and Human Rights Commission
GEO	Government Equalities Office
PSV	public service vehicle
RRA 1976	Race Relations Act 1976
SDA 1975	Sex Discrimination Act 1975
TULR(C)A 1992	Trade Union and Labour Relations (Consolidation) Act 1992

INTRODUCTION

The Equality Act 2010 harmonises the law on discrimination, bringing together the various strands which cover race, sex and disability, pregnancy and maternity, as well as the newer strands that have been developed during the 2000s, partly as a result of European intervention, and which cover age, gender reassignment, religion or belief, sexual orientation and the developments in pregnancy and maternity. The Act also includes a far-reaching public sector positive duty contained in Parts 1 and 11 to both combat socio-economic inequalities and impose a public sector equality duty. These provisions have already proved to be controversial as have some other provisions, in particular, those which impose a duty to publish equal pay information. The Act codifies the voluminous legislation, though it is to be supplemented by Codes of Practice and guidance, including the following:

- Equal Pay Act 1970 (c.41);
- Sex Discrimination Act 1975 (c.65);
- Race Relations Act 1976 (c.74);
- Disability Discrimination Act 1995 (c.50);
- Employment Equality (Religion or Belief) Regulations 2003, SI 2003/1660;
- Employment Equality (Sexual Orientation) Regulations 2003, SI 2003/166;
- Employment Equality (Age) Regulations 2006, SI 2006/1031.

The above legislation had been amended on a number of occasions to codify the concepts, extend its reach and to bring it into line with EU legislation, in particular, the Framework Directive of 2000 – Council Directive 2000/78/EC – as well as a raft of other Directives that have extended the concepts of discrimination. Paragraph 5 of the Explanatory Notes to the Act refers, in particular, to the following EU Directives:

- Council Directive 2000/43/EC implementing the principle of equal treatment between persons irrespective of racial or ethnic origin;
- Council Directive 2000/78/EC establishing a general framework for equal treatment in employment and occupation;
- Council Directive 2004/113/EC implementing the principle of equal treatment between men and women in the access to and supply of goods and services;
- European Parliament and Council Directive 2006/54/EC on the implementation of the principle of equal opportunities and equal treatment of men and

women in matters of employment and occupation (recast). Also relevant in this context is Article 157 of the Treaty on the Functioning of the European Union.

In addition, it is noted that there is a new draft Directive which was published in July 2008 and is under discussion.

The Act has had a long genesis. In February 2005, the Department for Trade and Industry (DTI) set up the Discrimination Law Review to consider creating a clearer and more streamlined discrimination law framework in order to produce better outcomes for those who experienced disadvantage. After the Review had been moved to the Communities and Local Government Department in May 2006, the Women and Equality Unit, on 12 June 2007, published *A Framework for Fairness; Proposals for a Single Equality Bill for Great Britain*. This was concerned with harmonising and modernising the law as well as making it more effective. However, it should be noted that there was a move to tackling disadvantage as much as legal prohibition of discrimination. The third Labour Government established an Equalities Review which reported in February 2007 and which contained an emphasis on the:

> aspirations of the British people: to live in a society that is fair and free, and which provides for each individual to realise his or her potential to the fullest. At root, this is what we should mean by an equal society. (*Fairness and Freedom: The Final Report of the Equalities Review*, Foreword)

It was apparent that a more interventionist approach was being proposed. The Equalities Review was chaired by Trevor Phillips who became Chair of the Commission for Equality and Human Rights, created by the Equality Act 2006. Whilst tensions developed about the direction of the legislation between Mr Phillips, other commissioners and the Joint Committee on Human Rights (see Equality and Human Rights Commission, HL Paper 72/HC 183, 15 March 2010) the cause was taken up by Harriet Harman QC, MP who, amongst other things, became the Minister for Women and the Cabinet Minister for Equality. The Woman and Equalities Unit became the Government Equalities Office and Harriet Harman took over on 12 October 2007. She was assisted by Maria Eagle MP, Minister of State for the Government Equalities Office (GEO) and Vera Baird QC, MP as Solicitor-General. On 26 June 2008, the White Paper on the Bill, *Framework for a Fairer Future – The Equalities Bill*, Cm 7431, was presented to Parliament, in which it was stated that:

> The agenda is for everyone, because fairness is the foundation for individual rights, a society at ease with itself, and a prosperous economy.

This White Paper set out the new equality duty on public bodies as well as prohibiting age discrimination in goods, facilities and services. There was extensive consultation and the Response was presented as Cm 7454. Further reports followed, including the Joint Committee on Human Rights producing the reports *Legislative Scrutiny; Equality Bill*, 2008–09, HL Paper169/HC 736 and *Legislative Scrutiny: Equality Bill (Second Report)*, 2009–10, HL Paper 73/HC 425, and the Delegated Powers and Regulatory Reform Committee reporting on the Bill twice.

The Bill was given its First Reading in the House of Commons on 27 April 2009, Second Reading on 11 May 2009 and was in Committee between 2 June and 7 July 2009. Although one of the aims of the Bill had been consolidation, there were major inconsistencies. Explanatory Notes were produced with the first draft of the Bill, but the notes themselves were not updated as the Bill went through Parliament. The Bill ran out of time and was then reintroduced on 19 November 2009. It went to the House of Lords on 3 December 2009 and had six days in Committee until 25 March 2010. Amendments were finally considered on 6 April 2010 and Royal Assent was given on 8 April, two days after the General Election had been called. The Act now consists of 218 sections and 28 Schedules.

Most of the Act is to come into force by ministerial order but, even during the General Election, it was announced that the Conservative Party would not bring in a number of provisions if it won the election, in particular, the socio-economic duty and the way in which equal pay and positive action is to be tackled. As this book goes to press the Government Equalities Office website states:

> The Government is currently considering how the different provisions will be commenced so that the Act is implemented in an effective and proportionate way. In the meantime, the Government Equalities Office continues to work on the basis of the previously announced timetable, which envisaged commencement of the Act's core provisions in October 2010.

In addition to the Act, there is provision for at least 30 sets of regulations in its 218 sections and more in the Schedules. There is further scope for guidance and Codes of Practice to be produced. At present, s.42 preserves the Codes of Practice that were issued by the separate commissions before the Equality and Human Rights Commission (EHRC) was formed in October 2007, and these will remain in force until revoked, though they only cover race, sex and disability.

The Explanatory Notes were published in April 2010 and consist of 1,026 paragraphs as well as providing a list of *Hansard* references at pp.214–15.

The Explanatory Notes (at para. 13) give a useful summary of the Act, as follows:

Part	Summary
Part 1	Imposes a duty on certain public bodies to have due regard to socio-economic considerations in making strategic decisions.
Part 2 including Schedule 1	Establishes the key concepts on which the Act is based including:
	■ the characteristics which are protected (age, disability, gender reassignment, marriage and civil partnership, pregnancy and maternity, race, religion or belief, sex and sexual orientation);

Part	Summary
	■ the definitions of direct discrimination (including because of a combination of two relevant protected characteristics), discrimination arising from disability, indirect discrimination, harassment and victimisation.
	These key concepts are then applied in the subsequent Parts of the Act.
Part 3 including Schedules 2 and 3	Makes it unlawful to discriminate against, harass or victimise a person when providing a service (which includes the provision of goods or facilities) or when exercising a public function.
Part 4 including Schedules 4 and 5	Makes it unlawful to discriminate against, harass or victimise a person when disposing of (for example, by selling or letting) or managing premises.
Part 5 including Schedules 6, 7, 8 and 9	Makes it unlawful to discriminate against, harass or victimise a person at work or in employment services. Also contains provisions relating to equal pay between men and women; pregnancy and maternity pay; provisions making it unlawful for an employment contract to prevent an employee disclosing his or her pay; and a power to require private sector employers to publish gender pay gap (the size of the difference between men and women's pay expressed as a percentage) information about differences in pay between men and women. It also contains provision restricting the circumstances in which potential employees can be asked questions about disability or health.
Part 6 including Schedules 10, 11, 12, 13 and 14	Makes it unlawful for education bodies to discriminate against, harass or victimise a school pupil or student or applicant for a place.
Part 7 including Schedules 15 and 16	Makes it unlawful for associations (for example, private clubs and political organisations) to discriminate against, harass or victimise members, associates or guests and contains a power to require political parties to publish information about the diversity of their candidates.
Part 8	Prohibits other forms of conduct, including discriminating against or harassing of an ex-employee or ex-pupil, for example: instructing a third party to discriminate against another; or helping someone discriminate against another. Also determines the liability of employers and principals in relation to the conduct of their employees or agents.

Part	Summary
Part 9 including Schedule 17	Deals with enforcement of the Act's provisions, through the civil courts (in relation to services and public functions; premises; education; and associations) and the employment tribunals (in relation to work and related areas, and equal pay).
Part 10	Makes terms in contracts, collective agreements or rules of undertakings unenforceable or void if they result in unlawful discrimination, harassment or victimisation.
Part 11 including Schedules 18 and 19	Establishes a general duty on public authorities to have due regard, when carrying out their functions, to the need: to eliminate unlawful discrimination, harassment or victimisation; to advance equality of opportunity; and to foster good relations. Also contains provisions which enable an employer or service provider or other organisation to take positive action to overcome or minimise a disadvantage arising from people possessing particular protected characteristics.
Part 12 including Schedule 20	Requires taxis, other private hire vehicles, public service vehicles (such as buses) and rail vehicles to be accessible to disabled people and to allow them to travel in reasonable comfort.
Part 13 including Schedule 21	Deals with consent to make reasonable adjustments to premises and improvements to let dwelling houses.
Part 14 including Schedules 22 and 23	Establishes exceptions to the prohibitions in the earlier parts of the Act in relation to a range of conduct, including action required by an enactment; protection of women; educational appointments; national security; the provision of benefits by charities and sporting competitions.
Part 15	Repeals or replaces rules of family property law which discriminated between husbands and wives.
Part 16 including Schedules 24, 25, 26, 27 and 28	Contains a power for a Minister of the Crown to harmonise certain provisions in the Act with changes required to comply with EU obligations. It contains general provisions on application to the Crown, subordinate legislation, interpretation, commencement and extent. It also contains amendments to the Civil Partnership Act 2004 to allow civil partnership registrations to take place on religious premises that are approved for that purpose.

An important point to note about the Act at this stage is that it leaves it to the courts and tribunals to decide when the Act applies in terms of territorial extent and application. This is considered further in the introduction to **Chapter 10** (Part 9 – Enforcement). It does, however, contain:

> a power to specify territorial application of Part 5 in relation to ships and hovercraft (section 81) and offshore work (section 82). In relation to the non-work provisions, the Act is again generally silent on territorial application, leaving it to the courts to determine whether the law applies. However, in a limited number of specific cases, express provision is made for particular provisions of the Act to apply (or potentially apply) outside the United Kingdom. Thus, section 29(9) provides for the prohibitions in respect of the provision of services or the exercise of public functions to apply in relation to race and religion or belief to the granting of entry clearance, even where the act in question takes place outside the United Kingdom. Also, section 30 contains a similar power to that in Part 5 to specify the territorial application of the services provisions of Part 3 in relation to ships and hovercraft. (Explanatory Notes, para. 15)

There are also detailed provisions as to the application of the Act to Scotland and Wales, which are set out in the commentary below, but the Act does not form part of the law of Northern Ireland with a few exceptions, though s.82 permits an Order in Council to apply it in the case of persons in offshore work, and the provisions of s.105 amend the Sex Discrimination (Election Candidates) Act 2002 with the effect that the extension of the expiry date for women-only shortlists will apply in Northern Ireland as well as Great Britain.

1 PARTS 1 AND 11

1.1 PART 1 – SOCIO-ECONOMIC INEQUALITIES

The 'fairness agenda', as set out in the White Paper, *Framework for a Fairer Future – The Equalities Bill*, is put at the forefront of the Act, with s.1 creating a new and general obligation on public authorities to consider inequalities of outcome that may result from 'socio-economic' disadvantage when making strategic decisions.

Section 1(1) of the Act provides that an authority to which the section applies:

> must, when making decisions of a strategic nature about how to exercise its functions, have due regard to the desirability of exercising them in a way that is designed to reduce the inequalities of outcome which result from socio-economic disadvantage.

The authority must decide how to carry out its functions in accordance with any guidance issued by a Minister of the Crown (s.1(2)).

The central duty therefore arises in relation to 'decisions of a strategic nature'. Section 1 was expected to come into force in 2011, but the change in government may mean that this will be postponed indefinitely as the Conservative Party has made it clear that it is opposed to the provision.

The duty is to have due regard to the desirability of exercising functions in a way which is designed to reduce the 'inequalities of outcome' resulting from socio-economic disadvantage. Section 1(6) provides that the reference to 'inequalities' in s.1(1) does not include those arising from being subject to immigration control within the meaning of s.115(9) of the Immigration and Asylum Act 1999. 'Due regard' is likely to have the meaning in *R (on the application of Baker)* v. *Secretary of State for Communities and Local Government* [2008] EWCA Civ 141, [2009] PTSR 809 as being the 'regard that is appropriate in all the circumstances' which will involve a balancing act between the effect of the disadvantage on the affected group and the factors relevant to the authority's functions, including financial constraints.

Section 1(3) lists 11 authorities to which the duty will apply (some of the descriptions are of a generic nature):

    (a) a Minister of the Crown;
    (b) a government department other than the Security Service, the Secret Intelligence Service or the Government Communications Headquarters;

(c)   a county council or district council in England;

(d)   the Greater London Authority;

(e)   a London borough council;

(f)   the Common Council of the City of London in its capacity as a local authority;

(g)   the Council of the Isles of Scilly;

(h)   a Strategic Health Authority established under section 13 of the National Health Service Act 2006, or continued in existence by virtue of that section;

(i)   a Primary Care Trust established under section 18 of that Act, or continued in existence by virtue of that section;

(j)   a regional development agency established by the Regional Development Agencies Act 1998;

(k)   a police authority established for an area in England.

Section 1 may be amended to add or remove a public authority, to make the duty apply only to certain functions of the public authority or to remove or alter such restrictions which may already apply (s.2(1)). In order to make clear that these amendment powers only apply to public functions, s.2(2) provides that a public authority is an authority that exercises functions of a public nature. However, a duty cannot be imposed in respect of any devolved Scottish or Welsh functions. Instead, the Scottish or Welsh Ministers may carry out the functions as set out in s.2(1) (s.2(3) and (4)). These powers may only be exercisable in relation to functions wholly exercisable in Scotland or Wales or wholly or mainly devolved and which correspond to the authorities set out in s.2(3) (s.2(5) and (6)). The Scottish or Welsh Ministers must consult a Minister of the Crown (s.2(7)). There is further power to make amendments to s.1 that appear necessary or expedient in consequence of any provision made under s.2(2) and to confer a power on Scottish or Welsh Ministers to issue guidance (s.2(8)–(10)).

Section 2(11) provides that a Scottish and Welsh function is a devolved function if it is exercisable as regards Scotland and does not relate to reserved matters within the meaning of the Scotland Act 1998 or it is a matter in respect of which functions are exercisable by the Welsh Ministers, the First Minister for Wales or the Counsel General to the Welsh Assembly Government or to a matter within the legislative competence of the National Assembly of Wales.

Section 3 provides that the duty under s.1 does *not* confer a cause of action at private law, so, for example, there is no power to bring a claim if an individual considers himself entitled to a flat in a new social housing development, ahead of other people whom he regards as less disadvantaged (Explanatory Notes, para. 33).

Part 1 is new. The Explanatory Notes give some examples of the application of s.1 at para. 27:

■   The Department of Health decides to improve the provision of primary care services. They find evidence that people suffering socio-economic disadvantage are less likely to access such services during working hours, due to their conditions of employment. The Department therefore advises that such services should be available at other times of the day.

■   Under the duty, a Regional Development Agency (RDA), when reviewing its funding programmes, could decide to amend the selection criteria for a programme designed to promote business development, to encourage more successful bids from deprived areas. The same RDA could also decide to continue a programme aimed at generating more jobs in the IT sector which, despite not contributing to a reduction in socio-economic inequalities, has wider economic benefits in attracting more well-paid jobs to the region. This decision would comply with the duty, because the RDA would have given due consideration to reducing socio-economic inequalities.

- The duty could lead a local education authority, when conducting a strategic review of its school applications process, to analyse the impact of its campaign to inform parents about the applications process, looking particularly at different neighbourhoods. If the results suggest that parents in more deprived areas are less likely to access or make use of the information provided, the authority could decide to carry out additional work in those neighbourhoods in future campaigns, to ensure that children from deprived areas have a better chance of securing a place at their school of choice.

1.2   PART 11 – ADVANCEMENT OF EQUALITY

Part 11 of the Act consists of two Chapters. Chapter 1 relates to the public sector equality duty whilst Chapter 2 relates to positive action. The Act continues the public sector duties that already existed in relation to race, disability and gender, but also extends them to cover age, sexual orientation, religion or belief, making it clear that pregnancy and maternity are also within the scope of the duty. In response to consultation the government noted that many authorities were adopting an integrated approach. It considered that the new Part would provide significant rationalisation as well as promoting more diverse public services to meet diverse needs better and place the achievement of equality outcomes at the heart of public services.

The existing legislation set out the duties on public authorities in different ways: the Race Relations Act 1976 contained a list whilst the Sex Discrimination Act 1975 and Disability Discrimination Act 1995 applied a general duty. Section 149 of the Act combines both approaches, so that there is a general duty underpinned by specific duties which, by s.153, will be set out in secondary legislation. There is also provision for Ministers to impose specific duties as set out below. Draft regulations are, supposedly, to be published in autumn 2010 and the government was proposing to publish, in due course, a duty to publish annual details of pay by reference to gender for public bodies with over 150 employees, ethnic minority employment rates and disability employment rates.

1.2.1   Public sector equality duty (section 149)

By s.149(1), a public authority must, in the exercise of its functions, have due regard to the need to:

(a)   eliminate discrimination, harassment, victimisation and any other conduct that is prohibited by or under this Act;
(b)   advance equality of opportunity between persons who share a relevant protected characteristic and persons who do not share it;
(c)   foster good relations between persons who share a relevant protected characteristic and persons who do not share it.

This duty involves having due regard, in particular, to the need to tackle prejudice and promote understanding (s.149(5)).

The duty also applies to a person who is not a public authority but who exercises public functions (s.149(2)).

By s.149(3), the duty to have due regard to the need to advance equality of opportunity between those persons who share a relevant protected characteristic and those persons who do not share it involves having due regard, in particular, to the need to:

(a)   remove or minimise disadvantages suffered by persons who share a relevant protected characteristic that are connected to that characteristic;
(b)   take steps to meet the needs of persons who share a relevant protected characteristic that are different from the needs of persons who do not share it;
(c)   encourage persons who share a relevant protected characteristic to participate in public life or in any other activity in which participation by such persons is disproportionately low.

Where the steps involved in meeting the needs of disabled persons are different, the public sector duty will involve, in particular, steps to take account of a person's disabilities (s.149(4)).

Compliance with the duties under s.149 may involve treating some persons more favourably, but s.149(6) makes it clear that this does not permit conduct which would otherwise be prohibited by the Act.

Section 149(7) confirms that the characteristics to which the section applies are age, disability, gender reassignment, pregnancy and maternity, race, religion or belief, sex and sexual orientation and the conduct that is prohibited, by s.149(8), includes a reference to a breach of an equality clause or rule and a breach of a non-discrimination rule.

There is a wide range of exceptions in Sched. 18 to the Act concerning children, immigration, judicial functions and a list of bodies which are not public authorities, but carry out public functions.

1.2.2   Schedule 18 – Public sector equality duty: exceptions

Children

In accordance with Sched. 18, para. 1, s.149, so far as it relates to *age*, does not apply to the exercise of functions relating to:

(a)   the provision of education to pupils in schools;
(b)   the provision of benefits, facilities or services to pupils in schools;

(c) the provision of accommodation, benefits, facilities or services in community homes pursuant to section 53(1) of the Children Act 1989;

(d) the provision of accommodation, benefits, facilities or services pursuant to arrangements under section 82(5) of that Act (arrangements by the Secretary of State relating to the accommodation of children);

(e) the provision of accommodation, benefits, facilities or services in residential establishments pursuant to section 26(1)(b) of the Children (Scotland) Act 1995.

Immigration

By Sched. 18, para. 2, s.149(1)(b) does not apply to the exercise of immigration and nationality functions in relation to the protected characteristics of age, race or religion or belief, but for that purpose 'race' means race so far as relating to nationality, or ethnic or national origins. Paragraph 2(2) sets out that immigration and nationality functions are those exercisable by virtue of:

(a) the Immigration Acts (excluding sections 28A to 28K of the Immigration Act 1971 so far as they relate to criminal offences),

(b) the British Nationality Act 1981,

(c) the British Nationality (Falkland Islands) Act 1983,

(d) the British Nationality (Hong Kong) Act 1990,

(e) the Hong Kong (War Wives and Widows) Act 1996,

(f) the British Nationality (Hong Kong) Act 1997,

(g) the Special Immigration Appeals Commission Act 1997, or

(h) a provision made under section 2(2) of the European Communities Act 1972, or of Community law, which relates to the subject matter of an enactment within paragraphs (a) to (g).

Judicial functions

Section 149 does not apply to the exercise of a judicial function or a function exercised on behalf of, or on the instructions of, a person exercising a judicial function (Sched. 18, para. 3). This includes functions conferred on a person other than a court or tribunal.

Section 149(2) exceptions

There are many bodies that are not regarded as a public authority, but which do, from time to time, perform public functions. Schedule 18, para. 4 contains a list of specific bodies and of specific functions that are excluded. Paragraph 4(2) excludes the following nine bodies:

(a) the House of Commons;

(b) the House of Lords;

(c) the Scottish Parliament;

(d) the National Assembly for Wales;

(e) the General Synod of the Church of England;

(f) the Security Service;

(g) the Secret Intelligence Service;

(h) the Government Communications Headquarters;

(i) a part of the armed forces which is, in accordance with a requirement of the Secretary of State, assisting the Government Communications Headquarters.

Paragraph 4(3) excludes the following functions:

(a) a function in connection with proceedings in the House of Commons or the House of Lords;

(b) a function in connection with proceedings in the Scottish Parliament (other than a function of the Scottish Parliamentary Corporate Body);

(c) a function in connection with proceedings in the National Assembly for Wales (other than a function of the Assembly Commission).

Paragraph 5 gives sweeping powers to a Minister of the Crown to add, vary or omit exceptions save in relation to judicial functions or to omit the exceptions under para. 4(2)(a)–(e) and the functions under para. 4(3) or to amend para. 5 itself to reduce the extent to which the exceptions apply.

The Explanatory Notes, at para. 492, give a number of examples of the operation of s.149:

■ The duty could lead a police authority to review its recruitment procedures to ensure they do not unintentionally deter applicants from ethnic minorities, with the aim of eliminating unlawful discrimination.

■ The duty could lead a local authority to target training and mentoring schemes at disabled people to enable them to stand as local councillors, with the aim of advancing equality of opportunity for different groups of people who have the same disability, and in particular encouraging their participation in public life.

■ The duty could lead a local authority to provide funding for a black women's refuge for victims of domestic violence, with the aim of advancing equality of opportunity for women, and in particular meeting the different needs of women from different racial groups.

■ The duty could lead a large government department, in its capacity as an employer, to provide staff with education and guidance, with the aim of fostering good relations between its transsexual staff and its non-transsexual staff.

■ The duty could lead a local authority to review its use of internet-only access to council services; or focus 'Introduction to Information Technology' adult learning courses on older people, with the aim of advancing equality of opportunity, in particular meeting different needs, for older people

■ The duty could lead a school to review its anti-bullying strategy to ensure that it addresses the issue of homophobic bullying, with the aim of fostering good relations, and in particular tackling prejudice against gay and lesbian people

■ The duty could lead a local authority to introduce measures to facilitate understanding and conciliation between Sunni and Shi'a Muslims living in a particular area, with the aim of fostering good relations between people of different religious beliefs.

1.2.3   Definitions of public authorities and duties (sections 150–152)

Sections 150–152 and Sched. 19 contain detailed definitions of public authorities, as well as powers under ss.153–155 to impose specific duties.

A public authority is a person who is specified in Sched. 19 (see s.150(1)). Section 150(2) provides that:

Part 1 specifies public authorities generally;
Part 2 specifies relevant Welsh authorities;
Part 3 specifies relevant Scottish authorities.

By s.150(3), a public authority specified in Sched. 19 is subject to the duty in s.149(1) in relation to all of the functions unless s.150(4) applies, whereby if a public authority specified in that Schedule relates to certain specified functions, it is only under a duty in respect of those functions.

Section 150(5) also provides that a public function is a function of a public nature for the purposes of the Human Rights Act 1998.

Schedule 19 contains the list of public authorities, relevant Welsh authorities and relevant Scottish authorities and the Schedule should be referred to for the complete list. Section 157, Interpretation, contains general definitions of a relevant Welsh authority and a relevant Scottish authority. A relevant Welsh authority is a person, other than the Assembly Commission, whose functions are exercisable only in or as regards Wales and are wholly or mainly devolved Welsh functions (s.157(2)) whilst a cross-border Welsh authority is a person other than a Welsh authority or the Assembly Commission who has any function that is exercisable in or as regards Wales and is a devolved Welsh function (s.157(3)). The definition of a Scottish authority differs. A relevant Scottish authority is a public body, public office or holder of a public office who is not a cross-border Scottish authority or the Scottish Parliamentary Corporate body, who has functions that are exercisable in or as regards Scotland and at least some of whose functions do not relate to reserved matters (s.157(6)). A cross-border Scottish authority is a cross-border authority defined in s.88(5) of the Scotland Act 1998 whilst a function is a devolved Scottish function if it is exercisable only in or as regards Scotland and does not relate to reserved matters (s.157(7)–(8)).

Section 151(1) contains powers to amend Sched. 19. A Minister of the Crown may amend the whole of Sched. 19 whilst a Welsh Minister may amend Part 2 and a Scottish Minister may amend Part 3. These powers may not be exercised so as to add an entry in Part 1 which relates to a cross-border authority or a Scottish or Welsh authority and an entry may not be made to Part 2 relating to a person who is not a Welsh authority or Part 3 relating to a person who is not a Scottish authority, though a Minister of the Crown may amend Sched. 19 so as to make provision relating to a cross-border Welsh or Scottish authority (s.151(4)–(5)). Section 151(6) provides that on the first exercise of the power to add an entry relating to a cross-border Welsh or Scottish authority, the Minister must add a Part 4 to the Schedule for cross-border authorities and add the cross-border Welsh or Scottish authority to that Part.

Under s.152, before making an order under s.151(1) and (5), the Minister of the Crown must consult before making an order as follows:

Provision	Consultees
Section 151(1)	The Commission
Section 151(1), so far as relating to a relevant Welsh authority	The Welsh Ministers
Section 151(1), so far as relating to a relevant Scottish authority	The Scottish Ministers
Section 151(5)	The Commission
Section 151(5), so far as relating to a cross-border Welsh authority	The Welsh Ministers
Section 151(5), so far as relating to a cross-border Scottish authority	The Scottish Ministers

Before the Welsh or Scottish Ministers may amend Part 2 or 3, they must obtain the consent of a Minister of the Crown and consult with the Commission (s.152(2)–(3)).

A Minister of the Crown has the power to impose specific duties on a public authority specified in Part 1 of Sched. 19 for the purpose of enabling the better performance of the duties under s.149, whilst the Welsh Ministers may impose duties on the authorities under Part 2 and the Scottish Ministers on the authorities under Part 3. These duties may be imposed by regulations but, before making such regulations, the person making them must consult the Commission (s.153). Where an entry is added by a Minister of the Crown under the power contained in s.151(5), the Minister must include, in the new Part 4, after the entry, a provision specifying the party which is to make regulations that impose specific duties and the procedural requirements (s.154). The entry will include the letter in the table below, in order to make it clear which person is to make the regulations and which procedure applies (s.154(1). The person making the regulations must consult with the Commission (s.154(4)). Section 154(3) sets out who may make the regulations and the procedural requirements in a table as follows:

Letter	Person by whom regulations may be made and procedural requirements
A	Regulations may be made by a Minister of the Crown in relation to the authority's functions that are not devolved Welsh functions.
	The Minister of the Crown must consult the Welsh Ministers before making the regulations.
	Regulations may be made by the Welsh Ministers in relation to the authority's devolved Welsh functions.
	The Welsh Ministers must consult a Minister of the Crown before making the regulations.
B	Regulations may be made by a Minister of the Crown in relation to the authority's functions that are not devolved Scottish functions.
	The Minister of the Crown must consult the Scottish Ministers before making the regulations.
	Regulations may be made by the Scottish Ministers in relation to the authority's devolved Scottish functions.
	The Scottish Ministers must consult a Minister of the Crown before making the regulations.
C	Regulations may be made by a Minister of the Crown in relation to the authority's functions that are neither devolved Welsh functions nor devolved Scottish functions.
	The Minister of the Crown must consult the Welsh Ministers and the Scottish Ministers before making the regulations.
	Regulations may be made by the Welsh Ministers in relation to the authority's devolved Welsh functions.
	The Welsh Ministers must consult a Minister of the Crown before making the regulations.
	Regulations may be made by the Scottish Ministers in relation to the authority's devolved Scottish functions.
	The Scottish Ministers must consult a Minister of the Crown before making the regulations.
D	The regulations may be made by a Minister of the Crown.
	The Minister of the Crown must consult the Welsh Ministers before making the regulations.

Section 156 makes it clear that a failure in respect of performance of a duty imposed by or under the above provisions does not confer a cause of action at private law (s.156).

1.2.4   Part 11, Chapter 2 – Positive action

Sections 158 and 159 of the Act contain general provisions which permit 'a person' to take positive action. Section 158(1) provides that the provisions for positive action come into play where a person reasonably believes that:

(a)   persons who share a protected characteristic suffer a disadvantage connected to the characteristic,
(b)   persons who share a protected characteristic have needs that are different from the needs of persons who do not share it, or
(c)   participation in an activity by persons who share a protected characteristic is disproportionately low.

Where any of the above situations pertain, s.158(2) provides that the person is not prohibited from taking action which is a proportionate means of achieving the aim of:

(a)   enabling or encouraging persons who share the protected characteristic to overcome or minimise that disadvantage,
(b)   meeting those needs, or
(c)   enabling or encouraging persons who share the protected characteristic to participate in that activity.

This is a general description of the aims of such action. Regulations may further specify action, or descriptions of action, to which the provisions of s.158(2) *do not apply* (s.158(3)). Moreover, the section does not apply to the provisions in relation to recruitment that are contained in s.159(3) or to action that is permitted under s.104 (which deals with selection of political candidates).

Section 158(6) makes it clear that the section does not permit the person to do anything that is prohibited by or under an enactment other than the Equality Act 2010.

Paragraph 525 of the Explanatory Notes gives two examples of the operation of s.158:

■   Having identified that its white male pupils are underperforming at maths, a school could run supplementary maths classes exclusively for them.
■   An NHS Primary Care Trust identifies that lesbians are less likely to be aware that they are at risk of cervical cancer and less likely to access health services such as national screening programmes. It is also aware that those who do not have children do not know that they are at an increased risk of breast cancer. Knowing this it could decide to establish local awareness campaigns for lesbians on the importance of cancer screening.

Section 159 contains provisions relating to positive action in relation to recruitment and promotion. The provisions apply where the person reasonably thinks that:

(a)   persons who share a protected characteristic suffer a disadvantage connected to the characteristic, or
(b)   participation in an activity by persons who share a protected characteristic is disproportionately low.

In such circumstances, Part 5 of the Act does not prohibit the person from treating a person (A) more favourably in connection with recruitment or promotion than another person (B) because A has the protected characteristic but B does not, where the aim of that more favourable treatment is to enable or encourage persons who share the protected characteristic to overcome or minimise that disadvantage or participate in that activity (s.159(2)–(3)).

The permitted positive action under s.159(2) only applies if A is as qualified as B to be recruited or promoted, the person does not have a policy of treating persons who share the protected characteristic more favourably in connection with recruitment or promotion than persons who do not share it, and taking the action in question is a proportionate means of achieving the aim referred to in s.159(2).

Section 159(5) provides a detailed definition of recruitment, which means a process for deciding whether to:

(a) offer employment to a person,
(b) make contract work available to a contract worker,
(c) offer a person a position as a partner in a firm or proposed firm,
(d) offer a person a position as a member of an LLP or proposed LLP,
(e) offer a person a pupillage or tenancy in barristers' chambers,
(f) take a person as an advocate's devil or offer a person membership of an advocate's stable,
(g) offer a person an appointment to a personal office,
(h) offer a person an appointment to a public office, recommend a person for such an appointment or approve a person's appointment to a public office, or
(i) offer a person a service for finding employment.

Section 159(6) makes it clear that the section does not permit the person to do anything that is prohibited by or under an enactment other than the Equality Act 2010.

The Explanatory Notes include examples of the operation of s.159, as follows:

■ A police service which employs disproportionately low numbers of people from an ethnic minority background identifies a number of candidates who are as qualified as each other for recruitment to a post, including a candidate from an under-represented ethnic minority background. It would not be unlawful to give preferential treatment to that candidate, provided the comparative merits of other candidates were also taken into consideration.

■ An employer offers a job to a woman on the basis that women are under-represented in the company's workforce when there was a male candidate who was more qualified. This would be unlawful direct discrimination. (para. 529)

2 PART 2, CHAPTER 1 – PROTECTED CHARACTERISTICS

2.1 PART 2 – EQUALITY: KEY CONCEPTS

Part 2 of the Act is divided into two Chapters:

- Chapter 1 sets out the protected characteristics. These are essentially the same as in previous discrimination statutes.
- Chapter 2 sets out the definitions of the prohibited types of discrimination. This introduces some new concepts, for example, 'dual discrimination' and 'discrimination arising from disability'.

Key aims of the Equality Act 2010 are to 'harmonise' these concepts across the various areas of existing discrimination law and to strengthen the law to support progress on equality (see Explanatory Notes, para. 10).

2.2 PROTECTED CHARACTERISTICS (SECTION 4)

The protected characteristics are listed in s.4 of the Act. The following characteristics are 'protected':

(a) age;
(b) disability;
(c) gender reassignment;
(d) marriage and civil partnership;
(e) pregnancy and maternity;
(f) race;
(g) religion or belief;
(h) sex;
(i) sexual orientation.

These characteristics are then further defined in ss.5–12. It is to be noted that the government rejected calls for characteristics such as genetic predisposition or Welsh speaking to be included.

2.3   AGE (SECTION 5)

The Framework Directive, Council Directive 2000/78/EC, does not contain any definition of 'age' or 'age group'. The concept of 'age group' in the Act is the same as that contained in the Employment Equality (Age) Regulations 2006 (the 'Age Regulations'), reg.3.

The definition of 'age group' in s.5(2) of the Act is identical to that in reg.3(1)(a) of the Age Regulations. Paragraph 36 of the Explanatory Notes also states that: 'An age group includes people of the same age and people of a particular range of ages. Where people fall in the same age group they share the protected characteristic of age'.

The Age Regulations contained no equivalent provision to s.5(1) of the Act which now separates out:

- a person's age; and
- 'persons who share a protected characteristic' who are defined as 'persons of the same age group'.

Regulation 3(3)(b) of the Age Regulations expressly specified that age included apparent age. This is not now specified but would, no doubt, be implied. The issue of age group banding has been a significant source of litigation in the sex discrimination and equal pay fields (see, for example, *Rutherford* v. *Secretary of State for Trade and Industry (No. 2)* [2006] UKHL 19, [2006] IRLR 553). It is likely that a similar line of case law will eventually develop for age discrimination.

This issue is potentially of greatest practical importance in cases where there are allegations of indirect discrimination, especially, for example, in the operation of a redundancy selection policy or where an employer is proposing alterations to an occupational pension scheme. If the claimant does not identify the relevant 'age group' for himself or herself, it is likely that the tribunal will select it by its own motion (see, for example, *Chief Constable of West Yorkshire Police and West Yorkshire Police Authority* v. *Homer* [2009] IRLR 262 [21], EAT; [2010] EWCA Civ 419; [2010] IRLR 619, CA). This may have a significant impact on whether the tribunal finds that the claimant's age group has been put at a substantial disadvantage.

2.4   DISABILITY (SECTION 6)

The definition of disability in s.6 of and Sched. 1 to the Equality Act 2010 is broadly similar to ss.1 and 2 of the Disability Discrimination Act 1995 (DDA 1995) and Sched. 1 to that Act.

The central formula remains (s.6(1)):

    (a)   P [a person] has a physical or mental impairment, and
    (b)   the impairment has a substantial and long-term adverse effect on P's ability to carry out normal day-to-day activities.

The Equality Act 2010 also protects those who have had a disability in the past (s.6(4)) except under Part 12 (Disabled persons: Transport) and s.190 (Improvements to let dwelling houses).

The DDA 1995 had been subject to much case law which defined the correct comparators for disability discrimination cases culminating in *Lewisham London Borough Council* v. *Malcolm* [2008] UKHL 43, [2008] 1 AC 1399. As noted at **13.4**, the Equality Act 2010 reverses the effect of the House of Lords' judgment in *Lewisham London Borough Council* v. *Malcolm*.

Section 6(3)(b) contains a further clarification of comparators: 'a reference to persons who share a protected characteristic is a reference to persons who have the same disability'. A similar provision did not exist under the DDA 1995.

The Framework Directive does not contain any definition of disability. In *Chacon Navas* v. *Eurest Colectividades SA* Case C–13/05 [2006] IRLR 706, the ECJ considered that:

(a) the European concept of disability was 'a limitation which results in particular from physical, mental or psychological impairments and which hinders the participation of the person concerned in professional life' (para. 43). The focus was on professional life rather than normal day-to-day activities.
(b) The ECJ held that there is a distinction within the Framework Directive between disability and sickness (paras. 44 and 46).
(c) 'it envisaged situations in which participation in professional life is hindered over a long period of time. In order for the limitation to fall within the concept of "disability", it must therefore be probable that it will last for a long time' (para. 45).

In *Coleman* v. *Attridge Law and Steve Law* Case C–303/06 [2008] IRLR 722, [2008] ICR 1128, the ECJ held that, for the purposes of the prohibition on direct discrimination and harassment, 'disability' in the Framework Directive did not only include protecting those who were themselves disabled. The Equality Act 2010 deals with this by a widened definition of discrimination, which is intended to include associative discrimination, see **3.2.1**.

2.5 GENDER REASSIGNMENT (SECTION 7)

Section 7 of the Equality Act 2010 on gender reassignment is broadly based on s.2A of the Sex Discrimination Act 1975 (SDA 1975) which was inserted in SDA 1975 in 2005. This amendment was to ensure compliance with the ECJ's judgment in *P* v. *S and Cornwall County Council* Case C–13/94 [1996] ECR I–02143, where discrimination on grounds of sex in the Equal Treatment Directive (then Directive 76/207/EEC) was interpreted as including discrimination on grounds of 'gender reassignment'.

Section 7 of the Act is more detailed than s.2A of the SDA 1975. In addition to protecting a person who is 'proposing to undergo, is undergoing or has undergone' gender reassignment, s.7(1) also applies to those proposing to undergo, undergoing or who have undergone 'part of a process' of gender reassignment. This means that it is no longer necessary for a person to be under medical supervision to come within the definition. Gender reassignment is defined as 'reassigning the person's sex by changing physiological or other attributes of sex'. Thus, it is not confined to a process of medical gender reassignment surgery.

Under s.7(3)(a), 'a reference to persons who share a protected characteristic is a reference to transsexual persons' – the comparators are expressly not limited to those who have changed sex in the same direction as the claimant. Therefore a male to female transsexual will 'share a protected characteristic' with a female to male transsexual.

2.6 MARRIAGE AND CIVIL PARTNERSHIP (SECTION 8)

Section 8 of the Act mirrors the similar provision in s.3 of the SDA 1975 which prohibited discrimination against married persons or civil partners in the employment field. SDA 1975, s.3(3) expressly stated that it applied equally to the treatment of men and women. This wording has not been reproduced in s.8 of the Equality Act 2010, but it is to be assumed that this provision will also protect men and women equally.

The Explanatory Notes make clear that the protection does not apply to people who are engaged to be married or those who have become divorced (para. 46).

Civil partnership is not a protected class under the Framework Directive. However, it is protected under the prohibition on indirect discrimination on grounds of sexual orientation (*Maruko* v. *Versorgungsanstalt der deutschen Bühnen* Case C–267/06 [2008] ECR I–01757).

2.7 RACE (SECTION 9)

Section 9(1) defines 'race' as including:

  (a) colour;
  (b) nationality;
  (c) ethnic or national origins.

The Race Relations Act 1976 (RRA 1976) contained the above characteristics though the Race Relations Act 1976 (Amendment) Regulations 2003, SI 2003/ 1626, made amendments to the RRA 1976 which drew a distinction between discrimination on grounds of race, ethnic or national origins and discrimination on the grounds of colour and nationality. Section 1A of the RRA 1976 (incorporated by the regulations) applied the definition of indirect discrimination based upon a provision, criterion or practice and the defence of 'proportionate means of achieving a legitimate aim' to race, ethnic or national origins, in accordance with European requirements, but not to colour and nationality as this was not required by the Directive. There was thus a two-tier approach to indirect discrimination in the RRA 1976 which has not been replicated in the 2010 Act.

The Race Directive, Directive 2000/43/EC, prohibits only discrimination on grounds of racial or ethnic origin (Article 1).

Section 9 of the Act has been drafted with a view to removing these distinctions. The same provisions will now apply to all types of race discrimination.

Section 9(2) makes clear that a reference to persons who share a protected characteristic is a reference to persons of the same racial group.

Section 9(4) states that the fact a racial group comprises two or more distinct racial groups does not prevent it from constituting a 'particular racial group'.

The Explanatory Notes contain the following examples (at para. 50):

- Colour includes being black or white.
- Nationality includes being a British, Australian or Swiss citizen.
- Ethnic or national origin includes being from a Roma background or of Chinese heritage.
- A racial group could be 'black Britons' which would encompass those people who are both black and who are British citizens.

At the Report Stage of the Act the House of Lords made an addition to s.9(5) and (6) so that the section now includes a power to make caste discrimination a form of race discrimination. The EHRC had considered such a power to be unnecessary. The government has commissioned research on the extent to which this is a problem so that, if the view is taken that there is discrimination in this area, a Minister of the Crown may add caste discrimination as one of the protected characteristics.

2.8   RELIGION OR BELIEF (SECTION 10)

Section 10 is based on the provisions of the Employment Equality (Religion or Belief) Regulations 2003, SI 2003/1660 (the 'Religion or Belief Regulations'), but is framed somewhat differently.

Prior to 30 April 2007, reg.2(1) of the Religion or Belief Regulations provided that a philosophical belief needed to be 'similar' to a religious belief. This provision was removed by the Equality Act 2006, s.77.

In *Grainger* v. *Nicholson* [2010] IRLR 4, the Employment Appeal Tribunal (Burton J presiding) directly applied the test imported from European Court of Human Rights (ECtHR) case law under Article 9 of the European Convention on Human Rights (ECHR) into the definition of a 'philosophical' belief (*Campbell and Cosans* v. *United Kingdom* [1982] 4 EHRR 293). In order to qualify for protection (*Grainger* [24]):

    (i)   the belief must be genuinely held;

    (ii) it must be a belief and not . . . an opinion or viewpoint based on the present state of information available;

(iii) it must be a belief as to a weighty and substantial aspect of human life and behaviour;

(iv) it must attain a certain level of cogency, seriousness, cohesion and importance; and

(v) it must be worthy of respect in a democratic society, be not incompatible with human dignity and not conflict with the fundamental rights of others.

The Framework Directive does not include a definition of religion or belief. However, the recitals refer to Article 9 of the ECHR (this was the route that enabled Burton J in *Grainger* to apply the ECtHR's approach in *Campbell* to the Religion or Belief Regulations).

The Explanatory Notes expressly refer to Article 9 of the ECHR. Paragraph 53 of the Explanatory Notes suggests that the Baha'i faith, Buddhism, Christianity, Hinduism, Islam, Jainism, Judaism, Rastafarianism, Sikhism and Zoroastrianism are all religions for the purposes of this provision and that beliefs such as humanism and atheism would be a belief for the purposes of this provision, but adherence to a particular football team would not be.

2.9   SEX (SECTION 11)

Section 11 of the Act provides:

In relation to the protected characteristic of sex –

(a)   a reference to a person who has a particular protected characteristic is a reference to a man or to a woman;

(b)   a reference to persons who share a protected characteristic is a reference to persons of the same sex.

This is a different approach from that contained in SDA 1975, ss.1 and 2, which defined sex discrimination as discrimination against a woman (s.1) on grounds of 'her sex', and then provided that references to sex discrimination 'are to be read as applying equally to the treatment of men' (s.2).

Section 11 is worded to make it clear (as had been clarified by case law under the SDA 1975) that sexual orientation discrimination is not sex discrimination (*Pearce* v. *Governing Body of Mayfield Secondary School*; *MacDonald* v. *Advocate General for Scotland* [2003] UKHL 34, [2003] IRLR 512; *Grant* v. *South-West Trains Ltd* Case C–249/96 [1998] ECR I–621, [1998] IRLR 206; *D and Sweden* v. *EU Council* [2001] ECR I–4319).

The Recast Directive, Directive 2006/54/EC, is framed in a different way by reference to the principle of 'equal opportunities and equal treatment of men and women' (Article 1). The Recast Directive also uses the term 'sex' in relation not only to the difference between men and women, but in relation to harassment of a 'sexual nature' (Article 2(1)(d)).

2.10   SEXUAL ORIENTATION (SECTION 12)

Section 12 is based on the exact wording of reg.2(1) of the Employment Equality (Sexual Orientation) Regulations 2003, SI 2003/166, including sexual orientation towards:

- persons of the same sex;
- persons of the opposite sex; or
- persons of the same sex and of the opposite sex.

In *English* v. *Thomas Sanderson Blinds* [2008] EWCA Civ 1421, [2009] IRLR 206, the Court of Appeal interpreted this definition as covering perceived as well as actual sexual orientation (Mr English was taunted for being homosexual when, in fact, he was heterosexual). The Court of Appeal also suggested (although this was not part of the reasoning of the Court) that the definition also covers those who are asexual (*English* [39]). This approach is likely to remain good law under the Equality Act 2010.

The Framework Directive does not contain any definition of sexual orientation. Only one ECJ case has considered the definition of sexual orientation: *Maruko* v. *Versorgungsanstalt der deutschen Bühnen* Case C–267/06 [2008] ECR I–01757. The discrimination arose from the fact that a widow's pension was not available to life partners (the German equivalent of civil partnership), so was potentially indirectly discriminatory.

The Explanatory Notes give the following examples at para. 57:

- A man who experiences sexual attraction towards both men and women is 'bisexual' in terms of sexual orientation even if he has only had relationships with women.
- A man and a woman who are both attracted only to people of the opposite sex from them share a sexual orientation.
- A man who is attracted only to other men is a gay man. A woman who is attracted only to other women is a lesbian. So a gay man and a lesbian share a sexual orientation.

3 PART 2, CHAPTER 2 – PROHIBITED CONDUCT

3.1 INTRODUCTION

Chapter 2 of the Equality Act 2010 sets out and defines the categories of prohibited conduct, which are:

- discrimination by way of less favourable treatment in its direct and indirect forms;
- failure to comply with a duty to make adjustments for disabled persons;
- harassment; and
- victimisation.

Because of the special rules and extensions that apply to discrimination in relation to disabled persons, the disability discrimination strand will be dealt with separately (see **Chapter 13** on Part 13 of the Act).

Discrimination is prohibited within each field covered by the Act, so, and by way of example, it is a contravention of the Act for an employer (A) to discriminate against a person (B) in the arrangements A makes for deciding whom to offer employment, both as to the terms on which employment is offered to B or if A does not offer B employment. This and the other specific applications of the general definitions of 'prohibited conduct' are dealt with field by field in the following chapters of this book.

3.2 DIRECT DISCRIMINATION (SECTION 13)

'Direct discrimination' is defined in s.13(1) of the Act. A person (A) discriminates against another (B) if:

- because of a protected characteristic,
- A treats B less favourably than A treats or would treat others.

The 'because of' form of words is new. The general form which was common to all strands of direct discrimination under the anti-discrimination statutes and statutory instruments which the Equality Act 2010 replaces was that A discriminated against B if:

- on the ground of the protected characteristic (sex, race, gender reassignment and disability)
- A treated B less favourably than he treated or would have treated someone not having that protected characteristic.

See SDA 1975, s.1(1)(a); RRA 1976, s.1(1)(a); Employment Equality (Religion or Belief) Regulations 2003, reg.3(1)(a); Employment Equality (Sexual Orientation) Regulations 2003, reg.3(1)(a); Employment Equality (Age) Regulations 2006, reg.3(1)(a).

It should be noted that:

- Article 2 of Directive 2006/54/EC proscribes 'direct discrimination' where one person is treated less favourably on grounds of sex than another is, has been or would be treated in a comparable situation;
- Article 2(1) of the Framework Directive, Directive 2000/78/EC (which lays down a general framework for combating discrimination on the grounds of religion or belief, disability, age or sexual orientation as regards employment and occupation) provides that direct discrimination shall be taken to occur where one person is treated less favourably than another is, or has been, or would be treated in a comparable situation, on any of the prohibited grounds;
- Article 2 of Directive 2000/43/EC provides that direct discrimination shall be taken to occur where one person is treated less favourably than another is, has been or would be treated in a comparable situation on grounds of racial or ethnic origin.

The change in the Act from 'on the ground' to 'because of' is not intended to change the scope or content of the prohibition, but to make the definition more accessible to the ordinary user of the Act. It is reasonable to suppose that the expressed intent will be fulfilled when the relevant words fall to be interpreted by the courts or tribunals, albeit that the English version of the prohibition in the relevant EU Directives is in the 'on the ground of' form. The new formulation does not require some form of conscious motivation.

The removal of the requirement that B must actually possess the protected characteristic means associative discrimination is covered (see further 3.2.1).

For a recent and detailed consideration of the law relating to direct discrimination, see *London Borough of Islington v. Ladele* [2009] IRLR 154, [2009] ICR 387, EAT, Elias P presiding. Particular points to note are:

- The motive for the less favourable treatment is irrelevant; the motive does not have to be hostile and it may be benign (*James v. Eastleigh BC* [1990] 1 QB 61; *European Roma Rights Centre v. Immigration Officer at Prague Airport* [2003] EWCA Civ 666, [2003] IRLR 577).
- The protected characteristic need not be the only ground upon which the less favourable treatment is given; it is sufficient that it is a 'significant influence' (*Nagarajan v. London Regional Transport* [1999] IRLR 572 at 576).
- The comparison between the claimant and a comparator must be a comparison

of like with like; the relevant circumstances of the two cases must be the same or at least not materially different (see s.23(1) and also *Shamoon v. Chief Constable of the Royal Ulster Constabulary* [2003] UKHL 11, [2003] IRLR 285 [4], per Lord Nicholls).

■ If the protected characteristic is sexual orientation, the fact that one person (whether or not the person referred to as B) is a civil partner while another is married is not a material difference between the circumstances (s.23(3)).

■ It may, in an appropriate case, be preferable to concentrate primarily on the reason why the claimant was treated in the way complained of rather than following a two-stage approach of determining whether there was less favourable treatment and then determining how an actual or hypothetical comparator was or would have been treated (*Shamoon* [11], per Lord Nicholls).

■ Where the protected characteristic is pregnancy or maternity, then there is no need for a comparator (actual or hypothetical), see **3.6** commenting on s.18 of the Act.

■ The Act expressly provides that the putative discriminator may have the protected characteristic himself (s.24(1)).

The judgment of the Employment Appeal Tribunal was upheld by the Court of Appeal: see *Ladele v. London Borough of Islington* [2009] EWCA Civ 1357; [2010] IRLR 211.

3.2.1   Associative discrimination

The Act proscribes associative discrimination, i.e. less favourable treatment by A of B on the ground of C's protected characteristic. Except in relation to the protected characteristic of marriage and civil partnership, the formula does not require that the victim, B, has the protected characteristic himself as long as the less favourable treatment of B is 'because of' the protected characteristic. Section 1(1)(a) of SDA 1975 required that the treatment of the complainant be on the ground of *her* sex albeit that the equivalent provisions in RRA 1976, s.1(1)(a), Religion or Belief Regulations, reg.3(1)(a) (as amended by Equality Act 2006, s.77), Sexual Orientation Regulations, reg.3(1)(a) and Age Regulations, reg.3(1)(a) did not make an analogous requirement. The use of this formula fulfils the requirement of the Framework Directive, Directive 2000/78/EC, as interpreted in the decision of the ECJ in *Coleman v. Attridge Law* [2008] IRLR 722 where the claimant contended that her resignation from the respondent was because she had received less favourable treatment, which had resulted from the consequences of her son's disability.

Where the less favourable treatment is because of marriage or civil partnership, then it is expressly provided by s.13(4) of the Act that the protected status must apply to the complainant. So B cannot complain because she or he has been less favourably treated by A because of C's status as a married person.

The Act also permits employers to restrict benefits relating to the provision of child care to children of a particular age group (Sched. 9, Part 2, para. 15) which will permit employers to continue to offer child care facilities up to the age of 16 without claims of indirect discrimination.

3.2.2   Victim of discrimination need not actually possess the protected characteristic

The formula is also intended to ensure that A will discriminate against B if he treats B less favourably because of a wrongly held belief that B (or C) possesses a protected characteristic (other than marriage or civil partnership). So, for example, less favourable treatment of B by A because A believes B is gay is still proscribed even if B is not, in fact, gay.

In *English v. Thomas Sanderson Blinds* [2008] EWCA Civ 1421, [2009] IRLR 206, the Court of Appeal held that the equivalent wording in the Sexual Orientation Regulations, as amended by the Equality Act 2006, s.77, proscribed discrimination by way of homophobic bullying even though the perpetrators knew that their victim was not a homosexual.

3.2.3   Segregation because of race

Segregation because of race is (always) discriminatory (s.13(5)).

3.2.4   Less favourable treatment of a woman who is breast-feeding

Section 13(6)(a) provides that in non-work cases (i.e. cases not within Part 5 (Work)), treating a woman less favourably because she is breast-feeding constitutes less favourable treatment of a woman because of her sex.

3.2.5   Treating a man less favourably than a woman who is pregnant/in connection with childbirth

A man cannot complain that he has been less favourably treated because of his gender by comparing the way in which he has been treated with the treatment given to an actual or hypothetical woman if that treatment has been in connection with pregnancy or childbirth (s.13(6)(b)).

3.2.6   Justification of less favourable treatment because of age

The general rule is that direct discrimination can never be justified. However, s.13(2) provides that A does not discriminate against B because of age if A can show that the treatment is a proportionate means of achieving a legitimate aim. This defence is dealt with in more detail at **3.7.1**, but it should be noted that the judgment of the ECJ in R *(on the application of the Incorporated Trustees of the National Council on Ageing (Age Concern England))* v. *Secretary of State for Business, Enterprise and Regulatory Reform* Case C–388/07 [2009] IRLR 373 (the 'Heyday' case challenging the inclusion of a retirement age within the Age Regulations) appears to indicate that where direct (as opposed to indirect) discrimination has to be justified, a higher standard of proof as to the legitimacy of the aim relied on as a justification will apply. See also *Seldon* v. *Clarkson Wright and Jakes* [2009] IRLR 267, Elias P.

3.3 'COMBINED' DIRECT DISCRIMINATION BECAUSE OF DUAL CHARACTERISTICS (SECTION 14)

The absence of a right to bring a claim of 'dual discrimination' was seen as a problem as highlighted by *Bahl* v. *Law Society* [2004] IRLR 799, and was first considered as meriting protection in the Consultation Paper, *Discrimination Law Review: A Framework for Fairness: Proposals for a Single Equality Bill for Great Britain*, June 2007). In April 2009, the Government Equalities Office published *Equality Bill: Assessing the Impact of a Multiple Discrimination Provision*. This resulted in s.14 of the Act.

Section 14 provides that A discriminates against B if, because of a combination of two relevant protected characteristics (i.e. age, disability, gender reassignment, race, religion or belief, sex, sexual orientation) A treats B less favourably than A treats or would treat a person who does not share either of those characteristics. Marriage and civil partnership, and pregnancy and maternity, which are covered elsewhere in the Act are not potential grounds of dual discrimination under s.14. The section only applies to claims of direct discrimination (s.14(7)).

As already noted above, where direct discrimination is one of several reasons for the less favourable treatment, the claimant only has to prove that the proscribed ground had 'a significant influence on the outcome' (*Nagarajan* v. *London Regional Transport* [2000] 1 AC 501; [1999] IRLR 572 at 576, per Lord Nicholls). It might therefore be thought that it would not be a bar to a successful claim that the claimant contended (and showed) that the less favourable treatment was on the ground of two protected characteristics as long as one was shown to have had a significant influence. Section 14 provides for the possibility that a claimant could not show that either of the protected characteristics was, in itself, a significant influence on the outcome. The Explanatory Notes give various hypothetical examples of combined claims including that of a black woman passed over for promotion to work on reception duties because her employer considers that black women do not perform well in customer service roles. The employer might be able to point to white women and black men as comparators to show that the treatment of the black woman has not been less favourable. Section 14(3) removes the requirement that the claimant needs to show that one, other or both of two claims based on separate strands would have succeeded. Section 14(4) provides that a claim of combined discrimination will not enable the claimant to side-step a defence which would have been available to the respondent if the claim had been based on a single strand, for example, genuine occupational qualification. A claim of direct disability discrimination which would come within s.116 (special educational needs) cannot be combined with another strand to make a combined discrimination claim under s.14. Section 14(6) creates a power to amend the combined discrimination provisions by statutory instrument.

As in cases of direct discrimination, the putative discriminator, A, may himself have either or both of the relevant protected characteristics (s.24(2)).

The government has estimated that 7.5 per cent of cases will include claims of dual discrimination and there will be a 10 per cent increase in discrimination cases once s.14 is in force.

The Explanatory Notes give the following examples (at para. 68):

- A black woman has been passed over for promotion to work on reception because her employer thinks black women do not perform well in customer service roles. Because the employer can point to a white woman of equivalent qualifications and experience who has been appointed to the role in question, as well as a black man of equivalent qualifications and experience in a similar role, the woman may need to be able to compare her treatment because of race and sex combined to demonstrate that she has been subjected to less favourable treatment because of her employer's prejudice against black women.
- A bus driver does not allow a Muslim man onto her bus, claiming that he could be a 'terrorist'. While it might not be possible for the man to demonstrate less favourable treatment because of either protected characteristic if considered separately, a dual discrimination claim will succeed if the reason for his treatment was the specific combination of sex and religion or belief, which resulted in him being stereotyped as a potential terrorist.
- A black woman is charged £100 for insurance. As white men are only charged £50 for the same insurance, she alleges this is dual discrimination because of the combination of sex and race. By comparing the claimant's treatment with a white woman who also pays £100, or a black man who pays £50, the insurance company is able to demonstrate that the difference in premium is entirely due to sex, not race. The insurance exception in Schedule 3 means that insurance companies can lawfully set different premiums for women and men in certain circumstances so provided the exception applies in this case, the treatment does not constitute dual discrimination. The less favourable treatment is because of sex and an exception makes the sex discrimination lawful.

3.4   ABSENCE FROM WORK BECAUSE OF GENDER REASSIGNMENT TREATMENT (SECTION 16)

Section 16 prohibits less favourable treatment at or in relation to work (i.e. under Part 5 of the Act) of persons who are absent from work arising out of gender reassignment. A discriminates against a transsexual person (B) in relation to B's absence from work where the absence is because B is proposing to undergo, is undergoing or has undergone a process of gender reassignment and either:

- A treats B less favourably than he would treat someone who was absent from work because of sickness or injury; *or*
- B's absence was for some other reason and it was not reasonable for B to be treated less favourably.

In effect, a transsexual claimant has a choice of comparators (and presumably would make the claim by reference to both – whether actual or hypothetical). Section 16 is a slightly simplified version of the prohibition previously contained in SDA 1975, s.2A.

3.5   PREGNANCY AND MATERNITY DISCRIMINATION: NON-WORK CASES (SECTION 17)

Sections 17 and 18 outlaw discrimination against women in relation to those situations where there can be no male comparator, i.e. pregnancy and maternity. The test is simply whether the woman has been treated 'unfavourably' on the ground of the protected characteristic and not whether she has been treated less favourably than a comparator. Similar provisions were contained in s.3B of SDA 1975, but s.17 extends the fields to which they apply beyond goods, facilities, services and premises.

Section 17 concerns discrimination against women by reason of maternity or pregnancy in non-work cases, i.e. for the purposes of Part 3 (Services and public functions); Part 4 (Premises); Part 6 (Education) and Part 7 (Associations). It provides that A discriminates against a woman if A treats her unfavourably because of a pregnancy of hers or if, in the period of 26 weeks beginning with the day on which she gives birth, A treats her unfavourably because she has given birth. This expressly includes treating a woman unfavourably because she is breast-feeding (s.17(4)). Section 17(6) prevents the making of direct sex discrimination claims under s.13 where such a claim can be made under s.17.

Paragraph 74 of the Explanatory Notes gives the following examples:

- A café owner must not ask a woman to leave his café because she is breast-feeding her baby.
- A shopkeeper must not refuse to sell cigarettes to a woman because she is pregnant.
- A school must not prevent a pupil taking an exam because she is pregnant.

3.6   PREGNANCY AND MATERNITY DISCRIMINATION: WORK CASES (SECTION 18)

In the work field a person discriminates against a woman if in the protected period in relation to a pregnancy of hers, he treats her unfavourably because of the pregnancy, or because of illness suffered by her as a result of it (s.18(2)). The government removed a provision that it was discrimination where the woman was treated less favourably 'than was reasonable', accepting the TUC view that this weakened the existing protection. If the treatment of a woman is in implementation of a decision taken in the protected period, the treatment is to be regarded as occurring in that period (even if the decision is not implemented until after the end of that period) (s.18(5)). Section 18(6) provides that the protected period begins when the pregnancy begins, and ends:

- if the woman has the right to ordinary and additional maternity leave, at the end of the additional maternity leave period or (if earlier) when she returns to work after the pregnancy;
- if the woman does not have that right, at the end of the period of two weeks beginning with the end of the pregnancy.

A person also discriminates against a woman if he treats her unfavourably because she is on compulsory maternity leave (s.18(3)) or because she is exercising or seeking to exercise, or has exercised or sought to exercise, the right to ordinary or additional maternity leave (s.18(5)). This latter provision means that it will be discrimination if the treatment is decided on during, but not implemented until after, the protected period. Section 18(7) prevents a direct sex discrimination claim being made under s.13 where such a claim can be made under s.18.

Similar provisions to those contained in s.18 of the Act were contained in SDA 1975, s.3A. There continues to be no requirement for a comparator in pregnancy and maternity cases.

3.7   INDIRECT DISCRIMINATION (SECTION 19)

Section 19 provides for a common form of definition for indirect discrimination in relation to the protected characteristics of age, disability, gender reassignment, marriage and civil partnership, race, religion or belief, sex and sexual orientation. The inclusion of the disability and gender reassignment strands is new. Indirect discrimination on the ground of disability is dealt with at 13.4. Indirect discrimination against women in relation to pregnancy or maternity leave will only be actionable if the claim can be brought as a claim of indirect sex discrimination.

Indirect discrimination looks beyond formal equality towards a more substantive equality of results: for example, criteria which appear neutral on their face may have a disproportionately adverse impact upon people of a particular colour, race, nationality or ethnic or national origins (R *(on the application of E)* v. *Governing Body of JFS* [2009] UKSC 15, [2010] IRLR 136 [56]).

The new single definition of indirect discrimination provides that a person (A) discriminates against another (B) if A applies to B a provision, criterion or practice (a 'PCP') which is discriminatory in relation to a relevant protected characteristic of B's. 'Provision', 'criterion' and 'practice' are alternatives and the concept of a PCP is a broad one: *British Airways plc* v. *Starmer* [2005] IRLR 862. A PCP is discriminatory in relation to a relevant protected characteristic of B's if A applies, or would apply, the PCP to persons with whom B does not share the characteristic, but:

(a) it puts, or would put, persons with whom B shares the characteristic at a particular disadvantage when compared with persons with whom B does not share it; and
(b) it actually puts, or would put, B at that disadvantage; and
(c) A cannot show the PCP to be a proportionate means of achieving a legitimate aim.

As in the case of direct discrimination, there must be no other material difference between the circumstances relating to the pool of persons who share the characteristic in issue with B and the pool of those who do not share that characteristic (s.23(1)). Coverage is extended to those who would be put at a disadvantage by the PCP, for instance, those who would have applied for a particular job but for the PCP. For an analysis of the concept of particular disadvantage, see *Homer* v. *Chief Constable of West Yorkshire Police* [2010] EWCA Civ 419, [2010] IRLR 619 (age discrimination). Note that it is not necessary to establish that the claimant and the group with which the protected characteristic is shared *cannot* comply with the PCP, only that they will be placed at a particular disadvantage by it. It must, however, be established that B is one of a group who are, or who would be, thus disadvantaged: *Eweida* v. *British Airways plc* [2010] EWCA Civ 80, [2010] IRLR 322: it is not sufficient that B himself is disadvantaged. The selection of the correct pool for comparison has caused considerable difficulty, see, in particular, *Secretary of State for Trade and Industry* v. *Rutherford (No. 2)* [2006] UKHL 19, [2006] ICR 785 and *Somerset County Council and Secretary of State for Children, Schools and Families* v. *Pike* [2009] EWCA Civ 808, [2009] IRLR 870 [18] – the pool for comparison must be those who have an interest in the advantage or disadvantage in question.

The following examples of indirect discrimination are set out in the Explanatory Notes at para. 81:

- A woman is forced to leave her job because her employer operates a practice that staff must work in a shift pattern which she is unable to comply with because she needs to look after her children at particular times of day, and no allowances are made because of those needs. This would put women (who are shown to be more likely to be responsible for childcare) at a disadvantage, and the employer will have indirectly discriminated against the woman unless the practice can be justified.
- An observant Jewish engineer who is seeking an advanced diploma decides (even though he is sufficiently qualified to do so) not to apply to a specialist training company because it invariably undertakes the selection exercises for the relevant course on Saturdays. The company will have indirectly discriminated against the engineer unless the practice can be justified.

3.7.1 Justification

The concept of indirect discrimination used in the EU Directives is:

> where an apparently neutral provision, criterion or practice would put persons having a particular religion or belief, a particular disability, a particular age, or a particular sexual orientation at a particular disadvantage compared with other persons unless… that provision, criterion or practice is objectively justified by a legitimate aim and the means of achieving that aim are appropriate and necessary.

The government rejected direct transposition of the 'appropriate and necessary' formula. In para. 7.26 of its response to Consultation on the Equality Bill the government explained that the wording 'appropriate and necessary' was 'problematic in domestic discrimination legislation because of the extreme exigency associated with "necessity" in domestic law'. There might, it was thought, be a risk that this would be interpreted by the courts as an 'overly-strict requirement', so that in order to satisfy the test, the provision, criterion or practice would have to be the only possible means of achieving the legitimate aim. It was therefore better to require that the justification be a 'proportionate means of achieving a legitimate aim'.

On the meaning of 'justifiable', see *Bilka-Kaufhaus GmbH* v. *Weber von Hartz* Case 170/84 [1986] IRLR 317, [1987] ICR 110 and *Hampson* v. *Department of Education and Science* [1989] IRLR 69, [1989] ICR 179, CA. Cost justifications are particularly problematic: *R (on the application of Elias)* v. *Secretary of State for Defence* [2005] EWHC 1435 (Admin), [2005] IRLR 788; *Redcar and Cleveland Borough Council* v. *Bainbridge* [2007] IRLR 91; *Cross* v. *British Airways plc* [2005] IRLR 423. As to proportionality, see *Hardys & Hansons plc* v. *Lax* [2005] EWCA Civ 846, [2005] IRLR 726: it is not necessary to establish that there was no alternative to the PCP that was applied, but the PCP has to be justified objectively notwithstanding its discriminatory effect. The principle of proportionality requires the tribunal to take into account the reasonable needs of the business but it has to make its own judgment, upon a fair and detailed analysis of the working practices and business considerations involved, as to whether the proposal is reasonably necessary.

3.8   HARASSMENT INCLUDING SEXUAL HARASSMENT (SECTION 26)

The relevant EU Directives proscribe harassment (and sexual harassment) in relation to the protected characteristics to which they relate.

Article 2(3) of Directive 2000/43/EC (racial or ethnic origin) states that:

> Harassment shall be deemed to be discrimination... when... unwanted conduct related to racial or ethnic origin takes place with the purpose or effect of violating the dignity of a person and of creating an intimidating, hostile, degrading, humiliating or offensive environment.

Article 2(3) of the Framework Directive, Directive 2000/78/EC (disability, age, religion or belief and sexual orientation) provides:

> Harassment shall be deemed to be a form of discrimination within the meaning of paragraph 1, when unwanted conduct related to any of the grounds referred to in Article 1 takes place with the purpose or effect of violating the dignity of a person and of creating an intimidating, hostile, degrading, humiliating or offensive environment.

'Harassment' is defined in Article 2(1)(c) of Directive 2006/54/EC (gender) as:

> where unwanted conduct related to the sex of a person occurs with the purpose or effect of violating the dignity of a person, and of creating an intimidating, hostile, degrading, humiliating or offensive environment.

In Article 2(1)(d) of that Directive, 'sexual harassment' takes place:

> where any form of unwanted verbal, non-verbal or physical conduct of a sexual nature occurs, with the purpose or effect of violating the dignity of a person, in particular when creating an intimidating, hostile, degrading, humiliating or offensive environment.

Section 26 of the Act provides a common definition for harassment which is proscribed in relation to the relevant protected characteristics of age, disability, gender reassignment, race, religion or belief, sex and sexual orientation (and, accordingly, not pregnancy or marriage/civil partnership).

There are three forms of harassment (of 'B' by 'A') which are defined in s.26(1)–(3). Subsections (1) and (2) of s.26 provide that harassment occurs where A engages in:

- unwanted conduct related to a relevant protected characteristic, or
- unwanted conduct of a sexual nature,

and the conduct has the purpose or effect of either:

- violating B's dignity, or
- creating an intimidating, hostile, degrading, humiliating or offensive environment for B.

Subsection (3) provides that harassment also occurs where A or another person engages in unwanted conduct of a sexual nature or that is related to gender reassignment or sex and the conduct has the purpose or effect of either:

- violating B's dignity, or
- creating an intimidating, hostile, degrading, humiliating or offensive environment for B.

and because of B's rejection of, or submission to, the conduct, A treats B less favourably than A would treat B if B had not rejected or submitted to the conduct.

As in the case of direct discrimination, it is not necessary that B (or anyone else) actually possesses the relevant protected characteristic, only that the conduct in issue was related to a relevant protected characteristic. It will not matter that A either made a mistake as to the existence of the relevant protected characteristic or indeed knew that the victim (or the third person, C) did not possess the relevant protected characteristic.

In deciding whether conduct has the effect of either violating B's dignity, or creating an intimidating, hostile, degrading, humiliating or offensive environment for B, a court or tribunal must take into account each and all of the following –

- the perception of B;
- the other circumstances of the case;
- whether it is reasonable for the conduct to have that effect.

Accordingly, the actual effect on B (whether or not B is particularly over-sensitive to the conduct) is but one ingredient which requires to be considered. For a general survey of the law relating to harassment under the pre-Equality Act anti-discrimination statutes and statutory instruments, see *Richmond Pharmacology* v. *Dhaliwal* [2009] IRLR 336. In particular, the Employment Appeal Tribunal made the following points at [11], [14]–[16]:

- 'There are – or will at least in some cases – be substantial overlaps between the questions that arise in relation to each element ... [and] between the two defined proscribed consequences.'

■ 'Nevertheless, it will be a healthy discipline for a tribunal ... specifically to address in its reasons each of the elements which we have identified, in order to establish whether any issue arises in relation to it and to ensure that clear factual findings are made on each element in relation to which an issue arises.'

■ 'A respondent may be held liable on the basis that the effect of his conduct has been to produce the proscribed consequences even if that was not his purpose; and, conversely, that he may be liable if he acted for the purposes of producing the proscribed consequences but did not in fact do so (or in any event has not been shown to have done so).'

■ '... a respondent should not be held liable merely because his conduct has had the effect of producing a proscribed consequence: it should be reasonable that that consequence has occurred. That ... creates an objective standard. ... The proscribed consequences are, of their nature, concerned with the feelings of the putative victim: that is, the victim must have felt, or perceived, her dignity to have been violated or an adverse environment to have been created, but overall the criterion is objective because what the tribunal is required to consider is whether, if the claimant has experienced those feelings or perceptions, it was reasonable for her to do so.'

■ 'Whether it was reasonable for a claimant to have felt her dignity to have been violated is quintessentially a matter for the factual assessment of the tribunal. It will be important for it to have regard to all the relevant circumstances, including the context of the conduct in question.'

■ 'One question that may be material is whether it should reasonably have been apparent whether the conduct was, or was not, intended to cause offence (or, more precisely, to produce the proscribed consequences): the same remark may have a very different weight if it was evidently innocently intended than if it was evidently intended to hurt.'

■ 'The inquiry into the perpetrator's grounds for acting as he did is logically distinct from any issue which may arise about whether he intended to produce the proscribed consequences: a perpetrator may intend to violate a claimant's dignity for reasons other than her race (or indeed any of the other reasons proscribed by the discrimination legislation).'

3.9   VICTIMISATION (SECTION 27)

Section 27 provides a common definition for victimisation which is in a form similar to that found in the predecessor statutes and statutory instruments save that the need for a comparison with the treatment accorded to an actual or hypothetical comparator who had not done a protected act is removed. It applies only where the person subjected to a detriment is an individual. A victimises B if A subjects B to a detriment because:

(a) B actually does a protected act, or
(b) A believes that B has done, or may do, a protected act.

The following are protected acts:

- bringing proceedings under the Equality Act;
- giving evidence or information in connection with proceedings under the Equality Act;
- doing any other thing for the purposes of or in connection with the Equality Act;
- making an allegation (whether or not express) that A or another person has contravened the Equality Act. (This includes a reference to committing a breach of an equality clause or rule (s.27(5)).)

However, giving *false* evidence or information, or making a false allegation, is not a protected act if the evidence or information is given, or the allegation is made, in bad faith.

3.10 SUPPLEMENTARY PROVISIONS (SECTIONS 23–25)

Sections 23–25 also contain general provisions with regard to discrimination.

Under s.23, like must be compared with like. Examples given in the Explanatory Notes are:

- A blind woman claims she was not short listed for a job involving computers because the employer wrongly assumed that blind people cannot use them. An appropriate comparator is a person who is not blind – it could be a non-disabled person or someone with a different disability – but who has the same ability to do the job as the claimant.
- A Muslim employee is put at a disadvantage by his employer's practice of not allowing requests for time off work on Fridays. The comparison that must be made is in terms of the impact of that practice on non-Muslim employees in similar circumstances to whom it is (or might be) applied. (para. 93)

By s.24 of the Act, it is no defence that the discriminator shares the protected characteristic with the victim. Examples are sharing the same religion or belief, or in the Explanatory Notes at para. 95:

> An employer cannot argue that because he is a gay man he is not liable for unlawful discrimination for rejecting a job application from another gay man because of the applicant's sexual orientation.

Section 25 explains what is meant by references to the types of discrimination referred to in the Act, so that references elsewhere in the Act to age, marriage and civil partnership, race, religious or belief-related, sex or sexual orientation discrimination include references to both direct and indirect discrimination because of any of these characteristics. Direct and indirect discrimination references to disability discrimination also include references to discrimination arising from disability and to a failure to comply with a duty to make reasonable adjustments; and references to gender reassignment discrimination also include discrimination within s.16 (gender reassignment discrimination: cases of absence from work). Finally, references to pregnancy and maternity discrimination have the meanings derived from ss.17 and 18.

4 PART 3 – SERVICES AND PUBLIC FUNCTIONS

4.1 INTRODUCTION

Part 3 concerning public services and functions consolidates much of the old law. The previous statutes had piecemeal coverage in this area. In general (subject to the exceptions noted below), it extends protection so that there is now a large measure of uniformity.

The most major substantive area of change is the prohibition on age discrimination in services and public functions. (This was the subject of specific consultation during the passage of the Bill. See *Equality Bill: Making it work: Ending age discrimination in services and public functions: Policy Statement*, January 2010, **www.equalities.gov.uk/pdf/GEO–EqualityBillAge–acc.pdf**.) It was planned that the prohibition on age discrimination would enter into force in 2012.

Some of the area covered by this Part is also covered by the Directives, for instance, Directive 2000/43/EC (the Race Directive) applies to goods and services (Article 3(1)(h)). However, Directive 2000/78/EC (the Framework Directive) only relates to employment and occupation as does Directive 2006/54/EC (the Recast Directive). In 2008, the Commission published a Communication on the social agenda, which, amongst other things, makes proposals for introducing further regulation of discrimination more widely (COM (2008) 412 Final. Communication from the Commission to the European Parliament, the Council, the European Economic and Social Committee and the Committee of the Regions: *Renewed social agenda: Opportunities, access and solidarity in 21st century Europe*). The proposed new Equal Treatment Directive is still going through the legislative process. Currently, the government says that it does not see the need to delay Part 3 of the Act until the Directive is finalised (Policy Statement, January 2010, above, at para. 5.5). However, there may be compatibility issues for Part 3 once the new Equal Treatment Directive is published.

4.2 THE PROHIBITION

Part 3 will prohibit discrimination in relation to the provision of services (whether or not for payment) and in the exercise of public functions. Section 29 prohibits a service provider from:

- not providing the protected person with the service (s.29(1));
- in providing the service, discriminating:
  - as to the terms on which the service provider provides the service (s.29(2)(a));
  - by terminating the provision of the service (s.29(2)(b));
  - by subjecting that person (called 'B') to any other detriment (s.29(2)(c));
- harassment (s.29(3)) – save for where it is on grounds of sexual orientation or religion or belief (s.29(8));
- victimisation (s.29(4) and (5));
- breaching the duty to make reasonable adjustments (s.29(7)).

Section 29(6) and (7) prohibits a person, who is exercising a public function (that is not the provision of a service to the public or a section of the public), from doing anything that constitutes discrimination, harassment or victimisation or failure to make reasonable adjustments.

Section 29(9) codifies the judgment of the House of Lords in *R (on the application of European Roma Rights Centre) v. Immigration Officer, Prague Airport* [2004] UKHL 55, [2005] 2 AC 1 to the effect that in the application of s.29, so far as relates to race discrimination, to the granting of entry clearance (within the meaning of the Immigration Act 1971), it does not matter whether an act is done within or outside the United Kingdom. The Equality Act extends the protection also to include religion and belief discrimination.

4.3   PUBLIC FUNCTIONS

Public function is defined in ss.31(4) and 150(5). The definition is identical to functions of a public nature for the purposes of the Human Rights Act 1998. The key case on the application of the Human Rights Act test is *YL v. Birmingham City Council* [2007] UKHL 27, [2008] 1 AC 95.

4.4   SERVICES

Unusually, 'services' includes the provision of goods or services (s.29(1)).

The examples given in the Explanatory Notes (at para. 116) are:

- A man and two female friends plan a night out at a local night club. At the entrance the man is charged £10 entry; the two women are charged £5 each. The owner explains the night club is trying to attract more women and has decided to charge them half the entrance fee. This would be direct sex discrimination.
- A company which organises outdoor activity breaks requires protective head-wear to be worn for certain activities, such as white water rafting and rock climbing. This requirement could be indirectly discriminatory against Sikhs unless it can be justified, for example on health and safety grounds.
- A man who suffers from long-standing and serious health problems, including partial paralysis and a severe sight impairment, is imprisoned. On his imprison-ment, the man is not allocated an adapted cell, despite being assessed as

requiring one within 24 hours of arriving at prison. Instead, he is allocated a standard cell. This would be discrimination resulting from a failure to make reasonable adjustments to take account of a person's disability.

■   A black man goes into a bar to watch a football match. He is served a pint of beer and takes a seat at an empty table. Whilst watching the football match the bartender and a number of customers make racist remarks about some of the footballers on the pitch. When the man complains he is then called a number of derogatory names. This would be harassment because of race.

Presumably, the last example would also constitute victimisation.

4.5   EXCEPTIONS

There are several important substantive exceptions to Part 3 of the Act. It does not apply to:

■   Discrimination, harassment or victimisation on grounds of being under the age of 18 (s.28(1)(a)).
■   Discrimination or harassment of people because they are married or in a civil partnership (s.28(1)(b)).
■   Harassment on grounds of sexual orientation or religion or belief (s.29(8)).
■   The functioning of:
    –   Parliament or in connection with proceedings in Parliament (Sched. 3, para. 1);
    –   a judicial function (Sched. 3, para. 2);
    –   the Security Services (Sched. 3, para. 5).
■   In relation to age, disability, gender reassignment, sex discrimination anything done for the purpose of ensuring the combat effectiveness of the armed forces (Sched. 3, para. 3). This exception does not include discrimination on grounds of sexual orientation, race, religion or belief, marriage and civil partnership and – perhaps oddly considering the sex exception – pregnancy and maternity.

Part 3 is a residual part of the Act. It does not apply:

■   where there are more specific provisions in the Act (s.28(2));
■   if circumstances are covered by an equality clause. (s.28(3));
■   in relation to age discrimination or religious or belief-related discrimination in various specific education-related powers (Sched. 3, para. 6).

4.6   DEFENCES

Schedule 3 already provides for various specific defences, for instance:

■   In health and care (Sched. 3, paras. 13–15) regarding:
    –   blood services (for blood and blood components, for example, plasma);
    –   pregnancy and health and safety;
    –   care within the family.
■   Immigration (Sched. 3, paras. 16–19) in relation to:

- disability;
- ethnic or national origins;
- religion or belief.
- Insurance (Sched. 3, paras. 20–23), in particular:
  - for new policies where protected characteristics are 'relevant' to the assessment of risk and it is 'reasonable' to rely on it or the policy;
  - existing policies will continue to be considered under the old law unless they are renewed or the terms are reviewed.
- Marriage and gender reassignment.
- Separate services for different sexes (Sched. 3, paras. 24–28).
- Television, radio and online broadcasting or distribution services under the Communications Act 2003.
- Disabled transport (Sched. 3, paras. 29–31).

The duties in Part 3 will also be subject to defences to be set out in specific regulations under Sched. 3. A government consultation on these ended in September 2009 (see GEO, *Equality Bill: Making it Work: Ending Age Discrimination in Services and Public Functions: Policy Statement*, January 2010, at **www.equalities. gov.uk/pdf/GEO–EqualityBillAge–acc.pdf January 2010**). Areas which are likely to be covered specifically are the application of defences to age discrimination in the fields of:

- health and social care;
- insurance and financial services;
- specialist holiday and holiday accommodation providers.

4.7 REASONABLE ADJUSTMENTS

Schedule 2 to the Equality Act 2010 alters some aspects of the duty to make reasonable adjustments by providers of services or public functions:

- The duty is owed not just to a specific disabled person but to 'disabled persons generally' (Sched. 2, para. 2(2)).
- The duty is not just to 'avoid the disadvantage', but also potentially 'to adopt a reasonable alternative method of providing the service or exercising the function' (Sched. 2, para. 2(5)).
- It extends to physical features of premises which the service-provider or body exercising a public function is not an 'occupier' (i.e. if a theatre company puts on a play in a theatre owned and run by another person).
- Service-providers are not required, under the duty to make reasonable adjustments, to do something which would fundamentally alter the nature of the service, trade or profession (Sched. 2, para. 2(7)).
- There are very particular, lengthy and complex glosses on the duties owed by transport operators (Sched. 2, paras. 3–4) which are intended to codify the existing law.

4.8   SHIPS AND HOVERCRAFT

Section 30 sets out the power to make regulations regarding particular circumstances to be prescribed in relation to transporting people by a ship or hovercraft or services on board ships or hovercraft. At present, the territorial applicability of the discrimination statutes on board ships and hovercraft is dealt with on a piecemeal basis. Paragraph 119 of the Explanatory Notes expresses the hope that:

> As the Bill is silent on the territorial application of the services provisions regulations made under this clause will ensure that there is clarity about when and on which ships and hovercraft the services provisions apply.

4.9   INTERPRETATION AND EXCEPTIONS

Section 31 contains provisions on interpretation and exceptions. It defines what is meant by the terms 'provision of a service' and 'public function' in the Act. The definition of a 'public function' is that which applies for the purposes of the Human Rights Act 1998. The public functions provisions apply only where what is being done does not fall within the definition of a 'service'. It also states that refusing to provide or not providing a service includes providing a person with a service of different quality, or in a different way (for example, hostile or less courteous) or on less favourable terms than the service would normally be provided. Provision of a service to a closed group of employees is also covered.

Examples are given in the Explanatory Notes at para. 125:

- Services include the provision of day care, the running of residential care homes and leisure centre facilities, whether provided by a private body or a local authority.
- Public functions, not involving the provision of a service, include licensing functions; Government and local authority public consultation exercises; the provision of public highways; planning permission decisions; and core functions of the prison service and the probation service.
- The definition of refusing to provide a service covers, for example, a bank which has a policy not to accept calls from customers through a third party. This could amount to indirect discrimination against a deaf person who uses a registered interpreter to call the bank.
- An employer arranges for an insurer to provide a group health insurance scheme to his employees. The insurer refuses to provide cover on the same terms to one of the employees because she is transsexual. This would be treated as direct discrimination in the provision of services by the insurer against the employee in the same way as if the insurance was available to the general public. However, if it was the employer, rather than the insurer, who decided that the transsexual employee should not be able to access the group health insurance scheme, such discrimination in the employee's access to benefits in the workplace would be covered by the provisions of Part 5 (Work).

5 PART 4 – PREMISES

5.1 INTRODUCTION

Part 4 (ss.32–38) of the Equality Act 2010 concerns discrimination in relation to the disposal and management of premises and reasonable adjustments in relation to leasehold and commonhold premises and common parts.

5.2 EXCLUSIONS (SECTION 32)

Section 32 defines the scope of the application of Part 4. The Part does not apply to age or marriage and civil partnership (s.32(1)) nor to discrimination, harassment or victimisation that is prohibited by Part 5 (Work) or Part 6 (Education) or that would be prohibited but for an express exception (s.32(2)).

The Part also does not apply to the provision of accommodation if the provision is generally for the purpose of short stays by individuals who live elsewhere or the accommodation is used for the purpose only of exercising a public function or providing a service to the public or a section of the public (s.32(3)). The references to the exercise of a public function and the provision of a service are to be construed in accordance with Part 3 (s.32(4)). Part 4 also does not apply to breaches of an equality clause or rule or anything that would be such a breach but for s.69 or Part 2 of Sched. 7 (the material factor defence in equal pay cases and the state retirement provisions relating to occupational pension schemes) (s.32(5)).

5.3 DISPOSAL OF PREMISES (SECTION 33)

Where a person, A, has the right to dispose of premises, he must not discriminate against another, B:

    (a) as to the terms on which A offers to dispose of the premises to B;
    (b) by not disposing of the premises to B;
    (c) in A's treatment of B with respect to things done in relation to persons seeking premises. (s.33(1))

This will include not being a party to the disposal where an interest in commonhold cannot be disposed of unless the person is a particular party to the disposal (s.33(2)).

Where the person has the right to dispose of premises, he must not harass a person who occupies them or applies for them in connection with anything relating to their occupation or disposal (s.33(3)). However, religion or belief and sexual orientation are not protected characteristics for the purposes of subs.(3) (s.33(6)).

Nor may the person, A, victimise another, B, as to the terms on which A offers to dispose of the premises to B, by not disposing of the premises to B or in A's treatment of B with respect to things done in relation to persons seeking premises (s.33(4)). This will include victimisation by not being party to the disposal where an interest in commonhold cannot be disposed of unless the person is a particular party to the disposal (s.33(5)).

Examples in the Explanatory Notes at para. 131 are:

- A landlord refuses to let a property to a prospective tenant because of her race. This is direct discrimination when disposing of premises.
- A vendor offers her property to a prospective buyer who is disabled at a higher sale price than she would to a non-disabled person, because of the person's disability. This is direct discrimination when disposing of premises.

5.4   PERMISSION TO DISPOSE OF PREMISES (SECTION 34)

By s.34(1), a person whose permission is required for the disposal of premises must not discriminate against another by not giving permission for the disposal of the premises to another. Nor may such a person harass a person who applies for permission to dispose of the premises or harass a person to whom the disposal would be made if permission was given (s.34(2)). However, religion or belief and sexual orientation are not protected characteristics for the purposes of this subs.(2) (s.34(3)). The person whose permission is required must also not victimise a person by refusing permission. The example given at para. 134 of the Explanatory Notes is:

A disabled tenant seeks permission from his landlord to sublet a room within his flat to help him pay his rent. The landlord tells him that he cannot because he is disabled. This is direct discrimination in permission for disposing of premises

Section 34 does not apply to anything done in the exercise of a judicial function (s.34(5)).

5.5   MANAGEMENT (SECTION 35)

Section 35 contains provisions against discrimination, harassment and victimisation in relation to the management of premises. By s.35(1), A, who manages premises, must not discriminate against B who occupies the premises:

(a) in the way in which A allows B, or by not allowing B, to make use of a benefit or facility;
(b) by evicting B (or taking steps for the purpose of securing B's eviction);
(c) by subjecting B to any other detriment.

The person who manages premises must, in addition, not harass a person who occupies them or who applies for them (s.35(2)), although, as with the other provisions above, religion or belief and sexual orientation are excluded (s.35(4)). The manager of the premises must also not victimise a person who occupies the premises:

(a) in the way in which A allows B, or by not allowing B, to make use of a benefit or facility;
(b) by evicting B (or taking steps for the purpose of securing B's eviction);
(c) by subjecting B to any other detriment. (s.35(3))

5.6 REASONABLE ADJUSTMENTS (SECTIONS 36 AND 37)

There is detailed provision in relation to reasonable adjustments in s.36 and in s.37 in so far as the latter section applies to Scotland.

By s.36(1), a duty to make reasonable adjustments applies to:

(a) a controller of let premises;
(b) a controller of premises to let;
(c) a commonhold association;
(d) a responsible person in relation to common parts.

The reference to letting includes sub-letting and, under s.36(1)(a) and (b), let premises also includes premises subject to a right to occupy (s.36(7)).

A controller of let premises is a person by whom premises are let or a person who manages such premises (s.36(2)). A controller of premises to let is a person who has premises to let or a person who manages them (s.36(3)). A commonhold association under s.36(1)(c) is the association in its capacity as the person who manages a commonhold unit (s.36(4)). A responsible person under s.36(1)(d) in relation to common parts is:

(a) where the premises to which the common parts relate are let (and are not part of commonhold land or in Scotland), a person by whom the premises are let;
(b) where the premises to which the common parts relate are part of commonhold land, the commonhold association.

Common parts are:

(a) in relation to let premises (which are not part of commonhold land or in Scotland), the structure and exterior of, and any common facilities within or used in connection with, the building or part of a building which includes the premises;
(b) in relation to commonhold land, every part of the commonhold which is not for the time being a commonhold unit in accordance with the commonhold community statement.

There is provision in s.36(8) for premises to be excluded by regulations.

The Explanatory Notes at para. 138 give the following example:

> An agency used by a landlord to let and manage leasehold premises, is a controller of premises under this provision and therefore is under the duty to make reasonable adjustments for disabled people, such as making information about the property available in accessible formats.

Section 37(1) provides that Scottish Ministers may, by regulations, provide that a disabled person is entitled to make relevant adjustments to common parts in relation to premises in Scotland after consultation with a Minister of the Crown (s.37(3)). Relevant adjustments are adjustments to avoid a substantial disadvantage to which the disabled person is put in using the common parts in comparison with a person who is not disabled (s.37(5)). Common parts are defined as the structure and exterior of, and any common facilities within or used in connection with, the building or part of a building which includes the premises but only in so far as the structure, exterior and common facilities are not solely owned by the owner of the premises (s.37(5)).

A disabled person is a person who is a tenant of premises, an owner of the premises or otherwise entitled to occupy the premises (s.37(2)).

Section 37(4) sets out matters that regulations made under s.37(1) may cover. The regulations may:

(a) prescribe things which are, or which are not, to be treated as relevant adjustments;
(b) prescribe circumstances in which the consent of an owner of the common parts is required before a disabled person may make an adjustment;
(c) provide that the consent to adjustments is not to be withheld unreasonably;
(d) prescribe matters to be taken into account, or to be disregarded, in deciding whether it is reasonable to consent to adjustments;
(e) prescribe circumstances in which consent to adjustments is to be taken to be withheld;
(f) make provision about the imposition of conditions on consent to adjustments;
(g) make provision as to circumstances in which the sheriff may make an order authorising a disabled person to carry out adjustments;
(h) make provision about the responsibility for costs arising (directly or indirectly) from an adjustment;
(i) make provision about the reinstatement of the common parts to the condition they were in before an adjustment was made;
(j) make provision about the giving of notice to the owners of the common parts and other persons;
(k) make provision about agreements between a disabled person and an owner of the common parts;
(l) make provision about the registration of information in the Land Register of Scotland or the recording of documents in the Register of Sasines relating to an entitlement of a disabled person or an obligation on an owner of the common parts;
(m) make provision about the effect of such registration or recording;
(n) make provision about who is to be treated as being, or as not being, a person entitled to occupy premises otherwise than as tenant or owner.

Section 37 is a new provision.

5.7   SUPPLEMENTARY PROVISIONS (SECTION 38)

Section 38 contains a number of definitions which set out the scope of the previous sections:

- Premises refers to the whole or part of premises (s.38(2)).
- Disposing of premises includes, in relation to a tenancy, assignment of the premises, sub-letting or parting with possession (s.38(3)).
- Disposal includes a reference to granting a right to occupy (s.38(4)).
- Disposing of an interest in a commonhold unit includes creating an interest in such a unit (s.38(5)).
- A tenancy includes a tenancy created by a lease or sub-lease, an agreement for a lease or sub-lease, a tenancy agreement or in pursuance of an enactment and a reference to tenant is to be so construed (s.38(6)).
- A reference to commonhold land, a commonhold association, a commonhold community statement, a commonhold unit or a unit-holder is to be construed in accordance with the Commonhold and Leasehold Reform Act 2002 (s.38(7)).

Schedule 4 contains detailed provisions on the manner in which reasonable adjustments are to apply to premises (s.38(8)) whilst Sched. 5 contains detailed exceptions. Schedule 4 also covers duties in relation to let premises and premises to let, the duty in relation to commonhold units, the duty in relation to common parts, consultation, agreement on adjustments relating to common parts, victimisation, and provision for the creation of regulations, whilst Sched. 5 provides for exceptions in relation to owner-occupiers and small premises.

6   PART 5 – WORK

6.1   PART 5, CHAPTER 1 – EMPLOYMENT, ETC.

Chapter 1 of Part 5 sets down the non-discrimination duties owed in relation to employment and occupation. This directly implements the duties in relation to employment and occupation conferred by the Race Directive (Directive 2000/43/ EC), the Framework Directive (Directive 2000/78/EC) and the Recast Directive (Directive 2006/54/EC).

6.1.1   Employees and applicants (section 39)

Section 39 relates to employees and applicants and sets out the provisions that make it unlawful for an employer to discriminate or victimise such persons. In addition, it states that a duty to make reasonable adjustments applies to an employer. The wording is not identical to all of the previous discrimination statutes; it would seem to have the same effect, but in plainer English.

Section 39 uses the formulation 'an employer (A) must not discriminate against a person (B)' as has been used, for instance, in the Employment Equality (Religion or Belief) Regulations 2003, SI 2003/1660.

Under s.39, an employer (A) must not discriminate or victimise a person (B):

- in the arrangements A makes for deciding to whom to offer employment;
- as to the terms on which A offers B employment;
- by not offering B employment;
- as to B's terms of employment;
- in the way A affords B access, or by not affording B access, to opportunities for promotion, transfer or training or for receiving any other benefit, facility or service,
- by dismissing B,
- by subjecting B to any other detriment.

Under s.39(7)(a) and (8), an employee will not be dismissed at the end of a fixed-term contract if immediately after the termination the employment is renewed on the same terms.

Section 39(6) simplifies the provisions which apply to terms and conditions during maternity leave which previously were contained in SDA 1975, s.6A.

'Employment' is defined by s.83(2) and s.212(1). The approach of the Court of Appeal in *Mingeley* v. *Pennock and Ivory* [2004] IRLR 373 under the RRA 1976 is likely to apply to the definition in the Equality Act 2010, as it has been in respect of the other older discrimination statutes.

The ECJ is currently determining the essence of 'employment' under the Framework Directive in *Mashi* v. *Awaz FM* S/116403/08 (referred by the Scottish Employment Tribunal: whether a volunteer can be an employee).

'Detriment' in discrimination law has previously been interpreted in a 'non-technical' manner. In *Shamoon* v. *Chief Constable of Royal Ulster Constabulary* [2003] UKHL 11, [2003] ICR 337, Lord Hope stated the test as being: 'Is there treatment of such a kind that a reasonable worker would or might take the view that in all the circumstances it was to his detriment?' ([2003] UKHL 11, [2003] ICR 337 [35]).

There are a number of examples set out at para. 147 of the Explanatory Notes:

- An employer decides not to shortlist for interview a disabled job applicant because of her epilepsy. This would be direct discrimination.
- An employer offers a woman a job on lower pay than the set rate because she is pregnant when she applies. She cannot bring an equality clause case as there is no comparator. However, she will be able to claim direct discrimination.
- An employer refuses to interview a man applying for promotion, because he previously supported a discrimination case against the employer brought by another employee. This would be victimisation.
- An employer enforces a 'no beards' policy by asking staff to shave. This could be indirect discrimination, because it would have a particular impact on Muslims or Orthodox Jews.

6.1.2   Harassment (section 40)

Section 40 is designed to replicate the provisions of the SDA 1975 regarding harassment by employers and to extend harassment to all the protected characteristics apart from marriage, civil partnership, pregnancy and maternity. This protects employees from harassment both by their employer and by third parties. In order to bring a claim of harassment by a third party, the claimant must show that the employer knows that the claimant has been subjected to harassment in the course of his or her employment on at least two occasions by a third party. It does not have to be the same third party on each occasion. Thus, the 'three strikes rule' applies and an employer will be liable if it does not protect the employee from repeated harassment. An example is given in para. 149 of the Explanatory Notes:

> A shop assistant with a strong Nigerian accent tells her manager that she is upset and humiliated by a customer who regularly uses the shop and each time makes derogatory remarks about Africans in her hearing. If her manager does nothing to try to stop it happening again, he would be liable for racial harassment.

6.1.3   Contract workers (section 41)

Section 41 applies similar duties to principals of contract workers as employers owe to their employees. Most of s.41 codifies existing law. Contract workers will also be protected under s.39 (employment) as regards the duties owed by their employers. Section 41(5)(b) codifies *Abbey Life Assurance* v. *Tansell* [2000] IRLR 387 in which the Court of Appeal held (under the provisions of the DDA 1995) that there need not be a direct contractual link between the principal and the employer. The extended duties in relation to third party harassment (s.40) do not apply to contract workers.

In the Committee stage of the Bill, questions were asked as to whether cl. 38 (now s.41) could overlap with Directive 2008/104/EC on temporary agency work (the Agency Worker Directive). The Solicitor-General confirmed it did not (Public Bill Committee, 23 June 2009, col. 377 at **www.publications.parliament.uk/pa/cm200 809/cmpublic/equality/090623/am/90623s01.htm#end**).

Examples given in the Explanatory Notes at para. 151 are:

- A hotel manager refuses to accept a black African contract worker sent to him by an agency because of fears that guests would be put off by his accent. This would be direct discrimination.
- A bank treats a female contract worker less well than her male counterparts, for example by insisting that as she is a woman she should make coffee for all meetings. This would be direct discrimination.

6.1.4   Police (sections 42 and 43)

Sections 42 and 43 set out specific provisions for claims brought by police officers and police cadets against the police. As police officers are, as a matter of common law, 'office holders' rather than employees, they do not automatically fit within s.39. Section 42 removes the requirement to pay out of police funds compensation and related costs arising from the personal liability of chief officers (or in Scotland, chief constables) for acts which are unlawful under the Act. Payments of compensation and related costs arising from the personal liability of chief officers (or in Scotland, chief constables) will instead be dealt with by the Police Act 1996 and the Police (Scotland) Act 1967, as for all other police officers.

A special constable, although not paid, holds the office of constable, so is protected in the same way under ss.42 and 43 (*Sheikh* v. *Chief Constable of Greater Manchester Police* [1989] ICR 373, CA).

As regards s.42, para. 156 of the Explanatory Notes gives the following example:

- A chief officer refuses to allocate protective equipment to female constables. The chief officer would be treated as the employer in a direct discrimination claim.

6.1.5   Partnerships (section 44)

Section 44 sets out the non-discrimination duties owed by firms, proposed firms and limited partnerships. A firm is defined in the Partnership Act 1890, s.4.

Separate provisions are needed because partners are mainly governed by the partnership agreements. The section replicates previous provisions, and applies to colour, race, nationality and ethnic or national origins whereas previously the scope of protection differed depending on whether the discrimination was for colour and nationality or was based on race or ethnic or national origin. The protection is now the same for all these characteristics. An example is given at para. 162 of the Explanatory Notes:

> ■ A firm refuses to accept an application for partnership from a black candidate, who is qualified to join, because he is of African origin. This would be direct discrimination.

6.1.6   Limited liability partnerships (section 45)

Limited liability partnerships (LLPs) have a different legal personality from a partnership, and therefore require special provision. Paragraph 164 of the Explanatory Notes states that the intention of s.45 is to replicate the liabilities of partnerships. Examples at para. 164 of the Explanatory Notes are:

> ■ An LLP refuses a member access to use of a company car because he has supported a discrimination or harassment claim against the LLP. This would be victimisation.
> ■ An LLP refuses a Muslim member access to its child care scheme because all the other children who attend the scheme have Christian parents. This would be direct discrimination.

6.1.7   Barristers and advocates (sections 47 and 48)

Sections 47 extends protection from discrimination, victimisation and harassment and the duty to make reasonable adjustments to barristers, pupils, tenants, squatters, clerks and door tenants and those applying to be tenants or pupils. Section 47(6) also protects barristers from discrimination, harassment or victimisation by persons instructing a barrister. The Explanatory Notes provide the following examples at para. 168:

> ■ A barrister treats a female pupil less favourably than his male pupils by allowing her to be involved in a narrower range of cases, because of assumptions about the kind of cases women can handle competently. This would be direct discrimination.
> ■ A clerk gives instructions to a Christian barrister in his chambers in preference to a Hindu barrister, because he fears that the barrister's religion would prevent him representing a Christian client properly. This would be direct discrimination.

Section 48 similarly protects advocates, devils and advocates' clerks from discrimination, victimisation and harassment, and confers the protection to make reasonable adjustments. Section 48(6) protects barristers from discrimination, victimisation or harassment by those instructing them. Examples given at para. 171 of the Explanatory Notes are:

- An advocate treats one devil less favourably than another by refusing to allow him to be involved in a particular case because he fears the devil's sexual orientation may affect his involvement in the case. This would be direct discrimination.
- An advocate puts pressure on a stable member to leave because the member is disabled and the advocate does not want to make reasonable adjustments. This would be direct discrimination.

These provisions replicate similar provisions in previous discrimination statutes, save that clients, solicitors and clerks are not protected under these sections from discrimination, harassment or victimisation by barristers or advocates. The Explanatory Notes state that this is because they are now protected under the services provisions or under other work provisions (see paras. 168 and 171).

6.1.8   Personal offices: appointments, etc. (section 49)

Section 49 applies in relation to personal offices. Under s.49(2), a personal office is an office or post to which a person is appointed to discharge a function personally under the direction of another person and in respect of which an appointed person is entitled to remuneration. Section 49 prohibits the same conduct as for employees, but only applies if the employment (or contract work, partnership, LLP, barristers, advocate, providers of work experience, etc.) provisions do not apply (Sched. 6, para. 1(2)).

Examples given at para. 176 of the Explanatory Notes are:

- A company board refuses to appoint a candidate as director because she is black. This would be direct discrimination.
- A company terminates the appointment of a director because it is discovered that she is pregnant. This would be direct discrimination.

The duties are imposed both on the person or persons with power to make the appointment to the office and also on those with power in relation to a personal office. The Explanatory Notes at para. 176 state that this is because sometimes an entirely different person can be responsible.

6.1.9   Public offices (sections 50 and 51)

Sections 50–51 contain similar provisions for public offices. However, unlike for private offices, a public office need not be for remuneration (s.50(2)). It applies to those appointing public offices as well as those who have powers in relation to them, but it also applies to a wider class – those empowered to make a recommendation or give approval for an appointment to public office.

Examples are provided in the Explanatory Notes (paras. 181 and 184):

- A Government Minister with the power to appoint the non-executive board members of a non-departmental public body fails to appoint a candidate because he is gay. This would be direct discrimination.
- It would be direct discrimination for the Government Minister responsible for approving the appointment of members of the BBC Trust to refuse to approve the appointment of a person because he has a hearing impairment.

Various public offices listed in Sched. 6 are excluded. Most notably a political office or a life peerage is neither a 'personal office' nor a 'public office' (Sched. 6, paras. 2(1) and 3).

6.1.10   Qualifications bodies (sections 53 and 54)

Sections 53 and 54 confer duties on qualifications bodies. A 'relevant qualification' for a qualifications body is an 'authorisation, qualification, recognition, registration, enrolment, approval or certification which is needed for, or facilitates engagement in, a particular trade or profession'(s.54(2)). Section 54(4) lists the bodies which are not 'qualifications bodies' for the purposes of s.53 of the Act, including schools, local education authorities and higher educational institutions.

See below examples from the Explanatory Notes for s.53 (at para. 188) and for s.54 (at para. 191):

- A body which confers diplomas certifying that people are qualified electricians refuses to confer the qualification on a man simply because he is gay. This would be direct discrimination.
- An organisation which maintains a register of professional trades people refuses to include a person's details on the register because her name does not sound English. This would be direct discrimination.
- Examples of qualifications bodies are the Public Carriage Office (which licenses cab drivers in London), the British Horseracing Authority and the General Medical Council. Also included is any body which confers a diploma on people pursuing a particular trade (for example, plumbers), even if the diploma is not strictly necessary to pursue a career in that trade but shows that the person has reached a certain standard.

The prohibited conduct is similar to that in the old discrimination statutes, although victimisation is now expressly prohibited (where it was not previously; see SDA 1975, s.13; RRA 1976, s.12; DDA 1995, s.14A; Religion or Belief Regulations, reg. 16; Sexual Orientation Regulations, reg.16; and Age Regulations, reg.19).

The EHRC in 2008 published a revised Code of Practice under the Disability Discrimination Act 1995 for Trade Organisations, Qualification Bodies and General Qualification Bodies which, until it is further revised, is likely to be applied by county courts dealing with complaints under the Equality Act 2010, s.53.

6.1.11   Employment service-providers (sections 55 and 56)

Sections 55 and 56 set out the non-discrimination provisions which apply to employment service-providers. This is a residual provision and does not apply if another provision of Part 5 applies (s.56(3)) or where the specific education provisions apply (s.56(4) and (5) – for example, work experience arranged by a school).

Most employment services are subject to the full range of non-discrimination, harassment, victimisation and reasonable adjustments duties under s.55.

'Employment services' include several types of 'vocational training' as defined in s.56(6). A reference to the provision of a vocational service is a reference to the provision of an employment service as listed in s.56(2)(a)–(d) (and (g) and (f), in so far as it is also an employment service within (a)–(d)). The duty to make reasonable adjustments in s.55(6) does not apply to the provision of 'vocational services'. Instead, the duty to make reasonable adjustments by vocational service-providers derives from the service provision duties under s.29 (see **4.4**). Enforcement, however, will be in the employment tribunal. This difficult legislative structure is explained by the Solicitor-General in the Public Bill Committee on 23 June 2009, col. 381, **www.publications.parliament.uk/pa/cm200809/cmpublic/equality/090 623/am/90623s02.htm**.

The Explanatory Notes give examples for s.55 at para. 193 and for s.56 at para. 194, which are:

- A company which provides courses to train people to be plumbers refuses to enrol women because its directors assume that very few people want to employ female plumbers. This would be direct discrimination.
- An agency which finds employment opportunities for teachers in schools offers placements only to white teachers based on the assumption that this is what parents in a particular area would prefer. This would be direct discrimination.
- An agency advertises job vacancies on its website. It will need to have the website checked for accessibility and make reasonable changes to enable disabled people using a variety of access software to use it.
- Examples of the types of activities covered under this section include providing CV writing classes, English or Maths classes to help adults into work; training in IT/keyboard skills; or providing work placements.

6.1.12   Trade organisations (section 57)

A trade organisation is defined in s.57(7) as an organisation of workers (such as a trade union) or employers (such as chambers of commerce), or an organisation whose members carry out a particular trade or profession (such as the Law Society or Bar Council).

The duties are intended to replicate those in existing legislation. As with qualifications bodies (see **6.1.10**), the previous legislation did not expressly proscribe victimisation. Section 57(5) of the Equality Act 2010 does.

Furthermore, the express wording of s.57(1) is different from some of the previous legislative provisions in that it protects those with prescribed characteristics from discrimination by the trade organisation as to whom 'to offer' membership (rather than 'to admit… to membership'. (The words 'to admit' were used in SDA 1975, s.12(2); RRA 1976, s.11(2); Religion or Belief Regulations, reg.15(1); Sexual Orientation Regulations, reg.15(1); Age Regulations, reg.18(1). DDA 1995, s.13(1)(a) used the word 'offer'.)

The examples in para. 197 of the Explanatory Notes are:

- A trade union restricts its membership to men. This would be direct discrimination.

- An organisation of employers varies membership subscriptions or access to conferences because of a person's race. This would be direct discrimination.

6.1.13   Local authority: official business (sections 58 and 59)

Sections 58 and 59 prohibit a local authority from discriminating, harassing or victimising a member of the authority in relation to the member's carrying out of official business, for example, in relation to access to training or any other detriment.

This protection was previously only contained in the DDA 1995 following an amendment to the Act in 2005 (DDA 1995, ss.15A–15C).

Members of a local authority are not protected when they are not carrying out official business (ss.58(1) and 59(4)), or where they are not appointed or elected to an office, committee, sub-committee or are not appointed or nominated in exercise of an appointment power of the authority (s.58(4)).

The relevant local authorities are listed in s.59(2) and may be amended by order (s.59(3)). The list includes district councils, borough councils, county councils and parish councils and the London Assembly (and mayor) but not the partly devolved Scottish Parliament or Welsh Assembly.

See the examples in the Explanatory Notes for s.58 (at para. 199) and s.59 (at para. 200):

- A local authority does not equip meeting rooms with hearing loops for a member who has a hearing impairment, in order to enable her to take full part in the business for which she has been elected. This would be discrimination if provision of hearing loops were considered to be a reasonable adjustment.
- A local authority member who is considering an application for planning permission while sitting on a council's Planning Committee would be undertaking 'official business'.

6.2   PART 5, CHAPTER 2 – OCCUPATIONAL PENSION SCHEMES

Sections 61–63 of the Act provide for non-discrimination in relation to occupational pension schemes.

By s.61(1), any occupational pension scheme must be taken to include a non-discrimination rule and s.60(3) provides that the provisions of an occupational scheme have effect subject to the rule. Section 61(2) describes a 'non-discrimination rule' as a provision by virtue of which a 'responsible person' (A):

(a) must not discriminate against another person (B) in carrying out any of A's functions in relation to the scheme;
(b) must not, in relation to the scheme, harass B;
(c) must not, in relation to the scheme, victimise B.

Responsible persons are the trustees or managers of the scheme, an employer whose employees are, or may be, members of the scheme or a person exercising an appointing function in relation to an office the holder of which is, or may be, a member of the scheme (s.61(4)). In relation to the latter, the appointing function is any of the following:

(a) the function of appointing a person;
(b) the function of terminating a person's appointment;
(c) the function of recommending a person for appointment;
(d) the function of approving an appointment.

It should be noted that a duty to make reasonable adjustments applies to a responsible person (s.61(11)).

Any breaches may be enforced under Part 9 (s.61(7)), but it will not be a breach of the non-discrimination rule to maintain or use in relation to the scheme rules, practices, actions or decisions relating to age which are of a description specified by order by a Minister of the Crown (s.61(8)). In other words, statutory authority may be a defence. However, such an order authorising the use of rules, practices, actions or decisions which are not in use before the order comes into force must not be made unless the Minister consults such persons as the Minister thinks appropriate (s.61(9)).

A non-discrimination rule will not have effect if an equality rule has effect in relation to the scheme or would have effect but for Part 2 of Sched. 7 (s.61(10)). This Part of Sched. 7 contains six paragraphs which provide as follows:

- By para. 3, the sex equality rule (which is to be found in Part 3 of Chapter 5) does not have effect in relation to a difference as between men and women in the effect of relevant matter if the difference is permitted by virtue of paras. 4–6. A 'relevant matter' has the meaning in s.67(8). It is therefore necessary to consider how the sex equality rule in s.67 interacts with Sched. 7, and this is considered at 6.3.

- Paragraph 4 permits different amounts to be paid by way of state retirement pensions in prescribed circumstances, where the different amounts are attributable only to differences between men and women in the retirement benefits to which, in prescribed circumstances, the man or woman are, or would be, entitled. Retirement benefits are as defined in ss.43–55 of the Social Security Contributions and Benefits Act 1992.

- By para. 5 (Actuarial factors), a difference as between men and woman is permitted if it consists of applying to the calculation of the employer's contributions to an occupational pension scheme actuarial factors which differ for men and women and are of such descriptions as may be prescribed.

- Paragraph 6 provides a power to amend Part 2 by regulations to add, vary or omit provision about cases where a difference as between men and women in the effect of a relevant matter is permitted, and to make provision about pensionable service on the date before the regulations come into force, but not about pensionable service before 17 May 1990.

Paragraph 215 of the Explanatory Notes gives an example under s.61:

A local authority member who is considering an application for planning permission while sitting on a council's Planning Committee would be undertaking 'official business'.

The general thrust of the above, therefore, is that there may be differential payments in respect of state retirement pensions based upon actuarial factors.

Section 62 goes on to provide that where there is no provision for the trustees to make non-discrimination alterations (s.62(1)) or there is a power but the procedure is liable to be unduly complex or protracted or involves obtaining consents which cannot be obtained or can only be obtained with undue delay or difficulty (s.62(2)), then the trustees *may by resolution* make non-discrimination alterations to the scheme (s.62(3)) which may have effect in relation to periods before the date of the resolution (s.62(4)). Section 62(5) makes it clear that the alterations are in order to ensure that s.61(3) is complied with.

The Explanatory Notes in para. 218 give an example under s.62:

> Changes to the scheme rules of a large scheme require consultation with all the members before they may be made. This is impracticable, particularly as some deferred members cannot be traced. Scheme trustees may make the necessary alteration to scheme rules relying on this power.

There is also provision for communication and operation of a dispute resolution procedure with a disabled person (s.63)).

6.3   PART 5, CHAPTER 3 – EQUALITY OF TERMS

The equal pay provisions of discrimination law have been considered to be in need of reform for some time and the cases being brought throughout the United Kingdom have highlighted the deficiencies in both substantive law and procedure. The EHRC in March 2009 had already published a press release arguing for reform and had included five proposals, of which three key reforms are now in the Act: (1) a ban on secrecy clauses; (2) a gender pay gap reporting requirement; and (3) the possibility of pay claims based upon hypothetical comparators (though (2) is controversial and it remains to be seen if it will be enacted). The other two proposals for representative actions and for tribunals to have a more sweeping power to make recommendations have not been taken up, though s.124 still permits general recommendations regarding the workforce as opposed to individual complainants. Section 124 does not, however, appear to bring in equal pay.

Chapter 3 of Part 5, which is entitled 'Equality of Terms', is itself divided into three sections:

- Sex equality, which is covered by ss.64–71. These sections are primarily concerned with equal pay and occupational pensions, derived from the Equal Pay Act 1970.
- Pregnancy and maternity equality, which is covered by ss.72–78.
- Supplementary provisions, which are primarily concerned with comparators (s.79) for the purposes of Chapter 3, as well as the interpretation and exceptions section (s.80).

6.3.1   Sex equality and equal pay (sections 64–71)

Section 64(1) provides that ss.64–70 apply where a person (A) is employed on work that is equal to work that a comparator of the opposite sex (B) does or where a person (A) holds a personal or public office that is equal to the work that a comparator (B) does. Section 64(2) states that s.64(1) is not restricted to work done contemporaneously. This subsection is designed to make it clear that the comparator may be a predecessor and to apply existing case law such as *McCarthy's Ltd* v. *Smith Case* C–129/79 [1980] ECR 1275.

Having defined the relevant types of work covered (s.64), s.65(1) sets out that work is equal if it is like work, work rated as equivalent or work of equal value (the provisions that were contained in the 1970 Act).

Like work

Section 65(2) provides that A's work is like B's work if A's work and B's work is the same or broadly similar, and such differences as there are between their work are not of practical importance in relation to the terms of their work. Section 65(3) then goes on to state that 'So', on a comparison of one person's work with another's for the purposes of s.65(2), it is necessary to have regard to the frequency with which differences between their work occur in practice and the nature and extent of the differences.

Work rated as equivalent

By s.65(4), work is rated as equivalent if a job evaluation study gives an equal value to A's job and B's job in terms of the demands made on a worker or would give an equal value to A's job and B's job in those terms were the evaluation not made on a sex-specific system. A system is sex specific if, for the purposes of one or more of the demands made on a worker, it sets values for men different from those it sets for women (s.65(5)). A job evaluation study is defined in s.80(5) as a study undertaken with a view to evaluating, in terms of the demands made on a person by reference to factors such as effort, skill and decision-making, the jobs to be done (a) by some or all of the workers in an undertaking or group of undertakings, or (b) in the case of the armed forces, by some or all of the members of the armed forces.

Equal value

By s.65(6), work is of equal value it if is neither like B's work nor rated as equivalent to B's work, but nevertheless is equal to B's work in terms of the demands made on A by reference to factors such as effort, skill and decision-making.

The sex equality clause

Section 66(1) provides that if the terms of A's work do not, by whatever means, include an equality clause, they are to be treated as including one. An equality clause under s.66(2) is a provision which has the effect that:

(a) if a term of A's is less favourable to A than a corresponding term of B's is to B, A's term is modified so as not to be less favourable. By s.66(3), this applies to membership or rights under an occupational pension scheme only in so far as a *sex equality rule* (defined in s.67) would have effect in relation to such terms;

(b) if A does not have a term which corresponds to a term of B's that benefits B, A's terms are modified so as to include such a term.

Where the work is rated as equivalent, but not all terms have been determined by the rating of the work, then the sex equality clause will be applicable (s.66(4)).

Sex equality rule

The sex equality rule is to be treated as applying to an occupational pension scheme if the scheme does not include such a rule (s.67(1)). A sex equality rule is defined by s.67(2) as a provision that has the effect that:

(a) if a relevant term is less favourable to A than it is to B, the term is modified so as not to be less favourable;

(b) if a term confers a relevant discretion capable of being exercised in a way that would be less favourable to A than to B, the term is modified so as to prevent the exercise of the discretion in that way.

The relevant term will be a term on which persons become members of the scheme or a term on which members of the scheme are treated (s.67(3)) including the way in which dependants of members are treated (s.67(5)). The exercise of discretion relates to the way in which persons become members of the scheme or are treated (s.67(4)) or the way in which dependants are treated (s.67(6)).

The Act also makes provision to ensure that if the effect of a relevant matter on persons of the same sex differs according to their family, marital or civil partnership status, a comparison for the purposes of s.67 of the effect of that matter on persons of the opposite sex must be with persons who have the same status (s.67(7)). A relevant matter for this purpose is a relevant term, a term conferring a relevant discretion or the exercise of a relevant discretion in relation to an occupational pension scheme (s.67(9)).

The above provisions do not apply to the terms on which persons *become members* in relation to pensionable service before 8 April 1976 (s.67(9)) or in relation to which *members of an occupational pension scheme are treated* before 17 May 1990. These dates reflect two ECJ decisions – the first, in 1976, when the ECJ in *Defrenne* v. *Sabena* [1976] ICR 547; [1976] ECR 455 decided that Article 141 had direct effect, and the second, the seminal case of *Barber* v. *Guardian Royal Exchange* [1990] ICR 616; [1990] IRLR 240, when, from 17 May 1990, it was held that claims could be made in relation to level of benefits but the ECJ applied a temporal limitation from that date.

Alteration of schemes

There is provision in relation to sex equality alterations of schemes in s.68 which is in similar terms to the non-discrimination alterations under s.62 of the Act.

The material factor defence

Section 69 of the Act contains provisions in relation the material factor defence. By s.69(1), the sex equality clause in A's terms has no effect in relation to a difference between A's terms and B's terms if the responsible person shows that the difference is because of a material factor reliance on which (a) does not involve treating A less favourably because of A's sex than the responsible person treats B, and (b) if the factor is within subs. (2), is a proportionate means of achieving a legitimate aim. Section 69(2) provides that the factor is within the subsection if A shows that, as a result of the factor, A and persons of the same sex doing work equal to A's work are put at a particular disadvantage when compared with persons of the opposite sex doing work equal to A's. The word 'genuine' which was contained in s.1(3) of the Equal Pay Act 1970 has been dropped as the government has taken the view that it adds nothing. The new wording does, however, make it clear that indirect discrimination is covered, so that it will require objective justification.

The Act expressly provides that the long-term objective of reducing inequality between the terms of work of men and women is always to be regarded as a legitimate aim (s.69(3)). This, in effect, adopts the case law that employers who implement a measure of pay protection whilst seeking to eliminate discrimination from their pay structures *may* be able to justify pay protection even though it prolongs the discriminatory pay practice on a temporary basis.

Provision is also made that the sex equality rule (i.e. the rule related to pensions) has no effect in relation to a relevant matter under s.67 if the trustees or managers of the scheme show that the difference is because of a material factor which is not the difference of sex (s.69(4)).

The material factor must be a material difference between A's case and B's case (s.69(6)).

Exclusion of sex discrimination provisions and sex discrimination in relation to contractual pay

As with the SDA 1975 and the Equal Pay Act 1970, the scheme of the Act is that claims under this Chapter are excluded from sex discrimination claims where there is contractual pay, i.e. it should be an equal pay claim. Therefore, the 'relevant sex discrimination provision', as defined in s.70(3), will have no effect in relation to a term of the contract that (a) is modified by, or included by virtue of, a sex equality clause or rule, or (b) would be so modified or included but for s.69 or Part 2 of Sched. 7, i.e. where the material factor defence applies or under the exceptions in the Schedule relating to occupational pensions.

Furthermore, it is not sex discrimination to include a term that is less favourable than that required by the equality clause provision of s.66(2). This is because the appropriate claim is one for equal pay.

Section 71 also provides that a term of a person's work that relates to pay, but in relation to which a sex equality clause or rule has no effect, is not covered by s.70, so that, in effect, claims may be brought as sex discrimination. The effect of s.71 would appear to permit claims to be brought for sex discrimination in relation to contractual pay under the direct discrimination and dual provisions, even though the comparator is hypothetical, thus, to a limited extent, getting round the requirement for a comparator otherwise needed in equal pay claims (cf. *Walton Centre for Neurology and Neuro Surgery NHS Trust* v. *Bewley* [2008] ICR 1041). The Explanatory Notes state that:

> This section deals with sex discrimination in relation to contractual pay in circumstances where a sex equality clause would not operate. This could be because there is no comparator doing equal work with whom a claimant can compare his or her pay or other terms. The section ensures that indirect sex discrimination in respect of contractual pay can be challenged only by means of an equality clause. However, the section for the first time enables a person who is treated less favourably than others by being paid less because of the person's sex or a combination of two protected characteristics including sex to pursue a claim for direct or dual discrimination where an equality clause does not operate. (para. 249)

6.3.2   Pregnancy and maternity equality (sections 72–76)

The pregnancy and maternity provisions apply where a woman is employed or holds a personal or public office (s.72). It should be noted that the provisions of ss.73–76 are concerned with pay and terms and conditions rather than leave, which is still to be found in the Employment Rights Act 1996 and associated regulations.

Section 73(1) provides that a maternity equality clause is deemed to be included in the terms of a woman's work, which is a provision that has the effect set out in s.74(1), (6) and (8). However, where this relates to membership of or rights under an occupational pension scheme, the maternity equality clause only has such effect as the maternity equality rule would have. As with the other provisions in this Chapter, the legislation distinguishes between the equality clause which relates to pay and the rule which relates to occupational pensions.

The maternity equality clause

By s.74(1), a term of the woman's work that provides for maternity-related pay to be calculated by reference to her pay at a particular time is, if each of the three conditions set out in s.74(2),(3) and (4) are satisfied, modified as mentioned in s.74(5).

The modification in s.74(5) is that maternity-related pay is to be subject to any increase in pay, mentioned in s.74(2)(a), or any increase as mentioned in s.74(2)(b). The simple effect of s.74 is that any pay increases which occur during maternity leave have to be taken into account. This is because s.74(2) provides that the first condition is that if, after the particular time mentioned in s.74(1) but before the end of the protected period, the pay increases or would have increased if the woman had not been on maternity leave, then s.74(5) means that these increases are taken into account.

Section 74(3) provides that the second condition is that the maternity-related pay is not what the woman's pay would have been if she was not on maternity leave or the difference between the amount of statutory maternity pay to which she is entitled and what her pay would have been had she not been on maternity leave.

The third condition is that the terms of the work do not provide for the maternity-related pay to be subject to the increase or an increase that would have occurred as set out in s.74(2).

There is further provision for modification of the terms in s.74(6) and (7) where the term of the work provides for pay, but does not provide for the woman to have been given the pay she would have been given if she had not been on maternity leave. For these purposes, pay is defined as pay, including bonus, in respect of times before the woman was on maternity leave, pay by way of bonus during the compulsory maternity leave period and pay in respect of bonus after the protected period. The contract is to be regarded as modified to include these sums. The contract is also to be regarded as modified to include for any pay increases to which pay would have been subject after the end of the protected period if the woman had not been on maternity leave (s.74(8)), i.e. it must include any pay rises awarded whilst the woman was on leave.

Maternity-related pay is pay to which a woman is entitled as a result of being pregnant or in respect of times she is on maternity leave (s.74(9)) and the protected period is as set out in s.18 (s.74(10)) (see **3.6**).

Examples in para. 260 of the Explanatory Notes include:

- Early in her maternity leave, a woman receiving maternity-related pay becomes entitled to an increase of pay. If her terms of employment do not already provide for the increase to be reflected in her maternity-related pay, the employer must recalculate her maternity pay to take account of the increment.
- A woman becomes entitled to a contractual bonus for work she undertook before she went on maternity leave. The employer cannot delay payment of the bonus and must pay it to her when it would have been paid had she not been on maternity leave.

The maternity equality rule

Section 75 contains detailed provision for a maternity equality rule to be incorporated into an occupational pension scheme if it does not contain such a rule (s.75(1)). By s.75(3), time spent on maternity leave must be treated in the same manner as when the woman is not on maternity leave and s.75(4) provides that a relevant discretion may not be exercised differently because the woman is on maternity leave. The relevant terms relate to membership, accrual of rights or terms providing for the determination of the amount of a benefit payable under the scheme (s.75(5)) and any exercise of discretion relates to these factors (s.75(6)).

Section 75(7) provides that a woman's contributions to the scheme whilst she is on maternity leave cannot be determined otherwise than by reference to what she is actually paid. There is also provision, because of the historical periods of time when a woman was paid whilst on ordinary maternity leave, that the section only applies where the expected week of childbirth was after 6 April 2003 (s.75(8)) and for additional maternity leave when she is not being paid that it does not apply to accrual of rights under the scheme and applies for other purposes only where the expected week of childbirth was after 5 October 2008 (s.75(9)).

References to payment include payment of statutory maternity pay (s.75(10)).

Examples in para. 268 of the Explanatory Notes include:

- A woman who is on maternity leave will be entitled to continuing membership of the scheme throughout the period of maternity leave whether or not she is paid.
- A woman who is paid whilst on maternity leave will be entitled to accrue rights in a scheme as though she were paid her usual salary but she will only be required to make contributions based on her actual pay.

Exclusions

As with sex discrimination and equal pay, the Act excludes the maternity and pregnancy discrimination provisions where the relevant term of a woman's work is modified by a maternity equality clause or rule (s.76(1) and (2)). The pregnancy and maternity provisions are those contained in ss.39(2), 49(6) and 50(6), i.e. those sections that prohibit discrimination against employees or in respect of a personal or public office. An example in para. 272 of the Explanatory Notes is:

A woman who is in line for promotion tells her employer that she is pregnant. The employer tells the woman he will not promote her because she is likely to be absent on maternity leave during a very busy period. This will be direct pregnancy discrimination.

6.3.3   Discussions about pay (section 77)

Although appearing in Part 5, Chapter 3 on equality of terms, s.77 contains a provision which is designed to make unenforceable any clause which aims to 'gag' any members of staff from talking about their pay. The government took the view in the White Paper that 'secrecy clauses' should be banned, which prevented an employee from discussing pay with his or her colleagues. It stated that where colleagues work closely together, on similar work, but are paid different amounts, they should be able to compare the amounts if they want (*Framework for a Fairer Future – The Equalities Bill*, Cm 7431, p.23).

Section 77(1) provides that a 'term of a person's work that purports to prevent or restrict the person (P) from disclosing or seeking to disclose information about the terms of P's work is unenforceable against P *in so far as P makes or seeks to make a relevant pay disclosure*' (emphasis added). The words in italics are rather more limited than the White Paper proposal since s.77(3) provides that a relevant pay disclosure is one that is made 'for the purpose of enabling the person who makes it, or the person to whom it is made, to find out whether or to what extent there is, in relation to the work in question, a connection between pay and having (or not having) a particular protected characteristic'. Any term which seeks to prevent such disclosure will be unenforceable (s.77(2)) and this will include any disclosure from a colleague or former colleague. The Act will therefore not prevent a clause in a contract which stops general discussion about pay but only where the discussions are aimed at establishing discrimination.

Such disclosures are protected acts (s.77(4)) and are covered by the victimisation provisions of the legislation (s.77(4)) as listed in s.77(5).

The Explanatory Notes (at para. 275) set out how this will work in practice:

- A female employee thinks she is underpaid compared with a male colleague. She asks him what he is paid, and he tells her. The employer takes disciplinary action against the man as a result. The man can bring a claim for victimisation against the employer for disciplining him.
- A female employee who discloses her pay to one of her employer's competitors with a view to getting a better offer could be in breach of a confidentiality clause in her contract. The employer could take action against her in relation to that breach.

6.3.4   Gender pay information (section 78)

The Labour Government was of the view that steps should be taken to seek to address pay inequality outside of the tribunal pay claim environment so that there is now provision in s.78(1) for regulations to be enacted which may require employers to 'publish information relating to the pay of employees for the purpose of showing whether, by reference to factors of such description as is prescribed, there are differences in the pay of male and female employees'. This will apply to an employer with over 250 employees but not to the public authorities listed in Sched. 19 or a government department or part of the armed forces not listed in that Schedule. The government is, in effect, excluded.

The regulations may prescribe:

(a)   descriptions of employer;
(b)   descriptions of employee;
(c)   how to calculate the number of employees that an employer has;
(d)   descriptions of information;
(e)   the time at which information is to be published;
(f)   the form and manner in which it is to be published.

The regulations cannot, however, after first publication of information, require that the information is published more frequently than on a 12-month basis (s.78(4)). There is also power for enforcement by criminal or other sanctions (s.78(5)).

It should be noted that the Labour Government stated that this power would not come into force until at least April 2013. The aim is to seek voluntary publishing and exercise the power if this does not work.

The EHRC has published recommendations as to how such voluntary disclosure should be made and is offering limited immunity for firms who take up this offer from investigation. The current coalition government is opposed to enacting these provisions.

6.3.5 Comparators and interpretation (sections 79 and 80)

Section 79 sets out the basis on which comparison is to be made for the purpose of Chapter 3. The scheme is as follows:

Where A is employed (s.79(2)), then B is the comparator if:

- under s.79(3), B is employed by A's employer or an associate of A's employer and A and B work at the same establishment;
- under s.79(4), B is employed by A's employer or an associate of A's employer, works at an establishment other than the one at which A works, and common terms apply at the establishments (either generally or as between A and B).

Where A holds a personal office or public office, B is a comparator if B holds a personal office or public office and the person responsible for paying A is also responsible for paying B.

There is also provision for House of Commons (s.79(6)) and House of Lords (s.79(7)) staff. A constable is to be treated as holding a public office (s.79(8)).

Under s.79(9), employers are associated if one is a company of which the other (directly or indirectly) has control, or both are companies of which a third person (directly or indirectly) has control. Associated employers are thus limited to companies.

Section 80 contains a number of relevant definitions that apply to Chapter 3:

- The terms of a person's work are defined as: (a) if the person is employed, the terms of the person's employment that are in the person's contract of employment, contract of apprenticeship or contract to do work personally; (b) if the person holds a personal or public office, the terms of the person's appointment to the office (s.80(2)).
- Where work is not done at an establishment, it will be treated as done at the establishment with which it has the closest connection (s.80(3)).
- A person is the 'responsible person' if that person is the other's employer or is responsible for paying remuneration in respect of a personal or public office that the other holds (s.80(4)).

It should also be noted that the exceptions set out in Sched. 7 (Equality of terms: exceptions) have effect under this Chapter. Part 2 of Sched. 7 has been considered at **6.2**. In addition, it should be noted that para. 1 of Sched. 7 excludes the sex and maternity equality clauses where there is the requirement to comply with laws regulating the employment or appointment of women to personal or public offices, and para. 2 provides that the sex equality clause does not have effect in respect of terms of work affording special treatment to women in connection with pregnancy or childbirth.

7 PART 6 – EDUCATION

7.1 PART 6, CHAPTER 1 – SCHOOLS

7.1.1 Application (section 84)

Section 84 provides that Chapter 1 does not apply to the protected characteristics of age or marriage and civil partnership. In this respect, s.84 is designed to ensure consistency with the previous legislative regime applying to schools. In addition, it extends protection from discrimination to transsexual pupils and pupils who become pregnant. At para. 295, the Explanatory Notes give examples of where there will not be discrimination, as follows:

- It is not unlawful discrimination for a school to organise a trip for pupils in one year group, but not for pupils in other years.
- It is not unlawful discrimination for a school to allow older pupils to have privileges for which younger pupils are not eligible, such as more choice of uniform or the right to leave school during the lunch period.

7.1.2 Principles of discrimination in the admission and treatment of pupils (section 85)

Section 85(1) prevents the responsible body of a school from discriminating against a person:

    (a)   in the arrangements it makes for deciding who is offered admission as a pupil;
    (b)   as to the terms on which it offers to admit the person as a pupil;
    (c)   by not admitting the person as a pupil.

Under s.85(2), the responsible body of a school must not discriminate against a pupil (defined in s.89(3)):

    (a)   in the way it provides education for the pupil;
    (b)   in the way it affords the pupil access to a benefit, facility or service;
    (c)   by not providing education for the pupil;
    (d)   by not affording the pupil access to a benefit, facility or service;
    (e)   by excluding the pupil from the school;
    (f)   by subjecting the pupil to any other detriment.

Harassment against a pupil or a person who has applied for admission as a pupil is proscribed by s.85(3). Importantly, the following are not protected characteristics for these purposes: (a) gender reassignment; (b) religion or belief; (c) sexual orientation. However, any harassment on these grounds is likely to constitute direct discrimination and therefore to be unlawful in any event.

Section 85(4) and (5) prohibits victimisation by the responsible body of a school. This should be read in conjunction with s.86 (see below).

By s.85(6), the duty to make reasonable adjustments applies to the responsible body of a school. Schedule 13 defines the ambit of this duty, restricting it to the first and third requirements (see s.20(3) and (5) respectively, adjustments as regards disabled persons). The third requirement will be new to most schools. In deciding whether it is reasonable to take a step for the purpose of complying with the first or third requirement, the responsible body must have regard to the relevant provisions of any Codes of Practice issued under s.14 of the Equality Act 2006 (see Sched. 7, para. 7).

The exceptions for admission to single-sex schools (in relation to sex), faith schools (in relation to religion and belief) and schools that select based on academic ability (in relation to disability) are dealt with in Sched. 11 (see 7.1.7).

In England and Wales, s.85 applies to:

- schools maintained by a local authority (in respect of which the 'responsible body' is the local authority or governing body); and
- independent educational institutions and special schools not maintained by a local authority (in respect of both of which the 'responsible body' is the proprietor).

The Explanatory Notes give examples at para. 299:

- A school refuses to let a gay pupil become a prefect because of his sexual orientation. This would be direct discrimination.
- A selective school imposes a higher standard for admission to applicants from an ethnic minority background, or to girls. This would be direct discrimination.
- A pupil alleges, in good faith, that his school has discriminated against him because of his religion (for example claiming that he is given worse marks than other pupils because he is Jewish), so the school punishes him by making him do a detention. This would be victimisation.
- A teacher ridicules a particular pupil in class because of his disability, or makes comments which have the result of making the girls in the class feel embarrassed and humiliated. This would be harassment.

7.1.3 Victimisation for conduct of parents, etc. (section 86)

Section 86 protects children in schools from victimisation as a result of a protected act (such as making a complaint of discrimination) done by their parent or sibling. The aim is that those responsible for the child will not feel discouraged from raising an issue of discrimination with a school because of a concern that their child may suffer a detriment as a result.

Section 86(3) and (4) addresses the situation of a parent apparently acting maliciously in supporting an untrue complaint. The approach under the Act mirrors the general approach to victimisation outside the education sphere:

(a) Where a parent or sibling maliciously makes or supports an untrue complaint, the child is still protected from victimisation, as long as the child has acted in good faith.

(b) Where the child has acted in bad faith, he or she is not protected, even where a parent or sibling makes or supports an untrue complaint in good faith.

Thus, if a pupil were to bring a case against her school claiming that she has suffered harassment by a member of staff because of her sex, the pupil's younger brother, at the same school, is protected against any less favourable treatment by the school because of this, even if it is later found that the older sister was not acting in good faith.

'Child' means a person who has not attained the age of 18 and 'sibling' includes a brother or sister, a half-brother or half-sister, or a stepbrother or stepsister (s.86(5)).

The Explanatory Notes give examples (at para. 302):

■   The parent of a pupil complains to the school that her daughter is suffering sex discrimination by not being allowed to participate in a metalwork class. The daughter is protected from being treated less favourably by the school in any way because of this complaint.

■   A pupil brings a case against his school claiming that he has suffered discrimination by a member of staff because of his sexual orientation. The pupil's younger brother, at the same school, is protected against any less favourable treatment by the school because of this case, even if it is later found that the older brother was not acting in good faith.

7.1.4   Application of powers under the Education Act 1996 (section 87)

By s.87, the Secretary of State is empowered to give directions, using powers under the Education Act 1996, to require a maintained school or a non-maintained special school to comply with its duties under s.85. The Secretary of State is thereby granted a level of autonomy in procuring the Act's application, for example, by requiring a school to stop a discriminatory practice or policy even if no complaint has been brought by a pupil or prospective pupil.

The Explanatory Notes at para. 304 give the following example:

■   The governing body of a school refuses as a matter of policy to let disabled pupils participate in school trips because of the extra risk management required. The Secretary of State could direct the governing body to change its policy so as to make reasonable adjustments to enable disabled pupils to participate.

Sections 496 and 497 of the Education Act 1996 empower the Secretary of State to give directions to local education authorities and to governing bodies of maintained schools to prevent them exercising their functions under the Education Acts unreasonably, or to require them to perform statutory duties where they are not doing so. This power had previously been extended to require compliance with the law on sex discrimination, and under s.87(2), now extends to all the protected characteristics covered by s.85.

7.1.5   Accessibility for disabled pupils (section 88)

Section 88 brings into effect Schedule 10, thereby requiring local authorities and schools to prepare and implement accessibility strategies and plans. The aim according to the Explanatory Notes is to increase disabled pupils' access to the school curriculum, improve the physical environment for such pupils and improve the provision of information to them. Strategies must be implemented after taking account of pupils' disabilities and any preferences expressed by them and their parents. The strategies should be reviewed regularly, and revised if needed.

7.1.6   Interpretation and exceptions (section 89)

Section 89 defines, by reference to pre-existing legislative provisions, certain terms used in the Act, such as 'pupil', 'school' and 'local authority'.

Importantly, s.89(2) expressly excludes from the scope of the Chapter anything done in connection with the content of the curriculum. According to the Explanatory Notes, this is designed to ensure that the Act does not stifle the ability of schools 'to include a full range of issues, ideas and materials in their syllabus and to expose pupils to thoughts and ideas of all kinds'. The reference to education in s.85(2)(a) should, in practical terms, ensure issues are taught in a way which does not subject pupils to discrimination.

Section 89(12) brings into effect Sched. 11, which in turn provides important amendments to the general scheme in the context of: (a) admission to single-sex schools; (b) single-sex boarding at schools; (c) single-sex schools turning co-educational; (d) schools with religious character; (e) curriculum/worship; and (f) permitted forms of selection for the purposes of s.85(1).

The Explanatory Notes give examples at para. 307:

- A school curriculum includes teaching of evolution in science lessons. This would not be religious discrimination against a pupil whose religious beliefs include creationism.
- A school curriculum includes The Taming of the Shrew on the syllabus. This would not be discrimination against a girl.

7.1.7   Schedule 11 – Schools: exceptions

Part 1: Sex discrimination

Part 1 of Sched. 11 is designed to replicate the effect of provisions in the SDA 1975. It makes exceptions from the s.85 prohibition on sex discrimination in order: (a) to allow for the existence of single-sex schools and single-sex boarding at schools, and (b) to make transitional provisions for single-sex schools which are turning co-educational. It defines a school as single-sex if it admits pupils of one sex only *or* if it admits a comparatively small number of pupils of the opposite sex on an exceptional basis or in relation to particular courses or classes only. A single-sex school is allowed to refuse to admit pupils of the opposite sex or to limit those pupils to particular courses or classes. However, other forms of sex discrimination by the school against its opposite-sex pupils would still be unlawful.

The Explanatory Notes provide the following examples at para. 873:

- A school which admits only boys is not discriminating unlawfully against girls.
- If the daughters of certain members of staff at a boys' school are allowed to attend, it is still regarded as a single-sex school.
- A boys' school which admits some girls to the Sixth Form, or which lets girls attend for a particular GCSE course not offered at their own school is still regarded as a single-sex school.
- A boys' school which admits girls to A-level science classes is not discriminating unlawfully if it refuses to admit them to A-level media studies or maths classes.
- A boys' school which admits girls to the Sixth Form but refuses to let them use the same cafeteria or go on the same visits as other Sixth Form pupils would be discriminating unlawfully against them.

Paragraph 2 of Sched. 11 provides that a mixed-sex school, some of whose pupils are boarders, may lawfully admit only pupils of one sex to be boarders. The exception applies even if some members of the other sex are admitted as boarders, so long as their numbers are small compared to the numbers of other pupils admitted as boarders.

Paragraphs 3 and 4 of the Schedule enable a school which is changing from a single-sex to a co-educational institution to apply for a transitional exemption order to enable it to continue to restrict admittance to a single sex until the transition from single-sex is complete.

Part 2: Religious or belief-related discrimination

Part 2 of Sched. 11 creates a number of exceptions to the prohibition on discrimination on grounds of religion or belief in relation to schools with a religious character, and to acts of worship or other religious observance in any school. According to the Explanatory Notes, these exceptions, in addition to the amending powers in para. 7, are designed to replicate the effect of provisions in Part 2 of the Equality Act 2006.

Paragraph 5 allows schools which have a religious character or ethos (commonly known as 'faith schools') to discriminate on grounds of religion or belief in relation to admissions and in access to any benefit, facility or service. Accordingly, a faith school may have admissions criteria which give preference to members of its own religion. Faith schools are also permitted to conduct themselves in a way which is compatible with their religious character or ethos, but are not permitted to discriminate on any other of the prohibited grounds, such as sex, race or sexual orientation.

Examples given by the Explanatory Notes (at para. 879) include the following:

- A Muslim school may give priority to Muslim pupils when choosing between applicants for admission (although the Admissions Code will not allow it to refuse to accept pupils of another or no religion unless it is oversubscribed). However, it may not discriminate between pupils on other prohibited grounds, such as by refusing to admit a child of the school's own faith because she is black or a lesbian.
- A Jewish school which provides spiritual instruction or pastoral care from a rabbi is not discriminating unlawfully by not making equivalent provision for pupils from other religious faiths.
- A Roman Catholic school which organises visits for pupils to sites of particular interest to its own faith, such as a cathedral, is not discriminating unlawfully by not arranging trips to sites of significance to the faiths of other pupils.
- A faith school would be acting unlawfully if it sought to penalise or exclude a pupil because he or she had renounced the faith of the school or joined a different religion or denomination.

Paragraph 6 disapplies the prohibition on religious discrimination from anything done in relation to acts of worship or other religious observance organised by or on behalf of a school, whether or not it is part of the curriculum. This exception applies to any school, not just faith schools. In this respect, it adopts the same position as the Equality Act 2006. Thus, parents can still remove their children from collective worship, and Sixth Form pupils may decide to withdraw themselves. Schools remain under no obligation to provide opportunities for separate worship for the different religions and beliefs represented among their pupils.

The Explanatory Notes give the following examples at para. 881:

- A school must allow Jewish or Hindu parents to withdraw their children from daily assemblies which include an element of worship of a mainly Christian character, but they will not be discriminating unlawfully against those children by not providing alternative assemblies including Jewish or Hindu worship.
- Schools are free to organise or to participate in ceremonies celebrating any faith, such as Christmas, Diwali, Chanukah or Eid, without being subject to claims of religious discrimination against children of other religions or of none.

Paragraph 7 provides a power for a Minister of the Crown to amend or repeal the religious discrimination exceptions.

Disability discrimination

Paragraph 8 of Sched. 11 provides that schools will not be discriminating against disabled children when applying a permitted form of selection (as defined). Permitted forms of selection are, broadly, the selective admission arrangements operated by grammar schools, and selection by ability and aptitude in accordance with the School Standards and Framework Act 1998.

By way of example: the parents of a disabled pupil cannot claim disability discrimination against a particular school if that pupil fails to meet any educational entry requirements set by the school.

Enforcement in respect of the rights of a disabled pupil is set out in Sched. 17.

7.2   PART 6, CHAPTER 2 – FURTHER AND HIGHER EDUCATION

This Chapter applies to the provision of further and higher education. 'Further education' has the meaning given in the Education Act 1996, s.2 and 'higher education' means education provided by means of a course described in Sched. 6 to the Education Reform Act 1988.

This Chapter does not apply to the protected characteristics of marriage and civil partnership (s.90).

As with schools, the provisions described below do not apply to anything done in connection with the content of the curriculum (s.94(2)), although the way in which the curriculum is taught is covered by these prohibitions.

7.2.1   Students: admission and treatment, etc. (section 91)

Although there are some changes, s.91 is designed to replicate the effect of provisions in the legislation that applied to schools prior to the Act coming into force. This section applies to universities, any other institutions within the higher education sector and institutions within the further education sector (s.91(10)).

By s.91(1), the responsible body of an institution providing further and higher education is prohibited from discriminating against a person:

    (a) in the arrangements it makes for deciding who is offered admission as a student;
    (b) as to the terms on which it offers to admit the person as a student;
    (c) by not admitting the person as a student.

Once that person becomes a student (as defined by s.94(3)), the responsible body must not discriminate against the student:

    (a) in the way it provides education for the student;
    (b) in the way it affords the student access to a benefit, facility or service;
    (c) by not providing education for the student;
    (d) by not affording the student access to a benefit. facility or service;
    (e) by excluding the student; or
    (f) by subjecting the student to any other detriment.

Section 91(3) prohibits discrimination in the context of conferring qualifications to disabled persons who are not enrolled at the institution.

Section 91(5) prohibits harassment of a student, a person who has applied for admission as a student or a disabled person who holds or has applied for a qualification conferred by the institution.

Section 91(6)–(8) prohibits victimisation by the responsible body.

Section 91(9) provides that the duty to make reasonable adjustments applies to the responsible body of an institution providing further or higher education. Paragraph 3(2) of Sched. 13 provides that this duty encompasses the first, second and third requirements (as defined in s.20(3) and (5)).

Examples given in the Explanatory Notes at paras. 313–315 are:

- A college refuses admission to a man who applies to be a student, because he is gay. This would be direct discrimination.
- A university refuses to provide residential accommodation to Jewish or Muslim students. This would be direct discrimination.
- A college puts an age limit on access to a particular course. This would be direct discrimination, unless the college could show that the age limit was objectively justified.

7.2.2 Further and higher education courses (section 92)

Section 92 replicates the effect of provisions in the DDA 1995 applying to further and higher education courses and extends them to all of the protected characteristics applying in the context of further and higher education. It applies to courses of further or higher education secured by a responsible body in England and Wales and courses of education provided by the governing body of a maintained school (as defined in s.20(7) of the School Standards and Framework Act 1998) under s.80 of the School Standards and Framework Act 1998.

Section 92 makes it unlawful for a local authority or a governing body of maintained schools to discriminate against (s.92(1)) or victimise (s.91(4)) a person: (a) in the arrangements it makes for deciding who is enrolled on the course, (b) as to the terms on which it offers to enrol the person on the course, or (c) by not accepting the person's application for enrolment.

Section 92(3) prohibits harassment of a person who seeks enrolment on a course, is enrolled on a course or is a user of services provided by the body in relation to the course.

Section 92(6) also imposes the duty to make reasonable adjustments for disabled students and prospective students. Paragraph 5(2) of Sched. 13 provides that local authorities are subject to the first, second and third requirements (as defined in s.20(3)–(5)), but governing bodies of maintained schools are only subject to the first and third requirements.

7.2.3 Recreational or training facilities (section 93)

Section 93 replicates the effect of provisions in the DDA 1995 applying to recreational or training facilities and extends these to all of the protected characteristics applying in further and higher education. The section makes it unlawful for a local authority providing recreational or training facilities to discriminate against (s.93(1)) or victimise (s.93(4)) a person: (a) in the arrangements it makes for deciding who is provided with the facilities, (b) as to the terms on which it offers to provide the facilities, or (c) by not accepting the person's application for provision of the facilities.

Section 93(3) prohibits harassment of a person who seeks to have the facilities provided, is provided with the facilities or is a user of services provided by the body in relation to the facilities.

The section encompasses facilities provided under ss.507A, 507B and 508 of the Education Act 1996 and includes, for example, centres, parks and sports facilities.

Section 93(6) also imposes the duty to make reasonable adjustments when offering facilities and service to disabled people. Paragraph 5(2) of Sched. 13 provides that local authorities are subject to the first, second and third requirements (as defined in s.20(3)–(5)).

7.3   PART 6, CHAPTER 3 – GENERAL QUALIFICATIONS BODIES

7.3.1   Application (section 95)

Section 95 provides that this Chapter does not apply to the protected characteristics of marriage and civil partnership.

7.3.2   Qualifications bodies (section 96)

This section makes it unlawful for a qualifications body (defined in s.97 as an authority or body which can confer a relevant qualification) to discriminate against (s.96(1)) or victimise (s.96(4)) a person: (a) in the arrangements it makes for deciding on whom to confer qualifications, (b) as to the terms on which it is prepared to confer a relevant qualification, and (c) by not conferring a relevant qualification.

Section 96(2) provides that a qualifications body must not discriminate against a person who has a qualification by withdrawing that qualification, varying the terms on which it is held or subjecting the person to any other detriment. Relevant qualifications are defined in s.97(3).

Section 96(3) prohibits harassment of a person who holds the qualification or who applies for it.

Section 96(6) places a duty on qualifications bodies to make reasonable adjustments for disabled people. The Explanatory Notes give the example of a visually impaired candidate being granted a modified paper (enlarged font) by a qualifications body in order that she can read her English GCSE exam (see Explanatory Notes, para. 328).

However, by s.96(7)–(10), an 'appropriate regulator' may be designated who can specify: (a) provisions, criteria and practices which are not subject to the duty to make reasonable adjustments; or (b) reasonable adjustments which should not be made. The regulator must consult with appropriate persons before specifying any such matter.

An example given in the Explanatory Notes (at para. 328) is the regulator publishing, after appropriate consultation, a requirement on qualifications bodies not to use a specific reasonable adjustment, such as a reader in the independent reading element of a GCSE English exam. This would then not be unlawful discrimination against a disabled candidate who would otherwise have been entitled to this specific adjustment.

8 PART 7 – ASSOCIATIONS

Sections 100–107 contain provisions in relation to discrimination by associations. This Part of the Act does not apply to the protected characteristic of marriage and civil partnership (s.100(1)). By s.107(2), an 'association' is an association of persons which has at least 25 members and to which admission of membership is regulated by the association's rules and involves a process of selection. The number of 25 may be amended by a Minister of the Crown (s.107(3)).

It does not make any difference whether the association is incorporated or whether the activities are carried out for profit (s.107(4)) and membership is membership of any description (s.107(5)). Further, a person is an 'associate' if the person is not a member but, in accordance with the rules, has some or all of the rights as a member as a result of being a member of another association (s.107(6)). Further, for the purposes of this Part, a registered political party is a party registered in Great Britain under Part 2 of the Political Parties, Elections and Referendums Act 2000.

Part 7 does not apply to discrimination, harassment or victimisation that is already covered by Parts 3, 4, 5 or 6 or that would be so prohibited but for an express exception (s.100(2)).

8.1 MEMBERSHIP AND GUESTS (SECTIONS 101–103)

Section 101(1) contains provision that an association must not discriminate against a person in the arrangements the association makes for deciding who to admit to membership, the terms of admission or by not accepting B's application for membership.

Section 101(2) prevents discrimination against a member, whilst s.101(3) prohibits discrimination against an associate:

- in the way that access is afforded or by not affording access to a benefit, facility or service;
- by depriving the member or associate of membership or rights as an associate;
- by varying terms of membership or rights as an associate;
- by subjecting the member or associate to a detriment.

Section 101(4) prevents harassment of a member, a person seeking to become a member or an associate.

Section 101(5) provides that A must not victimise B:

(a) in the arrangements A makes for deciding who to admit to membership;
(b) as to the terms on which A is prepared to admit B to membership;
(c) by not accepting B's application for membership.

Section 101(6) provides that A must not victimise a member, B, whilst s.101(7) provides that A must not victimise an associate, B:

(a) in the way A affords B access, or by not affording B access, to a benefit, facility or service (s.101(6)(a) and (7)(a))
(b) by depriving B of membership (s.101(6)(b)) or depriving B of B's rights as an associate (s.101(7)(b));
(c) by varying B's terms of membership (s.101(6)(c)) or by varying B's rights as an associate (s.101(7)(c));
(d) by subjecting B to any other detriment (s.101(6)(d) and (7)(e)).

Examples given in para. 337 of the Explanatory Notes are:

■   A gentlemen's club refuses to accept a man's application for membership or charges him a higher subscription rate because he is Muslim. This would be direct discrimination.
■   A private members' golf club, which has members of both sexes, requires its female members to play only on certain days while allowing male members to play at all times. This would be direct discrimination.

Section 102 contains similar provisions in relation to non-discrimination against guests in the arrangements for invitation and the terms on which guests are invited and against harassment or victimisation of guests. An example under para. 339 of the Explanatory Notes is:

An association refuses to invite the disabled wife of a member to attend an annual dinner, which is open to all members' partners, simply because she is a wheelchair user. This would be direct discrimination.

8.2   SPECIAL PROVISION FOR POLITICAL PARTIES (SECTIONS 104–106)

By s.104(1) and (2), a registered political party does not contravene Part 7 only by acting in accordance with selection arrangements. Such selection arrangements are arrangements:

(a) which the party makes for regulating the selection of its candidates in a relevant election;
(b) the purpose of which is to reduce inequality in the party's representation in the body concerned. This inequality is a reference to inequality between the number of the party's candidates elected to be members of the body who share a protected characteristic, and the number of the party's candidates so elected

who do not share that characteristic (s.104(4)). Persons share the selected characteristic of disability if they are disabled persons (s.104(5));

(c) which are a proportionate means of achieving that purpose.

Selection arrangements do not include shortlisting only such persons who have a protected characteristic (s.101(6)) but this does not apply to the protected characteristic of sex and (c) above does not apply to shortlisting (s.101(7)).

The relevant elections, for the purpose of s.104, are:

(a) Parliamentary Elections;
(b) elections to the European Parliament;
(c) elections to the Scottish Parliament;
(d) elections to the National Assembly for Wales;
(e) local government elections within the meaning of section 191, 203 or 204 of the Representation of the People Act 1983 (excluding elections for the Mayor of London).

Section 104(7) is time limited until 2030 unless an order is made otherwise (s.105).

Examples given under para. 345 of the Explanatory Notes include:

■ A political party can have a women-only shortlist of potential candidates to represent a particular constituency in Parliament, provided women remain under-represented in the party's Members of Parliament.
■ A political party cannot shortlist only black or Asian candidates for a local government by-election. However, if Asians are under-represented amongst a party's elected councillors on a particular Council, the party could choose to reserve a specific number of seats for Asian candidates on a by-election shortlist.

Under s.106, there is provision for regulations to be made which require registered political parties to publish information about the protected characteristics of persons who come within the description of persons prescribed in the regulations, which may cover:

(a) successful applicants for nomination as a candidate at the relevant election;
(b) unsuccessful applicants for nomination as a candidate at that election;
(c) candidates elected at that election;
(d) candidates who are not elected at that election.

The relevant elections (s.106(5)) are:

(a) Parliamentary Elections;
(b) elections to the European Parliament;
(c) elections to the Scottish Parliament;
(d) elections to the National Assembly for Wales.

However, this information should not enable a person to be identified from that information (s.106(4)) and the protected characteristics do not include marriage and civil partnership or pregnancy and maternity (s.106(6)).

The regulations may relate to all or only certain protected characteristics and must include a statement, in respect of each protected characteristic to which the information relates, of the proportion that the number of persons who provided the information to the party bears to the number of persons who were asked to provide it (s.106(7)) and the regulations may prescribe certain descriptions of information, political parties, the time at which information is to be published, the form and manner of the information and the period for which the information is to be published (s.106(8)). There is further provision to limit the regulations where parties have fewer candidates than a prescribed number (s.106(9)) and to regulate the duties for certain elections (s.106(10)).

A political party is not, however, authorised to require a person to provide information to it under this Part (s.106(11)).

An example of this new provision is given in para. 352 of the Explanatory Notes:

   ■   Regulations might require political parties fielding more than a specified
       number of candidates to publish six months after a general election
       anonymised diversity data relating to gender and race of all candidates who
       stood at that election.

9 PART 8 – PROHIBITED CONDUCT: ANCILLARY

Part 8 of the Act deals with two species of 'ancillary' liability. Section 108 addresses discrimination which occurs after a relationship has come to an end. Sections 109–112 deal with various forms of accessory liability.

9.1 RELATIONSHIPS THAT HAVE ENDED (SECTION 108)

Section 108 is designed to prohibit discrimination which occurs in the context of a relationship which has come to an end, when discrimination taking place within that relationship would be unlawful. The section therefore prohibits not only post-employment discrimination, but also, for example, discrimination by a school against a former pupil, or discrimination by a shop against a previous customer. This reflects the previous position in relation to most discrimination strands, but is an extension of protection in cases of sexual orientation discrimination and religion or belief discrimination. When the prohibition of age discrimination in the provision of goods, facilities, services and public functions comes into force in 2012, it will apply to discrimination occurring in the context of relationships that have ended.

Section 108 specifically prohibits harassment, as well as discrimination.

The discrimination/harassment will be unlawful where it 'arises out of and is closely connected' to the former relationship. This is the same statutory wording as that included by amendment in the SDA 1975 and other anti-discrimination legislation following the Court of Appeal decision in *Rhys-Harper* v. *Relaxion Group* [2001] EWCA Civ 634, [2001] ICR 1170, subsequently reversed by the House of Lords ([2003] UKHL 33, [2003] IRLR 484). It has been suggested that the statutory wording in relation to necessary connection between the alleged discrimination and the relationship is easier to satisfy than the test set out in *Rhys-Harper*, and post-2003 cases such as *South East Essex College* v. *Abegaze* [2006] ICR 486 will be relevant in both employment and non-employment cases.

In addition, s.108(4) provides that a duty to make reasonable adjustments continues to apply in circumstances where a disabled person continues to be placed at a substantial disadvantage as mentioned in s.20. This duty may arise, for example, where an employer provides recreational facilities for both current and retired employees, and a retired employee has mobility difficulties which can be accommo-dated by making adjustments to access provisions.

Section 108(7) expressly provides that conduct which also amounts to victimisa-tion is not in contravention of s.108. Such conduct will be actionable under the victimisation provisions contained in the Act.

Examples given at para. 362 of the Explanatory Notes include:

- A school or employer refuses to give a reference to an ex-pupil or ex-employee because of their religion or belief. This would be direct discrimination.
- A builder or plumber addresses abusive and hostile remarks to a previous customer because of her sex after their business relationship has ended. This would be harassment. It would not be harassment, however, where the reason for the treatment was not the customer's sex but, for example, a dispute over payment.
- A disabled former employee's benefits include life-time use of the company's in-house gym facilities. The employer or owner of the premises must make reasonable adjustments to enable the former employee to continue using the facilities even after she has retired.

9.2   ACCESSORY LIABILITY (SECTIONS 109–112)

9.2.1   Liability of employers and principals

Section 109 provides that anything done by an employee, or by an agent with authority, is to be treated as also being the act of the employer/principal. Subject to the exception mentioned below, this vicarious liability will attach to the employer/principal regardless of whether the employee/agent acted with the knowledge or approval of the employer/principal.

As with the previous discrimination legislation, there is a statutory defence pro-vided for employers or principals who can show that they 'took all reasonable steps' to prevent the employee or agent from doing either the specific act in question or anything of that description. This is a slight change in wording from the previous legislation which used the phrase 'took such steps as were reasonably practicable'. However, this is understood to be an example of the simplification of language which the consolidation has sought to achieve rather than a substantive change. It is to be expected that, as with the equivalent provisions in the former legislation, the statutory defence will be narrowly drawn and employers and principals will face difficulty in relying upon it.

Vicarious liability does not attach in respect of the criminal provisions of the Act, save for offences under Part 12 relating to transport provision for disabled persons (s.10(5)).

Examples given at para. 366 of the Explanatory Notes include:

- A landlord (the principal) instructs an agent to collect rent at a property. The agent harasses an Asian couple, who bring a claim in which the agent is held to have acted unlawfully. The principal may be held liable for breaching the harassment provisions even if he or she is unaware of the agent's actions.

■   A shop owner becomes aware that her employee is refusing to serve disabled customers. The employer tells the employee to treat disabled customers in the same way as other customers and sends the employee on a diversity training course. However, the employee continues to treat disabled customers less favourably. One such customer brings a claim against both the employee and the employer. The employer may avoid liability by showing that she took all reasonable steps to stop the employee from acting in a discriminatory way.

9.2.2   Liability of employees and agents

Section 110 is designed to work together with s.109 to ensure that both the individual carrying out an unlawful act and the person (individual or corporate) on whose behalf the individual was acting may be held liable.

The s.109/110 mechanism replicates that in the previous discrimination legislation in that s.109 attributes liability to the employer/principal and s.110 confers an accessory liability on the employee/agent where the action attributed to the employer/principal is unlawful under s.109. The effect of this is that a claimant may choose to bring a claim against the employer/principal, or the individual(s) alleged to have perpetrated the discrimination, or both.

Although the mechanism is the same, the precise wording and effect of the provisions are slightly different. In particular, the requirement to prove that an employee/agent acted 'knowingly' was a feature of the previous legislation, which cast the liability of the employee/agent in terms of 'aiding' the discrimination of the employer/principal. There is now no such requirement.

An exception to this principle arises in relation to disability claims in the context of education. The effect of s.110(7) is that claims for disability discrimination in schools cannot be brought against individuals.

The employee/agent has a defence if he can show that he reasonably relied on a statement by the employer/principal that the conduct in question would not contravene the Act. It is a criminal offence under the Act for an employer or principal to knowingly or recklessly make a false statement to that effect.

Examples given at para. 370 of the Explanatory Notes include:

■   A factory worker racially harasses her colleague. The factory owner would be liable for the worker's actions, but is able to show that he took all reasonable steps to stop the harassment. The colleague can still bring a claim against the factory worker in an employment tribunal.

■   A principal instructs an agent to sell products on her behalf. The agent discriminates against a disabled customer. Both the principal and the agent are liable, but the courts are able to determine that evidence provided by the principal indicate the authority given to the agent did not extend to carrying out an authorised act in a discriminatory manner. The disabled customer can still bring a claim against the agent.

9.2.3   Instructing, causing or inducing discrimination

Section 111 prohibits instructing, causing or inducing discrimination. The section adopts the terms 'basic contravention' to refer to the underlying act of discrimination and, as the heading suggests, it makes unlawful instructing, causing or inducing (whether directly or indirectly) a basic contravention. It does not matter whether or not the basic contravention actually takes place. However, the person giving the instruction and the person being asked to discriminate must be in a relationship such that discrimination within the relationship would be unlawful. Therefore, a bank manager instructing staff not to open joint accounts for gay couples would be caught by the section, but a remark by another customer that the bank should refuse to do so would not be.

Section 111(5) gives a right to claim to a third party who is subjected to a detriment, but also to the person who is instructed, caused or induced to discriminate, if he or she is subjected to a detriment.

The latter provision is designed to cover the scenarios such as employees in a service business who might be subjected to detriment as a result of refusing to discriminate against certain types of customer in accordance with their employer's instructions. Such cases had caused some problems under the wording of the previous legislation and, although the courts were generally able to find a way to achieve a remedy (see, for example, *Weathersfield Ltd* v. *Sergant* [1999] IRLR 94), this change should achieve more clarity and is to be welcomed.

Further, the previous legislation contained inconsistencies in relation to the extent of protection afforded in respect of the various discrimination strands. Section 111 extends protection to all strands in all areas covered by the Act.

As under previous legislation, the EHRC also has standing to bring actions under the section.

Paragraph 375 of the Explanatory Notes gives an example:

■   A GP instructs his receptionist not to register anyone with an Asian name. The receptionist would have a claim against the GP if subjected to a detriment for not doing so. A potential patient would also have a claim against the GP if she discovered the instruction had been given and was put off applying to register. The receptionist's claim against the GP would be brought before the employment tribunal as it relates to employment, while the potential patient's claim would be brought in the county court as it relates to services.

9.2.4   Aiding contraventions

Section 112 also adopts the terminology 'basic contravention' to refer to the primary breach or potential breach. The section makes it unlawful to knowingly aid another in conduct which amounts to a basic contravention.

As with s.110 in relation to employees/agents, there is a defence where the alleged aider reasonably relies on a statement that the conduct does not contravene the Act, and it is an offence to knowingly or recklessly make a false statement.

Again, as with s.110, there is an exclusion in relation to disability discrimination occurring in schools, and there is therefore no available cause of action against a person said to have aided such discrimination.

An example is provided at para. 379 of the Explanatory Notes:

■   On finding out that a new tenant is gay, a landlord discriminates against him by refusing him access to certain facilities, claiming that they are not part of the tenancy agreement. Another tenant knows this to be false but joins in with the landlord in refusing the new tenant access to the facilities in question. The new tenant can bring a discrimination claim against both the landlord and the tenant who helped him.

10 PART 9 – ENFORCEMENT

Part 9 is divided into five Chapters which deal with various aspects of enforcement of the Act. It should be noted that the Act is silent as to territorial scope. This leaves it to tribunals, as under the Employment Rights Act 1996, to determine whether the Act should apply in accordance with the test set out by the House of Lords in *Lawson* v. *Serco* [2006] UKHL 3, [2006] ICR 250, and the cases subsequent to it. The test is, however, narrower than existing legislation since the House of Lords excludes those recruited in Britain for a British business but who work outside Great Britain, unless they come within the narrow exceptions set out by the House of Lords (but cf. *Bleuse* v. *MBT Transport Ltd* [2008] ICR 488 and *Duncombe* v. *Secretary of State for Children, Schools and Families* [2009] EWCA Civ 1355, [2010] IRLR 331 where the test was modified to give effect to directly effective EU rights. Since non-discrimination is a fundamental feature of EU law, the wider test may be relied upon).

10.1 PART 9, CHAPTER 1 – INTRODUCTORY

Chapter 1 of Part 9 comprises only one section, s.113, which provides that proceedings relating to any alleged contravention of the Act must be brought in accordance with Part 9, save for various exceptional types of proceedings, specifically:

(a) the enforcement powers of the EHRC under Part 1 of the Equality Act 2006 remain unaffected;
(b) the right to bring judicial review proceedings (including, in Scotland, the right to apply to the supervisory jurisdiction of the Court of Session) is unaffected;
(c) proceedings under the Immigration Acts and Special Immigration Appeals Commission Act 1997 are unaffected;
(d) any proceedings in relation to an offence under the Act (including a penalty under Part 12 relating to the transport of disabled persons) will be brought in the criminal courts.

10.2   PART 9, CHAPTER 2 – CIVIL COURTS

10.2.1   Jurisdiction of civil courts (section 114)

The Act goes on, in s.114, to set out the jurisdiction of the county court (or sheriff in Scotland). Essentially, claims relating to provision of services, the exercise of public functions, disposal and management of premises, education (other than in relation to disability discrimination) and discrimination by associations are to be brought in the county court.

Special provision is made to avoid duplication of proceedings in immigration cases (discussed further at 10.2.2). Cases of disability discrimination within schools are heard in specially constituted tribunals. Detailed provision is made as to the tribunal system in Sched. 17. There is no jurisdiction for a county court to hear an allegation of alleged breach of regulations which may be promulgated to require political parties to publish diversity information about election candidates.

Specific provision is made within the Act to allocate jurisdiction in cases involving accessory liability. This is clearly set out and is largely a matter of common sense: to use an example given in the Explanatory Notes (at para. 375), if a GP instructs his receptionist not to register anyone with an Asian name, the receptionist would have a claim if she was subjected to detriment for refusing to comply. A patient who discovered the instruction and was put off applying to register would also have a claim. However, the receptionist's claim would fall within the jurisdiction of the employment tribunal and the potential patient's claim would fall within the jurisdiction of the county court.

Under s.114(7) and (8), there is a presumption that in a claim heard in the civil courts the judge will sit with an assessor. However, the judge may sit alone if there are good reasons for doing so. Under previous legislation, there was a requirement to have assessors in sex and race claims only – the Act therefore extends the use of assessors to the other discrimination strands. However, under the SDA 1975 and the RRA 1976, there was a specific requirement for two assessors, whereas it now appears that the appointment of one assessor will become the norm.

10.2.2   Immigration cases (section 115)

Section 115 provides that where an alleged contravention of the Act has been raised, or could have been raised, in immigration proceedings, the county court will have no jurisdiction to hear a claim relating to that alleged contravention. This provision is designed to avoid duplication of proceedings and replicates the effect of provisions in the current legislation.

10.2.3   Education cases (section 116)

Section 116, in conjunction with Sched. 17, sets out those claims in the educational arena which are to be determined by specialist tribunals, and which therefore fall outside the jurisdiction of both the county court and the employment tribunal. The claims affected are those where the allegation is of disability discrimination within a school. This carve-out reflects the current position in England and Wales, and Scotland gains a new Additional Support Needs Tribunal (Scotland) which will deal with this type of claim instead of the sheriff court, as had previously been the case.

10.2.4   National security (section 117)

Section 117 is an enabling provision which permits the Civil Procedure Rules Committee in England, and the Sheriff Court Rules Council in Scotland, to make rules enabling a court dealing with proceedings under the Act to exclude the claimant, his representative and/or an assessor from all or part of the proceedings where the court thinks it is expedient to do so in the interests of national security.

The section further provides that any such rules may confer a power to permit a claimant or representative who is excluded to make a statement to the court before the exclusion and may confer a power to keep the reasons (or part of the reasons) for the court's decision secret.

Finally, the section provides for the appointment of a special advocate to represent the claimant's interests in such cases.

This provision replicates present practice under most discrimination legislation, but had been absent from the Sexual Orientation Regulations and the Age Regulations.

10.2.5   Time limits (section 118)

Section 118 sets out the time limits applicable to claims in the county court.

The primary time limit is six months starting with the date of the act complained of. As in the previous legislation, s.118 provides both that conduct extending over a period is to be treated as done at the end of the period and a failure to do a thing is to be treated as occurring when the person in question decided on it. Also, in line with previous legislation, the court has a discretion to extend time where it is just and equitable to do so.

The extensive case law which has developed under the previous legislation (including in the employment arena) as to calculation of time, identifying continuing acts and omissions and extending time on just and equitable grounds will continue to be relevant.

Section 118(2)–(4) extends the primary time limit from six months to nine months in certain limited circumstances where formal complaints procedures are available to the claimant, either under the student complaints scheme in relation to qualifying educational institutions, or under the conciliation scheme operated by the EHRC under s.27 of the Equality Act 2006.

As noted above, s.114 provides that a county court will not have jurisdiction in relation to a complaint on a decision of an immigration authority unless a finding of discrimination is made in the course of immigration proceedings. In such a case, the time limit for bringing a claim in the county court is six months from the last date for appeal against the decision.

10.2.6   Remedies (section 119)

Section 119 enables the county court or sheriff to grant any remedy that would be available to the High Court or Court of Session, respectively, if the claim was in tort (reparation in Scotland) or in judicial review. Generally, the remedy sought will be damages, which s.119(4) expressly provides may include compensation for injury to feelings. However, in appropriate cases, injunctions and declarations may also be sought.

In cases of non-intentional indirect discrimination, s.119(6) provides that the court may not award damages without first considering whether another disposal is appropriate.

Section 119(7) provides that the court must not grant a remedy other than an award of damages or the making of a declaration where to do so may prejudice criminal proceedings.

These provisions replicate the current position as to remedies in the civil courts.

10.3   PART 9, CHAPTER 3 – EMPLOYMENT TRIBUNALS

10.3.1   Jurisdiction of employment tribunals (section 120)

Section 120 sets out the claims under the Act which an employment tribunal has jurisdiction to hear. The employment tribunal has jurisdiction in almost all cases where a contravention of Part 5 of the Act has occurred, i.e. cases arising in a work context. The only exception, set out at s.120(8), is in relation to alleged contraventions of s.60 which prohibits employers from requiring information as to the health of job applicants before making a job offer. Contraventions of s.60(1) are only enforceable by the EHRC. As discussed more fully elsewhere (see **Chapter 6**), Part 5 includes claims involving contract workers, partners, office-holders, barristers and advocates as well as employees.

In addition, claims under s.108 (discrimination after a relationship has ended), s.111 (instructing, causing or inducing discrimination) and s.112 (aiding discrimination) will be heard in the employment tribunal where they relate to a contravention of Part 5.

The employment tribunal also has jurisdiction in cases concerning collective agreements and rules of undertakings which are alleged to be unenforceable under s.145 as providing for discriminatory treatment.

Section 120 also gives jurisdiction to the employment tribunal to hear applications and claims relating to the operation of a non-discrimination rule in an occupational pension scheme.

These provisions are intended to replicate the position under previous legislation.

Examples given at para. 402 of the Explanatory Notes are:

- A worker is racially abused by a co-worker. She could bring a discrimination claim in the employment tribunal.
- A gay man has applied to become a partner in a firm of accountants but because he is gay he has not been invited for an interview despite being equally or better qualified than other candidates who were invited for an interview. He could bring a discrimination claim in the employment tribunal.

10.3.2   Armed forces cases (section 121)

Members of the armed forces who wish to pursue a claim under the Act in an employment tribunal must first pursue a service complaint (see Explanatory Notes, para. 404). Such a complaint is deemed to be withdrawn if no attempt is made to refer it to the Defence Council, either by the officers involved in handling the complaint or by the complainant.

The employment tribunal will only have jurisdiction to hear the complaint in circumstances where the service complaint has not been withdrawn. Section 121(5) specifically envisages that the service complaint will continue notwithstanding the commencement of employment tribunal proceedings.

Similar provision is made in respect of older complaints initially raised under the old service redress procedures.

These provisions are also intended to replicate the position under previous legislation.

10.3.3   References by court to tribunal, etc.

Section 122(1) provides that a civil court may strike out a claim or counter-claim before it if the claim or counter-claim relates to a non-discrimination rule and it appears to the court that it could be more conveniently dealt with in an employment tribunal.

Section 122(2) provides that if a question arises about the application of a non-discrimination rule in civil court proceedings, the court may refer the question to an employment tribunal for determination, either upon its own motion or on the application of a party, and may stay (or sist, in Scotland) the proceedings pending determination of the question.

These provisions are designed to deal with claims in which it is alleged that pension schemes operate in a discriminatory manner and give the civil courts flexibility in ensuring that such claims are determined in the most convenient forum.

These clauses reflect similar provisions in previous legislation.

10.3.4   Time limits (section 123)

Section 123 sets out the time limits applicable to claims in the employment tribunal.

The primary time limit is three months starting with the date of the act complained of. As in the previous legislation, s.123 provides both that conduct extending over a period is to be treated as done at the end of the period and a failure to do a thing is to be treated as occurring when the person in question decided on it. Also, in line with previous legislation, the employment tribunal has a discretion to extend time where it is just and equitable to do so.

The extensive case law which has developed under the previous legislation as to calculation of time, identifying continuing acts and omissions, and extending time on just and equitable grounds will continue to be relevant.

An exception to the usual three-month rule is provided by s.123(2) in relation to claims by members of the armed forces. As noted above, the employment tribunal only has jurisdiction in such cases where the service complaint procedure has been invoked prior to the claim being presented.

These provisions as to time limits do not apply to equal pay cases, which are dealt with separately under s.129.

These provisions are intended to replicate the position under previous legislation.

10.3.5   Remedies in employment tribunals (section 124)

Section 124 enables an employment tribunal to provide various remedies where a complaint of discrimination in respect of which the employment tribunal has jurisdiction is made out. Remedies in equal pay cases are dealt with separately (see **10.4.5** and **10.4.6**). The three remedies provided for are:

(a)   a declaration as to the rights of the complainant and the respondent;
(b)   an order that the respondent pay compensation to the complainant;
(c)   a recommendation.

Section 124(3) deals with recommendations in more detail, and it should be noted that the employment tribunal's powers in this respect have been broadened under the Act. A recommendation made under the Act will recommend that the respondent takes specified steps for the purpose of obviating or reducing the adverse effect of any matter to which the proceedings relate on the complainant or on any other person. The recommendation must also set out a specified time period for implementation. The government recognised that about 70 per cent of complainants leave the workforce so that recommendations may otherwise be of limited efficacy.

Previously, recommendations could only be made with a view to reducing or obviating the adverse effect upon the claimant in the action. As a high proportion of cases are heard after the particular employment has ended, the ability to make recommendations was of limited use and, in practical terms, was invoked only rarely, even in cases where employment continued. One of the aims of the new legislation is to encourage employment tribunals to consider carefully whether measures other than (or in addition to) compensation may be beneficial in combating discrimination.

Examples given in the Explanatory Notes as to recommendations which may be made under the new power include introducing or more effectively implementing equal opportunities or harassment policies and making public recruitment or promotion criteria. The scope for wide-ranging recommendations may potentially become a useful tactical weapon for claimants pursuing discrimination claims.

If a respondent fails, without reasonable excuse, to comply with a recommendation, then the employment tribunal may increase the compensation awarded or make an award of compensation if none was previously made (although only where the recommendation was specific to the individual). The previous legislation provided that the employment tribunal could take either of these steps where it was 'just and equitable' to do so, but the 'just and equitable' rubric has been lost from the Act. Nonetheless, it is clear from the use of the word 'may' that the section creates a discretion on the part of employment tribunals and there is no automatic uplift. In practice, the test is likely to be applied with similar results.

Section 124(4) and (5) deals specifically with cases of indirect discrimination and reflect the previous legislation in applying a presumption that where there is a finding of non-intentional indirect discrimination, compensation will not automatically follow. Rather, the employment tribunal must first consider whether a declaration or a recommendation would be more appropriate.

Section 124(6) provides, as previously, that the amount of compensation corresponds to the amount which may be awarded in a county court or sheriff as appropriate. Current authorities as to the calculation of compensation and the appropriate level of damages will be unaffected by the Act.

The Explanatory Notes give some examples of recommendations at para. 414:

A tribunal could recommend that the respondent:

■   introduces an equal opportunities policy;
■   ensures its harassment policy is more effectively implemented;
■   sets up a review panel to deal with equal opportunities and harassment/ grievance procedures;
■   re-trains staff; or
■   makes public the selection criteria used for transfer or promotion of staff.

10.3.6   Remedies in employment tribunals: national security (section 125)

The wide ambit of the employment tribunal to make recommendations under the Act is curtailed in respect of national security proceedings by s.125. This section provides that recommendations in respect of a person other than the claimant must not be made where to do so would affect anything done by the Security Service, the Secret Intelligence Service, the Government Communications Headquarters or a part of the armed forces assisting the Government Communications Headquarters. National security proceedings are defined within the section.

10.3.7   Remedies in employment tribunals: occupational pension schemes (section 126)

Specific provision is made for remedies in cases where the employment tribunal has found unlawful discrimination in the terms on which persons join, or are treated as members of, an occupational pension scheme.

The basic remedies of declaration, compensation and recommendation remain available, although, by virtue of s.126(3), compensation may only be awarded to reflect injury to feelings or as a result of a respondent's failure to implement a recommendation. In addition to these remedies, the employment tribunal may also order that a claimant has a right to be admitted to the scheme or has a right to membership of the scheme without discrimination (as appropriate). Such an order may provide for the terms on which the claimant is to enjoy admission or membership and may have retrospective effect.

These provisions are intended to replicate the position under previous legislation.

10.4   PART 9, CHAPTER 4 – EQUALITY OF TERMS

It will come as no surprise to those familiar with the complexities of equal pay litigation that the draftsmen of the Act have not attempted to accommodate equal pay cases in the general enforcement provisions, but have instead created a specific Chapter within Part 9 to deal with these cases. These provisions closely reflect those of the (much amended) Equal Pay Act 1970.

10.4.1   Jurisdiction of employment tribunals (section 127)

As provided for by s.127, matters which may broadly be described as equal pay matters may come before the employment tribunal in a number of ways. Most obviously, a worker may complain of an infringement. In addition, a 'responsible person' (the employer or other body responsible for remuneration (s.80)) may ask for a declaration as to the effect of an equality clause or rule where they are in dispute with a worker, and trustees or managers of occupational pension schemes may make similar applications. Finally, questions in relation to an equality clause or rule may be referred to the employment tribunal by the civil courts where they arise in the context of court proceedings.

As discussed at 10.3.2 in relation to standard discrimination proceedings, members of the armed forces must instigate internal service complaint proceedings before presenting a claim.

Section 127(8) expressly provides that the employer is to be treated as a party in any complaint relating to breach of an equality rule and is therefore entitled to appear and be heard.

These provisions are intended to replicate the position under previous legislation.

10.4.2   Reference by courts to tribunals (section 128)

As noted above, s.128(2) provides for a civil court to refer a question relating to an equality clause or rule to an employment tribunal for determination where the question arises in proceedings before the court. The court proceedings may (and generally will) be stayed (sisted, in Scotland) pending the resolution of the question by the employment tribunal.

Where the claim or counter-claim is such that it could more conveniently be resolved in its entirety in the employment tribunal, s.128(1) enables the civil court to strike it out.

These provisions are intended to replicate the position under previous legislation.

10.4.3   Time limits in equal pay cases (section 129)

Section 129, supplemented by further provisions in s.130, sets out the time limits within which proceedings must be brought where a worker alleges breach of an equality clause or rule, or where a responsible person or pension scheme trustee/ manager seeks a declaration under s.127(3) or (4).

In contrast to other types of discrimination cases, there is no provision for the employment tribunal to extend time, whether on just and equitable grounds or otherwise; hence in equal pay cases there are rather more complex provisions for determining whether a claim has been presented within the primary time limit.

The time limit in a standard case is six months beginning with the last day of the employment or appointment.

Over a number of years case law had developed to mitigate the effect of a strict six-month limitation period in a number of different types of case, largely to ensure compatibility with EU law. The Equal Pay Act 1970 was amended in 2003 to reflect the position which had been reached on the authorities and those provisions are essentially replicated in the Equality Act 2010.

In particular:

- In a 'stable work case' (defined in s.130(3)) which is not also a concealment and/or incapacity case, the claim must be brought within six months beginning with the day on which the stable working relationship ended.
- The provisions as to stable work cases are designed to allow workers employed on a series of fixed or short-term contracts to bring claims in respect of the entirety of the employment relationship.
- In a 'concealment case' the claim must be brought within six months beginning with the day on which the worker discovered (or could with reasonable diligence have discovered) the qualifying fact.
- In order to be considered a concealment case, there must be deliberate concealment by the employer (or pension scheme trustees or managers as appropriate) of a fact which is relevant to the complaint and without knowledge of which the worker could not reasonably be expected to bring the proceedings (s.130(4)).

- In an 'incapacity case' the claim must be brought within six months beginning with the day on which the worker ceased to have the incapacity.
- 'Incapacity' is defined in s.40 as applying to a person who is under the age of 18 or who lacks capacity within the meaning of the Mental Capacity Act 2005.
- Where a case is both a concealment and incapacity case, time will begin to run on the later of the relevant days if it had been merely one or the other.
- The large amount of current authority dealing with identifying different types of cases falling within these categories will remain relevant.
- In each case the time limit is extended by a further three months in proceedings relating to service in the armed forces.

These provisions are intended to replicate the position under previous legislation.

Examples given at para. 435 of the Explanatory Notes are:

- A woman's employment ends due to mental health problems which result in her temporary loss of capacity to make decisions for herself. She could make a claim for breach of an equality clause to an employment tribunal but is not well enough to do so. The six month time limit will start when she recovers sufficiently to make a claim.
- A woman suspects that her male colleagues who do the same work are better paid. Her employer reassures her that she and her colleagues get the same salary but he deliberately does not tell her that the men also receive performance bonuses under their contracts. Her male colleagues refuse to discuss their pay with her. The woman only discovers the discrepancy between her pay and the men's when one of the men tells her 18 months after she ceases employment. Within six months, she makes an equal pay claim to a tribunal based on the value of the bonus payments she would have received if her contract had provided for them. Although the woman's claim is made more than six months after her employment ends, she shows that her employer deliberately misled her into believing her salary was the same as the men's. She had no way of discovering the truth earlier. Her claim can proceed as a concealment case.

10.4.4   Assessment of whether work is of equal value (section 131)

Section 131 makes various provisions which are applicable where an employment tribunal has to decide if the work of the claimant and a comparator are of equal value. The employment tribunal is empowered to require an independent expert to prepare a report on the question of whether the work is of equal value. The employment tribunal must not determine the question of equal value in advance of receiving the report, unless it has previously withdrawn its request for a report. Where a request is withdrawn, s.131(3) provides that the employment tribunal may request the expert to provide documentation or make other requests connected to the withdrawal.

A panel of independent experts suitable to provide reports on equal value claims is maintained by ACAS.

Section 131 also deals with the position of job evaluation studies and provides that where jobs have been assessed as not being of equal value under a job evaluation study, the employment tribunal is obliged to come to the same conclusion unless it has reasonable grounds to suspect that the evaluation itself was discriminatory on grounds of sex or is otherwise unreliable.

These provisions are intended to replicate the position under previous legislation.

10.4.5   Remedies in non-pension cases (section 132)

Where a worker is successful in an equal pay claim, s.132 provides that an employment tribunal (or court as appropriate) may make a declaration as to the rights of the parties and/or may make an award by way of arrears of pay or damages.

Back pay recoverable as a result of a successful claim is generally subject to a longstop. In England, this is six years, save in incapacity or concealment cases where there is no longstop limit. In Scotland, the longstop is five years in a standard case, but 20 years in a concealment or incapacity case.

Section 132 is supplemented by s.135 which makes detailed provision for the calculation of the period in respect of which arrears of pay can be awarded in cases which are concealment cases, incapacity cases, or both.

These provisions are intended to replicate the position under previous legislation.

10.4.6   Remedies in pension cases (section 133)

In contrast to employment cases, the court or employment tribunal generally has no power to award arrears of benefits or damages or other compensation to the claimant in a pension case. Instead, the primary remedy is an order that the complainant be admitted to the scheme, or allowed to accrue the rights which discriminatory treatment has prevented him or her from accruing, with effect from a date determined by the court or employment tribunal.

Where there is an order for a claimant to be granted retrospective membership, the earliest date from which this can be ordered is 8 April 1976. This is the date of the ECJ's judgment in *Defrenne* v. *Sabena* [1976] ICR 547; [1976] ECR 455 in which the ECJ held that the right to equal pay was directly effective, but that claims should not be permitted in relation to periods prior to that date.

Where the complaint relates to the manner in which members of the scheme are treated and an order is made to secure the rights which would have accrued but for a breach, the earliest date from which the court can order that the rights are deemed to have accrued is 17 May 1990. This is the date of the ECJ's decision in *Barber* v. *Guardian Royal Exchange Assurance Group* [1990] ICR 616 which confirmed that the application of the equal treatment principle applied, but excluded retrospective claims in respect of service prior to the date of the judgment.

In such a case, s.133(8) provides that the employer must put the scheme in funds to secure the accrued rights ordered by the court or employment tribunal.

Section 133 is supplemented by s.135 which makes detailed provision for the calculation of the period in respect of which membership rights can be awarded in cases which are concealment cases, incapacity cases, or both.

These provisions are intended to replicate the position under previous legislation.

10.4.7   Remedies in claims for arrears brought by pensioner members (section 134)

Section 134 makes equivalent provisions in respect of claims against pension schemes brought by pensioner members to those set out at s.133. In such cases, compensation can be ordered in respect of arrears of pension benefits or damages. There is a longstop applicable in relation to the recovery period, which mirrors that set out in s.132 in relation to employment cases.

Section 134 is supplemented by s.135 which makes detailed provision for the calculation of the period in respect of which accrued benefits can be awarded in cases which are concealment cases, incapacity cases, or both.

These provisions are intended to replicate the position under previous legislation.

10.5   PART 9, CHAPTER 5 – MISCELLANEOUS

10.5.1   Burden of proof (section 136)

The birth and development of the shifting burden of proof in discrimination claims has been a notable strand in the evolution of discrimination law over the past 20 years. Section 136 of the Act puts in place at s.136(2) a (perhaps deceptively) simple formulation which applies to all prohibited grounds and to all types of unlawful discrimination. The only circumstances in which s.136 does not apply in determining whether there has been a contravention of the Act is in proceedings for an offence under the Act (s.136(5)).

This change excises from the law the various anomalous cases where there was previously no formal shifting burden of proof (or where the application of the shifting burden of proof had been doubted) – race discrimination cases brought on grounds of colour or nationality; victimisation claims under the RRA 1976; non-employment cases under the DDA 1995 and claims of sex discrimination relating to the exercise of public functions.

Experience of SDA 1975, s.63A, inserted in October 2001 to create a shifting burden of proof in sex discrimination claims, and of the equivalent provisions subsequently inserted into the other main discrimination statutes and regulations, suggests that although the concept can be expressed in simple terms, it is difficult to apply. Familiarity with the various glosses placed on the statutory provisions by decisions such as *Barton v. Investec Henderson Crosthwaite Securities Ltd* [2003] ICR 1205, *Igen v. Wong* [2005] ICR 931, *Madarassy v. Nomura International plc* [2007] ICR 867 and the numerous authorities referred to, or referring to, those cases, will remain essential. It is likely that the steady flow of authorities on the application of the shifting burden of proof will continue uninterrupted following the entry into force of the Act.

10.5.2   Previous findings (section 137)

Section 137 makes provision to ensure the finality of decisions made under predecessor legislation in order to prevent matters being litigated under the new Act.

10.5.3   Obtaining information (section 138)

Section 138 provides for the continuation of the questionnaire procedure adopted by the previous legislation to assist individuals who believed they may have been the subject of discrimination. As with the previous legislation, the Act itself contains an enabling provision with the form of the questionnaire to be determined by subordinate legislation.

As previously, a court or tribunal may (in most cases) draw an inference from a failure to answer a questionnaire. The Employment Appeal Tribunal has confirmed that there is no automatic presumption of discrimination in such cases, and the inference will only be drawn where it is appropriate to do so on the facts of the case (*D'Silva* v. *NATFHE* [2008] All ER (D) 163 (Mar)).

These provisions are intended to replicate the position under previous legislation.

10.5.4   Interest (section 139)

Section 139 is an enabling provision permitting regulations to be made to provide for interest in discrimination proceedings. It is expected that subordinate legislation will be promulgated in due course reflecting the current provisions in relation to interest.

10.5.5   Conduct giving rise to separate proceedings (section 140)

Section 140 enables a civil court to transfer proceedings to an employment tribunal and vice versa where the same conduct has given rise to two or more separate claims with at least one of those being a claim under s.111 (instructing, causing or inducing discrimination). The section expressly prohibits a court or employment tribunal from making a decision which is inconsistent with a previous decision arising out of the same conduct.

11

PART 10 – CONTRACTS

Sections 142–148 of Part 10 contain provisions whereby certain terms of a contract are rendered unenforceable or void as well as making provisions for compromise agreements.

11.1 CONTRACTS AND OTHER AGREEMENTS (SECTIONS 142–146)

By s.142(1), a term of a contract will be unenforceable against a person in so far as it constitutes, promotes or provides for treatment of that or another person that is of a description prohibited by the Act. A non-contractual term will also be unenforceable against a person in so far as it constitutes, promotes or provides for treatment of that or another person that is of a description prohibited by the Act, in so far as the Act relates to disability (s.142(2)). Non-contractual terms are terms that are not in a contract and relate to training, guidance or providing work or services under s.56(2)(a)–(e) or the provision of facilities by way of insurance under a group insurance arrangement.

The above prohibitions do not relate to equality clauses or maternity equality clauses (s.142(4)(a)) or to modification of a contract where it does not contain an equality clause (s.142(4)(b)) or to the duties under Part 1 or Chapter 1 of Part 11 (s.142(5)).

An example given in para. 468 of the Explanatory Notes of the operation of s.142 is:

- A term in a franchise agreement which included a requirement that the franchisee should only employ Asian people (which would be unlawful direct discrimination because of race unless an exception applied) could not be enforced by the franchisor. But the franchisee could still obtain any benefit he is due under the term, for example he could continue operating the franchise. However, if the franchisee complied with the discriminatory term, a person discriminated against under it could make a claim against the franchisee for unlawful discrimination under other provisions in the Act.

An application may be made by a person who has an interest in a contract or other agreement to the county court or sheriff for the unenforceable term to be modified or removed (s.143(1)), but such an order cannot be made unless every person who would be affected has been given notice of the application and afforded an opportunity to make representations (s.143(2)). The order may be retrospective (s.143(3)). An example can be found in para. 471 of the Explanatory Notes of the operation of s.143:

- A person renting an office in a serviced office block could ask for a term in the rental contract to be amended if the term discriminated indirectly, for example by including an unjustified requirement that people entering the premises remove any facial covering (thus discriminating against Muslim women). The term could be adjusted by the court or sheriff to allow special arrangements to be made to satisfy both genuine security needs of other users and the religious needs of Muslim women visiting the claimant.

Section 144 also prohibits contracting out by purporting to exclude or limit a provision of, or made under, the Act including non-contractual terms, unless there is a contract which settles a claim under s.114 (s.144(3)) or under s.120 if, in the latter case, it is made with the assistance of a conciliation officer or is a qualifying compromise agreement (s.144(4)) including a dispute submitted to arbitration under s.212A of the Trade Union and Labour Relations (Consolidation) Act 1992 (TULR(C)A 1992) and if submitted into arbitration in accordance with the scheme (s.144(6)). The latter can include a contract which settles a complaint relating to a breach of an equality clause or non-discrimination rule (s.144(5)). See para. 472 of the Explanatory Notes for examples of the operation of s.144:

- a contract settling a claim in an employment tribunal (including an agreement settling a claim for a breach of an equality clause) that has been negotiated with the help of a conciliation officer or which meets the standards set out in section 147 (meaning of qualifying compromise contract). This includes an arbitration agreement made in accordance with a scheme under section 212A of the Trade Union and Labour Relations (Consolidation) Act 1992 (where the parties agree to submit a dispute to arbitration);
- a contract settling a county or sheriff court claim.

Any term of a collective agreement (as defined by TULR(C)A 1992, s.178) will also be void in so far as it constitutes, promotes or provides for treatment of a description prohibited by the Act (s.145(1)) and a rule of an undertaking is unenforceable in so far as it constitutes, promotes or provides for treatment of the person that is of a description prohibited by the Act (s.145(2)). A rule of an undertaking is a rule made by a trade organisation or qualifications body for application to members or prospective members, persons on whom it has conferred a relevant qualification or persons seeking conferment by it of a relevant qualification, or a rule made by an employer for application to employees, persons who apply for employment or persons the employer considers for employment (s.148(6) and (7)). 'Trade organi- sation', 'qualifications body' and 'relevant qualification' each have the meaning given in Part 5. Examples are given at para. 478 of the Explanatory Notes of the operation of s.145:

- A collective agreement which required jobs in a particular part of a factory to be given only to men would be void, so a woman who applied could not be refused on those grounds.
- An indirectly discriminatory rule of a qualifications body (providing for exam- ple a professional qualification for plumbers) which required that applicants

must have two years' previous experience with a British firm would be unenforceable against a person who had the equivalent experience with a foreign firm. It would still be enforceable against a person who did not have the required experience at all (provided it was justified).

Section 146 makes provision for a qualifying person to apply to an employment tribunal that a term is void or a rule is unenforceable under s.145. This section only applies if the term or rule may have an effect on the qualifying person at some time in the future, and where the complaint alleges that the term or rule provides for treatment of a description prohibited by the Act, the qualifying person may in the future be subjected to treatment that would (if the qualifying person were subjected to it in present circumstances) be of that description (s.146(2)). The tribunal may make an order declaring that the term is void or the rule is unenforceable (s.146(3)) and the order may include a period before the date of the order (s.146(4)).

Where the complaint is about a term in a collective agreement and the term is made by or on behalf of a person of a description specified in the first column of the table (see below), a qualifying person is a person of a description specified in the second column.

Description of person who made collective agreement	Qualifying person
Employer	A person who is, or is seeking to be, an employee of that employer
Organisation of employers	A person who is, or is seeking to be, an employee of an employer who is a member of that organisation
Association of organisations of employers	A person who is, or is seeking to be, an employee of an employer who is a member of an organisation in that association

Where the complaint is about a rule of an undertaking where the rule is one made by or on behalf of a person of a description specified in the first column of the table (see below), a qualifying person is a person of a description specified in the second column.

Description of person who made rule of undertaking	Qualifying person
Employer	A person who is, or is seeking to be, an employee of that employer

Description of person who made rule of undertaking	Qualifying person
Trade organisation or qualifications body	A person who is, or is seeking to be, a member of the organisation or body
	A person upon whom the body has conferred a relevant qualification
	A person seeking conferment by the body of a relevant qualification

11.2   COMPROMISE AGREEMENTS (SECTION 147)

As noted at 11.1, compromise agreements are excluded from the provisions of Part 10. Section 147 contains a definition of 'qualifying compromise agreement' which is well known to employment lawyers. It is necessary for the conditions in s.147(3) to be met before the agreement will qualify. There are six conditions:

(a)   the contract is in writing,

(b)   the contract relates to the particular complaint,

(c)   the complainant has, before entering into the contract, received advice from an independent adviser about its terms and effect (including, in particular, its effect on the complainant's ability to pursue the complaint before an employment tribunal),

(d)   on the date of the giving of the advice, there is in force a contract of insurance, or an indemnity provided for members of a profession or professional body, covering the risk of a claim by the complainant in respect of loss arising from the advice,

(e)   the contract identifies the adviser, and

(f)   the contract states that the conditions in paragraphs (c) and (d) are met.

The independent adviser, mentioned in (c) above is, by s.147(4):

(a)   A qualified lawyer who is: (i) in relation to England and Wales, a person who, for the purposes of the Legal Services Act 2007, is an authorised person in relation to an activity which constitutes the exercise of a right of audience or the conduct of litigation; (ii) in relation to Scotland, an advocate (whether in practice as such or employed to give legal advice) or a solicitor who holds a practising certificate.

(b)   An officer, official, employee or member of an independent trade union certified in writing by the trade union as competent to give advice and as authorised to do so on its behalf. An 'independent trade union' has the meaning given in s.5 of TULR(C)A 1992.

(c)   A worker at an advice centre (whether as an employee or a volunteer) certified in writing by the centre as competent to give advice and as authorised to do so on its behalf.

(d)   A person of such description as may be specified by order.

However, under s.147(5), none of the following is an independent adviser in relation to a qualifying compromise contract:

(a) a person who is a party to the contract or the complaint;
(b) a person who is connected to a person within para. (a). Two persons are connected if:

- one is a company of which the other (directly or indirectly) has control, or
- both are companies of which a third person (directly or indirectly) has control,
- two persons are also connected in so far as a connection between them gives rise to a conflict of interest in relation to the contract or the complaint;

(c) a person who is employed by a person within para. (a) or (b);
(d) a person who is acting for a person within para. (a) or (b) in relation to the contract or the complaint;
(e) a person within s.147(4)(b) or (c), if the trade union or advice centre is a person within para. (a) or (b).
(f) a person within s.147(4)(c) to whom the complainant makes a payment for the advice.

Examples are given in para. 485 of the Explanatory Notes of the operation of s.147:

- An employee who settled a claim at an employment tribunal on the advice of a lawyer who works for the employer he was seeking to sue would still be able to pursue the claim (assuming a conciliation officer was not involved in the settlement). The settlement agreement would be unenforceable because the lawyer had a conflict of interest and therefore the agreement would not be a qualifying compromise contract.
- An employee who settled a claim of harassment in a contract which also provides that she will forgo all other claims arising under the Act in exchange for a fixed sum would still be able to pursue a claim for damages because of a discriminatory failure to promote her. The term of the contract precluding all claims would be unenforceable in respect of the discrimination claim because it is insufficiently tailored to the circumstances of the claim and therefore is not a qualifying compromise contract in respect of it.

12 PART 12 – DISABLED PERSONS AND TRANSPORT

Part 12 of the Equality Act 2010 contains and, in certain cases, extends various powers and provisions which were contained in the DDA 1995 (as amended by the DDA 2005) in relation to taxis, private hire vehicles, public service vehicles and trains. Section 172 of the DDA 1995 contains various definitions: 'taxi' means a vehicle which is licensed under the Town Police Clauses Act 1847, s.37 or the Metropolitan Public Carriage Act 1869, s.6 and, for the purposes of ss.162 and 165–167, also includes a taxi licensed under the Civic Government (Scotland) Act 1982, s.10, but does not include a vehicle drawn by a horse or other animal.

12.1 PART 12, CHAPTER 1 – TAXIS, ETC.

12.1.1 Power to make taxi accessibility regulations (section 160)

Section 160 of the Act re-enacts provisions previously contained in s.32 of the DDA 1995 (but never brought into force). Section 160 will enable the Secretary of State to make regulations ('taxi accessibility regulations') for securing that it is possible for disabled persons to:

- get into and out of taxis in safety and to do so while in wheelchairs;
- travel in taxis in safety and reasonable comfort and to do so while in wheelchairs.

The taxi accessibility regulations may, in particular, require a regulated taxi (i.e. a taxi to which taxi accessibility regulations are expressed to apply) to conform with provisions as to the size of a door opening for the use of passengers; the floor area of the passenger compartment (the meaning of that term will be defined in the taxi accessibility regulations); the amount of headroom in the passenger compartment; and the fitting of restraining devices designed to ensure the stability of a wheelchair while the taxi is moving. The taxi accessibility regulations may also require the driver of a regulated taxi which is plying for hire, or which has been hired, to comply with provisions as to the carrying of ramps or other devices designed to facilitate the loading and unloading of wheelchairs and require the driver of a regulated taxi in which a disabled person is being carried while in a wheelchair to comply with provisions as to the position in which the wheelchair is to be secured.

The driver of a regulated taxi which is plying for hire, or has which been hired, commits, an offence for which he or she will be liable on summary conviction to a fine not exceeding level 3 on the standard scale by failing to comply with a requirement of the regulations, or if the taxi fails to conform with any provision of the regulations with which it is required to conform.

12.1.2   Powers of licensing authorities to restrict number of licensed taxis: exception in favour of licences for vehicles which will be suitable for disabled users (section 161)

Section 161 is a new provision. Section 16 of the Transport Act 1985 and the Town Police Clauses Act 1847 permit licensing authorities to refuse a licence for a taxi if they do so to limit the number of licensed carriages in their area to the number considered necessary. Section 161 of the Act will disapply that power where:

■   the application under consideration is for a vehicle in respect of which it is possible for a disabled person to get into and out of the vehicle in safety and to travel in the vehicle in safety and reasonable comfort while in a wheelchair of a size prescribed by the Secretary of State; and
■   the proportion of taxis licensed in respect of the area to which the licence would (if granted) apply that conform to such requirements is less than the proportion that is prescribed by the Secretary of State.

12.1.3   Vehicles used in connection with designated transport facilities (section 162)

Section 162 of the Act re-enacts provisions previously contained in s.33 of the DDA 1995 (but never brought into force) concerning premises forming part of a port, airport, railway station or bus station. From a date to be appointed, s.162 will enable the Secretary of State (or in relation to transport facilities in Scotland, the Scottish Ministers) to make regulations for the application of any taxi provision contained in Chapter 1 of Part 12 of the Act (in Scotland, regulations made in pursuance of the Civic Government (Scotland) Act 1982, s.20(2A)) (with or without modification) to vehicles used for the provision of services under a franchise agreement or drivers of such vehicles. For these purposes, a franchise agreement is a contract entered into by the operator (a person who is concerned with the management or operation of the facility) of a designated transport facility for the provision, by the other party to the contract, of hire car services for members of the public using any part of the facility, and which involve vehicles entering any part of the facility. The precise meaning of 'hire car' will be prescribed in the regulations. 'Transport facility' refers to premises which form part of a port, airport, railway station or bus station.

12.1.4   Grant of taxi licences to be conditional on compliance with taxi accessibility regulations (section 163)

Section 163 of the Act re-enacts provisions previously contained in s.34 of the DDA 1995 (but never brought into force). It provides that a licence for a taxi to ply for hire must not be granted unless the vehicle conforms with the provisions of taxi accessibility regulations with which a vehicle is required to conform if it is licensed. However, this prohibition will not apply if a licence is in force in relation to the vehicle at any time during the period of 28 days immediately before the day on which the licence is granted. The Secretary of State may by order provide for this exception to cease to have effect on a specified date and such an order may be made to apply to particular areas or localities rather than the whole country.

12.1.5   Powers in respect of exemption from taxi accessibility regulations (section 164)

Section 164 of the Act re-enacts provisions previously contained in s.35 of the DDA 1995 (but never brought into force). The Secretary of State may by regulations provide for a relevant licensing authority to apply for an order (an 'exemption order') exempting the authority from the requirements of s.163. Such regulations may, in particular, make provision requiring an authority proposing to apply for an exemption order to:

- carry out such consultation as is specified;
- publish its proposals in the specified manner;
- consider representations made about the proposal before applying for the order;
- make the application in the form specified in the regulations.

An authority may apply for an exemption order only if it is satisfied that, having regard to the circumstances in its area, it is inappropriate for s.163 to apply, and that the application of that section would result in an unacceptable reduction in the number of taxis in its area.

After consulting the Disabled Persons Transport Advisory Committee and such other persons as he or she thinks appropriate, the Secretary of State may:

- make an exemption order in the terms of the application for the order; or
- make an exemption order in such other terms as the Secretary of State thinks appropriate; or
- refuse to make an exemption order.

Where an exemption order is made for an area, then the Secretary of State may by regulations make provision requiring a taxi plying for hire in that area to conform with provisions of the regulations as to the fitting and use of swivel seats. Those regulations may make provisions corresponding to those for which powers are given in s.163.

12.1.6   Duties of taxi and private hire vehicles in relation to passengers in wheelchairs (section 165)

Section 165 imposes duties on the driver of a designated taxi similar to those contained (but never brought into force) in s.36 of the DDA 1995, but extends them to a driver of a designated private hire vehicle. A taxi or private hire vehicle is 'designated' if it appears on a list maintained under s.167 and, for the purposes of ss.165, 166 and 167, a 'private hire vehicle' means a vehicle licensed under the Local Government (Miscellaneous Provisions) Act 1976, s.48, a vehicle licensed under the Private Hire Vehicles (London) Act 1998, s.7, a vehicle licensed under an equivalent provision of a local enactment, and a private hire car licensed under the Civic Government (Scotland) Act 1982, s.10.

In the case of a taxi, the duties in s.165 apply where the taxi has been hired by or for a disabled person who is in a wheelchair, or by another person who wishes to be accompanied by a disabled person who is in a wheelchair. In the case of a hire car, the duties are engaged where a person of either of these descriptions indicates to the driver that he or she wishes to travel in the vehicle. The duties are:

- to carry a disabled passenger while in a wheelchair;
- not to make an additional charge if that passenger chooses to sit in a passenger seat;
- to carry that passenger's wheelchair;
- to carry that passenger in safety and in reasonable comfort;
- to provide such assistance ('mobility assistance') as is reasonably required to enable that passenger to use the taxi including in relation to the loading of a wheelchair and luggage.

Section 165 does not require the driver (unless the vehicle is of a description prescribed by the Secretary of State) to carry more than one person in a wheelchair, or more than one wheelchair, on any one journey or to carry a person in circumstances in which it would otherwise be lawful for the driver to refuse to carry the person.

A driver of a designated taxi or designated private hire vehicle commits an offence if he fails to comply with a duty imposed on the driver by s.165 and is liable on summary conviction to a fine not exceeding level 3 on the standard scale.

It is a defence for the driver to show at the time of the alleged offence that the vehicle conformed to the accessibility requirements which applied to it, but it would not have been possible for the wheelchair to be carried safely in the vehicle.

Section 167 (re-enacting provisions formerly contained in DDA 1995, s.35A) provides that a licensing authority may maintain a list of vehicles which are either a taxi or a private hire vehicle, and conform to such accessibility requirements as the licensing authority thinks fit. 'Accessibility requirements' are requirements for securing that it is possible for disabled persons in wheelchairs to get into and out of vehicles in safety, and to travel in vehicles in safety and reasonable comfort either staying in their wheelchairs or not (depending on which they prefer). The Secretary

of State can issue guidance to licensing authorities as to the accessibility requirements which they should apply for the purposes of s.167 and any other aspect of
their functions under or by virtue of that section and a licensing authority which
maintains a list must have regard to any such guidance.

A licensing authority may, if it thinks fit, decide that a vehicle may be included on
the list of vehicles only if it is being used, or is to be used by the holder of a special
licence under that licence. 'Special licence' has the meaning given by s.12 of the
Transport Act 1985 which provides for restricted licences relating to the use of taxis
or hire cars in providing local services

A person who is aggrieved by the decision of a licensing authority to include a
vehicle on a list maintained under s.167 may appeal to a magistrates' court (or, in
Scotland, the sheriff) before the end of the period of 28 days beginning with the date
of the inclusion (s.172(4)).

12.1.7   Passengers in wheelchairs: exemption certificates for drivers of taxis and private hire vehicles (section 165)

A 'licensing authority', in relation to any area, means the authority responsible for
licensing taxis or, as the case may be, private hire vehicles in that area (ss.166 and
167). A licensing authority must issue a person with an exemption certificate
exempting the person from the duties imposed by s.165 if it is satisfied that it is
appropriate to do so on medical grounds or on the ground that the person's physical
condition makes it impossible or unreasonably difficult for the person to comply
with those duties. The exemption certificate will be valid for such period as is
specified in the certificate. The driver of a designated taxi or private hire vehicle is
exempt from the duties imposed by s.165 if an exemption certificate issued to the
driver is in force, and the prescribed notice of the exemption is exhibited on the taxi
or private hire vehicle in the prescribed manner.

Section 172 provides that a person who is aggrieved by the refusal of a licensing
authority in England and Wales to issue an exemption certificate under s.166 may
appeal to a magistrates' court before the end of the period of 28 days beginning with
the date of the refusal. A person who is aggrieved by the refusal of a licensing
authority in Scotland to issue an exemption certificate under s.166 may appeal to
the sheriff before the end of the period of 28 days beginning with the date of the
refusal.

On an appeal, the magistrates' court (or, in Scotland, the sheriff) may direct the
licensing authority to issue the exemption certificate to have effect for such period
as is specified in the direction.

12.1.8   Assistance dogs in taxis (sections 168 and 169)

Section 168 replicates s.37 of the DDA 1995 (which was never brought into force)
and imposes duties on the driver of a taxi in England and Wales which has been
hired by or for a disabled person who is accompanied by an assistance dog, or by

another person who wishes to be accompanied by a disabled person with an assistance dog. 'Assistance dog' is defined in s.173. It means a dog which has been trained to guide a blind person; a dog which has been trained to assist a deaf person; a dog which has been trained by a prescribed charity to assist a disabled person who has a disability that consists of epilepsy or otherwise affects the person's mobility, manual dexterity, physical co-ordination or ability to lift, carry or otherwise move everyday objects; or a dog of a prescribed category which has been trained to assist a disabled person who has a disability other than that prescribed kind. The Secretary of State may make regulations setting out such a prescribed category.

The driver of a taxi in these circumstances must carry the disabled person's dog and allow it to remain with that person and must not make any additional charge for doing so. The driver of a taxi commits an offence by failing to comply with the duty imposed by this section and is liable on summary conviction to a fine not exceeding level 3 on the standard scale.

Section 169 provides that a licensing authority must issue a person with an exemption certificate exempting the person from the duties imposed by s.168 if satisfied that it is appropriate to do so on medical grounds. Under this section, 'licensing authority' means, in relation to the area to which the Metropolitan Public Carriage Act 1869 applies, Transport for London and in relation to any other area in England and Wales, the authority responsible for licensing taxis in that area. In deciding whether to issue an exemption certificate, the authority must have regard, in particular, to the physical characteristics of the taxi which the person drives or those of any kind of taxi in relation to which the person requires the certificate. An exemption certificate is valid in respect of a specified taxi or a specified kind of taxi and for such period as is specified in the certificate.

The driver of a taxi will be exempt from the duties imposed by s.168 if an exemption certificate issued to the driver is in force with respect to the taxi, and the prescribed notice of the exemption is exhibited on the taxi in the manner prescribed by regulations to be made by the Secretary of State.

A right of appeal against refusal of an exemption certificate is provided in s.172.

12.1.9   Assistance dogs in private hire vehicles (sections 170 and 171)

Sections 170 and 171 contain similar provisions (formerly contained in DDA 1995, s.37A) in relation to assistance dogs in private hire vehicles in England and Wales as apply in relation to taxis. Duties are imposed in relation to private hire vehicle operators (for the definitions of 'private hire vehicle' and 'operator' as regards s.170, see s.170(5)). Private hire vehicle operators will commit an offence by failing or refusing to accept a booking for the vehicle if the booking is requested by or on behalf of a disabled person or a person who wishes to be accompanied by a disabled person, and the reason for the failure or refusal is that the disabled person will be accompanied by an assistance dog. An operator also commits an offence by making an additional charge for carrying an assistance dog which is accompanying a disabled person.

The driver of a private hire vehicle is a person who holds a licence under the Private Hire Vehicles (London) Act 1998, the Local Government (Miscellaneous Provisions) Act 1976, s.51, or an equivalent provision of a local enactment. The driver commits an offence by failing or refusing to carry out a booking accepted by the operator if the booking is made by or on behalf of a disabled person or a person who wishes to be accompanied by a disabled person, and the reason for the failure or refusal is that the disabled person is accompanied by an assistance dog.

Both offences carry a fine on conviction not exceeding level 3 on the standard scale.

A licensing authority (as defined in s.170(5)) must issue a driver with an exemption certificate exempting the driver from these offences if satisfied that it is appropriate to do so on medical grounds and, in deciding whether to issue an exemption certificate, the authority must have regard, in particular, to the physical characteristics of the private hire vehicle which the person drives or those of any kind of private hire vehicle in relation to which the person requires the certificate. An exemption certificate is valid in respect of a specified private hire vehicle or a specified kind of private hire vehicle and for such period as is specified in the certificate. A driver does not commit the offences if an exemption certificate issued to the driver is in force with respect to the private hire vehicle, and the prescribed notice of the exemption is exhibited on the vehicle in the prescribed manner. The power to make regulations as to the prescribed manner of display of certificates is exercisable by the Secretary of State.

A right of appeal against refusal of an exemption certificate is provided in s.172.

12.2   PART 12, CHAPTER 2 – PUBLIC SERVICE VEHICLES

12.2.1   PSV accessibility regulations (sections 174 and 175)

Section 40 of the DDA 1995 gave the Secretary of State a power to make regulations to ensure that public service vehicles were accessible to disabled people and the Public Service Vehicles Accessibility Regulations 2000, SI 2000/1970, were made under the section. Similar regulation-making powers are now enacted in s.174 of the Act. The Secretary of State may make regulations ('PSV accessibility regulations') for securing that it is possible for disabled persons to get on to and off regulated public service vehicles in safety and without unreasonable difficulty (and, in the case of disabled persons in wheelchairs, to do so while remaining in their wheelchairs), and to travel in such vehicles in safety and reasonable comfort. For the definition of a 'public service vehicle' and a 'regulated public service vehicle' in accordance with s.174, see s.174(3).

The regulations may, in particular, make provision as to the construction, use and maintenance of regulated public service vehicles, including provision as to:

- the fitting of equipment to vehicles;
- equipment to be carried by vehicles;
- the design of equipment to be fitted to, or carried by, vehicles;
- the fitting and use of restraining devices designed to ensure the stability of wheelchairs while vehicles are moving;
- the position in which wheelchairs are to be secured while vehicles are moving.

Guidance applicable to the regulations made under the 1995 Act has been published (see www.dft.gov.uk/transportforyou/access/buses/pubs/psvar/accessibili tyregulations20005993?page=1).

Different provision may be made as respects different classes or descriptions of vehicle and as respects the same class or description of vehicle in different circumstances. Consultation obligations are imposed in relation to this section and s.176 or s.177 in relation to the Disabled Persons Transport Advisory Committee and such other representative organisations as the Secretary of State thinks fit.

Section 175 provides for offences of:

- contravening a provision of PSV accessibility regulations;
- using on a road a regulated public service vehicle which does not conform with a provision of the regulations with which it is required to conform;
- causing or permitting such a regulated public service vehicle to be used on a road.

A fine at level 4 on the standard scale can be imposed on summary conviction.

If a body corporate commits such an offence with the consent or connivance of, or the commission of the offence is attributable to neglect on the part of, a 'responsible person', then the responsible person as well as the body corporate is guilty of the offence. In relation to a body corporate, a responsible person is a director, manager, secretary or similar officer or a person purporting to act in one of those capacities. In the case of a body corporate whose affairs are managed by its members, a member is a 'responsible person'. If, in Scotland, an offence committed by a partnership or an unincorporated association is committed with the consent or connivance of, or is attributable to neglect on the part of, a partner or person concerned in the management of the association, the partner or person as well as the partnership or association is guilty of the offence.

12.2.2   Accessibility certificates (section 176)

Section 176 re-enacts provisions formerly contained in DDA 1995, s.41. A regulated public service vehicle must not be used on a road unless a vehicle examiner has issued a certificate (an 'accessibility certificate') that such provisions of PSV accessibility regulations as are prescribed are satisfied in respect of the vehicle or, alternatively, if an approval certificate has been issued under s.177 in respect of the vehicle. The Secretary of State can make regulations which may make provision with respect to applications for, and the issue of, accessibility certificates, for providing for the examination of vehicles in respect of which applications have been made and with respect to the issue of copies of accessibility certificates which have been lost or destroyed (s.176(2)). (See the Public Service Vehicles Accessibility Regulations 2000, SI 2000/1970, as amended, for the regulations made under the DDA 1995.)

The operator of a regulated public service vehicle commits an offence if the vehicle is used without an accessibility certificate and a level 4 fine can be imposed on conviction. In accordance with s.176(6), 'operator' has the same meaning as in the Public Passenger Vehicles Act 1981.

12.2.3   Approval certificates in relation to type vehicles (section 177)

The Secretary of State may approve a vehicle for the purposes of s.177 if he is satisfied that such provisions of the PSV accessibility regulations as are prescribed for the purposes of s.176 are satisfied in respect of the vehicle and a vehicle which is so approved is referred to in this section as a 'type vehicle'. Similar provision was made by DDA 1995, s.42. Type approval may be withdrawn at any time and no further approval certificates are to be issued by reference to the type vehicle, but an approval certificate issued by reference to the type vehicle before the withdrawal continues to have effect for the purposes of s.176.

A vehicle examiner may issue a certificate in the prescribed form (an 'approval certificate') that a particular vehicle conforms to the type vehicle. A declaration in the prescribed form is made by an authorised person (a person authorised by the regulations) that a particular vehicle conforms in design, construction and equipment with a type vehicle.

The Secretary of State can make regulations with respect to applications for, and grants of, type approval, with respect to applications for, and the issue of, approval certificates, providing for the examination of vehicles in respect of which applications have been made and with respect to the issue of copies of approval certificates in place of certificates which have been lost or destroyed. The Public Service Vehicles Accessibility Regulations 2000, SI 2000/1970, were made under the equivalent DDA 1995 power.

12.2.4   Special authorisations (section 178)

Section 178(1) replicates powers given under DDA 1995, s.43 to the Secretary of State to make an order authorising the use on roads of a regulated public service vehicle of a class or description specified by the order, or a regulated public service vehicle which is so specified. Sections 174–177 will not prevent the use of a vehicle in accordance with such an authorisation order.

Section 178(3) also contains a power for the Secretary of State to make provision for securing that provisions of PSV accessibility regulations apply to regulated public service vehicles of a description specified by the order, subject to any modifications or exceptions specified by the order.

Orders under s.178(1) or (3) may make the authorisation or provision in question subject to such restrictions and conditions as are specified by or under the order (s.178(4)).

12.2.5   Reviews and appeals (section 179)

If the Secretary of State refuses an application for the approval of a vehicle under s.177(1) and, before the end of the prescribed period, the applicant asks the Secretary of State to review the decision, and pays any fee fixed under s.180, then the Secretary of State must review the decision and, in doing so, consider any representations made in writing by the applicant before the end of the prescribed period.

A person applying for an accessibility certificate or an approval certificate may appeal to the Secretary of State against the refusal of a vehicle examiner to issue the certificate. An appeal must be made within the prescribed time and in the pre-scribed manner. On the determination of an appeal, the Secretary of State may confirm, vary or reverse the decision appealed against and give directions to the vehicle examiner for giving effect to the Secretary of State's decision.

Regulations made by the Secretary of State may make provision as to the procedure to be followed in connection with appeals.

12.2.6   Fees (section 180)

The Secretary of State may charge such fees, payable at such times, as are prescribed in respect of applications for, and grants of, approval under s.177(1); applications for, and the issue of, accessibility certificates and approval certificates; copies of such certificates; and reviews and appeals under s.179. Such fees must be paid into the Consolidated Fund. The necessary regulations are to be made by the Secretary of State. The regulations may make provision for the repayment of fees, in whole or in part, in such circumstances as are prescribed. Before making the regulations, the Secretary of State must consult such representative organisations as the Secretary of State thinks fit (s.180(5)).

12.3   PART 12, CHAPTER 3 – RAIL VEHICLES

12.3.1   Rail vehicle accessibility regulations (section 182)

Section 182 contains powers formerly contained in DDA 1995, s.46 by which the Secretary of State may make 'rail vehicle accessibility regulations' for securing that it is possible for disabled persons:

- to get on to and off regulated rail vehicles (see definitions in s.182(4)) in safety and without unreasonable difficulty, and to do so while in wheelchairs;
- to travel in such vehicles in safety and reasonable comfort, and to do so while in wheelchairs.

The regulations may, in particular, make provision as to the construction, use and maintenance of regulated rail vehicles including provision as to:

- the fitting of equipment to vehicles;
- equipment to be carried by vehicles;
- the design of equipment to be fitted to, or carried by, vehicles;
- the use of equipment fitted to, or carried by, vehicles;
- the toilet facilities to be provided in vehicles;
- the location and floor area of the wheelchair accommodation to be provided in vehicles;
- assistance to be given to disabled persons.

The regulations may contain different provision as respects different classes or descriptions of rail vehicle; as respects the same class or description of rail vehicle in different circumstances and as respects different networks. 'Network' means any permanent way or other means of guiding or supporting rail vehicles, or any section of it (s.182(4)).

The power to make rail vehicle accessibility regulations must be exercised so as to secure that on and after 1 January 2020, every rail vehicle is a regulated rail vehicle although such regulations may continue to differentiate between different vehicles, classes of vehicles and so on.

Before making regulations under s.182(1) or s.183, the Secretary of State must consult the Disabled Persons Transport Advisory Committee and such other representative organisations as the Secretary of State thinks fit.

12.3.2 Exemptions from rail vehicle accessibility regulations (section 183)

The Secretary of State may make an 'exemption order':

- to authorise the use for carriage of a regulated rail vehicle even though the vehicle does not conform with the provisions of rail vehicle accessibility regulations with which it is required to conform;
- to authorise a regulated rail vehicle to be used for carriage otherwise than in conformity with the provisions of rail vehicle accessibility regulations with which use of the vehicle is required to conform.

A vehicle is used 'for carriage' if it is used for the carriage of passengers (s.187(2)).

An exemption order may be for:

- a regulated rail vehicle that is specified or of a specified description; or
- use in specified circumstances of a regulated rail vehicle, or
- use in specified circumstances of a regulated rail vehicle that is specified or of a specified description.

What is so 'specified' will be so specified in the exemption order.

The Secretary of State may by regulations make provision as to exemption orders including, in particular, provision as to:

- the persons by whom applications for exemption orders may be made;
- the form in which applications are to be made;
- information to be supplied in connection with applications;
- the period for which exemption orders are to continue in force;
- the revocation of exemption orders.

After consulting the Disabled Persons Transport Advisory Committee and such other persons as the Secretary of State thinks appropriate, the Secretary of State may:

- make an exemption order in the terms of the application for the order;
- make an exemption order in such other terms as the Secretary of State thinks appropriate;
- refuse to make an exemption order.

The Secretary of State may make an exemption order subject to such conditions and restrictions as are specified.

The procedure for making exemption orders is contained in s.184. By s.185, after the end of each calendar year, the Secretary of State must prepare a report on the exercise in that year of the power to make exemption orders and this must be laid before Parliament.

12.3.3   Rail vehicle accessibility: compliance (section 186)

Schedule 20 has effect under s.186. The Schedule re-enacts the provisions of DDA 1995, ss.47A–47M, as inserted by the Disability Discrimination Act 2005 (but never brought into force). Section 186 and Sched. 20 are to be repealed if not brought into force (either fully or to any extent) by 31 December 2010. However, it is most unlikely that they will be brought into force for the reasons set out in the Explanatory Note, paras. 938 onwards. Paragraphs 939–941 are set out below:

> 939. This Schedule was included in the Act because, during its passage through Parliament, the Department for Transport was consulting on draft regulations under section 46 of the Disability Discrimination Act 1995. These were prepared following a policy reappraisal which favoured a move away from compliance certification and civil enforcement powers for rail vehicle accessibility. The Government's preferred option, adoption of Health and Safety at Work etc Act 1974 enforcement powers with the Office of Rail Regulation being designated as enforcement authority, would make accessibility enforcement on light rail consistent with recent changes to accessibility enforcement on the main line rail system resulting from the introduction of new European standards which came into force in July 2008. The consultation period ended on 3 July 2009 but, in order not to pre-empt the outcome, the option to use compliance certification and civil enforcement powers was retained in the Act.
>
> 940. Consultation responses indicated that the Government's preferred option of non-commencement of this Schedule was widely supported by stakeholders. The Government therefore proceeded with the implementation of a package of secondary legislation under the Disability Discrimination Act 1995 which did not include compliance certification and replaced the originally envisaged civil enforcement regime with enforcement by the Office of Rail Regulation under their existing Health and Safety at Work etc Act 1974 powers. The enforcement

provisions were contained in the Rail Vehicle Accessibility (Non-Interoperable Rail System) Regulations 2010 (S.I. 2010/432) which came into force on 6 April 2010.

941. Government policy is therefore not to bring this Schedule into force.

12.4   PART 12, CHAPTER 4 – SUPPLEMENTARY

Section 188 of Chapter 4 makes it an offence to forge, alter or use a 'relevant document'; lends a relevant document to another person; allow a relevant document to be used by another person; or to make or have possession of a document which closely resembles a relevant document if this is done with 'intent to deceive'. A 'relevant document' is:

- an exemption certificate issued under s.166, 169 or 171;
- a notice of a kind mentioned in ss.166(3)(b), 169(4)(b) or 171(4)(b);
- an accessibility certificate (see s.176);
- an approval certificate (see s.177).

Summary conviction will lead to a fine not exceeding the statutory maximum; conviction on indictment, to imprisonment for a term not exceeding two years or to a fine or to both.

A person also commits an offence under s.188 by knowingly making a false statement for the purpose of obtaining an accessibility certificate or an approval certificate and will be liable on summary conviction to a fine not exceeding level 4 on the standard scale.

13 PART 13 – DISABILITY

The Equality Act 2010 has offered an opportunity to revisit the tangled web of disability discrimination. The original form of the DDA 1995 reflected a different approach to issues of discrimination to the traditional model of anti-discrimination legislation. In particular, it provided for differential positive treatment in favour of the disabled. The original form of the DDA 1995 was then subject to amendment to give effect to the obligations of EU law under the Framework Directive, Directive 2000/78/EC. This created a yet more complex structure. Added to that heady mix was the decision of the House of Lords in *Lewisham London Borough Council* v. *Malcolm* [2008] UKHL 43, [2008] 1 AC 1399, which placed a construction on parts of the Act which fettered the scope of protection which had previously been understood to have been provided by the Act. The Equality Act 2010 therefore provides an opportunity to address some of these issues and provide a more coherent structure.

13.1 THE DEFINITION OF DISABILITY

As set out at 2.2, s.4 of the Act defines disability as a protected characteristic. In this respect, disability is treated in the same way as other characteristics such as age, sex or race. Section 6(1) then defines disability in familiar terms for those who have been concerned with the application of DDA 1995, s.6(1), providing that:

A person (P) has a disability if –

(a) P has a physical or mental impairment, and
(b) the impairment has a substantial and long-term adverse effect on P's ability to carry out normal day-to-day activities.

A reference to a disabled person is a reference to a person who has a disability (s.6(2)).

In applying the Act when considering the protected characteristic of disability, s.6(3) provides:

(a) a reference to a person who has a particular protected characteristic is a reference to a person who has a particular disability;
(b) a reference to persons who share a protected characteristic is a reference to persons who have the same disability.

This definition is then supported by Part 1 of Sched. 1 to the Act. In similar form to the DDA 1995, this clarifies the meaning of disability.

In para. 2 of Sched. 1, 'long-term effects' are defined as:

(1)   The effect of an impairment is long-term if –

    (a)   it has lasted for at least 12 months,
    (b)   it is likely to last for at least 12 months, or
    (c)   it is likely to last for the rest of the life of the person affected.

(2)   If an impairment ceases to have a substantial adverse effect on a person's ability to carry out normal day-to-day activities, it is to be treated as continuing to have that effect if that effect is likely to recur.
(3)   For the purposes of sub-paragraph (2), the likelihood of an effect recurring is to be disregarded in such circumstances as may be prescribed.
(4)   Regulations may prescribe circumstances in which, despite sub-paragraph (1), an effect is to be treated as being, or as not being, long-term.

In the case of severe disfigurement, there is a deemed substantial adverse effect (Sched. 1, para. 3):

(1)   An impairment which consists of a severe disfigurement is to be treated as having a substantial adverse effect on the ability of the person concerned to carry out normal day-to-day activities.
(2)   Regulations may provide that in prescribed circumstances a severe disfigurement is not to be treated as having that effect.
(3)   The regulations may, in particular, make provision in relation to deliberately acquired disfigurement.

As to medical treatment (Sched. 1, para. 5):

(1)   An impairment is to be treated as having a substantial adverse effect on the ability of the person concerned to carry out normal day-to-day activities if –

    (a)   measures are being taken to treat or correct it, and
    (b)   but for that, it would be likely to have that effect.

(2)   'Measures' includes, in particular, medical treatment and the use of a prosthesis or other aid.
(3)   Sub-paragraph (1) does not apply –

    (a)   in relation to the impairment of a person's sight, to the extent that the impairment is, in the person's case, correctable by spectacles or contact lenses or in such other ways as may be prescribed;
    (b)   in relation to such other impairments as may be prescribed, in such circumstances as are prescribed.

Under para. 6(1) of Sched. 1, cancer, HIV infection and multiple sclerosis are each a disability. HIV infection is defined as an infection by a virus capable of causing the Acquired Immune Deficiency Syndrome.

Progressive conditions are dealt with under para. 8:

(1)   This paragraph applies to a person (P) if –

    (a)   P has a progressive condition,
    (b)   as a result of that condition P has an impairment which has (or had) an effect on P's ability to carry out normal day-to-day activities, but

(c)   the effect is not (or was not) a substantial adverse effect.

(2)   P is to be taken to have an impairment which has a substantial adverse effect if the condition is likely to result in P having such an impairment.

13.2   PAST DISABILITIES

One of the features of the DDA 1995 was that it extended the scope of protection to individuals who had had a disability but no longer suffered from the effect of the disability. This is mirrored by s.6(4) of the Act, which states:

> This Act (except Part 12 and section 190) applies in relation to a person who has had a disability as it applies in relation to a person who has the disability; accordingly (except in that Part and that section) –
>
> (a)   a reference (however expressed) to a person who has a disability includes a reference to a person who has had the disability, and
> (b)   a reference (however expressed) to a person who does not have a disability includes a reference to a person who has not had the disability.

As to the exclusions under Part 12 and s.190 referred to in s.6(4), these relate to transport for disabled persons and improvements to let dwelling houses, respectively. Under para. 9(2) of Sched. 1, when looking back to consider whether a person had a disability at a particular point in time, that may be a time before the Act came into force.

13.3   THE FORMS OF DISABILITY DISCRIMINATION

In common with other forms of discrimination, direct discrimination is defined by s.13 in the same manner as the protection is applied to other protected characteristics. Thus:

> (1)   A person (A) discriminates against another (B) if, because of a protected characteristic, A treats B less favourably than A treats or would treat others.

As noted at the beginning of this chapter, the DDA 1995 embraced the concept of more favourable treatment for the disabled where it was directed at removing a fetter upon them. Positive discrimination in favour of the disabled is now preserved by an exclusion for more favourable treatment under s.13(3):

> (3)   If the protected characteristic is disability, and B is not a disabled person, A does not discriminate against B only because A treats or would treat disabled persons more favourably than A treats B.

One aspect of the language adopted in the Act is that direct discrimination had been defined by reference to the phrase 'on the grounds of'. The Explanatory Notes to the Act indicate that the intention was not to change the developed case law on the meaning of 'on the grounds of' (see Explanatory Notes, para. 61). However, as the phrase adopted in the Act is 'because of', this appears to adopt a more causative approach to the question of discrimination. Therefore, earlier discriminatory treatment might be causative of a particular set of facts which leads to detrimental treatment. It may be, then, that the detrimental treatment itself is not on the grounds of disability (or indeed on the grounds of other protected characteristics), but it will still fall within the scope of s.13 as there is a causative connection between the detrimental treatment and the protected characteristic – thus, it can be said that the discriminatory treatment is because of the detrimental treatment. This would seem to broaden the scope of the protection.

The adoption of the 'because of' test may, however, present a problem of construction. The concept of associative discrimination could readily be brought within the formulation of 'on the grounds of'. It is clear from *Attridge LLP* v. *Coleman* [2010] ICR 242, following the decision of the ECJ in *Coleman* v. *Attridge Law* Case C–303/06 [2008] All ER (EC) 1105, that disability discrimination had to embrace associative discrimination. The Equality Act 2010 does not include an express provision to deal with this form of discrimination. The definition of direct discrimination is sufficiently wide enough to embrace associative discrimination – this is because of the use of the term 'because of' in relation to the characteristic. Thus, a carer may be directly discriminated against because of a protected characteristic, i.e. the disability of the person for whom they provide the care. Whilst a purposeful interpretation will be adopted, it is unfortunate that a specific provision was not included to make the law explicitly clear.

As referenced earlier at 3.3, disability in common with other protected characteristics may fall with the scope of the s.14 combined discrimination protection where discrimination arises because of the combination of a number of protected characteristics.

13.4   CONCEPTUAL DIFFICULTIES IN DIRECT DISABILITY DISCRIMINATION

In common with other forms of direct discrimination and consistent with the requirements of the Framework Directive, direct discrimination cannot be justified. In the amendments to the DDA 1995, which were made as a consequence of the Framework Directive, a form of direct discrimination was introduced. This adopted a difficult formulation which required the consideration of a hypothetical comparator who had the same capabilities as the claimant but was not disabled. Thus, if a one-armed typist was restricted in the speed at which he could type, a relevant comparator would be a person who had the same capabilities at typing, but was not disabled. It may be perceived that direct discrimination under the DDA 1995 was therefore directed at discrimination against the status of disability rather than against the limitations on the capabilities of the disabled person, which might legitimately present a reason why the individual claimant could not perform the required task. It should be noted, however, that before the decision of the House of Lords in *Lewisham London Borough Council* v. *Malcolm* above, any such disability-related discrimination would have to have been justified if it was not to be unlawful discrimination.

The former definition of direct disability discrimination under the DDA 1995 did lead to getting into conceptually difficult waters. For example, the relevant comparator for a blind person appeared to be an individual who could not see, so that he had the same capabilities as to vision as the claimant, but who was not blind. In part, this reflected the fact that under the DDA 1995, there was no section providing for comparison on the basis of materially similar circumstances when considering whether there has been discrimination.

The Act addresses this in a different manner. First, as already noted above, the cumbersome formulation of the DDA 1995 as to what constitutes direct discrimination is abandoned in favour of the simple 'because of' test. The concept of the comparator is applied to disability under s.23, which provides as follows:

> (1)   On a comparison of cases for the purposes of section 13, 14, or 19 there must be no material difference between the circumstances relating to each case.
> (2)   The circumstances relating to a case include a person's abilities if –
>   (a)   on a comparison for the purposes of section 13, the protected characteristic is disability;
>   (b)   on a comparison for the purposes of section 14, one of the protected characteristics in the combination is disability.

Thus, in approaching the question of the comparator, the focus is again on abilities when considering the question of comparative treatment. No doubt the intention was to accommodate the example given above of the individual who is blind, where the ability to see is a material circumstance which must be assumed to be the same as that of the comparator. However, on the simple wording of s.13, it would seem to render unlawful the refusal to allow a blind person to train as an airline pilot, without any defence of justification being available, because the detrimental treatment was because of the disability. On the face of it, s.23 does not take such conduct out of the scope of s.13.

13.5   DISABILITY-RELATED DISCRIMINATION

Under the DDA 1995, although capable of being justified, detrimental treatment for a disability-related reason was unlawful discrimination. Although not in an employment context, a majority of the House of Lords in *Lewisham London Borough Council* v. *Malcolm* [2008] UKHL 43, [2008] 1 AC 1399 placed a narrow construction on the approach to be adopted so that the breadth of the protection was significantly narrowed from that which had previously been understood to apply under the Court of Appeal decision in *Clark* v. *TDG Ltd (t/a Novacold Ltd)* [1999] 2 All ER 977. The Equality Act 2010 seeks to restore the scope of that protection by reversing the decision in *Lewisham London Borough Council* v. *Malcolm* by s.15, which states:

> (1)   A person (A) discriminates against a disabled person (B) if –
>   (a)   A treats B unfavourably because of something arising in consequence of B's disability, and

(b)   A cannot show that the treatment is a proportionate means of achieving a legitimate aim.

(2)   Subsection (1) does not apply if A shows that A did not know, and could not reasonably have been expected to know, that B had the disability.

The scope of s.15 can be seen from the use of the phrase 'something arising in consequence of B's disability'. Thus, to take the example of the disabled typist with the restriction on his ability to type a number of words per minute, refusing to employ that individual because of his typing speed is to do so because of something arising in consequence of his disability. Unless the putative employer could then show that the refusal was a proportionate means of achieving a legitimate aim, the employer will have discriminated against the claimant.

13.6   INDIRECT DISCRIMINATION

In accordance with the amendments made to the DDA 1995 to give effect to the Framework Directive, changes were made to the duty to make reasonable adjustments on the basis that it, together with disability-related discrimination, could give effect to the Directive's requirement that indirect discrimination in cases of disability should be unlawful. The Equality Act 2010 addresses the issue by directly bringing disability within the scope of the provisions on indirect discrimination which are applied to other protected characteristics. Thus, s.19 is applied to disability in common with other protected characteristics:

(1)   A person (A) discriminates against another (B) if A applies to B a provision, criterion or practice which is discriminatory in relation to a relevant protected characteristic of B's.

(2)   For the purposes of subsection (1), a provision, criterion or practice is discriminatory in relation to a relevant protected characteristic of B's if –

(a)   A applies, or would apply, it to persons with whom B does not share the characteristic,

(b)   it puts, or would put, persons with whom B shares the characteristic at a particular disadvantage when compared with persons with whom B does not share it,

(c)   it puts, or would put, B at that disadvantage, and

(d)   A cannot show it to be a proportionate means of achieving a legitimate aim.

The familiar form of indirect discrimination is therefore extended to disability discrimination. If, for example, a particular requirement is stipulated for appointment to a post such as a basic physical fitness standard, then this may place persons who share the claimant's disability at a particular disability when compared to others who are not disabled. Once again, if the claimant is placed at that disadvantage because he or she is not considered for the post, then it will be unlawful discrimination unless the employer can show that the requirement is a proportionate means of achieving a legitimate aim.

13.7   DUTY TO MAKE REASONABLE ADJUSTMENTS

The duty to make reasonable adjustments under the DDA 1995 was the primary obligation to mitigate against the effects of a disability. The duty embraced an obligation to take positive steps to make adjustments. Because of the structure of the original form of the DDA 1995 and, in particular, because disability-related discrimination could not be justified if the discrimination had arisen from a failure to make a reasonable adjustment, the logical starting point in any analysis was to consider whether a duty to make reasonable adjustment was engaged. Thus, the duty to make reasonable adjustments became the focus of much litigation.

Section 20 of the Equality Act 2010 imposes the same obligation under specific sections of the Act to make reasonable adjustments. Section 20 identifies three requirements where the duty applies.

13.7.1   The first requirement (section 20(3))

(3) The first requirement is a requirement, where a provision, criterion or practice of A's puts a disabled person at a substantial disadvantage in relation to a relevant matter in comparison with persons who are not disabled, to take such steps as it is reasonable to have to take to avoid the disadvantage.

The first requirement mirrors the obligations under indirect discrimination and imposes a requirement where a provision, criterion or practice of A's puts a disabled person at a substantial disadvantage in relation to a relevant matter in comparison with persons who are not disabled, to take such steps as it is reasonable to have to take to avoid the disadvantage. Taking again the example of the disabled person whose typing ability is restricted, a requirement that those employed in a personal assistant role have to have a specified level of typing speed would put the disabled person at a substantial disadvantage. It would consequently follow that there would be a duty to make reasonable adjustments to the job specification or the equipment, possibly by, for example, the use of voice dictation software so as remove the effect of this requirement.

13.7.2   The second requirement (section 20(4))

(4) The second requirement is a requirement, where a physical feature puts a disabled person at a substantial disadvantage in relation to a relevant matter in comparison with persons who are not disabled, to take such steps as it is reasonable to have to take to avoid the disadvantage.

The second requirement is focused upon physical features which place the disabled person at a substantial disadvantage. Thus, a wheelchair user would be placed at a substantial disadvantage in accessing premises if the only method of doing so was by a flight of steps.

13.7.3   The third requirement (section 20(5))

(5) The third requirement is a requirement, where a disabled person would, but for the provision of an auxiliary aid, be put at a substantial disadvantage in relation to a relevant matter in comparison with persons who are not disabled, to take such steps as it is reasonable to have to take to provide the auxiliary aid.

The third requirement specifically focuses upon the provision of an auxiliary aid, for example, a special chair for a person with a back-related condition, where the absence of the auxiliary aid would place the disabled person at a substantial disadvantage.

13.7.4   Scope of the adjustments

Section 20, together with ss.21 and 22, provide a wide definition of the scope of the adjustments which may be made and impose a specific duty not to impose any cost on the disabled person.

(6) Where the first or third requirement relates to the provision of information, the steps which it is reasonable for A to have to take include steps for ensuring that in the circumstances concerned the information is provided in an accessible format.

(7) A person (A) who is subject to a duty to make reasonable adjustments is not (subject to express provision to the contrary) entitled to require a disabled person, in relation to whom A is required to comply with the duty, to pay to any extent A's costs of complying with the duty.

(8) A reference in section 21 or 22 or an applicable Schedule to the first, second or third requirement is to be construed in accordance with this section.

(9) In relation to the second requirement, a reference in this section or an applicable Schedule to avoiding a substantial disadvantage includes a reference to –

(a) a feature arising from the design or construction of a building,

(b) a feature of an approach to, exit from or access to a building,

(c) a fixture or fitting, or furniture, furnishings, materials, equipment or other chattels, in or on premises, or

(d) any other physical element or quality.

(10) A reference in this section, section 21 or 22 or an applicable Schedule (apart from paragraphs 2 to 4 of Schedule 4) to a physical feature is a reference to –

(a) a feature arising from the design or construction of a building,

(b) a feature of an approach to, exit from or access to a building,

(c) a fixture or fitting, or furniture, furnishings, materials, equipment or other chattels, in or on premises, or

(d) any other physical element or quality.

(11) A reference in this section, section 21 or 22 or an applicable Schedule to an auxiliary aid includes a reference to an auxiliary service.

(12) A reference in this section or an applicable Schedule to chattels is to be read, in relation to Scotland, as a reference to moveable property.

(13) The applicable Schedule is, in relation to the Part of this Act specified in the first column of the Table, the Schedule specified in the second column.

Part of this Act	Applicable Schedule
Part 3 (services and public functions)	Schedule 2
Part 4 (premises)	Schedule 4
Part 5 (work)	Schedule 8
Part 6 (education)	Schedule 13
Part 7 (associations)	Schedule 15
Each of the Parts mentioned above	Schedule 21

As shown above, at the end of s.20, specific Schedules to the Act are then applied in the application of the reasonable adjustments duty in various Parts of the Act, and Sched. 21 is applied to all of these Parts. Thus, Sched. 2 is applied in the context of services and public functions. Schedule 2 modifies s.20 for the specific application to Part 3 and makes special provision about transport. Schedule 4 applies to premises and provides for specific obligations in respect of premises. Schedule 8 applies to Part 5 which is directed to work and deals with reasonable adjustment obligations. It specifically deals with the definition of the interested disabled person, for example, a person who has notified that she may be interested in applying for a job, where the duty to make reasonable adjustments will be engaged. Schedule 13 deals with education and Sched. 15 with associations. Some supplementary provisions within Sched. 21 are then applied to all the Parts.

The specific discriminatory act in failing to comply with a reasonable adjustment duty is defined by s.21, which provides that:

(1) A failure to comply with the first, second or third requirement is a failure to comply with a duty to make reasonable adjustments.

(2) A discriminates against a disabled person if A fails to comply with that duty in relation to that person

(3) A provision of an applicable Schedule which imposes a duty to comply with the first, second or third requirement applies only for the purpose of establishing whether A has contravened this Act by virtue of subsection (2); a failure to comply is, accordingly, not actionable by virtue of another provision of this Act or otherwise.

Section 22 provides a power for the making of regulations to amplify and define the reasonable adjustments duty further.

13.8   HARASSMENT AND VICTIMISATION

In common with other forms of protected characteristic, the scope of the protections under s.26 (harassment) and s.27 (victimisation) extends to disability.

13.9   RECRUITMENT

Of particular significance in the field of disability is the putative employer's knowledge of disability before employment. In the context of recruitment, knowledge of disability may have an adverse effect on potential employment in a manner which is difficult for the disabled person to prove.

The Act deals with this issue in s.60 by placing restrictions on the questions that may be asked by an employer who has received an application for work. Section 60(1) provides:

> (1)   A person (A) to whom an application for work is made must not ask about the health of the applicant (B) –
>
> (a)   before offering work to B, or
> (b)   where A is not in a position to offer work to B, before including B in a pool of applicants from whom A intends (when in a position to do so) to select a person to whom to offer work.

This is, under s.60(2), an unlawful act which is enforceable only by the Commission. Asking for the information does not involve the breach of any other Part of the Act, but, of course, it may be that there is, as a consequence of the information obtained, a breach of a specific provision such as the refusal of an application because of the disability. The asking of prohibited questions is specifically made of relevance for the purposes of considering the adverse inferences to be drawn to replies to a questionnaire under s.136 (see s.60(5)). This is of particular importance for a disabled person in seeking to show that the refusal of his application was because of his disability.

Under s.60(9), 'work' means employment, contract work, a position as a partner, a position as a member of an LLP, a pupillage or tenancy, being taken as a devil, membership of a stable, an appointment to a personal or public office, or the provision of an employment service; and the references in s.60(1) to offering a person work are, in relation to contract work, to be read as references to allowing a person to do the work. Further, under s.60(10), a reference to offering work is a reference to making a conditional or unconditional offer of work (and, in relation to contract work, is a reference to allowing a person to do the work subject to fulfilment of one or more conditions).

There are circumstances where it is proper that questions are asked about an individual's health and s.60(6) provides for s.60 not to apply in certain circumstances:

> (6)   This section does not apply to a question that A asks in so far as asking the question is necessary for the purpose of –
>
> (a)   establishing whether B will be able to comply with a requirement to undergo an assessment or establishing whether a duty to make reasonable adjustments is or will be imposed on A in relation to B in connection with a requirement to undergo an assessment,
> (b)   establishing whether B will be able to carry out a function that is intrinsic to the work concerned,

(c)   monitoring diversity in the range of persons applying to A for work,
(d)   taking action to which section 158 would apply if references in that section to persons who share (or do not share) a protected characteristic were references to disabled persons (or persons who are not disabled) and the reference to the characteristic were a reference to disability, or
(e)   if A applies in relation to the work a requirement to have a particular disability, establishing whether B has that disability.

These provisions have to be read in the wider context of the Act so that where, under s.60(6)(b), A reasonably believes that a duty to make reasonable adjustments would be imposed on A in relation to B in connection with the work, the reference to a function that is intrinsic to the work is to be read as a reference to a function that would be intrinsic to the work once A complied with the duty (s.60(7)). Thus, again, the first question must be 'could reasonable adjustments have been made?'. If they could, then the putative employer failed reasonably to take into account that reasonable adjustments could be made.

Section 60(6)(e) applies (see s.60(8)) only if A shows that, having regard to the nature or context of the work:

(a)   the requirement is an occupational requirement, and
(b)   the application of the requirement is a proportionate means of achieving a legitimate aim.

14 PARTS 14, 15 AND 16

14.1 PART 14 – GENERAL EXCEPTIONS

Part 14 contains seven sections that provide for general exceptions to the Act, which are supplemented by Scheds. 22 and 23. These exceptions are:

- Statutory provisions under s.191 and Sched. 22.
- National security under s.192.
- Charities under ss.193 and 194.
- Sport under s.195.
- The general provisions under s.196 and Sched. 23.
- Age under s.197.

14.1.1 Statutory provisions (section 191)

Section 191 states that Sched. 22 has effect. Schedule 22 contains five detailed paragraphs which set out various statutory exceptions.

Under para. 1(1), Statutory authority, there is no contravention relating to protected characteristics in the second column of the table set out where the person must do anything pursuant to a requirement specified in the third column:

Specified provision	Protected characteristic	Requirement
Parts 3 to 7	Age	A requirement of an enactment
Parts 3 to 7 and 12	Disability	A requirement of an enactment
		A relevant requirement or condition imposed by virtue of an enactment

Specified provision	Protected characteristic	Requirement
Parts 3 to 7	Religion or belief	A requirement of an enactment
		A relevant requirement or condition imposed by virtue of an enactment
Section 29(6) and Parts 6 and 7	Sex	A requirement of an enactment
Parts 3, 4, 6 and 7	Sexual orientation	A requirement of an enactment
		A relevant requirement or condition imposed by virtue of an enactment

However, the references to Part 6 do not include vocational training. An enactment includes a Measure of the General Synod of the Church of England and an enactment passed or made on or after the date on which the Act is passed.

A requirement or condition is a requirement or condition imposed by a Minister of the Crown, a member of the Scottish Executive; the National Assembly for Wales (constituted by the Government of Wales Act 1998); and the Welsh Ministers, the First Minister for Wales or the Counsel General to the Welsh Assembly Government.

Under para. 2, Protection of women, there is no contravention of a specified provision where the person is under a duty to comply with a pre-1975 enactment concerning the protection of women, a statutory provision under Part 1 of the Health and Safety at Work, etc. Act 1974 for the protection of women or a requirement of a provision in Sched. 1 to the Employment Act 1989. The protection of women relates to protection for the purposes of pregnancy or maternity or any other circumstances giving rise to risks specifically affecting women, though it does not matter whether the protection is restricted to women.

Under para. 3, Educational appointments, etc.: religious belief, a person does not contravene Part 5 only by doing a relevant act in connection with the employment of another in a relevant position. A relevant position is that of a head teacher or principal of an educational establishment; the head, a fellow or other member of the academic staff of a college, or institution in the nature of a college, in a university; or a professorship of a university which is a canon professorship or one to which a canonry is annexed. The relevant acts are anything necessary to comply with a requirement of an instrument relating to the establishment that the head teacher or principal must be a member of a particular religious order; a requirement of an instrument relating to the college or institution that the holder of the position must be a woman; or an Act or instrument in accordance with which the professorship is a canon professorship or one to which a canonry is annexed. Under para. 4, there is provision for dismissal of teachers because of failure to give religious education, religious considerations relating to certain appointments and preference for teachers at independent school of a religious character.

Paragraph 5 relates to Crown employment and provides that rules which restrict employment in the service of the Crown, employment by prescribed public bodies and holding a public office to persons of particular birth, nationality, descent or residence will not contravene the Act. There is a power to make regulations for this purpose.

14.1.2   National security (section 192)

Section 192 provides that a person does not contravene the Act by doing anything, for the purpose of national security, which is proportionate for that purpose.

14.1.3   Charities (section 193)

Section 193(1) and (2) provides that a person does not contravene the Act only by restricting the provision of benefits to persons who share a protected characteristic if the person acts in pursuance of a charitable instrument, and the provision of the benefits is a proportionate means of achieving a legitimate aim, or for the purpose of preventing or compensating for a disadvantage linked to the protected characteristic. There is also provision in relation to supported employment to treat persons who have the same disability or disability of a description (s.193(3)). It is also not a contravention of the Act for a charity to require members, or persons wishing to become members, to make a statement which asserts or implies membership or acceptance of a religion or belief; and for this purpose restricting the access by members to a benefit, facility or service to those who make such a statement is to be treated as imposing such a requirement (s.193(5)). However, ss.39–40 and 55 are excluded save as they relate to vocational training (s.193(9)) and the definition of race in so far as it relates to colour is excluded (s.194(2)). The definitions of 'charity' contained in the Charity Act 2006 are incorporated.

14.1.4   Sport (section 195)

By s.195, a person does not contravene the Act, so far as relating to sex, only by doing anything in relation to the participation of another as a competitor in a gender-affected activity, and a person does not contravene s.29, 33, 34 or 35, so far as relating to gender reassignment, only by doing anything in relation to the participation of a transsexual person as a competitor in a gender-affected activity if it is necessary to do so to secure in relation to the activity fair competition, or the safety of competitors.

A gender-affected sport is a sport, game or other activity of a competitive nature in circumstances in which the physical strength, stamina or physique of average persons of one sex would put them at a disadvantage compared to average persons of the other sex as competitors in events involving the activity and in considering whether a sport, game or other activity is gender-affected in relation to children, it is appropriate to take account of the age and stage of development of children who are likely to be competitors (s.195(3) and (4)).

There is also an exclusion for nationality or place of birth or length of residence in a particular area or place (s.195(5)) where selecting one or more persons to represent a country, place or area or a related association, in a sport or game or other activity of a competitive nature or where it relates to doing anything in pursuance of the rules of a competition so far as relating to eligibility to compete in a sport or game or other such activity (s.195(6)).

14.1.5   General (section 196)

Section 196 incorporates Sched. 23 which contains general exceptions. This Schedule has four broad heads:

- Acts authorised by statute or the executive. By para. 1, Parts 2, 3, 4 or 5 of the Act are not contravened where anything is done in relation to an enactment or instruments, or to comply with a requirement under an enactment or to comply with arrangements or conditions imposed by a Minister of the Crown. This includes provisions, criteria or practices which relate to residence.
- Organisations relating to religion or belief. Paragraph 2 contains detailed provisions whereby religious or belief organisations are excluded from paras. 3, 4 or 7 in relation to religion or belief or sexual orientation though it does not apply to commercial organisations.
- Communal accommodation. Paragraph 3 excludes sex discrimination or gender reassignment discrimination relating to communal accommodation which is residential accommodation, including dormitories or shared sleeping accommodation which for reasons of privacy should be used only by persons of the same sex or benefits facilities or services which are linked and which cannot be properly and effectively provided except for those using the accommodation.
- Training provided to non-EEA residents, etc. By para. 4, there will not be a breach where a person, so far as relating to nationality, provides a non-resident with training, where the person thinks that the non-resident does not intend to exercise in Great Britain skills obtained as a result of that training. A non-resident is someone not ordinarily resident in a non-EEA state.

14.1.6   Age (section 197)

Section 197(1) gives a Minister of the Crown the power by order to amend the Act to provide that specified conduct, anything done for a specified purpose and anything done in pursuance of arrangements of a specified description will not contravene the Act as regards age. However, this does not include references to work or further and higher education (s.197(9)). Specified conduct is conduct of a specified description, carried out in specified circumstances, or by or in relation to a person of a specified description (s.197(2)). This new exception is designed to allow exceptions to be made from the new prohibitions on age discrimination in the provision of services and the exercise of public functions. Appropriate age-based treatment may include the following:

- concessionary travel for older and young people;
- disease prevention programmes such as cancer screening targeted at people in particular age groups on the basis of clinical evidence;
- age differences in the calculation of annuities and insurance programmes which are reasonable and based on adequate evidence of the underlying difference in risk;
- holidays for particular age groups.

Such order may include provision for guidance (s.197(3)) and there is provision for consultation (s.197(5)) and content of the guidance (s.197(6)).

The section is not affected by any provisions of the Act which make special provision in relation to age (s.197(8)).

14.2   PART 15 – FAMILY PROPERTY

By s.198, the rule of common law that a husband must maintain his wife is abolished. The presumption of advancement, by which, for example, a husband is presumed to be making a gift to his wife if he transfers property to her or purchases property in her name is also abolished (s.199(1)) though this does not have effect in relation to anything done before the commencement or any obligation incurred before the commencement of the section (s.199(2)).

Amendments are also made to the housekeeping allowance provisions under the Married Women's Property Act 1964 (s.200) and to provide that the same position applies to a civil partnership as to that between husband and wife (s.201). Money and property derived from a housekeeping allowance will, in the absence of an agreement to the contrary, be owned by the husband and wife in equal shares regardless of who paid or received the allowance. The provision does not apply to any allowance paid before it comes into force.

14.3   PART 16 – GENERAL AND MISCELLANEOUS

Part 16 (ss.202–218) covers various miscellaneous matters, general definitions and rule-making powers as well as provisions for harmonisation. The rule-making powers are self-explanatory and set out the powers to be exercisable by a Minister of the Crown, the Welsh Ministers and the Scottish Ministers. The general interpretation provisions set out in s.121 should, in particular, be referred to, though it should be noted that they mainly refer back to the definitions contained in earlier Parts of the Act.

The provisions for harmonisation, contained in s.203, are intended to create a power to amend the Act by ministerial order when the United Kingdom becomes under an obligation to implement EU law relating to a Directive that relates to this Act or the Equality Act 2006 and it is considered appropriate by a Minister to make a harmonising provision. There are procedures for consultation and for at least 12 weeks to pass and the requirement for an affirmative resolution in both houses. A Minister must report to Parliament every two years on the use of this power.

Section 216 provides that most of the sections are to come into force on such date as the Minister of the Crown may by order appoint.

Appendix
EQUALITY ACT 2010

2010 Chapter 15

CONTENTS

Part 3   Services and public functions

Preliminary

28.   Application of this Part

Provision of services, etc.

29.   Provision of services, etc.

Supplementary

30.   Ships and hovercraft
31.   Interpretation and exceptions

Part 4   Premises

Preliminary

32.   Application of this Part

Disposal and management

33.   Disposals, etc.
34.   Permission for disposal
35.   Management

Reasonable adjustments

36.   Leasehold and commonhold premises and common parts
37.   Adjustments to common parts in Scotland

Supplementary

38.   Interpretation and exceptions

Part 5   Work

Chapter 1 – Employment, etc.

Employees

39.   Employees and applicants
40.   Employees and applicants: harassment
41.   Contract workers

Police officers

42.   Identity of employer
43.   Interpretation

Partners

44.   Partnerships
45.   Limited liability partnerships
46.   Interpretation

The Bar

47.   Barristers
48.   Advocates

Office-holders

49.   Personal offices: appointments, etc.
50.   Public offices: appointments, etc.
51.   Public offices: recommendations for appointments, etc.
52.   Interpretation and exceptions

Qualifications

53.   Qualifications bodies
54.   Interpretation

An Act to make provision to require Ministers of the Crown and others when making strategic decisions about the exercise of their functions to have regard to the desirability of reducing socio-economic inequalities; to reform and harmonise equality law and restate the greater part of the enactments relating to discrimination and harassment related to certain personal characteristics; to enable certain employers to be required to publish information about the differences in pay between male and female employees; to prohibit victimisation in certain circumstances; to require the exercise of certain functions to be with regard to the need to eliminate discrimination and other prohibited conduct; to enable duties to be imposed in relation to the exercise of public procurement functions; to increase equality of opportunity; to amend the law relating to rights and responsibilities in family relationships; and for connected purposes. [8th April 2010]

BE IT ENACTED by the Queen's most Excellent Majesty, by and with the advice and consent of the Lords Spiritual and Temporal, and Commons, in this present Parliament assembled, and by the authority of the same, as follows: –

PART 1   SOCIO-ECONOMIC INEQUALITIES

1   Public sector duty regarding socio-economic inequalities

(1)   An authority to which this section applies must, when making decisions of a strategic nature about how to exercise its functions, have due regard to the desirability of exercising them in a way that is designed to reduce the inequalities of outcome which result from socio-economic disadvantage.

(2)   In deciding how to fulfil a duty to which it is subject under subsection (1), an authority must take into account any guidance issued by a Minister of the Crown.

(3)   The authorities to which this section applies are –

    (a)   a Minister of the Crown;

    (b)   a government department other than the Security Service, the Secret Intelligence Service or the Government Communications Headquarters;

    (c)   a county council or district council in England;

    (d)   the Greater London Authority;

    (e)   a London borough council;

    (f)   the Common Council of the City of London in its capacity as a local authority;

    (g)   the Council of the Isles of Scilly;

    (h)   a Strategic Health Authority established under section 13 of the National Health Service Act 2006, or continued in existence by virtue of that section;

    (i)   a Primary Care Trust established under section 18 of that Act, or continued in existence by virtue of that section;

    (j)   a regional development agency established by the Regional Development Agencies Act 1998;

    (k)   a police authority established for an area in England.

(4)   This section also applies to an authority that –

    (a)   is a partner authority in relation to a responsible local authority, and

    (b)   does not fall within subsection (3),

but only in relation to its participation in the preparation or modification of a sustainable community strategy.

(5)   In subsection (4) –

'partner authority' has the meaning given by section 104 of the Local Government and Public Involvement in Health Act 2007;

'responsible local authority' has the meaning given by section 103 of that Act;

'sustainable community strategy' means a strategy prepared under section 4 of the Local Government Act 2000.

(6) The reference to inequalities in subsection (1) does not include any inequalities experienced by a person as a result of being a person subject to immigration control within the meaning given by section 115(9) of the Immigration and Asylum Act 1999.

2   Power to amend section 1

(1) A Minister of the Crown may by regulations amend section 1 so as to –

   (a)   add a public authority to the authorities that are subject to the duty under subsection (1) of that section;
   (b)   remove an authority from those that are subject to the duty;
   (c)   make the duty apply, in the case of a particular authority, only in relation to certain functions that it has;
   (d)   in the case of an authority to which the application of the duty is already restricted to certain functions, remove or alter the restriction.

(2) In subsection (1) 'public authority' means an authority that has functions of a public nature.

(3) Provision made under subsection (1) may not impose a duty on an authority in relation to any devolved Scottish functions or devolved Welsh functions.

(4) The Scottish Ministers or the Welsh Ministers may by regulations amend section 1 so as to –

   (a)   add a relevant authority to the authorities that are subject to the duty under subsection (1) of that section;
   (b)   remove a relevant authority from those that are subject to the duty;
   (c)   make the duty apply, in the case of a particular relevant authority, only in relation to certain functions that it has;
   (d)   in the case of a relevant authority to which the application of the duty is already restricted to certain functions, remove or alter the restriction.

(5) For the purposes of the power conferred by subsection (4) on the Scottish Ministers, 'relevant authority' means an authority whose functions –

   (a)   are exercisable only in or as regards Scotland,
   (b)   are wholly or mainly devolved Scottish functions, and
   (c)   correspond or are similar to those of an authority for the time being specified in section 1 (3).

(6) For the purposes of the power conferred by subsection (4) on the Welsh Ministers, 'relevant authority' means an authority whose functions –

   (a)   are exercisable only in or as regards Wales,
   (b)   are wholly or mainly devolved Welsh functions, and
   (c)   correspond or are similar to those of an authority for the time being specified in subsection (3) of section 1 or referred to in subsection (4) of that section.

(7) Before making regulations under this section, the Scottish Ministers or the Welsh Ministers must consult a Minister of the Crown.

(8) Regulations under this section may make any amendments of section 1 that appear to the Minister or Ministers to be necessary or expedient in consequence of provision made under subsection (1) or (as the case may be) subsection (4).

(9) Provision made by the Scottish Ministers or the Welsh Ministers in reliance on subsection (8) may, in particular, amend section 1 so as to –

   (a)   confer on the Ministers a power to issue guidance;
   (b)   require a relevant authority to take into account any guidance issued under a power conferred by virtue of paragraph (a);
   (c)   disapply section 1(2) in consequence of the imposition of a requirement by virtue of paragraph (b).

(10) Before issuing guidance under a power conferred by virtue of subsection (9)(a), the Ministers must –

    (a)   take into account any guidance issued by a Minister of the Crown under section 1;

    (b)   consult a Minister of the Crown.

(11) For the purposes of this section –

    (a)   a function is a devolved Scottish function if it is exercisable in or as regards Scotland and it does not relate to reserved matters (within the meaning of the Scotland Act 1998);

    (b)   a function is a devolved Welsh function if it relates to a matter in respect of which functions are exercisable by the Welsh Ministers, the First Minister for Wales or the Counsel General to the Welsh Assembly Government, or to a matter within the legislative competence of the National Assembly for Wales.

3   Enforcement

A failure in respect of a performance of a duty under section 1 does not confer a cause of action at private law.

PART 2   EQUALITY: KEY CONCEPTS

CHAPTER 1   PROTECTED CHARACTERISTICS

4   The protected characteristics

The following characteristics are protected characteristics –

    age;
    disability;
    gender reassignment;
    marriage and civil partnership;
    pregnancy and maternity;
    race;
    religion or belief;
    sex;
    sexual orientation.

5   Age

(1)   In relation to the protected characteristic of age –

    (a)   a reference to a person who has a particular protected characteristic is a reference to a person of a particular age group;

    (b)   a reference to persons who share a protected characteristic is a reference to persons of the same age group.

(2)   A reference to an age group is a reference to a group of persons defined by reference to age, whether by reference to a particular age or to a range of ages.

6   Disability

(1)   A person (P) has a disability if –

    (a)   P has a physical or mental impairment, and

    (b)   the impairment has a substantial and long-term adverse effect on P's ability to carry out normal day-to-day activities.

(2)   A reference to a disabled person is a reference to a person who has a disability.

(3) In relation to the protected characteristic of disability –

   (a)   a reference to a person who has a particular protected characteristic is a reference to a person who has a particular disability;

   (b)   a reference to persons who share a protected characteristic is a reference to persons who have the same disability.

(4) This Act (except Part 12 and section 190) applies in relation to a person who has had a disability as it applies in relation to a person who has the disability; accordingly (except in that Part and that section) –

   (a)   a reference (however expressed) to a person who has a disability includes a reference to a person who has had the disability, and

   (b)   a reference (however expressed) to a person who does not have a disability includes a reference to a person who has not had the disability.

(5) A Minister of the Crown may issue guidance about matters to be taken into account in deciding any question for the purposes of subsection (1).

(6) Schedule 1 (disability: supplementary provision) has effect.

7   Gender reassignment

(1) A person has the protected characteristic of gender reassignment if the person is proposing to undergo, is undergoing or has undergone a process (or part of a process) for the purpose of reassigning the person's sex by changing physiological or other attributes of sex.

(2) A reference to a transsexual person is a reference to a person who has the protected characteristic of gender reassignment.

(3) In relation to the protected characteristic of gender reassignment –

   (a)   a reference to a person who has a particular protected characteristic is a reference to a transsexual person;

   (b)   a reference to persons who share a protected characteristic is a reference to transsexual persons.

8   Marriage and civil partnership

(1) A person has the protected characteristic of marriage and civil partnership if the person is married or is a civil partner.

(2) In relation to the protected characteristic of marriage and civil partnership –

   (a)   a reference to a person who has a particular protected characteristic is a reference to a person who is married or is a civil partner;

   (b)   a reference to persons who share a protected characteristic is a reference to persons who are married or are civil partners.

9   Race

(1) Race includes –

   (a)   colour;
   (b)   nationality;
   (c)   ethnic or national origins.

(2) In relation to the protected characteristic of race –

   (a)   a reference to a person who has a particular protected characteristic is a reference to a person of a particular racial group;

   (b)   a reference to persons who share a protected characteristic is a reference to persons of the same racial group.

(3) A racial group is a group of persons defined by reference to race; and a reference to a person's racial group is a reference to a racial group into which the person falls.

(4) The fact that a racial group comprises two or more distinct racial groups does not prevent it from constituting a particular racial group.

(5) A Minister of the Crown may by order –

    (a)   amend this section so as to provide for caste to be an aspect of race;

    (b)   amend this Act so as to provide for an exception to a provision of this Act to apply, or not to apply, to caste or to apply, or not to apply, to caste in specified circumstances.

(6) The power under section 207(4)(b), in its application to subsection (5), includes power to amend this Act.

10 Religion or belief

(1) Religion means any religion and a reference to religion includes a reference to a lack of religion.

(2) Belief means any religious or philosophical belief and a reference to belief includes a reference to a lack of belief.

(3) In relation to the protected characteristic of religion or belief –

    (a)   a reference to a person who has a particular protected characteristic is a reference to a person of a particular religion or belief;

    (b)   a reference to persons who share a protected characteristic is a reference to persons who are of the same religion or belief.

11 Sex

In relation to the protected characteristic of sex –

    (a)   a reference to a person who has a particular protected characteristic is a reference to a man or to a woman;

    (b)   a reference to persons who share a protected characteristic is a reference to persons of the same sex.

12 Sexual orientation

(1) Sexual orientation means a person's sexual orientation towards –

    (a)   persons of the same sex,

    (b)   persons of the opposite sex, or

    (c)   persons of either sex.

(2) In relation to the protected characteristic of sexual orientation –

    (a)   a reference to a person who has a particular protected characteristic is a reference to a person who is of a particular sexual orientation;

    (b)   a reference to persons who share a protected characteristic is a reference to persons who are of the same sexual orientation.

CHAPTER 2   PROHIBITED CONDUCT

Discrimination

13 Direct discrimination

(1) A person (A) discriminates against another (B) if, because of a protected characteristic, A treats B less favourably than A treats or would treat others.

(2) If the protected characteristic is age, A does not discriminate against B if A can show A's treatment of B to be a proportionate means of achieving a legitimate aim.

(3) If the protected characteristic is disability, and B is not a disabled person, A does not

discriminate against B only because A treats or would treat disabled persons more favourably than A treats B.

(4) If the protected characteristic is marriage and civil partnership, this section applies to a contravention of Part 5 (work) only if the treatment is because it is B who is married or a civil partner.

(5) If the protected characteristic is race, less favourable treatment includes segregating B from others.

(6) If the protected characteristic is sex –

(a)   less favourable treatment of a woman includes less favourable treatment of her because she is breast-feeding;

(b)   in a case where B is a man, no account is to be taken of special treatment afforded to a woman in connection with pregnancy or childbirth.

(7) Subsection (6)(a) does not apply for the purposes of Part 5 (work).

(8) This section is subject to sections 17(6) and 18(7).

14   Combined discrimination: dual characteristics

(1) A person (A) discriminates against another (B) if, because of a combination of two relevant protected characteristics, A treats B less favourably than A treats or would treat a person who does not share either of those characteristics.

(2) The relevant protected characteristics are –

(a)   age;
(b)   disability;
(c)   gender reassignment;
(d)   race
(e)   religion or belief;
(f)   sex;
(g)   sexual orientation.

(3) For the purposes of establishing a contravention of this Act by virtue of subsection (1), B need not show that A's treatment of B is direct discrimination because of each of the characteristics in the combination (taken separately).

(4) But B cannot establish a contravention of this Act by virtue of subsection (1) if, in reliance on another provision of this Act or any other enactment, A shows that A's treatment of B is not direct discrimination because of either or both of the characteristics in the combination.

(5) Subsection (1) does not apply to a combination of characteristics that includes disability in circumstances where, if a claim of direct discrimination because of disability were to be brought, it would come within section 116 (special educational needs).

(6) A Minister of the Crown may by order amend this section so as to –

(a)   make further provision about circumstances in which B can, or in which B cannot, establish a contravention of this Act by virtue of subsection (1);

(b)   specify other circumstances in which subsection (1) does not apply.

(7) The references to direct discrimination are to a contravention of this Act by virtue of section 13.

15   Discrimination arising from disability

(1) A person (A) discriminates against a disabled person (B) if –

(a)   A treats B unfavourably because of something arising in consequence of B's disability, and

(b)   A cannot show that the treatment is a proportionate means of achieving a legitimate aim.

(2)   Subsection (1) does not apply if A shows that A did not know, and could not reasonably have been expected to know, that B had the disability.

16   Gender reassignment discrimination: cases of absence from work

(1)   This section has effect for the purposes of the application of Part 5 (work) to the protected characteristic of gender reassignment.

(2)   A person (A) discriminates against a transsexual person (B) if, in relation to an absence of B's that is because of gender reassignment, A treats B less favourably than A would treat B if –

(a)   B's absence was because of sickness or injury, or

(b)   B's absence was for some other reason and it is not reasonable for B to be treated less favourably.

(3)   A person's absence is because of gender reassignment if it is because the person is proposing to undergo, is undergoing or has undergone the process (or part of the process) mentioned in section 7(1).

17   Pregnancy and maternity discrimination: non-work cases

(1)   This section has effect for the purposes of the application to the protected characteristic of pregnancy and maternity of –

(a)   Part 3 (services and public functions);

(b)   Part 4 (premises);

(c)   Part 6 (education);

(d)   Part 7 (associations).

(2)   A person (A) discriminates against a woman if A treats her unfavourably because of a pregnancy of hers.

(3)   A person (A) discriminates against a woman if, in the period of 26 weeks beginning with the day on which she gives birth, A treats her unfavourably because she has given birth.

(4)   The reference in subsection (3) to treating a woman unfavourably because she has given birth includes, in particular, a reference to treating her unfavourably because she is breast-feeding.

(5)   For the purposes of this section, the day on which a woman gives birth is the day on which –

(a)   she gives birth to a living child, or

(b)   she gives birth to a dead child (more than 24 weeks of the pregnancy having passed).

(6)   Section 13, so far as relating to sex discrimination, does not apply to anything done in relation to a woman in so far as –

(a)   it is for the reason mentioned in subsection (2), or

(b)   it is in the period, and for the reason, mentioned in subsection (3).

18   Pregnancy and maternity discrimination: work cases

(1)   This section has effect for the purposes of the application of Part 5 (work) to the protected characteristic of pregnancy and maternity.

(2)   A person (A) discriminates against a woman if, in the protected period in relation to a pregnancy of hers, A treats her unfavourably –

(a)   because of the pregnancy, or

(b)   because of illness suffered by her as a result of it.

(3)   A person (A) discriminates against a woman if A treats her unfavourably because she is on compulsory maternity leave.

(4)   A person (A) discriminates against a woman if A treats her unfavourably because she is

exercising or seeking to exercise, or has exercised or sought to exercise, the right to ordinary or additional maternity leave.

(5)   For the purposes of subsection (2), if the treatment of a woman is in implementation of a decision taken in the protected period, the treatment is to be regarded as occurring in that period (even if the implementation is not until after the end of that period).

(6)   The protected period, in relation to a woman's pregnancy, begins when the pregnancy begins, and ends –

(a)   if she has the right to ordinary and additional maternity leave, at the end of the additional maternity leave period or (if earlier) when she returns to work after the pregnancy;

(b)   if she does not have that right, at the end of the period of 2 weeks beginning with the end of the pregnancy.

(7)   Section 13, so far as relating to sex discrimination, does not apply to treatment of a woman in so far as –

(a)   it is in the protected period in relation to her and is for a reason mentioned in paragraph (a) or (b) of subsection (2), or

(b)   it is for a reason mentioned in subsection (3) or (4).

19   Indirect discrimination

(1)   A person (A) discriminates against another (B) if A applies to B a provision, criterion or practice which is discriminatory in relation to a relevant protected characteristic of B's.

(2)   For the purposes of subsection (1), a provision, criterion or practice is discriminatory in relation to a relevant protected characteristic of B's if –

(a)   A applies, or would apply, it to persons with whom B does not share the characteristic,

(b)   it puts, or would put, persons with whom B shares the characteristic at a particular disadvantage when compared with persons with whom B does not share it,

(c)   it puts, or would put, B at that disadvantage, and

(d)   A cannot show it to be a proportionate means of achieving a legitimate aim.

(3)   The relevant protected characteristics are –

age;
disability;
gender reassignment;
marriage and civil partnership;
race;
religion or belief;
sex;
sexual orientation.

Adjustments for disabled persons

20   Duty to make adjustments

(1)   Where this Act imposes a duty to make reasonable adjustments on a person, this section, sections 21 and 22 and the applicable Schedule apply; and for those purposes, a person on whom the duty is imposed is referred to as A.

(2)   The duty comprises the following three requirements.

(3)   The first requirement is a requirement, where a provision, criterion or practice of A's puts a disabled person at a substantial disadvantage in relation to a relevant matter in comparison with persons who are not disabled, to take such steps as it is reasonable to have to take to avoid the disadvantage.

(4)   The second requirement is a requirement, where a physical feature puts a disabled

person at a substantial disadvantage in relation to a relevant matter in comparison with persons who are not disabled, to take such steps as it is reasonable to have to take to avoid the disadvantage.

(5) The third requirement is a requirement, where a disabled person would, but for the provision of an auxiliary aid, be put at a substantial disadvantage in relation to a relevant matter in comparison with persons who are not disabled, to take such steps as it is reasonable to have to take to provide the auxiliary aid.

(6) Where the first or third requirement relates to the provision of information, the steps which it is reasonable for A to have to take include steps for ensuring that in the circumstances concerned the information is provided in an accessible format.

(7) A person (A) who is subject to a duty to make reasonable adjustments is not (subject to express provision to the contrary) entitled to require a disabled person, in relation to whom A is required to comply with the duty, to pay to any extent A's costs of complying with the duty.

(8) A reference in section 21 or 22 or an applicable Schedule to the first, second or third requirement is to be construed in accordance with this section.

(9) In relation to the second requirement, a reference in this section or an applicable Schedule to avoiding a substantial disadvantage includes a reference to –

(a)   removing the physical feature in question,
(b)   altering it, or
(c)   providing a reasonable means of avoiding it.

(10) A reference in this section, section 21 or 22 or an applicable Schedule (apart from paragraphs 2 to 4 of Schedule 4) to a physical feature is a reference to –

(a)   a feature arising from the design or construction of a building,
(b)   a feature of an approach to, exit from or access to a building,
(c)   a fixture or fitting, or furniture, furnishings, materials, equipment or other chattels, in or on premises, or
(d)   any other physical element or quality.

(11) A reference in this section, section 21 or 22 or an applicable Schedule to an auxiliary aid includes a reference to an auxiliary service.

(12) A reference in this section or an applicable Schedule to chattels is to be read, in relation to Scotland, as a reference to moveable property.

(13) The applicable Schedule is, in relation to the Part of this Act specified in the first column of the Table, the Schedule specified in the second column.

Part of this Act	Applicable Schedule
Part 3 (services and public functions)	Schedule 2
Part 4 (premises)	Schedule 4
Part 5 (work)	Schedule 8
Part 6 (education)	Schedule 13
Part 7 (associations)	Schedule 15
Each of the Parts mentioned above	Schedule 21

21   Failure to comply with duty

(1) A failure to comply with the first, second or third requirement is a failure to comply with a duty to make reasonable adjustments.

(2) A discriminates against a disabled person if A fails to comply with that duty in relation to that person.
(3) A provision of an applicable Schedule which imposes a duty to comply with the first, second or third requirement applies only for the purpose of establishing whether A has contravened this Act by virtue of subsection (2); a failure to comply is, accordingly, not actionable by virtue of another provision of this Act or otherwise.

22   Regulations
(1) Regulations may prescribe –

(a)   matters to be taken into account in deciding whether it is reasonable for A to take a step for the purposes of a prescribed provision of an applicable Schedule;
(b)   descriptions of persons to whom the first, second or third requirement does not apply.

(2) Regulations may make provision as to –

(a)   circumstances in which it is, or in which it is not, reasonable for a person of a prescribed description to have to take steps of a prescribed description;
(b)   what is, or what is not, a provision, criterion or practice;
(c)   things which are, or which are not, to be treated as physical features;
(d)   things which are, or which are not, to be treated as alterations of physical features;
(e)   things which are, or which are not, to be treated as auxiliary aids.

(3) Provision made by virtue of this section may amend an applicable Schedule.

Discrimination: supplementary

23   Comparison by reference to circumstances
(1) On a comparison of cases for the purposes of section 13, 14, or 19 there must be no material difference between the circumstances relating to each case.
(2) The circumstances relating to a case include a person's abilities if –

(a)   on a comparison for the purposes of section 13, the protected characteristic is disability;
(b)   on a comparison for the purposes of section 14, one of the protected characteristics in the combination is disability.

(3) If the protected characteristic is sexual orientation, the fact that one person (whether or not the person referred to as B) is a civil partner while another is married is not a material difference between the circumstances relating to each case.

24   Irrelevance of alleged discriminator's characteristics
(1) For the purpose of establishing a contravention of this Act by virtue of section 13(1), it does not matter whether A has the protected characteristic.
(2) For the purpose of establishing a contravention of this Act by virtue of section 14(1), it does not matter –

(a)   whether A has one of the protected characteristics in the combination;
(b)   whether A has both.

25   References to particular strands of discrimination
(1) Age discrimination is –

(a)   discrimination within section 13 because of age;
(b)   discrimination within section 19 where the relevant protected characteristic is age.

(2) Disability discrimination is –

    (a)   discrimination within section 13 because of disability;

    (b)   discrimination within section 15;

    (c)   discrimination within section 19 where the relevant protected characteristic is disability;

    (d)   discrimination within section 21.

(3) Gender reassignment discrimination is –

    (a)   discrimination within section 13 because of gender reassignment;

    (b)   discrimination within section 16;

    (c)   discrimination within section 19 where the relevant protected characteristic is gender reassignment.

(4) Marriage and civil partnership discrimination is –

    (a)   discrimination within section 13 because of marriage and civil partnership;

    (b)   discrimination within section 19 where the relevant protected characteristic is marriage and civil partnership.

(5) Pregnancy and maternity discrimination is discrimination within section 17 or 18.

(6) Race discrimination is –

    (a)   discrimination within section 13 because of race;

    (b)   discrimination within section 19 where the relevant protected characteristic is race.

(7) Religious or belief-related discrimination is –

    (a)   discrimination within section 13 because of religion or belief;

    (b)   discrimination within section 19 where the relevant protected characteristic is religion or belief.

(8) Sex discrimination is –

    (a)   discrimination within section 13 because of sex;

    (b)   discrimination within section 19 where the relevant protected characteristic is sex.

(9) Sexual orientation discrimination is –

    (a)   discrimination within section 13 because of sexual orientation;

    (b)   discrimination within section 19 where the relevant protected characteristic is sexual orientation.

Other prohibited conduct

26   Harassment

(1) A person (A) harasses another (B) if –

    (a)   A engages in unwanted conduct related to a relevant protected characteristic, and

    (b)   the conduct has the purpose or effect of –

        (i)   violating B's dignity, or

        (ii)   creating an intimidating, hostile, degrading, humiliating or offensive environment for B.

(2) A also harasses B if –

    (a)   A engages in unwanted conduct of a sexual nature, and

    (b)   the conduct has the purpose or effect referred to in subsection (1)(b).

(3) A also harasses B if –

(a)   A or another person engages in unwanted conduct of a sexual nature or that is related to gender reassignment or sex,

(b)   the conduct has the purpose or effect referred to in subsection (1)(b), and

(c)   because of B's rejection of or submission to the conduct, A treats B less favourably than A would treat B if B had not rejected or submitted to the conduct.

(4)   In deciding whether conduct has the effect referred to in subsection (1)(b), each of the following must be taken into account –

(a)   the perception of B;

(b)   the other circumstances of the case;

(c)   whether it is reasonable for the conduct to have that effect.

(5)   The relevant protected characteristics are –

age;
disability;
gender reassignment;
race;
religion or belief;
sex;
sexual orientation.

27   Victimisation

(1)   A person (A) victimises another person (B) if A subjects B to a detriment because –

(a)   B does a protected act, or

(b)   A believes that B has done, or may do, a protected act.

(2)   Each of the following is a protected act –

(a)   bringing proceedings under this Act;

(b)   giving evidence or information in connection with proceedings under this Act;

(c)   doing any other thing for the purposes of or in connection with this Act;

(d)   making an allegation (whether or not express) that A or another person has contravened this Act.

(3)   Giving false evidence or information, or making a false allegation, is not a protected act if the evidence or information is given, or the allegation is made, in bad faith.

(4)   This section applies only where the person subjected to a detriment is an individual.

(5)   The reference to contravening this Act includes a reference to committing a breach of an equality clause or rule.

PART 3   SERVICES AND PUBLIC FUNCTIONS

Preliminary

28   Application of this Part

(1)   This Part does not apply to the protected characteristic of –

(a)   age, so far as relating to persons who have not attained the age of 18;

(b)   marriage and civil partnership.

(2)   This Part does not apply to discrimination, harassment or victimisation –

(a)   that is prohibited by Part 4 (premises), 5 (work) or 6 (education), or

(b)   that would be so prohibited but for an express exception.

(3)   This Part does not apply to –

(a)   a breach of an equality clause or rule;

(b)   anything that would be a breach of an equality clause or rule but for section 69 or Part 2 of Schedule 7;

(c)   a breach of a non-discrimination rule.

Provision of services, etc.

29   Provision of services, etc.

(1)   A person (a 'service-provider') concerned with the provision of a service to the public or a section of the public (for payment or not) must not discriminate against a person requiring the service by not providing the person with the service.

(2)   A service-provider (A) must not, in providing the service, discriminate against a person (B) –

(a)   as to the terms on which A provides the service to B;

(b)   by terminating the provision of the service to B;

(c)   by subjecting B to any other detriment.

(3)   A service-provider must not, in relation to the provision of the service, harass –

(a)   a person requiring the service, or

(b)   a person to whom the service-provider provides the service.

(4)   A service-provider must not victimise a person requiring the service by not providing the person with the service.

(5)   A service-provider (A) must not, in providing the service, victimise a person (B) –

(a)   as to the terms on which A provides the service to B;

(b)   by terminating the provision of the service to B;

(c)   by subjecting B to any other detriment.

(6)   A person must not, in the exercise of a public function that is not the provision of a service to the public or a section of the public, do anything that constitutes discrimination, harassment or victimisation.

(7)   A duty to make reasonable adjustments applies to –

(a)   a service-provider (and see also section 55(7));

(b)   a person who exercises a public function that is not the provision of a service to the public or a section of the public.

(8)   In the application of section 26 for the purposes of subsection (3), and subsection (6) as it relates to harassment, neither of the following is a relevant protected characteristic –

(a)   religion or belief;

(b)   sexual orientation.

(9)   In the application of this section, so far as relating to race or religion or belief, to the granting of entry clearance (within the meaning of the Immigration Act 1971), it does not matter whether an act is done within or outside the United Kingdom.

(10) Subsection (9) does not affect the application of any other provision of this Act to conduct outside England and Wales or Scotland.

Supplementary

30   Ships and hovercraft

(1)   This Part (subject to subsection (2)) applies only in such circumstances as are prescribed in relation to –

(a)   transporting people by ship or hovercraft;

(b)   a service provided on a ship or hovercraft.

(2)   Section 29(6) applies in relation to the matters referred to in paragraphs (a) and (b) of

subsection (1); but in so far as it relates to disability discrimination, section 29(6) applies to those matters only in such circumstances as are prescribed.

(3) It does not matter whether the ship or hovercraft is within or outside the United Kingdom.

(4) 'Ship' has the same meaning as in the Merchant Shipping Act 1995.

(5) 'Hovercraft' has the same meaning as in the Hovercraft Act 1968.

(6) Nothing in this section affects the application of any other provision of this Act to conduct outside England and Wales or Scotland.

31   Interpretation and exceptions

(1) This section applies for the purposes of this Part.

(2) A reference to the provision of a service includes a reference to the provision of goods or facilities.

(3) A reference to the provision of a service includes a reference to the provision of a service in the exercise of a public function.

(4) A public function is a function that is a function of a public nature for the purposes of the Human Rights Act 1998.

(5) Where an employer arranges for another person to provide a service only to the employer's employees –

   (a)   the employer is not to be regarded as the service-provider, but
   (b)   the employees are to be regarded as a section of the public.

(6) A reference to a person requiring a service includes a reference to a person who is seeking to obtain or use the service.

(7) A reference to a service-provider not providing a person with a service includes a reference to –

   (a)   the service-provider not providing the person with a service of the quality that the service-provider usually provides to the public (or the section of it which includes the person), or
   (b)   the service-provider not providing the person with the service in the manner in which, or on the terms on which, the service-provider usually provides the service to the public (or the section of it which includes the person).

(8) In relation to the provision of a service by either House of Parliament, the service-provider is the Corporate Officer of the House concerned; and if the service involves access to, or use of, a place in the Palace of Westminster which members of the public are allowed to enter, both Corporate Officers are jointly the service-provider.

(9) Schedule 2 (reasonable adjustments) has effect.

(10) Schedule 3 (exceptions) has effect.

PART 4   PREMISES

Preliminary

32   Application of this Part

(1) This Part does not apply to the following protected characteristics –

   (a)   age;
   (b)   marriage and civil partnership.

(2) This Part does not apply to discrimination, harassment or victimisation –

   (a)   that is prohibited by Part 5 (work) or Part 6 (education), or
   (b)   that would be so prohibited but for an express exception.

(3) This Part does not apply to the provision of accommodation if the provision –

(a)   is generally for the purpose of short stays by individuals who live elsewhere, or

(b)   is for the purpose only of exercising a public function or providing a service to the public or a section of the public.

(4)   The reference to the exercise of a public function, and the reference to the provision of a service, are to be construed in accordance with Part 3.

(5)   This Part does not apply to –

(a)   a breach of an equality clause or rule;

(b)   anything that would be a breach of an equality clause or rule but for section 69 or Part 2 of Schedule 7;

(c)   a breach of a non-discrimination rule.

Disposal and management

33   Disposals, etc.

(1)   A person (A) who has the right to dispose of premises must not discriminate against another (B) –

(a)   as to the terms on which A offers to dispose of the premises to B;

(b)   by not disposing of the premises to B;

(c)   in A's treatment of B with respect to things done in relation to persons seeking premises.

(2)   Where an interest in a commonhold unit cannot be disposed of unless a particular person is a party to the disposal, that person must not discriminate against a person by not being a party to the disposal.

(3)   A person who has the right to dispose of premises must not, in connection with anything done in relation to their occupation or disposal, harass –

(a)   a person who occupies them;

(b)   a person who applies for them.

(4)   A person (A) who has the right to dispose of premises must not victimise another (B) –

(a)   as to the terms on which A offers to dispose of the premises to B;

(b)   by not disposing of the premises to B;

(c)   in A's treatment of B with respect to things done in relation to persons seeking premises.

(5)   Where an interest in a commonhold unit cannot be disposed of unless a particular person is a party to the disposal, that person must not victimise a person by not being a party to the disposal.

(6)   In the application of section 26 for the purposes of subsection (3), neither of the following is a relevant protected characteristic –

(a)   religion or belief;

(b)   sexual orientation.

34   Permission for disposal

(1)   A person whose permission is required for the disposal of premises must not discriminate against another by not giving permission for the disposal of the premises to the other.

(2)   A person whose permission is required for the disposal of premises must not, in relation to an application for permission to dispose of the premises, harass a person –

(a)   who applies for permission to dispose of the premises, or

(b)   to whom the disposal would be made if permission were given.

(3)   A person whose permission is required for the disposal of premises must not victimise another by not giving permission for the disposal of the premises to the other.

(4) In the application of section 26 for the purposes of subsection (2), neither of the following is a relevant protected characteristic –

    (a)   religion or belief;
    (b)   sexual orientation.

(5) This section does not apply to anything done in the exercise of a judicial function.

35   Management

(1) A person (A) who manages premises must not discriminate against a person (B) who occupies the premises –

    (a)   in the way in which A allows B, or by not allowing B, to make use of a benefit or facility;
    (b)   by evicting B (or taking steps for the purpose of securing B's eviction);
    (c)   by subjecting B to any other detriment.

(2) A person who manages premises must not, in relation to their management, harass –

    (a)   a person who occupies them;
    (b)   a person who applies for them.

(3) A person (A) who manages premises must not victimise a person (B) who occupies the premises –

    (a)   in the way in which A allows B, or by not allowing B, to make use of a benefit or facility;
    (b)   by evicting B (or taking steps for the purpose of securing B's eviction);
    (c)   by subjecting B to any other detriment.

(4) In the application of section 26 for the purposes of subsection (2), neither of the following is a relevant protected characteristic –

    (a)   religion or belief;
    (b)   sexual orientation.

Reasonable adjustments

36   Leasehold and commonhold premises and common parts

(1) A duty to make reasonable adjustments applies to –

    (a)   a controller of let premises;
    (b)   a controller of premises to let;
    (c)   a commonhold association;
    (d)   a responsible person in relation to common parts.

(2) A controller of let premises is –

    (a)   a person by whom premises are let, or
    (b)   a person who manages them.

(3) A controller of premises to let is –

    (a)   a person who has premises to let, or
    (b)   a person who manages them.

(4) The reference in subsection (1)(c) to a commonhold association is a reference to the association in its capacity as the person who manages a commonhold unit.

(5) A responsible person in relation to common parts is –

    (a)   where the premises to which the common parts relate are let (and are not part of commonhold land or in Scotland), a person by whom the premises are let;
    (b)   where the premises to which the common parts relate are part of commonhold land, the commonhold association.

(6) Common parts are –

(a)   in relation to let premises (which are not part of commonhold land or in Scotland), the structure and exterior of, and any common facilities within or used in connection with, the building or part of a building which includes the premises;

(b)   in relation to commonhold land, every part of the commonhold which is not for the time being a commonhold unit in accordance with the commonhold community statement.

(7) A reference to letting includes a reference to sub-letting; and for the purposes of subsection (1)(a) and (b), a reference to let premises includes premises subject to a right to occupy.

(8) This section does not apply to premises of such description as may be prescribed.

37   Adjustments to common parts in Scotland

(1) The Scottish Ministers may by regulations provide that a disabled person is entitled to make relevant adjustments to common parts in relation to premises in Scotland.

(2) The reference in subsection (1) to a disabled person is a reference to a disabled person who –

(a)   is a tenant of the premises,

(b)   is an owner of the premises, or

(c)   is otherwise entitled to occupy the premises, and uses or intends to use the premises as the person's only or main home.

(3) Before making regulations under subsection (1), the Scottish Ministers must consult a Minister of the Crown.

(4) Regulations under subsection (1) may, in particular –

(a)   prescribe things which are, or which are not, to be treated as relevant adjustments;

(b)   prescribe circumstances in which the consent of an owner of the common parts is required before a disabled person may make an adjustment;

(c)   provide that the consent to adjustments is not to be withheld unreasonably;

(d)   prescribe matters to be taken into account, or to be disregarded, in deciding whether it is reasonable to consent to adjustments;

(e)   prescribe circumstances in which consent to adjustments is to be taken to be withheld;

(f)   make provision about the imposition of conditions on consent to adjustments;

(g)   make provision as to circumstances in which the sheriff may make an order authorising a disabled person to carry out adjustments;

(h)   make provision about the responsibility for costs arising (directly or indirectly) from an adjustment;

(i)   make provision about the reinstatement of the common parts to the condition they were in before an adjustment was made;

(j)   make provision about the giving of notice to the owners of the common parts and other persons;

(k)   make provision about agreements between a disabled person and an owner of the common parts;

(l)   make provision about the registration of information in the Land Register of Scotland or the recording of documents in the Register of Sasines relating to an entitlement of a disabled person or an obligation on an owner of the common parts;

(m)   make provision about the effect of such registration or recording;

(n)   make provision about who is to be treated as being, or as not being, a person entitled to occupy premises otherwise than as tenant or owner.

(5) In this section –

'common parts' means, in relation to premises, the structure and exterior of, and any common facilities within or used in connection with, the building or part of a building which includes the premises but only in so far as the structure, exterior and common facilities are not solely owned by the owner of the premises;

'relevant adjustments' means, in relation to a disabled person, alterations or additions which are likely to avoid a substantial disadvantage to which the disabled person is put in using the common parts in comparison with persons who are not disabled.

Supplementary

38   Interpretation and exceptions

(1) This section applies for the purposes of this Part.
(2) A reference to premises is a reference to the whole or part of the premises.
(3) A reference to disposing of premises includes, in the case of premises subject to a tenancy, a reference to –

(a)   assigning the premises,
(b)   sub-letting them, or
(c)   parting with possession of them.

(4) A reference to disposing of premises also includes a reference to granting a right to occupy them.
(5) A reference to disposing of an interest in a commonhold unit includes a reference to creating an interest in a commonhold unit.
(6) A reference to a tenancy is to a tenancy created (whether before or after the passing of this Act) –

(a)   by a lease or sub-lease,
(b)   by an agreement for a lease or sub-lease,
(c)   by a tenancy agreement, or
(d)   in pursuance of an enactment,

and a reference to a tenant is to be construed accordingly.

(7) A reference to commonhold land, a commonhold association, a commonhold community statement, a commonhold unit or a unit-holder is to be construed in accordance with the Commonhold and Leasehold Reform Act 2002.
(8) Schedule 4 (reasonable adjustments) has effect.
(9) Schedule 5 (exceptions) has effect.

PART 5   WORK

CHAPTER 1   EMPLOYMENT, ETC.

Employees

39   Employees and applicants

(1) An employer (A) must not discriminate against a person (B) –

(a)   in the arrangements A makes for deciding to whom to offer employment;
(b)   as to the terms on which A offers B employment;
(c)   by not offering B employment.

(2) An employer (A) must not discriminate against an employee of A's (B) –

(a)   as to B's terms of employment;

    (b)   in the way A affords B access, or by not affording B access, to opportunities for promotion, transfer or training or for receiving any other benefit, facility or service;

    (c)   by dismissing B;

    (d)   by subjecting B to any other detriment.

(3)   An employer (A) must not victimise a person (B) –

    (a)   in the arrangements A makes for deciding to whom to offer employment;

    (b)   as to the terms on which A offers B employment;

    (c)   by not offering B employment.

(4)   An employer (A) must not victimise an employee of A's (B) –

    (a)   as to B's terms of employment;

    (b)   in the way A affords B access, or by not affording B access, to opportunities for promotion, transfer or training or for any other benefit, facility or service;

    (c)   by dismissing B;

    (d)   by subjecting B to any other detriment.

(5)   A duty to make reasonable adjustments applies to an employer.

(6)   Subsection (1)(b), so far as relating to sex or pregnancy and maternity, does not apply to a term that relates to pay –

    (a)   unless, were B to accept the offer, an equality clause or rule would have effect in relation to the term, or

    (b)   if paragraph (a) does not apply, except in so far as making an offer on terms including that term amounts to a contravention of subsection (1)(b) by virtue of section 13, 14 or 18.

(7)   In subsections (2)(c) and (4)(c), the reference to dismissing B includes a reference to the termination of B's employment –

    (a)   by the expiry of a period (including a period expiring by reference to an event or circumstance);

    (b)   by an act of B's (including giving notice) in circumstances such that B is entitled, because of A's conduct, to terminate the employment without notice.

(8)   Subsection (7)(a) does not apply if, immediately after the termination, the employment is renewed on the same terms.

40   Employees and applicants: harassment

(1)   An employer (A) must not, in relation to employment by A, harass a person (B) –

    (a)   who is an employee of A's;

    (b)   who has applied to A for employment.

(2)   The circumstances in which A is to be treated as harassing B under subsection (1) include those where –

    (a)   a third party harasses B in the course of B's employment, and

    (b)   A failed to take such steps as would have been reasonably practicable to prevent the third party from doing so.

(3)   Subsection (2) does not apply unless A knows that B has been harassed in the course of B's employment on at least two other occasions by a third party; and it does not matter whether the third party is the same or a different person on each occasion.

(4)   A third party is a person other than –

    (a)   A, or

    (b)   an employee of A's.

41   Contract workers

(1)   A principal must not discriminate against a contract worker –

(a)   as to the terms on which the principal allows the worker to do the work;
(b)   by not allowing the worker to do, or to continue to do, the work;
(c)   in the way the principal affords the worker access, or by not affording the worker access, to opportunities for receiving a benefit, facility or service;
(d)   by subjecting the worker to any other detriment.

(2)   A principal must not, in relation to contract work, harass a contract worker.
(3)   A principal must not victimise a contract worker –

(a)   as to the terms on which the principal allows the worker to do the work;
(b)   by not allowing the worker to do, or to continue to do, the work;
(c)   in the way the principal affords the worker access, or by not affording the worker access, to opportunities for receiving a benefit, facility or service;
(d)   by subjecting the worker to any other detriment.

(4)   A duty to make reasonable adjustments applies to a principal (as well as to the employer of a contract worker).
(5)   A 'principal' is a person who makes work available for an individual who is –

(a)   employed by another person, and
(b)   supplied by that other person in furtherance of a contract to which the principal is a party (whether or not that other person is a party to it).

(6)   'Contract work' is work such as is mentioned in subsection (5).
(7)   A 'contract worker' is an individual supplied to a principal in furtherance of a contract such as is mentioned in subsection (5)(b).

Police officers

42   Identity of employer

(1)   For the purposes of this Part, holding the office of constable is to be treated as employment –

(a)   by the chief officer, in respect of any act done by the chief officer in relation to a constable or appointment to the office of constable;
(b)   by the responsible authority, in respect of any act done by the authority in relation to a constable or appointment to the office of constable.

(2)   For the purposes of this Part, holding an appointment as a police cadet is to be treated as employment –

(a)   by the chief officer, in respect of any act done by the chief officer in relation to a police cadet or appointment as one;
(b)   by the responsible authority, in respect of any act done by the authority in relation to a police cadet or appointment as one.

(3)   Subsection (1) does not apply to service with the Civil Nuclear Constabulary (as to which, see section 55(2) of the Energy Act 2004).
(4)   Subsection (1) does not apply to a constable at SOCA, SPSA or SCDEA.
(5)   A constable at SOCA or SPSA is to be treated as employed by it, in respect of any act done by it in relation to the constable.
(6)   A constable at SCDEA is to be treated as employed by the Director General of SCDEA, in respect of any act done by the Director General in relation to the constable.

43   Interpretation

(1)   This section applies for the purposes of section 42.
(2)   'Chief officer' means –

(a)   in relation to an appointment under a relevant Act, the chief officer of police for the police force to which the appointment relates;

(b)   in relation to any other appointment, the person under whose direction and control the body of constables or other persons to which the appointment relates is;

(c)   in relation to a constable or other person under the direction and control of a chief officer of police, that chief officer of police;

(d)   in relation to any other constable or any other person, the person under whose direction and control the constable or other person is.

(3) 'Responsible authority' means –

(a)   in relation to an appointment under a relevant Act, the police authority that maintains the police force to which the appointment relates;

(b)   in relation to any other appointment, the person by whom a person would (if appointed) be paid;

(c)   in relation to a constable or other person under the direction and control of a chief officer of police, the police authority that maintains the police force for which that chief officer is the chief officer of police;

(d)   in relation to any other constable or any other person, the person by whom the constable or other person is paid.

(4) 'Police cadet' means a person appointed to undergo training with a view to becoming a constable.

(5) 'SOCA' means the Serious Organised Crime Agency; and a reference to a constable at SOCA is a reference to a constable seconded to it to serve as a member of its staff.

(6) 'SPSA' means the Scottish Police Services Authority; and a reference to a constable at SPSA is a reference to a constable –

(a)   seconded to it to serve as a member of its staff, and

(b)   not at SCDEA.

(7) 'SCDEA' means the Scottish Crime and Drugs Enforcement Agency; and a reference to a constable at SCDEA is a reference to a constable who is a police member of it by virtue of paragraph 7(2)(a) or (b) of Schedule 2 to the Police, Public Order and Criminal Justice (Scotland) Act 2006 (asp 10) (secondment).

(8) For the purposes of this section, the relevant Acts are –

(a)   the Metropolitan Police Act 1829;

(b)   the City of London Police Act 1839;

(c)   the Police (Scotland) Act 1967;

(d)   the Police Act 1996.

(9) A reference in subsection (2) or (3) to a chief officer of police includes, in relation to Scotland, a reference to a chief constable.

Partners

44   Partnerships

(1) A firm or proposed firm must not discriminate against a person –

(a)   in the arrangements it makes for deciding to whom to offer a position as a partner;

(b)   as to the terms on which it offers the person a position as a partner;

(c)   by not offering the person a position as a partner.

(2) A firm (A) must not discriminate against a partner (B) –

(a)   as to the terms on which B is a partner;

(b)   in the way A affords B access, or by not affording B access, to opportunities for promotion, transfer or training or for receiving any other benefit, facility or service;

(c)   by expelling B;

(d)   by subjecting B to any other detriment.

(3) A firm must not, in relation to a position as a partner, harass –

(a)   a partner;
(b)   a person who has applied for the position.

(4) A proposed firm must not, in relation to a position as a partner, harass a person who has applied for the position.

(5) A firm or proposed firm must not victimise a person –

(a)   in the arrangements it makes for deciding to whom to offer a position as a partner;
(b)   as to the terms on which it offers the person a position as a partner;
(c)   by not offering the person a position as a partner.

(6) A firm (A) must not victimise a partner (B) –

(a)   as to the terms on which B is a partner;
(b)   in the way A affords B access, or by not affording B access, to opportunities for promotion, transfer or training or for receiving any other benefit, facility or service;
(c)   by expelling B;
(d)   by subjecting B to any other detriment.

(7) A duty to make reasonable adjustments applies to –

(a)   a firm;
(b)   a proposed firm.

(8) In the application of this section to a limited partnership within the meaning of the Limited Partnerships Act 1907, 'partner' means a general partner within the meaning of that Act.

45   Limited liability partnerships

(1) An LLP or proposed LLP must not discriminate against a person –

(a)   in the arrangements it makes for deciding to whom to offer a position as a member;
(b)   as to the terms on which it offers the person a position as a member;
(c)   by not offering the person a position as a member.

(2) An LLP (A) must not discriminate against a member (B) –

(a)   as to the terms on which B is a member;
(b)   in the way A affords B access, or by not affording B access, to opportunities for promotion, transfer or training or for receiving any other benefit, facility or service;
(c)   by expelling B;
(d)   by subjecting B to any other detriment.

(3) An LLP must not, in relation to a position as a member, harass –

(a)   a member;
(b)   a person who has applied for the position.

(4) A proposed LLP must not, in relation to a position as a member, harass a person who has applied for the position.

(5) An LLP or proposed LLP must not victimise a person –

(a)   in the arrangements it makes for deciding to whom to offer a position as a member;
(b)   as to the terms on which it offers the person a position as a member;
(c)   by not offering the person a position as a member.

(6)   An LLP (A) must not victimise a member (B) –

   (a)   as to the terms on which B is a member;
   (b)   in the way A affords B access, or by not affording B access, to opportunities for promotion, transfer or training or for receiving any other benefit, facility or service;
   (c)   by expelling B;
   (d)   by subjecting B to any other detriment.

(7)   A duty to make reasonable adjustments applies to –

   (a)   an LLP;
   (b)   a proposed LLP.

46   Interpretation

(1)   This section applies for the purposes of sections 44 and 45.
(2)   'Partnership' and 'firm' have the same meaning as in the Partnership Act 1890.
(3)   'Proposed firm' means persons proposing to form themselves into a partnership.
(4)   'LLP' means a limited liability partnership (within the meaning of the Limited Liability Partnerships Act 2000).
(5)   'Proposed LLP' means persons proposing to incorporate an LLP with themselves as members.
(6)   A reference to expelling a partner of a firm or a member of an LLP includes a reference to the termination of the person's position as such –

   (a)   by the expiry of a period (including a period expiring by reference to an event or circumstance);
   (b)   by an act of the person (including giving notice) in circumstances such that the person is entitled, because of the conduct of other partners or members, to terminate the position without notice;
   (c)   (in the case of a partner of a firm) as a result of the dissolution of the partnership.

(7)   Subsection (6)(a) and (c) does not apply if, immediately after the termination, the position is renewed on the same terms.

The Bar

47   Barristers

(1)   A barrister (A) must not discriminate against a person (B) –

   (a)   in the arrangements A makes for deciding to whom to offer a pupillage or tenancy;
   (b)   as to the terms on which A offers B a pupillage or tenancy;
   (c)   by not offering B a pupillage or tenancy.

(2)   A barrister (A) must not discriminate against a person (B) who is a pupil or tenant –

   (a)   as to the terms on which B is a pupil or tenant;
   (b)   in the way A affords B access, or by not affording B access, to opportunities for training or gaining experience or for receiving any other benefit, facility or service;
   (c)   by terminating the pupillage;
   (d)   by subjecting B to pressure to leave chambers;
   (e)   by subjecting B to any other detriment.

(3)   A barrister must not, in relation to a pupillage or tenancy, harass –

   (a)   the pupil or tenant;
   (b)   a person who has applied for the pupillage or tenancy.

(4) A barrister (A) must not victimise a person (B) –

   (a)   in the arrangements A makes for deciding to whom to offer a pupillage or tenancy;
   (b)   as to the terms on which A offers B a pupillage or tenancy;
   (c)   by not offering B a pupillage or tenancy.

(5) A barrister (A) must not victimise a person (B) who is a pupil or tenant –

   (a)   as to the terms on which B is a pupil or tenant;
   (b)   in the way A affords B access, or by not affording B access, to opportunities for training or gaining experience or for receiving any other benefit, facility or service;
   (c)   by terminating the pupillage;
   (d)   by subjecting B to pressure to leave chambers;
   (e)   by subjecting B to any other detriment.

(6) A person must not, in relation to instructing a barrister –

   (a)   discriminate against a barrister by subjecting the barrister to a detriment;
   (b)   harass the barrister;
   (c)   victimise the barrister.

(7) A duty to make reasonable adjustments applies to a barrister.

(8) The preceding provisions of this section (apart from subsection (6)) apply in relation to a barrister's clerk as they apply in relation to a barrister; and for that purpose the reference to a barrister's clerk includes a reference to a person who carries out the functions of a barrister's clerk.

(9) A reference to a tenant includes a reference to a barrister who is permitted to work in chambers (including as a squatter or door tenant); and a reference to a tenancy is to be construed accordingly.

48   Advocates

(1) An advocate (A) must not discriminate against a person (B) –

   (a)   in the arrangements A makes for deciding who to take as A's devil or to whom to offer membership of a stable;
   (b)   as to the terms on which A offers to take B as A's devil or offers B membership of a stable;
   (c)   by not offering to take B as A's devil or not offering B membership of a stable.

(2) An advocate (A) must not discriminate against a person (B) who is a devil or a member of a stable –

   (a)   as to the terms on which B is a devil or a member of the stable;
   (b)   in the way A affords B access, or by not affording B access, to opportunities for training or gaining experience or for receiving any other benefit, facility or service;
   (c)   by terminating A's relationship with B (where B is a devil);
   (d)   by subjecting B to pressure to leave the stable;
   (e)   by subjecting B to any other detriment.

(3) An advocate must not, in relation to a relationship with a devil or membership of a stable, harass –

   (a)   a devil or member;
   (b)   a person who has applied to be taken as the advocate's devil or to become a member of the stable.

(4) An advocate (A) must not victimise a person (B) –

    (a)   in the arrangements A makes for deciding who to take as A's devil or to whom to offer membership of a stable;

    (b)   as to the terms on which A offers to take B as A's devil or offers B membership of a stable;

    (c)   by not offering to take B as A's devil or not offering B membership of a stable.

(5) An advocate (A) must not victimise a person (B) who is a devil or a member of a stable –

    (a)   as to the terms on which B is a devil or a member of the stable;

    (b)   in the way A affords B access, or by not affording B access, to opportunities for training or gaining experience or for receiving any other benefit, facility or service;

    (c)   by terminating A's relationship with B (where B is a devil);

    (d)   by subjecting B to pressure to leave the stable;

    (e)   by subjecting B to any other detriment.

(6) A person must not, in relation to instructing an advocate –

    (a)   discriminate against the advocate by subjecting the advocate to a detriment;

    (b)   harass the advocate;

    (c)   victimise the advocate.

(7) A duty to make reasonable adjustments applies to an advocate.

(8) This section (apart from subsection (6)) applies in relation to an advocate's clerk as it applies in relation to an advocate; and for that purpose the reference to an advocate's clerk includes a reference to a person who carries out the functions of an advocate's clerk.

(9) 'Advocate' means a practising member of the Faculty of Advocates.

Office-holders

49   Personal offices: appointments, etc.

(1) This section applies in relation to personal offices.

(2) A personal office is an office or post –

    (a)   to which a person is appointed to discharge a function personally under the direction of another person, and

    (b)   in respect of which an appointed person is entitled to remuneration.

(3) A person (A) who has the power to make an appointment to a personal office must not discriminate against a person (B) –

    (a)   in the arrangements A makes for deciding to whom to offer the appointment;

    (b)   as to the terms on which A offers B the appointment;

    (c)   by not offering B the appointment.

(4) A person who has the power to make an appointment to a personal office must not, in relation to the office, harass a person seeking, or being considered for, the appointment.

(5) A person (A) who has the power to make an appointment to a personal office must not victimise a person (B) –

    (a)   in the arrangements A makes for deciding to whom to offer the appointment;

    (b)   as to the terms on which A offers B the appointment;

    (c)   by not offering B the appointment.

(6) A person (A) who is a relevant person in relation to a personal office must not discriminate against a person (B) appointed to the office –

    (a)   as to the terms of B's appointment;

    (b)   in the way A affords B access, or by not affording B access, to opportunities for promotion, transfer or training or for receiving any other benefit, facility or service;

(c)   by terminating B's appointment;

(d)   by subjecting B to any other detriment.

(7)   A relevant person in relation to a personal office must not, in relation to that office, harass a person appointed to it.

(8)   A person (A) who is a relevant person in relation to a personal office must not victimise a person (B) appointed to the office –

(a)   as to the terms of B's appointment;

(b)   in the way A affords B access, or by not affording B access, to opportunities for promotion, transfer or training or for receiving any other benefit, facility or service;

(c)   by terminating B's appointment;

(d)   by subjecting B to any other detriment.

(9)   A duty to make reasonable adjustments applies to –

(a)   a person who has the power to make an appointment to a personal office;

(b)   a relevant person in relation to a personal office.

(10)   For the purposes of subsection (2)(a), a person is to be regarded as discharging functions personally under the direction of another person if that other person is entitled to direct the person as to when and where to discharge the functions.

(11)   For the purposes of subsection (2)(b), a person is not to be regarded as entitled to remuneration merely because the person is entitled to payments –

(a)   in respect of expenses incurred by the person in discharging the functions of the office or post, or

(b)   by way of compensation for the loss of income or benefits the person would or might have received had the person not been discharging the functions of the office or post.

(12)   Subsection (3)(b), so far as relating to sex or pregnancy and maternity, does not apply to a term that relates to pay –

(a)   unless, were B to accept the offer, an equality clause or rule would have effect in relation to the term, or

(b)   if paragraph (a) does not apply, except in so far as making an offer on terms including that term amounts to a contravention of subsection (3)(b) by virtue of section 13, 14 or 18.

50   Public offices: appointments, etc.

(1)   This section and section 51 apply in relation to public offices.

(2)   A public office is –

(a)   an office or post, appointment to which is made by a member of the executive;

(b)   an office or post, appointment to which is made on the recommendation of, or subject to the approval of, a member of the executive;

(c)   an office or post, appointment to which is made on the recommendation of, or subject to the approval of, the House of Commons, the House of Lords, the National Assembly for Wales or the Scottish Parliament.

(3)   A person (A) who has the power to make an appointment to a public office within subsection (2)(a) or (b) must not discriminate against a person (B) –

(a)   in the arrangements A makes for deciding to whom to offer the appointment;

(b)   as to the terms on which A offers B the appointment;

(c)   by not offering B the appointment.

(4)   A person who has the power to make an appointment to a public office within subsection (2)(a) or (b) must not, in relation to the office, harass a person seeking, or being considered for, the appointment.

(5) A person (A) who has the power to make an appointment to a public office within subsection (2)(a) or (b) must not victimise a person (B) –

    (a)   in the arrangements A makes for deciding to whom to offer the appointment;

    (b)   as to the terms on which A offers B the appointment;

    (c)   by not offering B the appointment.

(6) A person (A) who is a relevant person in relation to a public office within subsection (2)(a) or (b) must not discriminate against a person (B) appointed to the office –

    (a)   as to B's terms of appointment;

    (b)   in the way A affords B access, or by not affording B access, to opportunities for promotion, transfer or training or for receiving any other benefit, facility or service;

    (c)   by terminating the appointment;

    (d)   by subjecting B to any other detriment.

(7) A person (A) who is a relevant person in relation to a public office within subsection (2)(c) must not discriminate against a person (B) appointed to the office –

    (a)   as to B's terms of appointment;

    (b)   in the way A affords B access, or by not affording B access, to opportunities for promotion, transfer or training or for receiving any other benefit, facility or service;

    (c)   by subjecting B to any other detriment (other than by terminating the appointment).

(8) A relevant person in relation to a public office must not, in relation to that office, harass a person appointed to it.

(9) A person (A) who is a relevant person in relation to a public office within subsection (2)(a) or (b) must not victimise a person (B) appointed to the office –

    (a)   as to B's terms of appointment;

    (b)   in the way A affords B access, or by not affording B access, to opportunities for promotion, transfer or training or for receiving any other benefit, facility or service;

    (c)   by terminating the appointment;

    (d)   by subjecting B to any other detriment.

(10) A person (A) who is a relevant person in relation to a public office within subsection (2)(c) must not victimise a person (B) appointed to the office –

    (a)   as to B's terms of appointment;

    (b)   in the way A affords B access, or by not affording B access, to opportunities for promotion, transfer or training or for receiving any other benefit, facility or service;

    (c)   by subjecting B to any other detriment (other than by terminating the appointment).

(11) A duty to make reasonable adjustments applies to –

    (a)   a relevant person in relation to a public office;

    (b)   a person who has the power to make an appointment to a public office within subsection (2)(a) or (b).

(12) Subsection (3)(b), so far as relating to sex or pregnancy and maternity, does not apply to a term that relates to pay –

    (a)   unless, were B to accept the offer, an equality clause or rule would have effect in relation to the term, or

    (b)   if paragraph (a) does not apply, except in so far as making an offer on terms including that term amounts to a contravention of subsection (3)(b) by virtue of section 13, 14 or 18.

51   Public offices: recommendations for appointments, etc.

(1)   A person (A) who has the power to make a recommendation for or give approval to an appointment to a public office within section 50(2)(a) or (b), must not discriminate against a person (B) –

   (a)   in the arrangements A makes for deciding who to recommend for appointment or to whose appointment to give approval;
   (b)   by not recommending B for appointment to the office;
   (c)   by making a negative recommendation of B for appointment to the office;
   (d)   by not giving approval to the appointment of B to the office.

(2)   A person who has the power to make a recommendation for or give approval to an appointment to a public office within section 50(2)(a) or (b) must not, in relation to the office, harass a person seeking or being considered for the recommendation or approval.

(3)   A person (A) who has the power to make a recommendation for or give approval to an appointment to a public office within section 50(2)(a) or (b), must not victimise a person (B) –

   (a)   in the arrangements A makes for deciding who to recommend for appointment or to whose appointment to give approval;
   (b)   by not recommending B for appointment to the office;
   (c)   by making a negative recommendation of B for appointment to the office;
   (d)   by not giving approval to the appointment of B to the office.

(4)   A duty to make reasonable adjustments applies to a person who has the power to make a recommendation for or give approval to an appointment to a public office within section 50(2)(a) or (b).

(5)   A reference in this section to a person who has the power to make a recommendation for or give approval to an appointment to a public office within section 50(2)(a) is a reference only to a relevant body which has that power; and for that purpose 'relevant body' means a body established –

   (a)   by or in pursuance of an enactment, or
   (b)   by a member of the executive.

52   Interpretation and exceptions

(1)   This section applies for the purposes of sections 49 to 51.
(2)   'Personal office' has the meaning given in section 49.
(3)   'Public office' has the meaning given in section 50.
(4)   An office or post which is both a personal office and a public office is to be treated as being a public office only.
(5)   Appointment to an office or post does not include election to it.
(6)   'Relevant person', in relation to an office, means the person who, in relation to a matter specified in the first column of the table, is specified in the second column (but a reference to a relevant person does not in any case include the House of Commons, the House of Lords, the National Assembly for Wales or the Scottish Parliament).

Matter	Relevant person
A term of appointment	The person who has the power to set the term.
Access to an opportunity	The person who has the power to afford access to the opportunity (or, if there is no such person, the person who has the power to make the appointment).

Matter	Relevant person
Terminating an appointment	The person who has the power to terminate the appointment.
Subjecting an appointee to any other detriment	The person who has the power in relation to the matter to which the conduct in question relates (or, if there is no such person, the person who has the power to make the appointment).
Harassing an appointee	The person who has the power in relation to the matter to which the conduct in question relates.

(7) A reference to terminating a person's appointment includes a reference to termination of the appointment –

  (a)   by the expiry of a period (including a period expiring by reference to an event or circumstance);

  (b)   by an act of the person (including giving notice) in circumstances such that the person is entitled, because of the relevant person's conduct, to terminate the appointment without notice.

(8) Subsection (7)(a) does not apply if, immediately after the termination, the appointment is renewed on the same terms.

(9) Schedule 6 (excluded offices) has effect.

Qualifications

53   Qualifications bodies

(1) A qualifications body (A) must not discriminate against a person (B) –

  (a)   in the arrangements A makes for deciding upon whom to confer a relevant qualification;

  (b)   as to the terms on which it is prepared to confer a relevant qualification on B;

  (c)   by not conferring a relevant qualification on B.

(2) A qualifications body (A) must not discriminate against a person (B) upon whom A has conferred a relevant qualification –

  (a)   by withdrawing the qualification from B;

  (b)   by varying the terms on which B holds the qualification;

  (c)   by subjecting B to any other detriment.

(3) A qualifications body must not, in relation to conferment by it of a relevant qualification, harass –

  (a)   a person who holds the qualification, or

  (b)   a person who applies for it.

(4) A qualifications body (A) must not victimise a person (B) –

  (a)   in the arrangements A makes for deciding upon whom to confer a relevant qualification;

  (b)   as to the terms on which it is prepared to confer a relevant qualification on B;

  (c)   by not conferring a relevant qualification on B.

(5) A qualifications body (A) must not victimise a person (B) upon whom A has conferred a relevant qualification –

      (a)   by withdrawing the qualification from B;

      (b)   by varying the terms on which B holds the qualification;

      (c)   by subjecting B to any other detriment.

(6)   A duty to make reasonable adjustments applies to a qualifications body.

(7)   The application by a qualifications body of a competence standard to a disabled person is not disability discrimination unless it is discrimination by virtue of section 19.

54   Interpretation

(1)   This section applies for the purposes of section 53.

(2)   A qualifications body is an authority or body which can confer a relevant qualification.

(3)   A relevant qualification is an authorisation, qualification, recognition, registration, enrolment, approval or certification which is needed for, or facilitates engagement in, a particular trade or profession.

(4)   An authority or body is not a qualifications body in so far as –

      (a)   it can confer a qualification to which section 96 applies,

      (b)   it is the responsible body of a school to which section 85 applies,

      (c)   it is the governing body of an institution to which section 91 applies,

      (d)   it exercises functions under the Education Acts, or

      (e)   it exercises functions under the Education (Scotland) Act 1980.

(5)   A reference to conferring a relevant qualification includes a reference to renewing or extending the conferment of a relevant qualification.

(6)   A competence standard is an academic, medical or other standard applied for the purpose of determining whether or not a person has a particular level of competence or ability.

Employment services

55   Employment service-providers

(1)   A person (an 'employment service-provider') concerned with the provision of an employment service must not discriminate against a person –

      (a)   in the arrangements the service-provider makes for selecting persons to whom to provide, or to whom to offer to provide, the service;

      (b)   as to the terms on which the service-provider offers to provide the service to the person;

      (c)   by not offering to provide the service to the person.

(2)   An employment service-provider (A) must not, in relation to the provision of an employment service, discriminate against a person (B) –

      (a)   as to the terms on which A provides the service to B;

      (b)   by not providing the service to B;

      (c)   by terminating the provision of the service to B;

      (d)   by subjecting B to any other detriment.

(3)   An employment service-provider must not, in relation to the provision of an employment service, harass –

      (a)   a person who asks the service-provider to provide the service;

      (b)   a person for whom the service-provider provides the service.

(4)   An employment service-provider (A) must not victimise a person (B) –

      (a)   in the arrangements A makes for selecting persons to whom to provide, or to whom to offer to provide, the service;

      (b)   as to the terms on which A offers to provide the service to B;

      (c)   by not offering to provide the service to B.

(5) An employment service-provider (A) must not, in relation to the provision of an employment service, victimise a person (B) –

    (a)   as to the terms on which A provides the service to B;

    (b)   by not providing the service to B;

    (c)   by terminating the provision of the service to B;

    (d)   by subjecting B to any other detriment.

(6) A duty to make reasonable adjustments applies to an employment service-provider, except in relation to the provision of a vocational service.

(7) The duty imposed by section 29(7)(a) applies to a person concerned with the provision of a vocational service; but a failure to comply with that duty in relation to the provision of a vocational service is a contravention of this Part for the purposes of Part 9 (enforcement).

56   Interpretation

(1) This section applies for the purposes of section 55.

(2) The provision of an employment service includes –

    (a)   the provision of vocational training;

    (b)   the provision of vocational guidance;

    (c)   making arrangements for the provision of vocational training or vocational guidance;

    (d)   the provision of a service for finding employment for persons;

    (e)   the provision of a service for supplying employers with persons to do work;

    (f)   the provision of a service in pursuance of arrangements made under section 2 of the Employment and Training Act 1973 (functions of the Secretary of State relating to employment);

    (g)   the provision of a service in pursuance of arrangements made or a direction given under section 10 of that Act (careers services);

    (h)   the exercise of a function in pursuance of arrangements made under section 2(3) of the Enterprise and New Towns (Scotland) Act 1990 (functions of Scottish Enterprise, etc. relating to employment);

    (i)   an assessment related to the conferment of a relevant qualification within the meaning of section 53 above (except in so far as the assessment is by the qualifications body which confers the qualification).

(3) This section does not apply in relation to training or guidance in so far as it is training or guidance in relation to which another provision of this Part applies.

(4) This section does not apply in relation to training or guidance for pupils of a school to which section 85 applies in so far as it is training or guidance to which the responsible body of the school has power to afford access (whether as the responsible body of that school or as the responsible body of any other school at which the training or guidance is provided).

(5) This section does not apply in relation to training or guidance for students of an institution to which section 91 applies in so far as it is training or guidance to which the governing body of the institution has power to afford access.

(6) 'Vocational training' means –

    (a)   training for employment, or

    (b)   work experience (including work experience the duration of which is not agreed until after it begins).

(7) A reference to the provision of a vocational service is a reference to the provision of an employment service within subsection (2)(a) to (d) (or an employment service within subsection (2)(f) or (g) in so far as it is also an employment service within subsection (2)(a) to (d)); and for that purpose –

(a)   the references to an employment service within subsection (2)(a) do not include a reference to vocational training within the meaning given by subsection (6)(b), and

(b)   the references to an employment service within subsection (2)(d) also include a reference to a service for assisting persons to retain employment.

(8) A reference to training includes a reference to facilities for training.

Trade organisations

57   Trade organisations

(1) A trade organisation (A) must not discriminate against a person (B) –

(a)   in the arrangements A makes for deciding to whom to offer membership of the organisation;

(b)   as to the terms on which it is prepared to admit B as a member;

(c)   by not accepting B's application for membership.

(2) A trade organisation (A) must not discriminate against a member (B) –

(a)   in the way it affords B access, or by not affording B access, to opportunities for receiving a benefit, facility or service;

(b)   by depriving B of membership;

(c)   by varying the terms on which B is a member;

(d)   by subjecting B to any other detriment.

(3) A trade organisation must not, in relation to membership of it, harass –

(a)   a member, or

(b)   an applicant for membership.

(4) A trade organisation (A) must not victimise a person (B) –

(a)   in the arrangements A makes for deciding to whom to offer membership of the organisation;

(b)   as to the terms on which it is prepared to admit B as a member;

(c)   by not accepting B's application for membership.

(5) A trade organisation (A) must not victimise a member (B) –

(a)   in the way it affords B access, or by not affording B access, to opportunities for receiving a benefit, facility or service;

(b)   by depriving B of membership;

(c)   by varying the terms on which B is a member;

(d)   by subjecting B to any other detriment.

(6) A duty to make reasonable adjustments applies to a trade organisation.

(7) A trade organisation is –

(a)   an organisation of workers,

(b)   an organisation of employers, or

(c)   any other organisation whose members carry on a particular trade or profession for the purposes of which the organisation exists.

Local authority members

58   Official business of members

(1) A local authority must not discriminate against a member of the authority in relation to the member's carrying out of official business –

(a)   in the way the authority affords the member access, or by not affording the member access, to opportunities for training or for receiving any other facility;

(b)   by subjecting the member to any other detriment.

(2) A local authority must not, in relation to a member's carrying out of official business, harass the member.

(3) A local authority must not victimise a member of the authority in relation to the member's carrying out of official business –

(a)   in the way the authority affords the member access, or by not affording the member access, to opportunities for training or for receiving any other facility;

(b)   by subjecting the member to any other detriment.

(4) A member of a local authority is not subjected to a detriment for the purposes of subsection (1)(b) or (3)(b) only because the member is –

(a)   not appointed or elected to an office of the authority,

(b)   not appointed or elected to, or to an office of, a committee or sub-committee of the authority, or

(c)   not appointed or nominated in exercise of an appointment power of the authority.

(5) In subsection (4)(c), an appointment power of a local authority is a power of the authority, or of a group of bodies including the authority, to make –

(a)   appointments to a body;

(b)   nominations for appointment to a body.

(6) A duty to make reasonable adjustments applies to a local authority.

59   Interpretation

(1) This section applies for the purposes of section 58.

(2) 'Local authority' means –

(a)   a county council in England;

(b)   a district council in England;

(c)   the Greater London Authority;

(d)   a London borough council;

(e)   the Common Council of the City of London;

(f)   the Council of the Isles of Scilly;

(g)   a parish council in England;

(h)   a county council in Wales;

(i)   a community council in Wales;

(j)   a county borough council in Wales;

(k)   a council constituted under section 2 of the Local Government etc. (Scotland) Act 1994;

(l)   a community council in Scotland.

(3) A Minister of the Crown may by order amend subsection (2) so as to add, vary or omit a reference to a body which exercises functions that have been conferred on a local authority within paragraph (a) to (l).

(4) A reference to the carrying-out of official business by a person who is a member of a local authority is a reference to the doing of anything by the person –

(a)   as a member of the authority,

(b)   as a member of a body to which the person is appointed by, or appointed following nomination by, the authority or a group of bodies including the authority, or

(c)   as a member of any other public body.

(5) 'Member', in relation to the Greater London Authority, means –

(a)   the Mayor of London;

(b)   a member of the London Assembly.

Recruitment

60   Enquiries about disability and health

(1)   A person (A) to whom an application for work is made must not ask about the health of the applicant (B) –

    (a)   before offering work to B, or

    (b)   where A is not in a position to offer work to B, before including B in a pool of applicants from whom A intends (when in a position to do so) to select a person to whom to offer work.

(2)   A contravention of subsection (1) (or a contravention of section 111 or 112 that relates to a contravention of subsection (1)) is enforceable as an unlawful act under Part 1 of the Equality Act 2006 (and, by virtue of section 120(8), is enforceable only by the Commission under that Part).

(3)   A does not contravene a relevant disability provision merely by asking about B's health; but A's conduct in reliance on information given in response may be a contravention of a relevant disability provision.

(4)   Subsection (5) applies if B brings proceedings before an employment tribunal on a complaint that A's conduct in reliance on information given in response to a question about B's health is a contravention of a relevant disability provision.

(5)   In the application of section 136 to the proceedings, the particulars of the complaint are to be treated for the purposes of subsection (2) of that section as facts from which the tribunal could decide that A contravened the provision.

(6)   This section does not apply to a question that A asks in so far as asking the question is necessary for the purpose of –

    (a)   establishing whether B will be able to comply with a requirement to undergo an assessment or establishing whether a duty to make reasonable adjustments is or will be imposed on A in relation to B in connection with a requirement to undergo an assessment,

    (b)   establishing whether B will be able to carry out a function that is intrinsic to the work concerned,

    (c)   monitoring diversity in the range of persons applying to A for work,

    (d)   taking action to which section 158 would apply if references in that section to persons who share (or do not share) a protected characteristic were references to disabled persons (or persons who are not disabled) and the reference to the characteristic were a reference to disability, or

    (e)   if A applies in relation to the work a requirement to have a particular disability, establishing whether B has that disability.

(7)   In subsection (6)(b), where A reasonably believes that a duty to make reasonable adjustments would be imposed on A in relation to B in connection with the work, the reference to a function that is intrinsic to the work is to be read as a reference to a function that would be intrinsic to the work once A complied with the duty.

(8)   Subsection (6)(e) applies only if A shows that, having regard to the nature or context of the work –

    (a)   the requirement is an occupational requirement, and

    (b)   the application of the requirement is a proportionate means of achieving a legitimate aim.

(9)   'Work' means employment, contract work, a position as a partner, a position as a member of an LLP, a pupillage or tenancy, being taken as a devil, membership of a stable, an appointment to a personal or public office, or the provision of an employment service; and the references in subsection (1) to offering a person work are, in relation to contract work, to be read as references to allowing a person to do the work.

(10) A reference to offering work is a reference to making a conditional or unconditional

offer of work (and, in relation to contract work, is a reference to allowing a person to do the work subject to fulfilment of one or more conditions).

(11) The following, so far as relating to discrimination within section 13 because of disability, are relevant disability provisions –

 (a) section 39(1)(a) or (c);
 (b) section 41(1)(b);
 (c) section 44(1)(a) or (c);
 (d) section 45(1)(a) or (c);
 (e) section 47(1)(a) or (c);
 (f) section 48(1)(a) or (c);
 (g) section 49(3)(a) or (c);
 (h) section 50(3)(a) or (c);
 (i) section 51(1);
 (j) section 55(1)(a) or (c).

(12) An assessment is an interview or other process designed to give an indication of a person's suitability for the work concerned.

(13) For the purposes of this section, whether or not a person has a disability is to be regarded as an aspect of that person's health.

(14) This section does not apply to anything done for the purpose of vetting applicants for work for reasons of national security.

CHAPTER 2   OCCUPATIONAL PENSION SCHEMES

61   Non-discrimination rule

(1) An occupational pension scheme must be taken to include a non-discrimination rule.

(2) A non-discrimination rule is a provision by virtue of which a responsible person (A) –

 (a) must not discriminate against another person (B) in carrying out any of A's functions in relation to the scheme;
 (b) must not, in relation to the scheme, harass B;
 (c) must not, in relation to the scheme, victimise B.

(3) The provisions of an occupational pension scheme have effect subject to the non-discrimination rule.

(4) The following are responsible persons –

 (a) the trustees or managers of the scheme;
 (b) an employer whose employees are, or may be, members of the scheme;
 (c) a person exercising an appointing function in relation to an office the holder of which is, or may be, a member of the scheme.

(5) A non-discrimination rule does not apply in relation to a person who is a pension credit member of a scheme.

(6) An appointing function is any of the following –

 (a) the function of appointing a person;
 (b) the function of terminating a person's appointment;
 (c) the function of recommending a person for appointment;
 (d) the function of approving an appointment.

(7) A breach of a non-discrimination rule is a contravention of this Part for the purposes of Part 9 (enforcement).

(8) It is not a breach of a non-discrimination rule for the employer or the trustees or managers of a scheme to maintain or use in relation to the scheme rules, practices, actions or decisions relating to age which are of a description specified by order by a Minister of the Crown.

(9) An order authorising the use of rules, practices, actions or decisions which are not in use

before the order comes into force must not be made unless the Minister consults such persons as the Minister thinks appropriate.

(10) A non-discrimination rule does not have effect in relation to an occupational pension scheme in so far as an equality rule has effect in relation to it (or would have effect in relation to it but for Part 2 of Schedule 7).

(11) A duty to make reasonable adjustments applies to a responsible person.

62   Non-discrimination alterations

(1)   This section applies if the trustees or managers of an occupational pension scheme do not have power to make non-discrimination alterations to the scheme.

(2)   This section also applies if the trustees or managers of an occupational pension scheme have power to make non-discrimination alterations to the scheme but the procedure for doing so –

    (a)   is liable to be unduly complex or protracted, or

    (b)   involves obtaining consents which cannot be obtained or which can be obtained only with undue delay or difficulty.

(3)   The trustees or managers may by resolution make non-discrimination alterations to the scheme.

(4)   Non-discrimination alterations may have effect in relation to a period before the date on which they are made.

(5)   Non-discrimination alterations to an occupational pension scheme are such alterations to the scheme as may be required for the provisions of the scheme to have the effect that they have in consequence of section 61(3).

63   Communications

(1)   In their application to communications the following provisions apply in relation to a disabled person who is a pension credit member of an occupational pension scheme as they apply in relation to a disabled person who is a deferred member or pensioner member of the scheme –

    (a)   section 61;

    (b)   section 120;

    (c)   section 126;

    (d)   paragraph 19 of Schedule 8 (and such other provisions of that Schedule as apply for the purposes of that paragraph).

(2)   Communications include –

    (a)   the provision of information;

    (b)   the operation of a dispute resolution procedure.

CHAPTER 3   EQUALITY OF TERMS

Sex equality

64   Relevant types of work

(1)   Sections 66 to 70 apply where –

    (a)   a person (A) is employed on work that is equal to the work that a comparator of the opposite sex (B) does;

    (b)   a person (A) holding a personal or public office does work that is equal to the work that a comparator of the opposite sex (B) does.

(2)   The references in subsection (1) to the work that B does are not restricted to work done contemporaneously with the work done by A.

65   **Equal work**

(1) For the purposes of this Chapter, A's work is equal to that of B if it is –

   (a)   like B's work,
   (b)   rated as equivalent to B's work, or
   (c)   of equal value to B's work.

(2) A's work is like B's work if –

   (a)   A's work and B's work are the same or broadly similar, and
   (b)   such differences as there are between their work are not of practical importance in relation to the terms of their work.

(3) So on a comparison of one person's work with another's for the purposes of subsection (2), it is necessary to have regard to –

   (a)   the frequency with which differences between their work occur in practice, and
   (b)   the nature and extent of the differences.

(4) A's work is rated as equivalent to B's work if a job evaluation study –

   (a)   gives an equal value to A's job and B's job in terms of the demands made on a worker, or
   (b)   would give an equal value to A's job and B's job in those terms were the evaluation not made on a sex-specific system.

(5) A system is sex-specific if, for the purposes of one or more of the demands made on a worker, it sets values for men different from those it sets for women.

(6) A's work is of equal value to B's work if it is –

   (a)   neither like B's work nor rated as equivalent to B's work, but
   (b)   nevertheless equal to B's work in terms of the demands made on A by reference to factors such as effort, skill and decision-making.

66   **Sex equality clause**

(1) If the terms of A's work do not (by whatever means) include a sex equality clause, they are to be treated as including one.

(2) A sex equality clause is a provision that has the following effect –

   (a)   if a term of A's is less favourable to A than a corresponding term of B's is to B, A's term is modified so as not to be less favourable;
   (b)   if A does not have a term which corresponds to a term of B's that benefits B, A's terms are modified so as to include such a term.

(3) Subsection (2)(a) applies to a term of A's relating to membership of or rights under an occupational pension scheme only in so far as a sex equality rule would have effect in relation to the term.

(4) In the case of work within section 65(1)(b), a reference in subsection (2) above to a term includes a reference to such terms (if any) as have not been determined by the rating of the work (as well as those that have).

67   **Sex equality rule**

(1) If an occupational pension scheme does not include a sex equality rule, it is to be treated as including one.

(2) A sex equality rule is a provision that has the following effect –

   (a)   if a relevant term is less favourable to A than it is to B, the term is modified so as not to be less favourable;
   (b)   if a term confers a relevant discretion capable of being exercised in a way that would be less favourable to A than to B, the term is modified so as to prevent the exercise of the discretion in that way.

(3) A term is relevant if it is –

(a)   a term on which persons become members of the scheme, or
(b)   a term on which members of the scheme are treated.

(4) A discretion is relevant if its exercise in relation to the scheme is capable of affecting –

(a)   the way in which persons become members of the scheme, or
(b)   the way in which members of the scheme are treated.

(5) The reference in subsection (3)(b) to a term on which members of a scheme are treated includes a reference to the term as it has effect for the benefit of dependants of members.

(6) The reference in subsection (4)(b) to the way in which members of a scheme are treated includes a reference to the way in which they are treated as the scheme has effect for the benefit of dependants of members.

(7) If the effect of a relevant matter on persons of the same sex differs according to their family, marital or civil partnership status, a comparison for the purposes of this section of the effect of that matter on persons of the opposite sex must be with persons who have the same status.

(8) A relevant matter is –

(a)   a relevant term;
(b)   a term conferring a relevant discretion;
(c)   the exercise of a relevant discretion in relation to an occupational pension scheme.

(9) This section, so far as relating to the terms on which persons become members of an occupational pension scheme, does not have effect in relation to pensionable service before 8 April 1976.

(10) This section, so far as relating to the terms on which members of an occupational pension scheme are treated, does not have effect in relation to pensionable service before 17 May 1990.

68   Sex equality rule: consequential alteration of schemes

(1) This section applies if the trustees or managers of an occupational pension scheme do not have power to make sex equality alterations to the scheme.

(2) This section also applies if the trustees or managers of an occupational pension scheme have power to make sex equality alterations to the scheme but the procedure for doing so –

(a)   is liable to be unduly complex or protracted, or
(b)   involves obtaining consents which cannot be obtained or which can be obtained only with undue delay or difficulty.

(3) The trustees or managers may by resolution make sex equality alterations to the scheme.

(4) Sex equality alterations may have effect in relation to a period before the date on which they are made.

(5) Sex equality alterations to an occupational pension scheme are such alterations to the scheme as may be required to secure conformity with a sex equality rule.

69   Defence of material factor

(1) The sex equality clause in A's terms has no effect in relation to a difference between A's terms and B's terms if the responsible person shows that the difference is because of a material factor reliance on which –

(a)   does not involve treating A less favourably because of A's sex than the responsible person treats B, and
(b)   if the factor is within subsection (2), is a proportionate means of achieving a legitimate aim.

(2) A factor is within this subsection if A shows that, as a result of the factor, A and persons of the same sex doing work equal to A's are put at a particular disadvantage when compared with persons of the opposite sex doing work equal to A's.

(3) For the purposes of subsection (1), the long-term objective of reducing inequality between men's and women's terms of work is always to be regarded as a legitimate aim.

(4) A sex equality rule has no effect in relation to a difference between A and B in the effect of a relevant matter if the trustees or managers of the scheme in question show that the difference is because of a material factor which is not the difference of sex.

(5) 'Relevant matter' has the meaning given in section 67.

(6) For the purposes of this section, a factor is not material unless it is a material difference between A's case and B's.

70   Exclusion of sex discrimination provisions

(1) The relevant sex discrimination provision has no effect in relation to a term of A's that –

    (a)   is modified by, or included by virtue of, a sex equality clause or rule, or

    (b)   would be so modified or included but for section 69 or Part 2 of Schedule 7.

(2) Neither of the following is sex discrimination for the purposes of the relevant sex discrimination provision –

    (a)   the inclusion in A's terms of a term that is less favourable as referred to in section 66(2) (a);

    (b)   the failure to include in A's terms a corresponding term as referred to in section 66(2)(b).

(3) The relevant sex discrimination provision is, in relation to work of a description given in the first column of the table, the provision referred to in the second column so far as relating to sex.

Description of work	Provision
Employment	Section 39(2)
Appointment to a personal office	Section 49(6)
Appointment to a public office	Section 50(6)

71   Sex discrimination in relation to contractual pay

(1) This section applies in relation to a term of a person's work –

    (a)   that relates to pay, but

    (b)   in relation to which a sex equality clause or rule has no effect.

(2) The relevant sex discrimination provision (as defined by section 70) has no effect in relation to the term except in so far as treatment of the person amounts to a contravention of the provision by virtue of section 13 or 14.

Pregnancy and maternity equality

72   Relevant types of work

Sections 73 to 76 apply where a woman –

(a) is employed, or

(b) holds a personal or public office.

73   Maternity equality clause

(1) If the terms of the woman's work do not (by whatever means) include a maternity equality clause, they are to be treated as including one.

(2) A maternity equality clause is a provision that, in relation to the terms of the woman's work, has the effect referred to in section 74(1), (6) and (8).

(3) In the case of a term relating to membership of or rights under an occupational pension scheme, a maternity equality clause has only such effect as a maternity equality rule would have.

74   Maternity equality clause: pay

(1) A term of the woman's work that provides for maternity-related pay to be calculated by reference to her pay at a particular time is, if each of the following three conditions is satisfied, modified as mentioned in subsection (5).

(2) The first condition is that, after the time referred to in subsection (1) but before the end of the protected period –

  (a)   her pay increases, or
  (b)   it would have increased had she not been on maternity leave.

(3) The second condition is that the maternity-related pay is not –

  (a)   what her pay would have been had she not been on maternity leave, or
  (b)   the difference between the amount of statutory maternity pay to which she is entitled and what her pay would have been had she not been on maternity leave.

(4) The third condition is that the terms of her work do not provide for the maternity-related pay to be subject to –

  (a)   an increase as mentioned in subsection (2)(a), or
  (b)   an increase that would have occurred as mentioned in subsection (2)(b).

(5) The modification referred to in subsection (1) is a modification to provide for the maternity-related pay to be subject to –

  (a)   any increase as mentioned in subsection (2)(a), or
  (b)   any increase that would have occurred as mentioned in subsection (2)(b).

(6) A term of her work that –

  (a)   provides for pay within subsection (7), but
  (b)   does not provide for her to be given the pay in circumstances in which she would have been given it had she not been on maternity leave,

  is modified so as to provide for her to be given it in circumstances in which it would normally be given.

(7) Pay is within this subsection if it is –

  (a)   pay (including pay by way of bonus) in respect of times before the woman is on maternity leave,
  (b)   pay by way of bonus in respect of times when she is on compulsory maternity leave, or
  (c)   pay by way of bonus in respect of times after the end of the protected period.

(8) A term of the woman's work that –

  (a)   provides for pay after the end of the protected period, but
  (b)   does not provide for it to be subject to an increase to which it would have been subject had she not been on maternity leave,

  is modified so as to provide for it to be subject to the increase.

(9) Maternity-related pay is pay (other than statutory maternity pay) to which a woman is entitled –

(a)   as a result of being pregnant, or

(b)   in respect of times when she is on maternity leave.

(10) A reference to the protected period is to be construed in accordance with section 18.

75   Maternity equality rule

(1) If an occupational pension scheme does not include a maternity equality rule, it is to be treated as including one.

(2) A maternity equality rule is a provision that has the effect set out in subsections (3) and (4).

(3) If a relevant term does not treat time when the woman is on maternity leave as it treats time when she is not, the term is modified so as to treat time when she is on maternity leave as time when she is not.

(4) If a term confers a relevant discretion capable of being exercised so that time when she is on maternity leave is treated differently from time when she is not, the term is modified so as not to allow the discretion to be exercised in that way.

(5) A term is relevant if it is –

(a)   a term relating to membership of the scheme,

(b)   a term relating to the accrual of rights under the scheme, or

(c)   a term providing for the determination of the amount of a benefit payable under the scheme.

(6) A discretion is relevant if its exercise is capable of affecting –

(a)   membership of the scheme,

(b)   the accrual of rights under the scheme, or

(c)   the determination of the amount of a benefit payable under the scheme.

(7) This section does not require the woman's contributions to the scheme in respect of time when she is on maternity leave to be determined otherwise than by reference to the amount she is paid in respect of that time.

(8) This section, so far as relating to time when she is on ordinary maternity leave but is not being paid by her employer, applies only in a case where the expected week of childbirth began on or after 6 April 2003.

(9) This section, so far as relating to time when she is on additional maternity leave but is not being paid by her employer –

(a)   does not apply to the accrual of rights under the scheme in any case;

(b)   applies for other purposes only in a case where the expected week of childbirth began on or after 5 October 2008.

(10) In this section –

(a)   a reference to being on maternity leave includes a reference to having been on maternity leave, and

(b)   a reference to being paid by the employer includes a reference to receiving statutory maternity pay from the employer.

76   Exclusion of pregnancy and maternity discrimination provisions

(1) The relevant pregnancy and maternity discrimination provision has no effect in relation to a term of the woman's work that is modified by a maternity equality clause or rule.

(2) The inclusion in the woman's terms of a term that requires modification by virtue of section 73(2) or (3) is not pregnancy and maternity discrimination for the purposes of the relevant pregnancy and maternity discrimination provision.

(3) The relevant pregnancy and maternity discrimination provision is, in relation to a description of work given in the first column of the table, the provision referred to in the second column so far as relating to pregnancy and maternity.

Description of work	Provision
Employment	Section 39(2)
Appointment to a personal office	Section 49(6)
Appointment to a public office	Section 50(6)

Disclosure of information

77   Discussions about pay

(1) A term of a person's work that purports to prevent or restrict the person (P) from disclosing or seeking to disclose information about the terms of P's work is unenforceable against P in so far as P makes or seeks to make a relevant pay disclosure.

(2) A term of a person's work that purports to prevent or restrict the person (P) from seeking disclosure of information from a colleague about the terms of the colleague's work is unenforceable against P in so far as P seeks a relevant pay disclosure from the colleague; and 'colleague' includes a former colleague in relation to the work in question.

(3) A disclosure is a relevant pay disclosure if made for the purpose of enabling the person who makes it, or the person to whom it is made, to find out whether or to what extent there is, in relation to the work in question, a connection between pay and having (or not having) a particular protected characteristic.

(4) The following are to be treated as protected acts for the purposes of the relevant victimisation provision –

(a)   seeking a disclosure that would be a relevant pay disclosure;
(b)   making or seeking to make a relevant pay disclosure;
(c)   receiving information disclosed in a relevant pay disclosure.

(5) The relevant victimisation provision is, in relation to a description of work specified in the first column of the table, section 27 so far as it applies for the purposes of a provision mentioned in the second column.

Description of work	Provision by virtue of which section 27 has effect
Employment	Section 39(3) or (4)
Appointment to a personal office	Section 49(5) or (8)
Appointment to a public office	Section 50(5) or (9)

78   Gender pay gap information

(1) Regulations may require employers to publish information relating to the pay of employees for the purpose of showing whether, by reference to factors of such description as is prescribed, there are differences in the pay of male and female employees.

(2) This section does not apply to –

(a)   an employer who has fewer than 250 employees;
(b)   a person specified in Schedule 19;
(c)   a government department or part of the armed forces not specified in that Schedule.

(3) The regulations may prescribe –

    (a)   descriptions of employer;
    (b)   descriptions of employee;
    (c)   how to calculate the number of employees that an employer has;
    (d)   descriptions of information;
    (e)   the time at which information is to be published;
    (f)   the form and manner in which it is to be published.

(4) Regulations under subsection (3)(e) may not require an employer, after the first publication of information, to publish information more frequently than at intervals of 12 months.

(5) The regulations may make provision for a failure to comply with the regulations –

    (a)   to be an offence punishable on summary conviction by a fine not exceeding level 5 on the standard scale;
    (b)   to be enforced, otherwise than as an offence, by such means as are prescribed.

(6) The reference to a failure to comply with the regulations includes a reference to a failure by a person acting on behalf of an employer.

Supplementary

79   Comparators

(1) This section applies for the purposes of this Chapter.
(2) If A is employed, B is a comparator if subsection (3) or (4) applies.
(3) This subsection applies if –

    (a)   B is employed by A's employer or by an associate of A's employer, and
    (b)   A and B work at the same establishment.

(4) This subsection applies if –

    (a)   B is employed by A's employer or an associate of A's employer,
    (b)   B works at an establishment other than the one at which A works, and
    (c)   common terms apply at the establishments (either generally or as between A and B).

(5) If A holds a personal or public office, B is a comparator if –

    (a)   B holds a personal or public office, and
    (b)   the person responsible for paying A is also responsible for paying B.

(6) If A is a relevant member of the House of Commons staff, B is a comparator if –

    (a)   B is employed by the person who is A's employer under subsection (6) of section 195 of the Employment Rights Act 1996, or
    (b)   if subsection (7) of that section applies in A's case, B is employed by the person who is A's employer under that subsection.

(7) If A is a relevant member of the House of Lords staff, B is a comparator if B is also a relevant member of the House of Lords staff.

(8) Section 42 does not apply to this Chapter; accordingly, for the purposes of this Chapter only, holding the office of constable is to be treated as holding a personal office.

(9) For the purposes of this section, employers are associated if –

    (a)   one is a company of which the other (directly or indirectly) has control, or
    (b)   both are companies of which a third person (directly or indirectly) has control.

80   Interpretation and exceptions

(1) This section applies for the purposes of this Chapter.
(2) The terms of a person's work are –

    (a)   if the person is employed, the terms of the person's employment that are in the person's contract of employment, contract of apprenticeship or contract to do work personally;

    (b)   if the person holds a personal or public office, the terms of the person's appointment to the office.

(3)   If work is not done at an establishment, it is to be treated as done at the establishment with which it has the closest connection.

(4)   A person (P) is the responsible person in relation to another person if –

    (a)   P is the other's employer;

    (b)   P is responsible for paying remuneration in respect of a personal or public office that the other holds.

(5)   A job evaluation study is a study undertaken with a view to evaluating, in terms of the demands made on a person by reference to factors such as effort, skill and decision-making, the jobs to be done –

    (a)   by some or all of the workers in an undertaking or group of undertakings, or

    (b)   in the case of the armed forces, by some or all of the members of the armed forces.

(6)   In the case of Crown employment, the reference in subsection (5)(a) to an undertaking is to be construed in accordance with section 191(4) of the Employment Rights Act 1996.

(7)   'Civil partnership status' has the meaning given in section 124(1) of the Pensions Act 1995.

(8)   Schedule 7 (exceptions) has effect.

CHAPTER 4   SUPPLEMENTARY

81   Ships and hovercraft

(1)   This Part applies in relation to –

    (a)   work on ships,

    (b)   work on hovercraft, and

    (c)   seafarers,

only in such circumstances as are prescribed.

(2)   For the purposes of this section, it does not matter whether employment arises or work is carried out within or outside the United Kingdom.

(3)   'Ship' has the same meaning as in the Merchant Shipping Act 1995.

(4)   'Hovercraft' has the same meaning as in the Hovercraft Act 1968.

(5)   'Seafarer' means a person employed or engaged in any capacity on board a ship or hovercraft.

(6)   Nothing in this section affects the application of any other provision of this Act to conduct outside England and Wales or Scotland.

82   Offshore work

(1)   Her Majesty may by Order in Council provide that in the case of persons in offshore work –

    (a)   specified provisions of this Part apply (with or without modification);

    (b)   Northern Ireland legislation making provision for purposes corresponding to any of the purposes of this Part applies (with or without modification).

(2)   The Order may –

    (a)   provide for these provisions, as applied by the Order, to apply to individuals (whether or not British citizens) and bodies corporate (whether or not incorporated under the law of a part of the United Kingdom), whether or not such application affects activities outside the United Kingdom;

(b)   make provision for conferring jurisdiction on a specified court or class of court or on employment tribunals in respect of offences, causes of action or other matters arising in connection with offshore work;

(c)   exclude from the operation of section 3 of the Territorial Waters Jurisdiction Act 1878 (consents required for prosecutions) proceedings for offences under the provisions mentioned in subsection (1) in connection with offshore work;

(d)   provide that such proceedings must not be brought without such consent as may be required by the Order.

(3) 'Offshore work' is work for the purposes of –

(a)   activities in the territorial sea adjacent to the United Kingdom,

(b)   activities such as are mentioned in subsection (2) of section 11 of the Petroleum Act 1998 in waters within subsection (8)(b) or (c) of that section, or

(c)   activities mentioned in paragraphs (a) and (b) of section 87(1) of the Energy Act 2004 in waters to which that section applies.

(4) Work includes employment, contract work, a position as a partner or as a member of an LLP, or an appointment to a personal or public office.

(5) Northern Ireland legislation includes an enactment contained in, or in an instrument under, an Act that forms part of the law of Northern Ireland.

(6) In the application to Northern Ireland of subsection (2)(b), the reference to employment tribunals is to be read as a reference to industrial tribunals.

(7) Nothing in this section affects the application of any other provision of this Act to conduct outside England and Wales or Scotland.

83   Interpretation and exceptions

(1) This section applies for the purposes of this Part.

(2) 'Employment' means –

(a)   employment under a contract of employment, a contract of apprenticeship or a contract personally to do work;

(b)   Crown employment;

(c)   employment as a relevant member of the House of Commons staff;

(d)   employment as a relevant member of the House of Lords staff.

(3) This Part applies to service in the armed forces as it applies to employment by a private person; and for that purpose –

(a)   references to terms of employment, or to a contract of employment, are to be read as including references to terms of service;

(b)   references to associated employers are to be ignored.

(4) A reference to an employer or an employee, or to employing or being employed, is (subject to section 212(11)) to be read with subsections (2) and (3); and a reference to an employer also includes a reference to a person who has no employees but is seeking to employ one or more other persons.

(5) 'Relevant member of the House of Commons staff' has the meaning given in section 195 of the Employment Rights Act 1996; and such a member of staff is an employee of –

(a)   the person who is the employer of that member under subsection (6) of that section, or

(b)   if subsection (7) of that section applies in the case of that member, the person who is the employer of that member under that subsection.

(6) 'Relevant member of the House of Lords staff' has the meaning given in section 194 of

that Act (which provides that such a member of staff is an employee of the Corporate Officer of the House of Lords).

(7) In the case of a person in Crown employment, or in employment as a relevant member of the House of Commons staff, a reference to the person's dismissal is a reference to the termination of the person's employment.

(8) A reference to a personal or public office, or to an appointment to a personal or public office, is to be construed in accordance with section 52.

(9) 'Crown employment' has the meaning given in section 191 of the Employment Rights Act 1996.

(10) Schedule 8 (reasonable adjustments) has effect.

(11) Schedule 9 (exceptions) has effect.

PART 6   EDUCATION

CHAPTER 1   SCHOOLS

84   Application of this Chapter

This Chapter does not apply to the following protected characteristics –

(a) age;

(b) marriage and civil partnership.

85   Pupils: admission and treatment, etc.

(1) The responsible body of a school to which this section applies must not discriminate against a person –

    (a)   in the arrangements it makes for deciding who is offered admission as a pupil;

    (b)   as to the terms on which it offers to admit the person as a pupil;

    (c)   by not admitting the person as a pupil.

(2) The responsible body of such a school must not discriminate against a pupil –

    (a)   in the way it provides education for the pupil;

    (b)   in the way it affords the pupil access to a benefit, facility or service;

    (c)   by not providing education for the pupil;

    (d)   by not affording the pupil access to a benefit, facility or service;

    (e)   by excluding the pupil from the school;

    (f)   by subjecting the pupil to any other detriment.

(3) The responsible body of such a school must not harass –

    (a)   a pupil;

    (b)   a person who has applied for admission as a pupil.

(4) The responsible body of such a school must not victimise a person –

    (a)   in the arrangements it makes for deciding who is offered admission as a pupil;

    (b)   as to the terms on which it offers to admit the person as a pupil;

    (c)   by not admitting the person as a pupil.

(5) The responsible body of such a school must not victimise a pupil –

    (a)   in the way it provides education for the pupil;

    (b)   in the way it affords the pupil access to a benefit, facility or service;

    (c)   by not providing education for the pupil;

    (d)   by not affording the pupil access to a benefit, facility or service;

    (e)   by excluding the pupil from the school;

    (f)   by subjecting the pupil to any other detriment.

(6) A duty to make reasonable adjustments applies to the responsible body of such a school.

(7) In relation to England and Wales, this section applies to –

(a) a school maintained by a local authority;
(b) an independent educational institution (other than a special school);
(c) a special school (not maintained by a local authority).

(8) In relation to Scotland, this section applies to –

(a) a school managed by an education authority;
(b) an independent school;
(c) a school in respect of which the managers are for the time being receiving grants under section 73(c) or (d) of the Education (Scotland) Act 1980.

(9) The responsible body of a school to which this section applies is –

(a) if the school is within subsection (7)(a), the local authority or governing body;
(b) if it is within subsection (7)(b) or (c), the proprietor;
(c) if it is within subsection (8)(a), the education authority;
(d) if it is within subsection (8)(b), the proprietor;
(e) if it is within subsection (8)(c), the managers.

(10) In the application of section 26 for the purposes of subsection (3), none of the following is a relevant protected characteristic –

(a) gender reassignment;
(b) religion or belief;
(c) sexual orientation.

86   Victimisation of pupils, etc. for conduct of parents, etc.

(1) This section applies for the purposes of section 27 in its application to section 85(4) or (5).

(2) The references to B in paragraphs (a) and (b) of subsection (1) of section 27 include a reference to a parent or sibling of the child in question.

(3) Giving false evidence or information, or making a false allegation, in good faith is not a protected act in a case where –

(a) the evidence or information is given, or the allegation is made, by a parent or sibling of the child, and
(b) the child has acted in bad faith.

(4) Giving false evidence or information, or making a false allegation, in bad faith, is a protected act in a case where –

(a) the evidence or information is given, or the allegation is made, by a parent or sibling of the child, and
(b) the child has acted in good faith.

(5) In this section –

'child' means a person who has not attained the age of 18;

'sibling' means a brother or sister, a half-brother or half-sister, or a stepbrother or stepsister.

87   Application of certain powers under Education Act 1996

(1) Sections 496 and 497 of the Education Act 1996 (powers to give directions where responsible body of school in default of obligations, etc.) apply to the performance of a duty under section 85.

(2) But neither of sections 496 and 497 of that Act applies to the performance of a duty under that section by the proprietor of an independent educational institution (other than a special school).

88   Disabled pupils: accessibility

Schedule 10 (accessibility) has effect.

89   Interpretation and exceptions

(1)   This section applies for the purposes of this Chapter.
(2)   Nothing in this Chapter applies to anything done in connection with the content of the curriculum.
(3)   'Pupil' –

    (a)   in relation to England and Wales, has the meaning given in section 3(1) of the Education Act 1996;
    (b)   in relation to Scotland, has the meaning given in section 135(1) of the Education (Scotland) Act 1980.

(4)   'Proprietor' –

    (a)   in relation to a school in England and Wales, has the meaning given in section 579(1) of the Education Act 1996;
    (b)   in relation to a school in Scotland, has the meaning given in section 135(1) of the Education (Scotland) Act 1980.

(5)   'School' –

    (a)   in relation to England and Wales, has the meaning given in section 4 of the Education Act 1996;
    (b)   in relation to Scotland, has the meaning given in section 135(1) of the Education (Scotland) Act 1980.

(6)   A reference to a school includes a reference to an independent educational institution in England; and a reference to an independent educational institution in England is to be construed in accordance with Chapter 1 of Part 4 of the Education and Skills Act 2008.
(7)   A reference to an independent educational institution is a reference to –

    (a)   an independent educational institution in England, or
    (b)   an independent school in Wales.

(8)   'Independent school' –

    (a)   in relation to Wales, has the meaning given in section 463 of the Education Act 1996;
    (b)   in relation to Scotland, has the meaning given in section 135(1) of the Education (Scotland) Act 1980.

(9)   'Special school' has the meaning given in section 337 of the Education Act 1996.
(10) 'Local authority' means –

    (a)   in relation to England, an English local authority within the meaning of section 162 of the Education and Inspections Act 2006;
    (b)   in relation to Wales, a Welsh local authority within the meaning of that section.

(11) 'Education authority', in relation to Scotland, has the meaning given in section 135(1) of the Education (Scotland) Act 1980.
(12) Schedule 11 (exceptions) has effect.

CHAPTER 2   FURTHER AND HIGHER EDUCATION

90   Application of this Chapter

This Chapter does not apply to the protected characteristic of marriage and civil partnership.

91   Students: admission and treatment, etc.

(1)   The responsible body of an institution to which this section applies must not discriminate against a person –

    (a)   in the arrangements it makes for deciding who is offered admission as a student;

    (b)   as to the terms on which it offers to admit the person as a student;

    (c)   by not admitting the person as a student.

(2)   The responsible body of such an institution must not discriminate against a student –

    (a)   in the way it provides education for the student;

    (b)   in the way it affords the student access to a benefit, facility or service;

    (c)   by not providing education for the student;

    (d)   by not affording the student access to a benefit, facility or service;

    (e)   by excluding the student;

    (f)   by subjecting the student to any other detriment.

(3)   The responsible body of such an institution must not discriminate against a disabled person –

    (a)   in the arrangements it makes for deciding upon whom to confer a qualification;

    (b)   as to the terms on which it is prepared to confer a qualification on the person;

    (c)   by not conferring a qualification on the person;

    (d)   by withdrawing a qualification from the person or varying the terms on which the person holds it.

(4)   Subsection (3) applies only to disability discrimination.

(5)   The responsible body of such an institution must not harass –

    (a)   a student;

    (b)   a person who has applied for admission as a student;

    (c)   a disabled person who holds or has applied for a qualification conferred by the institution.

(6)   The responsible body of such an institution must not victimise a person –

    (a)   in the arrangements it makes for deciding who is offered admission as a student;

    (b)   as to the terms on which it offers to admit the person as a student;

    (c)   by not admitting the person as a student.

(7)   The responsible body of such an institution must not victimise a student –

    (a)   in the way it provides education for the student;

    (b)   in the way it affords the student access to a benefit, facility or service;

    (c)   by not providing education for the student;

    (d)   by not affording the student access to a benefit, facility or service;

    (e)   by excluding the student;

    (f)   by subjecting the student to any other detriment.

(8)   The responsible body of such an institution must not victimise a disabled person –

    (a)   in the arrangements it makes for deciding upon whom to confer a qualification;

    (b)   as to the terms on which it is prepared to confer a qualification on the person;

    (c)   by not conferring a qualification on the person;

    (d)   by withdrawing a qualification from the person or varying the terms on which the person holds it.

(9)   A duty to make reasonable adjustments applies to the responsible body of such an institution.

(10) In relation to England and Wales, this section applies to –

    (a)   a university;

    (b)   any other institution within the higher education sector;

    (c)   an institution within the further education sector.

(11) In relation to Scotland, this section applies to –

    (a)   a university;

    (b)   a designated institution;

(c)   a college of further education.

(12) A responsible body is –

(a)   in the case of an institution within subsection (10)(a), (b) or (c), the governing body;

(b)   in the case of an institution within subsection (11)(a) or (b), the governing body;

(c)   in the case of a college of further education under the management of a board of management, the board of management;

(d)   in the case of any other college of further education, any board of governors of the college or any person responsible for the management of the college, whether or not formally constituted as a governing body or board of governors.

92   Further and higher education courses

(1)   The responsible body in relation to a course to which this section applies must not discriminate against a person –

(a)   in the arrangements it makes for deciding who is enrolled on the course;

(b)   as to the terms on which it offers to enrol the person on the course;

(c)   by not accepting the person's application for enrolment.

(2)   The responsible body in relation to such a course must not discriminate against a person who is enrolled on the course in the services it provides or offers to provide.

(3)   The responsible body in relation to such a course must not harass a person who –

(a)   seeks enrolment on the course;

(b)   is enrolled on the course;

(c)   is a user of services provided by the body in relation to the course.

(4)   The responsible body in relation to such a course must not victimise a person –

(a)   in the arrangements it makes for deciding who is enrolled on the course;

(b)   as to the terms on which it offers to enrol the person on the course;

(c)   by not accepting the person's application for enrolment.

(5)   The responsible body in relation to such a course must not victimise a person who is enrolled on the course in the services it provides or offers to provide.

(6)   A duty to make reasonable adjustments applies to the responsible body.

(7)   This section applies to –

(a)   a course of further or higher education secured by a responsible body in England or Wales;

(b)   a course of education provided by the governing body of a maintained school under section 80 of the School Standards and Framework Act 1998;

(c)   a course of further education secured by an education authority in Scotland.

(8)   A responsible body is –

(a)   a local authority in England or Wales, for the purposes of subsection (7)(a);

(b)   the governing body of a maintained school, for the purposes of subsection (7)(b);

(c)   an education authority in Scotland, for the purposes of subsection (7)(c).

(9)   In this section –

'course', in relation to further education, includes each component part of a course if there is no requirement imposed on persons registered for a component part of the course to register for another component part of the course;

'enrolment' includes registration for a component part of a course;

'maintained school' has the meaning given in section 20(7) of the School Standards and Framework Act 1998;

'services' means services of any description which are provided wholly or mainly for persons enrolled on a course to which this section applies.

93   Recreational or training facilities

(1) The responsible body in relation to facilities to which this section applies must not discriminate against a person –

(a)   in the arrangements it makes for deciding who is provided with the facilities;
(b)   as to the terms on which it offers to provide the facilities to the person;
(c)   by not accepting the person's application for provision of the facilities.

(2) The responsible body in relation to such facilities must not discriminate against a person who is provided with the facilities in the services it provides or offers to provide.

(3) The responsible body in relation to such facilities must not harass a person who –

(a)   seeks to have the facilities provided;
(b)   is provided with the facilities;
(c)   is a user of services provided by the body in relation to the facilities.

(4) The responsible body in relation to such facilities must not victimise a person –

(a)   in the arrangements it makes for deciding who is provided with the facilities;
(b)   as to the terms on which it offers to provide the facilities to the person;
(c)   by not accepting the person's application for provision of the facilities.

(5) The responsible body in relation to such facilities must not victimise a person who is provided with the facilities in the services it provides or offers to provide.

(6) A duty to make reasonable adjustments applies to the responsible body.

(7) This section applies to –

(a)   facilities secured by a local authority in England under section 507A or 507B of the Education Act 1996;
(b)   facilities secured by a local authority in Wales under section 508 of that Act;
(c)   recreational or training facilities provided by an education authority in Scotland.

(8) A responsible body is –

(a)   a local authority in England, for the purposes of subsection (7)(a);
(b)   a local authority in Wales, for the purposes of subsection (7)(b);
(c)   an education authority in Scotland, for the purposes of subsection (7)(c).

(9) This section does not apply to the protected characteristic of age, so far as relating to persons who have not attained the age of 18.

94   Interpretation and exceptions

(1) This section applies for the purposes of this Chapter.

(2) Nothing in this Chapter applies to anything done in connection with the content of the curriculum.

(3) A reference to a student, in relation to an institution, is a reference to a person for whom education is provided by the institution.

(4) A reference to a university includes a reference to a university college and a college, school or hall of a university.

(5) A reference to an institution within the further or higher education sector is to be construed in accordance with section 91 of the Further and Higher Education Act 1992.

(6) 'Further education' –

(a)   in relation to England and Wales, has the meaning given in section 2 of the Education Act 1996;
(b)   in relation to Scotland, has the meaning given in section 1(3) of the Further and Higher Education (Scotland) Act 1992.

(7) 'Higher education' –

  (a)   in relation to England and Wales, means education provided by means of a course of a description mentioned in Schedule 6 to the Education Reform Act 1988;

  (b)   in relation to Scotland, has the meaning given in section 38 of the Further and Higher Education (Scotland) Act 1992.

(8) 'College of further education' has the meaning given in section 36 of the Further and Higher Education (Scotland) Act 1992.

(9) 'Designated institution' has the meaning given in section 44 of that Act.

(10) 'Local authority' means –

  (a)   in relation to England, an English local authority within the meaning of section 162 of the Education and Inspections Act 2006;

  (b)   in relation to Wales, a Welsh local authority within the meaning of that section.

(11) 'Education authority' has the meaning given by section 135(1) of the Education (Scotland) Act 1980.

(12) Schedule 12 (exceptions) has effect.

CHAPTER 3   GENERAL QUALIFICATIONS BODIES

95   Application of this Chapter

This Chapter does not apply to the protected characteristic of marriage and civil partnership.

96   Qualifications bodies

(1) A qualifications body (A) must not discriminate against a person (B) –

  (a)   in the arrangements A makes for deciding upon whom to confer a relevant qualification;

  (b)   as to the terms on which it is prepared to confer a relevant qualification on B;

  (c)   by not conferring a relevant qualification on B.

(2) A qualifications body (A) must not discriminate against a person (B) upon whom A has conferred a relevant qualification –

  (a)   by withdrawing the qualification from B;

  (b)   by varying the terms on which B holds the qualification;

  (c)   by subjecting B to any other detriment.

(3) A qualifications body must not, in relation to conferment by it of a relevant qualification, harass –

  (a)   a person who holds the qualification, or

  (b)   a person who applies for it.

(4) A qualifications body (A) must not victimise a person (B) –

  (a)   in the arrangements A makes for deciding upon whom to confer a relevant qualification;

  (b)   as to the terms on which it is prepared to confer a relevant qualification on B;

  (c)   by not conferring a relevant qualification on B.

(5) A qualifications body (A) must not victimise a person (B) upon whom A has conferred a relevant qualification –

  (a)   by withdrawing the qualification from B;

  (b)   by varying the terms on which B holds the qualification;

  (c)   by subjecting B to any other detriment.

(6) A duty to make reasonable adjustments applies to a qualifications body.

(7) Subsection (6) does not apply to the body in so far as the appropriate regulator specifies provisions, criteria or practices in relation to which the body –

(a) is not subject to a duty to make reasonable adjustments;

(b) is subject to a duty to make reasonable adjustments, but in relation to which such adjustments as the regulator specifies should not be made.

(8) For the purposes of subsection (7) the appropriate regulator must have regard to –

(a) the need to minimise the extent to which disabled persons are disadvantaged in attaining the qualification because of their disabilities;

(b) the need to secure that the qualification gives a reliable indication of the knowledge, skills and understanding of a person upon whom it is conferred;

(c) the need to maintain public confidence in the qualification.

(9) The appropriate regulator –

(a) must not specify any matter for the purposes of subsection (7) unless it has consulted such persons as it thinks appropriate;

(b) must publish matters so specified (including the date from which they are to have effect) in such manner as is prescribed.

(10) The appropriate regulator is –

(a) in relation to a qualifications body that confers qualifications in England, a person prescribed by a Minister of the Crown;

(b) in relation to a qualifications body that confers qualifications in Wales, a person prescribed by the Welsh Ministers;

(c) in relation to a qualifications body that confers qualifications in Scotland, a person prescribed by the Scottish Ministers.

(11) For the purposes of subsection (10), a qualification is conferred in a part of Great Britain if there are, or may reasonably be expected to be, persons seeking to obtain the qualification who are or will be assessed for those purposes wholly or mainly in that part.

97 Interpretation

(1) This section applies for the purposes of section 96.

(2) A qualifications body is an authority or body which can confer a relevant qualification.

(3) A relevant qualification is an authorisation, qualification, approval or certification of such description as may be prescribed –

(a) in relation to conferments in England, by a Minister of the Crown;

(b) in relation to conferments in Wales, by the Welsh Ministers;

(c) in relation to conferments in Scotland, by the Scottish Ministers.

(4) An authority or body is not a qualifications body in so far as –

(a) it is the responsible body of a school to which section 85 applies,

(b) it is the governing body of an institution to which section 91 applies,

(c) it exercises functions under the Education Acts, or

(d) it exercises functions under the Education (Scotland) Act 1980.

(5) A qualifications body does not include an authority or body of such description, or in such circumstances, as may be prescribed.

(6) A reference to conferring a relevant qualification includes a reference –

(a) to renewing or extending the conferment of a relevant qualification;

(b) to authenticating a relevant qualification conferred by another person.

(7) A reference in section 96(8), (10) or (11) to a qualification is a reference to a relevant qualification.

(8)   Subsection (11) of section 96 applies for the purposes of subsection (3) of this section as it applies for the purposes of subsection (10) of that section.

CHAPTER 4   MISCELLANEOUS

98   Reasonable adjustments

Schedule 13 (reasonable adjustments) has effect.

99   Educational charities and endowments

Schedule 14 (educational charities and endowments) has effect.

PART 7   ASSOCIATIONS

Preliminary

100   Application of this Part

(1)   This Part does not apply to the protected characteristic of marriage and civil partnership.
(2)   This Part does not apply to discrimination, harassment or victimisation –

    (a)   that is prohibited by Part 3 (services and public functions), Part 4 (premises), Part 5 (work) or Part 6 (education), or
    (b)   that would be so prohibited but for an express exception.

Membership, etc.

101   Members and associates

(1)   An association (A) must not discriminate against a person (B) –

    (a)   in the arrangements A makes for deciding who to admit to membership;
    (b)   as to the terms on which A is prepared to admit B to membership;
    (c)   by not accepting B's application for membership.

(2)   An association (A) must not discriminate against a member (B) –

    (a)   in the way A affords B access, or by not affording B access, to a benefit, facility or service;
    (b)   by depriving B of membership;
    (c)   by varying B's terms of membership;
    (d)   by subjecting B to any other detriment.

(3)   An association (A) must not discriminate against an associate (B) –

    (a)   in the way A affords B access, or by not affording B access, to a benefit, facility or service;
    (b)   by depriving B of B's rights as an associate;
    (c)   by varying B's rights as an associate;
    (d)   by subjecting B to any other detriment.

(4)   An association must not harass –

    (a)   a member;
    (b)   a person seeking to become a member;
    (c)   an associate.

(5)   An association (A) must not victimise a person (B) –

    (a)   in the arrangements A makes for deciding who to admit to membership;

(b)   as to the terms on which A is prepared to admit B to membership;

(c)   by not accepting B's application for membership.

(6) An association (A) must not victimise a member (B) –

(a)   in the way A affords B access, or by not affording B access, to a benefit, facility or service;

(b)   by depriving B of membership;

(c)   by varying B's terms of membership;

(d)   by subjecting B to any other detriment.

(7) An association (A) must not victimise an associate (B) –

(a)   in the way A affords B access, or by not affording B access, to a benefit, facility or service;

(b)   by depriving B of B's rights as an associate;

(c)   by varying B's rights as an associate;

(d)   by subjecting B to any other detriment.

102   Guests

(1) An association (A) must not discriminate against a person (B) –

(a)   in the arrangements A makes for deciding who to invite, or who to permit to be invited, as a guest;

(b)   as to the terms on which A is prepared to invite B, or to permit B to be invited, as a guest;

(c)   by not inviting B, or not permitting B to be invited, as a guest.

(2) An association (A) must not discriminate against a guest (B) invited by A or with A's permission (whether express or implied) –

(a)   in the way A affords B access, or by not affording B access, to a benefit, facility or service;

(b)   by subjecting B to any other detriment.

(3) An association must not harass –

(a)   a guest;

(b)   a person seeking to be a guest.

(4) An association (A) must not victimise a person (B) –

(a)   in the arrangements A makes for deciding who to invite, or who to permit to be invited, as a guest;

(b)   as to the terms on which A is prepared to invite B, or to permit B to be invited, as a guest;

(c)   by not inviting B, or not permitting B to be invited, as a guest.

(5) An association (A) must not victimise a guest (B) invited by A or with A's permission (whether express or implied) –

(a)   in the way A affords B access, or by not affording B access, to a benefit, facility or service;

(b)   by subjecting B to any other detriment.

103   Sections 101 and 102: further provision

(1) A duty to make reasonable adjustments applies to an association.

(2) In the application of section 26 for the purposes of section 101(4) or 102(3), neither of the following is a relevant protected characteristic –

(a)   religion or belief;

(b)   sexual orientation.

Special provision for political parties

104   Selection of candidates

(1)   This section applies to an association which is a registered political party.

(2)   A person does not contravene this Part only by acting in accordance with selection arrangements.

(3)   Selection arrangements are arrangements –

    (a)   which the party makes for regulating the selection of its candidates in a relevant election,

    (b)   the purpose of which is to reduce inequality in the party's representation in the body concerned, and

    (c)   which, subject to subsection (7), are a proportionate means of achieving that purpose.

(4)   The reference in subsection (3)(b) to inequality in a party's representation in a body is a reference to inequality between –

    (a)   the number of the party's candidates elected to be members of the body who share a protected characteristic, and

    (b)   the number of the party's candidates so elected who do not share that characteristic.

(5)   For the purposes of subsection (4), persons share the protected characteristic of disability if they are disabled persons (and section 6(3)(b) is accordingly to be ignored).

(6)   Selection arrangements do not include short-listing only such persons as have a particular protected characteristic.

(7)   But subsection (6) does not apply to the protected characteristic of sex; and subsection (3)(c) does not apply to short-listing in reliance on this subsection.

(8)   The following elections are relevant elections –

    (a)   Parliamentary Elections;

    (b)   elections to the European Parliament;

    (c)   elections to the Scottish Parliament;

    (d)   elections to the National Assembly for Wales;

    (e)   local government elections within the meaning of section 191, 203 or 204 of the Representation of the People Act 1983 (excluding elections for the Mayor of London).

105   Time-limited provision

(1)   Section 104(7) and the words ', subject to subsection (7),' in section 104(3)(c) are repealed at the end of 2030 unless an order is made under subsection (2).

(2)   At any time before the end of 2030, a Minister of the Crown may by order provide that subsection (1) is to have effect with the substitution of a later time for that for the time being specified there.

(3)   In section 3 of the Sex Discrimination (Election Candidates) Act 2002 (expiry of that Act), in subsection (1) for '2015' substitute '2030'.

(4)   The substitution made by subsection (3) does not affect the power to substitute a later time by order under section 3 of that Act.

106   Information about diversity in range of candidates, etc.

(1)   This section applies to an association which is a registered political party.

(2)   If the party had candidates at a relevant election, the party must, in accordance with regulations, publish information relating to protected characteristics of persons who come within a description prescribed in the regulations in accordance with subsection (3).

(3) One or more of the following descriptions may be prescribed for the purposes of subsection (2) –

    (a)   successful applicants for nomination as a candidate at the relevant election;
    (b)   unsuccessful applicants for nomination as a candidate at that election;
    (c)   candidates elected at that election;
    (d)   candidates who are not elected at that election.

(4) The duty imposed by subsection (2) applies only in so far as it is possible to publish information in a manner that ensures that no person to whom the information relates can be identified from that information.

(5) The following elections are relevant elections –

    (a)   Parliamentary Elections;
    (b)   elections to the European Parliament;
    (c)   elections to the Scottish Parliament;
    (d)   elections to the National Assembly for Wales.

(6) This section does not apply to the following protected characteristics –

    (a)   marriage and civil partnership;
    (b)   pregnancy and maternity.

(7) The regulations may provide that the information to be published –

    (a)   must (subject to subsection (6)) relate to all protected characteristics or only to such as are prescribed;
    (b)   must include a statement, in respect of each protected characteristic to which the information relates, of the proportion that the number of persons who provided the information to the party bears to the number of persons who were asked to provide it.

(8) Regulations under this section may prescribe –

    (a)   descriptions of information;
    (b)   descriptions of political party to which the duty is to apply;
    (c)   the time at which information is to be published;
    (d)   the form and manner in which information is to be published;
    (e)   the period for which information is to be published.

(9) Provision by virtue of subsection (8)(b) may, in particular, provide that the duty imposed by subsection (2) does not apply to a party which had candidates in fewer constituencies in the election concerned than a prescribed number.

(10) Regulations under this section –

    (a)   may provide that the duty imposed by subsection (2) applies only to such relevant elections as are prescribed;
    (b)   may provide that a by-election or other election to fill a vacancy is not to be treated as a relevant election or is to be so treated only to a prescribed extent;
    (c)   may amend this section so as to provide for the duty imposed by subsection (2) to apply in the case of additional descriptions of election.

(11) Nothing in this section authorises a political party to require a person to provide information to it.

Supplementary

107   Interpretation and exceptions

(1) This section applies for the purposes of this Part.

(2) An 'association' is an association of persons –

    (a)   which has at least 25 members, and

(b)   admission to membership of which is regulated by the association's rules and involves a process of selection.

(3) A Minister of the Crown may by order amend subsection (2)(a) so as to substitute a different number for that for the time being specified there.

(4) It does not matter –

(a)   whether an association is incorporated;

(b)   whether its activities are carried on for profit.

(5) Membership is membership of any description; and a reference to a member is to be construed accordingly.

(6) A person is an 'associate', in relation to an association, if the person –

(a)   is not a member of the association, but

(b)   in accordance with the association's rules, has some or all of the rights as a member as a result of being a member of another association.

(7) A reference to a registered political party is a reference to a party registered in the Great Britain register under Part 2 of the Political Parties, Elections and Referendums Act 2000.

(8) Schedule 15 (reasonable adjustments) has effect.

(9) Schedule 16 (exceptions) has effect.

PART 8   PROHIBITED CONDUCT: ANCILLARY

108   Relationships that have ended

(1) A person (A) must not discriminate against another (B) if –

(a)   the discrimination arises out of and is closely connected to a relationship which used to exist between them, and

(b)   conduct of a description constituting the discrimination would, if it occurred during the relationship, contravene this Act.

(2) A person (A) must not harass another (B) if –

(a)   the harassment arises out of and is closely connected to a relationship which used to exist between them, and

(b)   conduct of a description constituting the harassment would, if it occurred during the relationship, contravene this Act.

(3) It does not matter whether the relationship ends before or after the commencement of this section.

(4) A duty to make reasonable adjustments applies to A in so far as B continues to be placed at a substantial disadvantage as mentioned in section 20.

(5) For the purposes of subsection (4), sections 20, 21 and 22 and the applicable Schedules are to be construed as if the relationship had not ended.

(6) For the purposes of Part 9 (enforcement), a contravention of this section relates to the Part of this Act that would have been contravened if the relationship had not ended.

(7) But conduct is not a contravention of this section in so far as it also amounts to victimisation of B by A.

109   Liability of employers and principals

(1) Anything done by a person (A) in the course of A's employment must be treated as also done by the employer.

(2) Anything done by an agent for a principal, with the authority of the principal, must be treated as also done by the principal.

(3) It does not matter whether that thing is done with the employer's or principal's knowledge or approval.

(4)   In proceedings against A's employer (B) in respect of anything alleged to have been done by A in the course of A's employment it is a defence for B to show that B took all reasonable steps to prevent A –

(a)   from doing that thing, or
(b)   from doing anything of that description.

(5)   This section does not apply to offences under this Act (other than offences under Part 12 (disabled persons: transport)).

110   Liability of employees and agents

(1)   A person (A) contravenes this section if –

(a)   A is an employee or agent,
(b)   A does something which, by virtue of section 109(1) or (2), is treated as having been done by A's employer or principal (as the case may be), and
(c)   the doing of that thing by A amounts to a contravention of this Act by the employer or principal (as the case may be).

(2)   It does not matter whether, in any proceedings, the employer is found not to have contravened this Act by virtue of section 109(4).

(3)   A does not contravene this section if –

(a)   A relies on a statement by the employer or principal that doing that thing is not a contravention of this Act, and
(b)   it is reasonable for A to do so.

(4)   A person (B) commits an offence if B knowingly or recklessly makes a statement mentioned in subsection (3)(a) which is false or misleading in a material respect.

(5)   A person guilty of an offence under subsection (4) is liable on summary conviction to a fine not exceeding level 5 on the standard scale.

(6)   Part 9 (enforcement) applies to a contravention of this section by A as if it were the contravention mentioned in subsection (1)(c).

(7)   The reference in subsection (1)(c) to a contravention of this Act does not include a reference to disability discrimination in contravention of Chapter 1 of Part 6 (schools).

111   Instructing, causing or inducing contraventions

(1)   A person (A) must not instruct another (B) to do in relation to a third person (C) anything which contravenes Part 3, 4, 5, 6 or 7 or section 108(1) or (2) or 112(1) (a basic contravention).

(2)   A person (A) must not cause another (B) to do in relation to a third person (C) anything which is a basic contravention.

(3)   A person (A) must not induce another (B) to do in relation to a third person (C) anything which is a basic contravention.

(4)   For the purposes of subsection (3), inducement may be direct or indirect.

(5)   Proceedings for a contravention of this section may be brought –

(a)   by B, if B is subjected to a detriment as a result of A's conduct;
(b)   by C, if C is subjected to a detriment as a result of A's conduct;
(c)   by the Commission.

(6)   For the purposes of subsection (5), it does not matter whether –

(a)   the basic contravention occurs;
(b)   any other proceedings are, or may be, brought in relation to A's conduct.

(7)   This section does not apply unless the relationship between A and B is such that A is in a position to commit a basic contravention in relation to B.

(8)   A reference in this section to causing or inducing a person to do something includes a reference to attempting to cause or induce the person to do it.

(9)   For the purposes of Part 9 (enforcement), a contravention of this section is to be treated as relating –

    (a)   in a case within subsection (5)(a), to the Part of this Act which, because of the relationship between A and B, A is in a position to contravene in relation to B;

    (b)   in a case within subsection (5)(b), to the Part of this Act which, because of the relationship between B and C, B is in a position to contravene in relation to C.

112   Aiding contraventions

(1)   A person (A) must not knowingly help another (B) to do anything which contravenes Part 3, 4, 5, 6 or 7 or section 108(1) or (2) or 111 (a basic contravention).

(2)   It is not a contravention of subsection (1) if –

    (a)   A relies on a statement by B that the act for which the help is given does not contravene this Act, and

    (b)   it is reasonable for A to do so.

(3)   B commits an offence if B knowingly or recklessly makes a statement mentioned in subsection (2)(a) which is false or misleading in a material respect.

(4)   A person guilty of an offence under subsection (3) is liable on summary conviction to a fine not exceeding level 5 on the standard scale.

(5)   For the purposes of Part 9 (enforcement), a contravention of this section is to be treated as relating to the provision of this Act to which the basic contravention relates.

(6)   The reference in subsection (1) to a basic contravention does not include a reference to disability discrimination in contravention of Chapter 1 of Part 6 (schools).

PART 9   ENFORCEMENT

CHAPTER 1   INTRODUCTORY

113   Proceedings

(1)   Proceedings relating to a contravention of this Act must be brought in accordance with this Part.

(2)   Subsection (1) does not apply to proceedings under Part 1 of the Equality Act 2006.

(3)   Subsection (1) does not prevent –

    (a)   a claim for judicial review;

    (b)   proceedings under the Immigration Acts;

    (c)   proceedings under the Special Immigration Appeals Commission Act 1997;

    (d)   in Scotland, an application to the supervisory jurisdiction of the Court of Session.

(4)   This section is subject to any express provision of this Act conferring jurisdiction on a court or tribunal.

(5)   The reference to a contravention of this Act includes a reference to a breach of an equality clause or rule.

(6)   Chapters 2 and 3 do not apply to proceedings relating to an equality clause or rule except in so far as Chapter 4 provides for that.

(7)   This section does not apply to –

    (a)   proceedings for an offence under this Act;

    (b)   proceedings relating to a penalty under Part 12 (disabled persons: transport).

CHAPTER 2   CIVIL COURTS

114   Jurisdiction

(1)   A county court or, in Scotland, the sheriff has jurisdiction to determine a claim relating to –

    (a)   a contravention of Part 3 (services and public functions);

    (b)   a contravention of Part 4 (premises);

    (c)   a contravention of Part 6 (education);

    (d)   a contravention of Part 7 (associations);

    (e)   a contravention of section 108, 111 or 112 that relates to Part 3, 4, 6 or 7.

(2) Subsection (1)(a) does not apply to a claim within section 115.

(3) Subsection (1)(c) does not apply to a claim within section 116.

(4) Subsection (1)(d) does not apply to a contravention of section 106.

(5) For the purposes of proceedings on a claim within subsection (1)(a) –

    (a)   a decision in proceedings on a claim mentioned in section 115(1) that an act is a contravention of Part 3 is binding;

    (b)   it does not matter whether the act occurs outside the United Kingdom.

(6) The county court or sheriff –

    (a)   must not grant an interim injunction or interdict unless satisfied that no criminal matter would be prejudiced by doing so;

    (b)   must grant an application to stay or sist proceedings under subsection (1) on grounds of prejudice to a criminal matter unless satisfied the matter will not be prejudiced.

(7) In proceedings in England and Wales on a claim within subsection (1), the power under section 63(1) of the County Courts Act 1984 (appointment of assessors) must be exercised unless the judge is satisfied that there are good reasons for not doing so.

(8) In proceedings in Scotland on a claim within subsection (1), the power under rule 44.3 of Schedule 1 to the Sheriff Court (Scotland) Act 1907 (appointment of assessors) must be exercised unless the sheriff is satisfied that there are good reasons for not doing so.

(9) The remuneration of an assessor appointed by virtue of subsection (8) is to be at a rate determined by the Lord President of the Court of Session.

115   Immigration cases

(1) A claim is within this section if it relates to the act of an immigration authority in taking a relevant decision and –

    (a)   the question whether the act is a contravention of Part 3 has been or could be raised on an appeal which is pending, or could be brought, under the immigration provisions, or

    (b)   it has been decided on an appeal under those provisions that the act is not a contravention of Part 3.

(2) The relevant decision is not –

    (a)   subject to challenge in proceedings on a claim within section 114(1)(a), or

    (b)   affected by the decision of a court in such proceedings.

(3) For the purposes of subsection (1)(a) a power to grant permission to appeal out of time must be ignored.

(4) Each of the following is an immigration authority –

    (a)   the Secretary of State;

    (b)   an immigration officer;

    (c)   a person responsible for the grant or refusal of entry clearance (within the meaning of section 33(1) of the Immigration Act 1971).

(5) The immigration provisions are –

    (a)   the Special Immigration Appeals Commission Act 1997, or

    (b)   Part 5 of the Nationality, Immigration and Asylum Act 2002.

(6) A relevant decision is –

(a)   a decision under the Immigration Acts relating to the entitlement of a person to enter or remain in the United Kingdom;

(b)   a decision on an appeal under the immigration provisions relating to a decision within paragraph (a).

(7)   An appeal is pending if it is pending for the purposes of section 104 of the Nationality, Immigration and Asylum Act 2002 or (as the case may be) for the purposes of that section as it is applied by section 2(2)(j) of the Special Immigration Appeals Commission Act 1997.

116   Education cases

(1)   A claim is within this section if it may be made to –

(a)   the First-tier Tribunal in accordance with Part 2 of Schedule 17,

(b)   the Special Educational Needs Tribunal for Wales in accordance with Part 2 of that Schedule, or

(c)   an Additional Support Needs Tribunal for Scotland in accordance with Part 3 of that Schedule.

(2)   A claim is also within this section if it must be made in accordance with appeal arrangements within the meaning of Part 4 of that Schedule.

(3)   Schedule 17 (disabled pupils: enforcement) has effect.

117   National security

(1)   Rules of court may, in relation to proceedings on a claim within section 114, confer power as mentioned in subsections (2) to (4); but a power so conferred is exercisable only if the court thinks it expedient to do so in the interests of national security.

(2)   The rules may confer power to exclude from all or part of the proceedings –

(a)   the claimant or pursuer;

(b)   a representative of the claimant or pursuer;

(c)   an assessor.

(3)   The rules may confer power to permit a claimant, pursuer or representative who has been excluded to make a statement to the court before the commencement of the proceedings, or part of the proceedings, to which the exclusion relates.

(4)   The rules may confer power to take steps to keep secret all or part of the reasons for the court's decision.

(5)   The Attorney General or, in Scotland, the Advocate General for Scotland may appoint a person to represent the interests of a claimant or pursuer in, or in any part of, proceedings to which an exclusion by virtue of subsection (2)(a) or (b) relates.

(6)   A person (P) may be appointed under subsection (5) only if –

(a)   in relation to proceedings in England and Wales, P is a person who, for the purposes of the Legal Services Act 2007, is an authorised person in relation to an activity which constitutes the exercise of a right of audience or the conduct of litigation;

(b)   in relation to proceedings in Scotland, P is an advocate or qualified to practice as a solicitor in Scotland.

(7)   P is not responsible to the person whose interests P is appointed to represent.

118   Time limits

(1)   Proceedings on a claim within section 114 may not be brought after the end of –

(a)   the period of 6 months starting with the date of the act to which the claim relates, or

(b)   such other period as the county court or sheriff thinks just and equitable.

(2) If subsection (3) or (4) applies, subsection (1)(a) has effect as if for '6 months' there were substituted '9 months'.

(3) This subsection applies if –

(a) the claim relates to the act of a qualifying institution, and

(b) a complaint relating to the act is referred under the student complaints scheme before the end of the period of 6 months starting with the date of the act.

(4) This subsection applies if –

(a) the claim relates to a dispute referred for conciliation in pursuance of arrangements under section 27 of the Equality Act 2006, and

(b) subsection (3) does not apply.

(5) If it has been decided under the immigration provisions that the act of an immigration authority in taking a relevant decision is a contravention of Part 3 (services and public functions), subsection (1) has effect as if for paragraph (a) there were substituted –

'(a) the period of 6 months starting with the day after the expiry of the period during which, as a result of section 114(2), proceedings could not be brought in reliance on section 114(1)(a);'.

(6) For the purposes of this section –

(a) conduct extending over a period is to be treated as done at the end of the period;

(b) failure to do something is to be treated as occurring when the person in question decided on it.

(7) In the absence of evidence to the contrary, a person (P) is to be taken to decide on failure to do something –

(a) when P does an act inconsistent with doing it, or

(b) if P does no inconsistent act, on the expiry of the period in which P might reasonably have been expected to do it.

(8) In this section –

'immigration authority', 'immigration provisions' and 'relevant decision' each have the meaning given in section 115;

'qualifying institution' has the meaning given in section 11 of the Higher Education Act 2004;

'the student complaints scheme' means a scheme for the review of qualifying complaints (within the meaning of section 12 of that Act) that is provided by the designated operator (within the meaning of section 13(5)(b) of that Act).

119 Remedies

(1) This section applies if a county court or the sheriff finds that there has been a contravention of a provision referred to in section 114(1).

(2) The county court has power to grant any remedy which could be granted by the High Court –

(a) in proceedings in tort;

(b) on a claim for judicial review.

(3) The sheriff has power to make any order which could be made by the Court of Session –

(a) in proceedings for reparation;

(b) on a petition for judicial review.

(4) An award of damages may include compensation for injured feelings (whether or not it includes compensation on any other basis).

(5) Subsection (6) applies if the county court or sheriff –

(a)   finds that a contravention of a provision referred to in section 114(1) is established by virtue of section 19, but

(b)   is satisfied that the provision, criterion or practice was not applied with the intention of discriminating against the claimant or pursuer.

(6)   The county court or sheriff must not make an award of damages unless it first considers whether to make any other disposal.

(7)   The county court or sheriff must not grant a remedy other than an award of damages or the making of a declaration unless satisfied that no criminal matter would be prejudiced by doing so.

CHAPTER 3   EMPLOYMENT TRIBUNALS

120   Jurisdiction

(1)   An employment tribunal has, subject to section 121, jurisdiction to determine a complaint relating to –

(a)   a contravention of Part 5 (work);

(b)   a contravention of section 108, 111 or 112 that relates to Part 5.

(2)   An employment tribunal has jurisdiction to determine an application by a responsible person (as defined by section 61) for a declaration as to the rights of that person and a worker in relation to a dispute about the effect of a non-discrimination rule.

(3)   An employment tribunal also has jurisdiction to determine an application by the trustees or managers of an occupational pension scheme for a declaration as to their rights and those of a member in relation to a dispute about the effect of a non-discrimination rule.

(4)   An employment tribunal also has jurisdiction to determine a question that –

(a)   relates to a non-discrimination rule, and

(b)   is referred to the tribunal by virtue of section 122.

(5)   In proceedings before an employment tribunal on a complaint relating to a breach of a non-discrimination rule, the employer –

(a)   is to be treated as a party, and

(b)   is accordingly entitled to appear and be heard.

(6)   Nothing in this section affects such jurisdiction as the High Court, a county court, the Court of Session or the sheriff has in relation to a non-discrimination rule.

(7)   Subsection (1)(a) does not apply to a contravention of section 53 in so far as the act complained of may, by virtue of an enactment, be subject to an appeal or proceedings in the nature of an appeal.

(8)   In subsection (1), the references to Part 5 do not include a reference to section 60(1).

121   Armed forces cases

(1)   Section 120(1) does not apply to a complaint relating to an act done when the complainant was serving as a member of the armed forces unless –

(a)   the complainant has made a service complaint about the matter, and

(b)   the complaint has not been withdrawn.

(2)   If the complaint is made under the service complaint procedures, it is to be treated for the purposes of subsection (1)(b) as withdrawn if –

(a)   neither the officer to whom it is made nor a superior officer refers it to the Defence Council, and

(b)   the complainant does not apply for it to be referred to the Defence Council.

(3)   If the complaint is made under the old service redress procedures, it is to be treated for

the purposes of subsection (1)(b) as withdrawn if the complainant does not submit it to the Defence Council under those procedures.

(4) The reference in subsection (3) to the old service redress procedures is a reference to the procedures (other than those relating to the making of a report on a complaint to Her Majesty) referred to in –

   (a)   section 180 of the Army Act 1955,
   (b)   section 180 of the Air Force Act 1955, or
   (c)   section 130 of the Naval Discipline Act 1957.

(5) The making of a complaint to an employment tribunal in reliance on subsection (1) does not affect the continuation of the service complaint procedures or (as the case may be) the old service redress procedures.

122   References by court to tribunal, etc.

(1) If it appears to a court in which proceedings are pending that a claim or counter-claim relating to a non-discrimination rule could more conveniently be determined by an employment tribunal, the court may strike out the claim or counter-claim.

(2) If in proceedings before a court a question arises about a non-discrimination rule, the court may (whether or not on an application by a party to the proceedings) –

   (a)   refer the question, or direct that it be referred by a party to the proceedings, to an employment tribunal for determination, and
   (b)   stay or sist the proceedings in the meantime.

123   Time limits

(1) Proceedings on a complaint within section 120 may not be brought after the end of –

   (a)   the period of 3 months starting with the date of the act to which the complaint relates, or
   (b)   such other period as the employment tribunal thinks just and equitable.

(2) Proceedings may not be brought in reliance on section 121(1) after the end of –

   (a)   the period of 6 months starting with the date of the act to which the proceedings relate, or
   (b)   such other period as the employment tribunal thinks just and equitable.

(3) For the purposes of this section –

   (a)   conduct extending over a period is to be treated as done at the end of the period;
   (b)   failure to do something is to be treated as occurring when the person in question decided on it.

(4) In the absence of evidence to the contrary, a person (P) is to be taken to decide on failure to do something –

   (a)   when P does an act inconsistent with doing it, or
   (b)   if P does no inconsistent act, on the expiry of the period in which P might reasonably have been expected to do it.

124   Remedies: general

(1) This section applies if an employment tribunal finds that there has been a contravention of a provision referred to in section 120(1).

(2) The tribunal may –

   (a)   make a declaration as to the rights of the complainant and the respondent in relation to the matters to which the proceedings relate;
   (b)   order the respondent to pay compensation to the complainant;
   (c)   make an appropriate recommendation.

(3)   An appropriate recommendation is a recommendation that within a specified period the respondent takes specified steps for the purpose of obviating or reducing the adverse effect of any matter to which the proceedings relate –

    (a)   on the complainant;

    (b)   on any other person.

(4)   Subsection (5) applies if the tribunal –

    (a)   finds that a contravention is established by virtue of section 19, but

    (b)   is satisfied that the provision, criterion or practice was not applied with the intention of discriminating against the complainant.

(5)   It must not make an order under subsection (2)(b) unless it first considers whether to act under subsection (2)(a) or (c).

(6)   The amount of compensation which may be awarded under subsection (2)(b) corresponds to the amount which could be awarded by a county court or the sheriff under section 119.

(7)   If a respondent fails, without reasonable excuse, to comply with an appropriate recommendation in so far as it relates to the complainant, the tribunal may –

    (a)   if an order was made under subsection (2)(b), increase the amount of compensation to be paid;

    (b)   if no such order was made, make one.

125   Remedies: national security

(1)   In national security proceedings, an appropriate recommendation (as defined by section 124) must not be made in relation to a person other than the complainant if the recommendation would affect anything done by –

    (a)   the Security Service,

    (b)   the Secret Intelligence Service,

    (c)   the Government Communications Headquarters, or

    (d)   a part of the armed forces which is, in accordance with a requirement of the Secretary of State, assisting the Government Communications Headquarters.

(2)   National security proceedings are –

    (a)   proceedings to which a direction under section 10(3) of the Employment Tribunals Act 1996 (national security) relates;

    (b)   proceedings to which an order under section 10(4) of that Act relates;

    (c)   proceedings (or the part of proceedings) to which a direction pursuant to regulations made under section 10(5) of that Act relates;

    (d)   proceedings (or the part of proceedings) in relation to which an employment tribunal acts pursuant to regulations made under section 10(6) of that Act.

126   Remedies: occupational pension schemes

(1)   This section applies if an employment tribunal finds that there has been a contravention of a provision referred to in section 120(1) in relation to –

    (a)   the terms on which persons become members of an occupational pension scheme, or

    (b)   the terms on which members of an occupational pension scheme are treated.

(2)   In addition to anything which may be done by the tribunal under section 124 the tribunal may also by order declare –

    (a)   if the complaint relates to the terms on which persons become members of a scheme, that the complainant has a right to be admitted to the scheme;

(b)   if the complaint relates to the terms on which members of the scheme are treated, that the complainant has a right to membership of the scheme without discrimination.

(3) The tribunal may not make an order under subsection (2)(b) of section 124 unless –

(a)   the compensation is for injured feelings, or
(b)   the order is made by virtue of subsection (7) of that section.

(4) An order under subsection (2) –

(a)   may make provision as to the terms on which or the capacity in which the claimant is to enjoy the admission or membership;
(b)   may have effect in relation to a period before the order is made.

CHAPTER 4   EQUALITY OF TERMS

127   Jurisdiction

(1) An employment tribunal has, subject to subsection (6), jurisdiction to determine a complaint relating to a breach of an equality clause or rule.
(2) The jurisdiction conferred by subsection (1) includes jurisdiction to determine a complaint arising out of a breach of an equality clause or rule; and a reference in this Chapter to a complaint relating to such a breach is to be read accordingly.
(3) An employment tribunal also has jurisdiction to determine an application by a responsible person for a declaration as to the rights of that person and a worker in relation to a dispute about the effect of an equality clause or rule.
(4) An employment tribunal also has jurisdiction to determine an application by the trustees or managers of an occupational pension scheme for a declaration as to their rights and those of a member in relation to a dispute about the effect of an equality rule.
(5) An employment tribunal also has jurisdiction to determine a question that –

(a)   relates to an equality clause or rule, and
(b)   is referred to the tribunal by virtue of section 128(2).

(6) This section does not apply to a complaint relating to an act done when the complainant was serving as a member of the armed forces unless –

(a)   the complainant has made a service complaint about the matter, and
(b)   the complaint has not been withdrawn.

(7) Subsections (2) to (5) of section 121 apply for the purposes of subsection (6) of this section as they apply for the purposes of subsection (1) of that section.
(8) In proceedings before an employment tribunal on a complaint relating to a breach of an equality rule, the employer –

(a)   is to be treated as a party, and
(b)   is accordingly entitled to appear and be heard.

(9) Nothing in this section affects such jurisdiction as the High Court, a county court, the Court of Session or the sheriff has in relation to an equality clause or rule.

128   References by court to tribunal, etc.

(1) If it appears to a court in which proceedings are pending that a claim or counter-claim relating to an equality clause or rule could more conveniently be determined by an employment tribunal, the court may strike out the claim or counter-claim.
(2) If in proceedings before a court a question arises about an equality clause or rule, the court may (whether or not on an application by a party to the proceedings) –

(a)   refer the question, or direct that it be referred by a party to the proceedings, to an employment tribunal for determination, and

(b)   stay or sist the proceedings in the meantime.

129   Time limits

(1) This section applies to –

(a)   a complaint relating to a breach of an equality clause or rule;
(b)   an application for a declaration referred to in section 127(3) or (4).

(2) Proceedings on the complaint or application may not be brought in an employment tribunal after the end of the qualifying period.

(3) If the complaint or application relates to terms of work other than terms of service in the armed forces, the qualifying period is, in a case mentioned in the first column of the table, the period mentioned in the second column.

Case	Qualifying period
A standard case	The period of 6 months beginning with the last day of the employment or appointment.
A stable work case (but not if it is also a concealment or incapacity case (or both))	The period of 6 months beginning with the day on which the stable working relationship ended.
A concealment case (but not if it is also an incapacity case)	The period of 6 months beginning with the day on which the worker discovered (or could with reasonable diligence have discovered) the qualifying fact.
An incapacity case (but not if it is also a concealment case)	The period of 6 months beginning with the day on which the worker ceased to have the incapacity.
A case which is a concealment case and an incapacity case.	The period of 6 months beginning with the later of the days on which the period would begin if the case were merely a concealment or incapacity case.

(4) If the complaint or application relates to terms of service in the armed forces, the qualifying period is, in a case mentioned in the first column of the table, the period mentioned in the second column.

Case	Qualifying period
A standard case	The period of 9 months beginning with the last day of the period of service during which the complaint arose.
A concealment case (but not if it is also an incapacity case)	The period of 9 months beginning with the day on which the worker discovered (or could with reasonable diligence have discovered) the qualifying fact.
An incapacity case (but not if it is also a concealment case)	The period of 9 months beginning with the day on which the worker ceased to have the incapacity.

Case	Qualifying period
A case which is a concealment case and an incapacity case.	The period of 9 months beginning with the later of the days on which the period would begin if the case were merely a concealment or incapacity case.

130   Section 129: supplementary

(1) This section applies for the purposes of section 129.

(2) A standard case is a case which is not –

    (a)   a stable work case,

    (b)   a concealment case,

    (c)   an incapacity case, or

    (d)   a concealment case and an incapacity case.

(3) A stable work case is a case where the proceedings relate to a period during which there was a stable working relationship between the worker and the responsible person (including any time after the terms of work had expired).

(4) A concealment case in proceedings relating to an equality clause is a case where –

    (a)   the responsible person deliberately concealed a qualifying fact from the worker, and

    (b)   the worker did not discover (or could not with reasonable diligence have discovered) the qualifying fact until after the relevant day.

(5) A concealment case in proceedings relating to an equality rule is a case where –

    (a)   the employer or the trustees or managers of the occupational pension scheme in question deliberately concealed a qualifying fact from the member, and

    (b)   the member did not discover (or could not with reasonable diligence have discovered) the qualifying fact until after the relevant day.

(6) A qualifying fact for the purposes of subsection (4) or (5) is a fact –

    (a)   which is relevant to the complaint, and

    (b)   without knowledge of which the worker or member could not reasonably have been expected to bring the proceedings.

(7) An incapacity case in proceedings relating to an equality clause with respect to terms of work other than terms of service in the armed forces is a case where the worker had an incapacity during the period of 6 months beginning with the later of –

    (a)   the relevant day, or

    (b)   the day on which the worker discovered (or could with reasonable diligence have discovered) the qualifying fact deliberately concealed from the worker by the responsible person.

(8) An incapacity case in proceedings relating to an equality clause with respect to terms of service in the armed forces is a case where the worker had an incapacity during the period of 9 months beginning with the later of –

    (a)   the last day of the period of service during which the complaint arose, or

    (b)   the day on which the worker discovered (or could with reasonable diligence have discovered) the qualifying fact deliberately concealed from the worker by the responsible person.

(9) An incapacity case in proceedings relating to an equality rule is a case where the member

of the occupational pension scheme in question had an incapacity during the period of 6 months beginning with the later of –

(a)   the relevant day, or

(b)   the day on which the member discovered (or could with reasonable diligence have discovered) the qualifying fact deliberately concealed from the member by the employer or the trustees or managers of the scheme.

(10) The relevant day for the purposes of this section is –

(a)   the last day of the employment or appointment, or

(b)   the day on which the stable working relationship between the worker and the responsible person ended.

131   Assessment of whether work is of equal value

(1)   This section applies to proceedings before an employment tribunal on –

(a)   a complaint relating to a breach of an equality clause or rule, or

(b)   a question referred to the tribunal by virtue of section 128(2).

(2)   Where a question arises in the proceedings as to whether one person's work is of equal value to another's, the tribunal may, before determining the question, require a member of the panel of independent experts to prepare a report on the question.

(3)   The tribunal may withdraw a requirement that it makes under subsection (2); and, if it does so, it may –

(a)   request the panel member to provide it with specified documentation;

(b)   make such other requests to that member as are connected with the withdrawal of the requirement.

(4)   If the tribunal requires the preparation of a report under subsection (2) (and does not withdraw the requirement), it must not determine the question unless it has received the report.

(5)   Subsection (6) applies where –

(a)   a question arises in the proceedings as to whether the work of one person (A) is of equal value to the work of another (B), and

(b)   A's work and B's work have been given different values by a job evaluation study.

(6)   The tribunal must determine that A's work is not of equal value to B's work unless it has reasonable grounds for suspecting that the evaluation contained in the study –

(a)   was based on a system that discriminates because of sex, or

(b)   is otherwise unreliable.

(7)   For the purposes of subsection (6)(a), a system discriminates because of sex if a difference (or coincidence) between values that the system sets on different demands is not justifiable regardless of the sex of the person on whom the demands are made.

(8)   A reference to a member of the panel of independent experts is a reference to a person –

(a)   who is for the time being designated as such by the Advisory, Conciliation and Arbitration Service (ACAS) for the purposes of this section, and

(b)   who is neither a member of the Council of ACAS nor one of its officers or members of staff.

(9)   'Job evaluation study' has the meaning given in section 80(5).

132   Remedies in non-pensions cases

(1)   This section applies to proceedings before a court or employment tribunal on a complaint relating to a breach of an equality clause, other than a breach with respect to membership of or rights under an occupational pension scheme.

(2)   If the court or tribunal finds that there has been a breach of the equality clause, it may –

(a)   make a declaration as to the rights of the parties in relation to the matters to which the proceedings relate;

(b)   order an award by way of arrears of pay or damages in relation to the complainant.

(3) The court or tribunal may not order a payment under subsection (2)(b) in respect of a time before the arrears day.

(4) In relation to proceedings in England and Wales, the arrears day is, in a case mentioned in the first column of the table, the day mentioned in the second column.

Case	Arrears day
A standard case	The day falling 6 years before the day on which the proceedings were instituted.
A concealment case or an incapacity case (or a case which is both).	The day on which the breach first occurred.

(5) In relation to proceedings in Scotland, the arrears day is the first day of –

(a)   the period of 5 years ending with the day on which the proceedings were commenced, or

(b)   if the case involves a relevant incapacity, or a relevant fraud or error, the period of 20 years ending with that day.

133   Remedies in pensions cases

(1) This section applies to proceedings before a court or employment tribunal on a complaint relating to –

(a)   a breach of an equality rule, or

(b)   a breach of an equality clause with respect to membership of, or rights under, an occupational pension scheme.

(2) If the court or tribunal finds that there has been a breach as referred to in subsection (1) –

(a)   it may make a declaration as to the rights of the parties in relation to the matters to which the proceedings relate;

(b)   it must not order arrears of benefits or damages or any other amount to be paid to the complainant.

(3) Subsection (2)(b) does not apply if the proceedings are proceedings to which section 134 applies.

(4) If the breach relates to a term on which persons become members of the scheme, the court or tribunal may declare that the complainant is entitled to be admitted to the scheme with effect from a specified date.

(5) A date specified for the purposes of subsection (4) must not be before 8 April 1976.

(6) If the breach relates to a term on which members of the scheme are treated, the court or tribunal may declare that the complainant is, in respect of a specified period, entitled to secure the rights that would have accrued if the breach had not occurred.

(7) A period specified for the purposes of subsection (6) must not begin before 17 May 1990.

(8) If the court or tribunal makes a declaration under subsection (6), the employer must provide such resources to the scheme as are necessary to secure for the complainant (without contribution or further contribution by the complainant or other members) the rights referred to in that subsection.

134   Remedies in claims for arrears brought by pensioner members

(1) This section applies to proceedings before a court or employment tribunal on a

complaint by a pensioner member of an occupational pension scheme relating to a breach of an equality clause or rule with respect to a term on which the member is treated.

(2) If the court or tribunal finds that there has been a breach referred to in subsection (1), it may –

    (a)   make a declaration as to the rights of the complainant and the respondent in relation to the matters to which the proceedings relate;

    (b)   order an award by way of arrears of benefits or damages or of any other amount in relation to the complainant.

(3) The court or tribunal must not order an award under subsection (2)(b) in respect of a time before the arrears day.

(4) If the court or tribunal orders an award under subsection (2)(b), the employer must provide such resources to the scheme as are necessary to secure for the complainant (without contribution or further contribution by the complainant or other members) the amount of the award.

(5) In relation to proceedings in England and Wales, the arrears day is, in a case mentioned in the first column of the table, the day mentioned in the second column.

Case	Arrears day
A standard case	The day falling 6 years before the day on which the proceedings were commenced.
A concealment case or an incapacity case (or a case which is both).	The day on which the breach first occurred.

(6) In relation to proceedings in Scotland, the arrears day is the first day of –

    (a)   the period of 5 years ending with the day on which the proceedings were commenced, or

    (b)   if the case involves a relevant incapacity, or a relevant fraud or error, the period of 20 years ending with that day.

135 Supplementary

(1) This section applies for the purposes of sections 132 to 134.

(2) A standard case is a case which is not –

    (a)   a concealment case,

    (b)   an incapacity case, or

    (c)   a concealment case and an incapacity case.

(3) A concealment case in relation to an equality clause is a case where –

    (a)   the responsible person deliberately concealed a qualifying fact (as defined by section 130) from the worker, and

    (b)   the worker commenced the proceedings before the end of the period of 6 years beginning with the day on which the worker discovered (or could with reasonable diligence have discovered) the qualifying fact.

(4) A concealment case in relation to an equality rule is a case where –

    (a)   the employer or the trustees or managers of the occupational pension scheme in question deliberately concealed a qualifying fact (as defined by section 130) from the member, and

    (b)   the member commenced the proceedings before the end of the period of 6 years beginning with the day on which the member discovered (or could with reasonable diligence have discovered) the qualifying fact.

(5) An incapacity case is a case where the worker or member –

(a) had an incapacity when the breach first occurred, and

(b) commenced the proceedings before the end of the period of 6 years beginning with the day on which the worker or member ceased to have the incapacity.

(6) A case involves a relevant incapacity or a relevant fraud or error if the period of 5 years referred to in section 132(5)(a) is, as a result of subsection (7) below, reckoned as a period of more than 20 years.

(7) For the purposes of the reckoning referred to in subsection (6), no account is to be taken of time when the worker or member –

(a) had an incapacity, or

(b) was induced by a relevant fraud or error to refrain from commencing proceedings (not being a time after the worker or member could with reasonable diligence have discovered the fraud or error).

(8) For the purposes of subsection (7) –

(a) a fraud is relevant in relation to an equality clause if it is a fraud on the part of the responsible person;

(b) an error is relevant in relation to an equality clause if it is induced by the words or conduct of the responsible person;

(c) a fraud is relevant in relation to an equality rule if it is a fraud on the part of the employer or the trustees or managers of the scheme;

(d) an error is relevant in relation to an equality rule if it is induced by the words or conduct of the employer or the trustees or managers of the scheme.

(9) A reference in subsection (8) to the responsible person, the employer or the trustees or managers includes a reference to a person acting on behalf of the person or persons concerned.

(10) In relation to terms of service, a reference in section 132(5) or subsection (3) or (5)(b) of this section to commencing proceedings is to be read as a reference to making a service complaint.

(11) A reference to a pensioner member of a scheme includes a reference to a person who is entitled to the present payment of pension or other benefits derived through a member.

(12) In relation to proceedings before a court –

(a) a reference to a complaint is to be read as a reference to a claim, and

(b) a reference to a complainant is to be read as a reference to a claimant.

CHAPTER 5   MISCELLANEOUS

136   Burden of proof

(1) This section applies to any proceedings relating to a contravention of this Act.

(2) If there are facts from which the court could decide, in the absence of any other explanation, that a person (A) contravened the provision concerned, the court must hold that the contravention occurred.

(3) But subsection (2) does not apply if A shows that A did not contravene the provision.

(4) The reference to a contravention of this Act includes a reference to a breach of an equality clause or rule.

(5) This section does not apply to proceedings for an offence under this Act.

(6) A reference to the court includes a reference to –

(a) an employment tribunal;

(b) the Asylum and Immigration Tribunal;

(c)   the Special Immigration Appeals Commission;
(d)   the First-tier Tribunal;
(e)   the Special Educational Needs Tribunal for Wales;
(f)   an Additional Support Needs Tribunal for Scotland.

137   Previous findings

(1)   A finding in relevant proceedings in respect of an act which has become final is to be treated as conclusive in proceedings under this Act.
(2)   Relevant proceedings are proceedings before a court or employment tribunal under any of the following –

(a)   section 19 or 20 of the Race Relations Act 1968;
(b)   the Equal Pay Act 1970;
(c)   the Sex Discrimination Act 1975;
(d)   the Race Relations Act 1976;
(e)   section 6(4A) of the Sex Discrimination Act 1986;
(f)   the Disability Discrimination Act 1995;
(g)   Part 2 of the Equality Act 2006;
(h)   the Employment Equality (Religion and Belief) Regulations 2003 (S.I. 2003/1660);
(i)   the Employment Equality (Sexual Orientation) Regulations 2003 (S.I. 2003/1661);
(j)   the Employment Equality (Age) Regulations 2006 (S.I. 2006/1031);
(k)   the Equality Act (Sexual Orientation) Regulations 2007 (S.I. 2007/1263).

(3)   A finding becomes final –

(a)   when an appeal against the finding is dismissed, withdrawn or abandoned, or
(b)   when the time for appealing expires without an appeal having been brought.

138   Obtaining information, etc.

(1)   In this section –

(a)   P is a person who thinks that a contravention of this Act has occurred in relation to P;
(b)   R is a person who P thinks has contravened this Act.

(2)   A Minister of the Crown must by order prescribe –

(a)   forms by which P may question R on any matter which is or may be relevant;
(b)   forms by which R may answer questions by P.

(3)   A question by P or an answer by R is admissible as evidence in proceedings under this Act (whether or not the question or answer is contained in a prescribed form).
(4)   A court or tribunal may draw an inference from –

(a)   a failure by R to answer a question by P before the end of the period of 8 weeks beginning with the day on which the question is served;
(b)   an evasive or equivocal answer.

(5)   Subsection (4) does not apply if –

(a)   R reasonably asserts that to have answered differently or at all might have prejudiced a criminal matter;
(b)   R reasonably asserts that to have answered differently or at all would have revealed the reason for not commencing or not continuing criminal proceedings;
(c)   R's answer is of a kind specified for the purposes of this paragraph by order of a Minister of the Crown;

    (d)   R's answer is given in circumstances specified for the purposes of this paragraph by order of a Minister of the Crown;

    (e)   R's failure to answer occurs in circumstances specified for the purposes of this paragraph by order of a Minister of the Crown.

(6)   The reference to a contravention of this Act includes a reference to a breach of an equality clause or rule.

(7)   A Minister of the Crown may by order –

    (a)   prescribe the period within which a question must be served to be admissible under subsection (3);

    (b)   prescribe the manner in which a question by P, or an answer by R, may be served.

(8)   This section –

    (a)   does not affect any other enactment or rule of law relating to interim or preliminary matters in proceedings before a county court, the sheriff or an employment tribunal, and

    (b)   has effect subject to any enactment or rule of law regulating the admissibility of evidence in such proceedings.

139   Interest

(1)   Regulations may make provision –

    (a)   for enabling an employment tribunal to include interest on an amount awarded by it in proceedings under this Act;

    (b)   specifying the manner in which, and the periods and rate by reference to which, the interest is to be determined.

(2)   Regulations may modify the operation of an order made under section 14 of the Employment Tribunals Act 1996 (power to make provision as to interest on awards) in so far as it relates to an award in proceedings under this Act.

140   Conduct giving rise to separate proceedings

(1)   This section applies in relation to conduct which has given rise to two or more separate proceedings under this Act, with at least one being for a contravention of section 111 (instructing, causing or inducing contraventions).

(2)   A court may transfer proceedings to an employment tribunal.

(3)   An employment tribunal may transfer proceedings to a court.

(4)   A court or employment tribunal is to be taken for the purposes of this Part to have jurisdiction to determine a claim or complaint transferred to it under this section; accordingly –

    (a)   a reference to a claim within section 114(1) includes a reference to a claim transferred to a court under this section, and

    (b)   a reference to a complaint within section 120(1) includes a reference to a complaint transferred to an employment tribunal under this section.

(5)   A court or employment tribunal may not make a decision that is inconsistent with an earlier decision in proceedings arising out of the conduct.

(6)   'Court' means –

    (a)   in relation to proceedings in England and Wales, a county court;

    (b)   in relation to proceedings in Scotland, the sheriff.

141   Interpretation, etc.

(1)   This section applies for the purposes of this Part.

(2) A reference to the responsible person, in relation to an equality clause or rule, is to be construed in accordance with Chapter 3 of Part 5.

(3) A reference to a worker is a reference to the person to the terms of whose work the proceedings in question relate; and, for the purposes of proceedings relating to an equality rule or a non-discrimination rule, a reference to a worker includes a reference to a member of the occupational pension scheme in question.

(4) A reference to the terms of a person's work is to be construed in accordance with Chapter 3 of Part 5.

(5) A reference to a member of an occupational pension scheme includes a reference to a prospective member.

(6) In relation to proceedings in England and Wales, a person has an incapacity if the person –

(a) has not attained the age of 18, or
(b) lacks capacity (within the meaning of the Mental Capacity Act 2005).

(7) In relation to proceedings in Scotland, a person has an incapacity if the person –

(a) has not attained the age of 16, or
(b) is incapable (within the meaning of the Adults with Incapacity (Scotland) Act 2000 (asp 4)).

(8) 'Service complaint' means a complaint under section 334 of the Armed Forces Act 2006; and 'service complaint procedures' means the procedures prescribed by regulations under that section (except in so far as relating to references under section 337 of that Act).

(9) 'Criminal matter' means –

(a) an investigation into the commission of an alleged offence;
(b) a decision whether to commence criminal proceedings;
(c) criminal proceedings.

PART 10   CONTRACTS, ETC.

Contracts and other agreements

142   Unenforceable terms

(1) A term of a contract is unenforceable against a person in so far as it constitutes, promotes or provides for treatment of that or another person that is of a description prohibited by this Act.

(2) A relevant non-contractual term is unenforceable against a person in so far as it constitutes, promotes or provides for treatment of that or another person that is of a description prohibited by this Act, in so far as this Act relates to disability.

(3) A relevant non-contractual term is a term which –

(a) is a term of an agreement that is not a contract, and
(b) relates to the provision of an employment service within section 56(2)(a) to (e) or to the provision under a group insurance arrangement of facilities by way of insurance.

(4) A reference in subsection (1) or (2) to treatment of a description prohibited by this Act does not include –

(a) a reference to the inclusion of a term in a contract referred to in section 70(2)(a) or 76(2), or
(b) a reference to the failure to include a term in a contract as referred to in section 70(2)(b).

(5) Subsection (4) does not affect the application of section 148(2) to this section.

143   Removal or modification of unenforceable terms

(1)   A county court or the sheriff may, on an application by a person who has an interest in a contract or other agreement which includes a term that is unenforceable as a result of section 142, make an order for the term to be removed or modified.

(2)   An order under this section must not be made unless every person who would be affected by it –

(a)   has been given notice of the application (except where notice is dispensed with in accordance with rules of court), and

(b)   has been afforded an opportunity to make representations to the county court or sheriff.

(3)   An order under this section may include provision in respect of a period before the making of the order.

144   Contracting out

(1)   A term of a contract is unenforceable by a person in whose favour it would operate in so far as it purports to exclude or limit a provision of or made under this Act.

(2)   A relevant non-contractual term (as defined by section 142) is unenforceable by a person in whose favour it would operate in so far as it purports to exclude or limit a provision of or made under this Act, in so far as the provision relates to disability.

(3)   This section does not apply to a contract which settles a claim within section 114.

(4)   This section does not apply to a contract which settles a complaint within section 120 if the contract –

(a)   is made with the assistance of a conciliation officer, or

(b)   is a qualifying compromise contract.

(5)   A contract within subsection (4) includes a contract which settles a complaint relating to a breach of an equality clause or rule or of a non-discrimination rule.

(6)   A contract within subsection (4) includes an agreement by the parties to a dispute to submit the dispute to arbitration if –

(a)   the dispute is covered by a scheme having effect by virtue of an order under section 212A of the Trade Union and Labour Relations (Consolidation) Act 1992, and

(b)   the agreement is to submit the dispute to arbitration in accordance with the scheme.

Collective agreements and rules of undertakings

145   Void and unenforceable terms

(1)   A term of a collective agreement is void in so far as it constitutes, promotes or provides for treatment of a description prohibited by this Act.

(2)   A rule of an undertaking is unenforceable against a person in so far as it constitutes, promotes or provides for treatment of the person that is of a description prohibited by this Act.

146   Declaration in respect of void term, etc.

(1)   A qualifying person (P) may make a complaint to an employment tribunal that a term is void, or that a rule is unenforceable, as a result of section 145.

(2)   But subsection (1) applies only if –

(a)   the term or rule may in the future have effect in relation to P, and

(b)   where the complaint alleges that the term or rule provides for treatment of a description prohibited by this Act, P may in the future be subjected to treatment that would (if P were subjected to it in present circumstances) be of that description.

(3) If the tribunal finds that the complaint is well-founded, it must make an order declaring that the term is void or the rule is unenforceable.

(4) An order under this section may include provision in respect of a period before the making of the order.

(5) In the case of a complaint about a term of a collective agreement, where the term is one made by or on behalf of a person of a description specified in the first column of the table, a qualifying person is a person of a description specified in the second column.

Description of person who made collective agreement	Qualifying person
Employer	A person who is, or is seeking to be, an employee of that employer
Organisation of employers	A person who is, or is seeking to be, an employee of an employer who is a member of that organisation
Association of organisations of employers	A person who is, or is seeking to be, an employee of an employer who is a member of an organisation in that association

(6) In the case of a complaint about a rule of an undertaking, where the rule is one made by or on behalf of a person of a description specified in the first column of the table, a qualifying person is a person of a description specified in the second column.

Description of person who made rule of undertaking	Qualifying person
Employer	A person who is, or is seeking to be, an employee of that employer
Trade organisation or qualifications body	A person who is, or is seeking to be, a member of the organisation or body
	A person upon whom the body has conferred a relevant qualification
	A person seeking conferment by the body of a relevant qualification

Supplementary

147   Meaning of 'qualifying compromise contract'

(1) This section applies for the purposes of this Part.

(2) A qualifying compromise contract is a contract in relation to which each of the conditions in subsection (3) is met.

(3) Those conditions are that –

(a)   the contract is in writing,

(b)   the contract relates to the particular complaint,

(c)   the complainant has, before entering into the contract, received advice from an independent adviser about its terms and effect (including, in particular, its effect on the complainant's ability to pursue the complaint before an employment tribunal),

(d)   on the date of the giving of the advice, there is in force a contract of insurance, or an indemnity provided for members of a profession or professional body, covering the risk of a claim by the complainant in respect of loss arising from the advice,

(e)   the contract identifies the adviser, and

(f)   the contract states that the conditions in paragraphs (c) and (d) are met.

(4) Each of the following is an independent adviser –

(a)   a qualified lawyer;

(b)   an officer, official, employee or member of an independent trade union certified in writing by the trade union as competent to give advice and as authorised to do so on its behalf;

(c)   a worker at an advice centre (whether as an employee or a volunteer) certified in writing by the centre as competent to give advice and as authorised to do so on its behalf;

(d)   a person of such description as may be specified by order.

(5) Despite subsection (4), none of the following is an independent adviser in relation to a qualifying compromise contract –

(a)   a person who is a party to the contract or the complaint;

(b)   a person who is connected to a person within paragraph (a);

(c)   a person who is employed by a person within paragraph (a) or (b);

(d)   a person who is acting for a person within paragraph (a) or (b) in relation to the contract or the complaint;

(e)   a person within subsection (4)(b) or (c), if the trade union or advice centre is a person within paragraph (a) or (b);

(f)   a person within subsection (4)(c) to whom the complainant makes a payment for the advice.

(6) A 'qualified lawyer', for the purposes of subsection (4)(a), is –

(a)   in relation to England and Wales, a person who, for the purposes of the Legal Services Act 2007, is an authorised person in relation to an activity which constitutes the exercise of a right of audience or the conduct of litigation;

(b)   in relation to Scotland, an advocate (whether in practice as such or employed to give legal advice) or a solicitor who holds a practising certificate.

(7) 'Independent trade union' has the meaning given in section 5 of the Trade Union and Labour Relations (Consolidation) Act 1992.

(8) Two persons are connected for the purposes of subsection (5) if –

(a)   one is a company of which the other (directly or indirectly) has control, or

(b)   both are companies of which a third person (directly or indirectly) has control.

(9) Two persons are also connected for the purposes of subsection (5) in so far as a connection between them gives rise to a conflict of interest in relation to the contract or the complaint.

148   Interpretation

(1) This section applies for the purposes of this Part.

(2) A reference to treatment of a description prohibited by this Act does not include treatment in so far as it is treatment that would contravene –

(a)   Part 1 (public sector duty regarding socio-economic inequalities), or

(b)   Chapter 1 of Part 11 (public sector equality duty).

(3) 'Group insurance arrangement' means an arrangement between an employer and another person for the provision by that other person of facilities by way of insurance to the employer's employees (or a class of those employees).

(4) 'Collective agreement' has the meaning given in section 178 of the Trade Union and Labour Relations (Consolidation) Act 1992.

(5) A rule of an undertaking is a rule within subsection (6) or (7).

(6) A rule within this subsection is a rule made by a trade organisation or a qualifications body for application to –

(a)   its members or prospective members,

(b)   persons on whom it has conferred a relevant qualification, or

(c)   persons seeking conferment by it of a relevant qualification.

(7) A rule within this subsection is a rule made by an employer for application to –

(a)   employees,

(b)   persons who apply for employment, or

(c)   persons the employer considers for employment.

(8) 'Trade organisation', 'qualifications body' and 'relevant qualification' each have the meaning given in Part 5 (work).

PART 11   ADVANCEMENT OF EQUALITY

CHAPTER 1   PUBLIC SECTOR EQUALITY DUTY

149   Public sector equality duty

(1) A public authority must, in the exercise of its functions, have due regard to the need to –

(a)   eliminate discrimination, harassment, victimisation and any other conduct that is prohibited by or under this Act;

(b)   advance equality of opportunity between persons who share a relevant protected characteristic and persons who do not share it;

(c)   foster good relations between persons who share a relevant protected characteristic and persons who do not share it.

(2) A person who is not a public authority but who exercises public functions must, in the exercise of those functions, have due regard to the matters mentioned in subsection (1).

(3) Having due regard to the need to advance equality of opportunity between persons who share a relevant protected characteristic and persons who do not share it involves having due regard, in particular, to the need to –

(a)   remove or minimise disadvantages suffered by persons who share a relevant protected characteristic that are connected to that characteristic;

(b)   take steps to meet the needs of persons who share a relevant protected characteristic that are different from the needs of persons who do not share it;

(c)   encourage persons who share a relevant protected characteristic to participate in public life or in any other activity in which participation by such persons is disproportionately low.

(4) The steps involved in meeting the needs of disabled persons that are different from the needs of persons who are not disabled include, in particular, steps to take account of disabled persons' disabilities.

(5) Having due regard to the need to foster good relations between persons who share a relevant protected characteristic and persons who do not share it involves having due regard, in particular, to the need to –

      (a)   tackle prejudice, and

      (b)   promote understanding.

(6)   Compliance with the duties in this section may involve treating some persons more favourably than others; but that is not to be taken as permitting conduct that would otherwise be prohibited by or under this Act.

(7)   The relevant protected characteristics are –

age;
disability;
gender reassignment;
pregnancy and maternity;
race;
religion or belief;
sex;
sexual orientation.

(8)   A reference to conduct that is prohibited by or under this Act includes a reference to –

      (a)   a breach of an equality clause or rule;

      (b)   a breach of a non-discrimination rule.

(9)   Schedule 18 (exceptions) has effect.

150   Public authorities and public functions

(1)   A public authority is a person who is specified in Schedule 19.

(2)   In that Schedule –

Part 1 specifies public authorities generally;
Part 2 specifies relevant Welsh authorities;
Part 3 specifies relevant Scottish authorities.

(3)   A public authority specified in Schedule 19 is subject to the duty imposed by section 149(1) in relation to the exercise of all of its functions unless subsection (4) applies.

(4)   A public authority specified in that Schedule in respect of certain specified functions is subject to that duty only in respect of the exercise of those functions.

(5)   A public function is a function that is a function of a public nature for the purposes of the Human Rights Act 1998.

151   Power to specify public authorities

(1)   A Minister of the Crown may by order amend Part 1, 2 or 3 of Schedule 19.

(2)   The Welsh Ministers may by order amend Part 2 of Schedule 19.

(3)   The Scottish Ministers may by order amend Part 3 of Schedule 19.

(4)   The power under subsection (1), (2) or (3) may not be exercised so as to –

      (a)   add an entry to Part 1 relating to a relevant Welsh or Scottish authority or a cross-border Welsh or Scottish authority;

      (b)   add an entry to Part 2 relating to a person who is not a relevant Welsh authority;

      (c)   add an entry to Part 3 relating to a person who is not a relevant Scottish authority.

(5)   A Minister of the Crown may by order amend Schedule 19 so as to make provision relating to a cross-border Welsh or Scottish authority.

(6)   On the first exercise of the power under subsection (5) to add an entry relating to a cross-border Welsh or Scottish authority to Schedule 19, a Minister of the Crown must –

      (a)   add a Part 4 to the Schedule for cross-border authorities, and

      (b)   add the cross-border Welsh or Scottish authority to that Part.

(7)   Any subsequent exercise of the power under subsection (5) to add an entry relating to a cross-border Welsh or Scottish authority to Schedule 19 must add that entry to Part 4 of the Schedule.

(8) An order may not be made under this section so as to extend the application of section 149 unless the person making it considers that the extension relates to a person by whom a public function is exercisable.

(9) An order may not be made under this section so as to extend the application of section 149 to –

    (a)   the exercise of a function referred to in paragraph 3 of Schedule 18 (judicial functions, etc);

    (b)   a person listed in paragraph 4(2)(a) to (e) of that Schedule (Parliament, devolved legislatures and General Synod);

    (c)   the exercise of a function listed in paragraph 4(3) of that Schedule (proceedings in Parliament or devolved legislatures).

152   Power to specify public authorities: consultation and consent

(1) Before making an order under a provision specified in the first column of the Table, a Minister of the Crown must consult the person or persons specified in the second column.

Provision	Consultees
Section 151(1)	The Commission
Section 151(1), so far as relating to a relevant Welsh authority	The Welsh Ministers
Section 151(1), so far as relating to a relevant Scottish authority	The Scottish Ministers
Section 151(5)	The Commission
Section 151(5), so far as relating to a cross-border Welsh authority	The Welsh Ministers
Section 151(5), so far as relating to a cross-border Scottish authority	The Scottish Ministers

(2) Before making an order under section 151(2), the Welsh Ministers must –

    (a)   obtain the consent of a Minister of the Crown, and

    (b)   consult the Commission.

(3) Before making an order under section 151(3), the Scottish Ministers must –

    (a)   obtain the consent of a Minister of the Crown, and

    (b)   consult the Commission.

153   Power to impose specific duties

(1) A Minister of the Crown may by regulations impose duties on a public authority specified in Part 1 of Schedule 19 for the purpose of enabling the better performance by the authority of the duty imposed by section 149(1).

(2) The Welsh Ministers may by regulations impose duties on a public authority specified in Part 2 of Schedule 19 for that purpose.

(3) The Scottish Ministers may by regulations impose duties on a public authority specified in Part 3 of Schedule 19 for that purpose.

(4) Before making regulations under this section, the person making them must consult the Commission.

154   Power to impose specific duties: cross-border authorities

(1) If a Minister of the Crown exercises the power in section 151(5) to add an entry for a public authority to Part 4 of Schedule 19, the Minister must include after the entry a letter specified in the first column of the Table in subsection (3).

(2) Where a letter specified in the first column of the Table in subsection (3) is included after an entry for a public authority in Part 4 of Schedule 19, the person specified in the second column of the Table –

  (a) may by regulations impose duties on the authority for the purpose of enabling the better performance by the authority of the duty imposed by section 149(1), subject to such limitations as are specified in that column;

  (b) must in making the regulations comply with the procedural requirement specified in that column.

(3) This is the Table –

Letter	Person by whom regulations may be made and procedural requirements
A	Regulations may be made by a Minister of the Crown in relation to the authority's functions that are not devolved Welsh functions.
	The Minister of the Crown must consult the Welsh Ministers before making the regulations.
	Regulations may be made by the Welsh Ministers in relation to the authority's devolved Welsh functions.
	The Welsh Ministers must consult a Minister of the Crown before making the regulations.
B	Regulations may be made by a Minister of the Crown in relation to the authority's functions that are not devolved Scottish functions.
	The Minister of the Crown must consult the Scottish Ministers before making the regulations.
	Regulations may be made by the Scottish Ministers in relation to the authority's devolved Scottish functions.
	The Scottish Ministers must consult a Minister of the Crown before making the regulations.
C	Regulations may be made by a Minister of the Crown in relation to the authority's functions that are neither devolved Welsh functions nor devolved Scottish functions.
	The Minister of the Crown must consult the Welsh Ministers and the Scottish Ministers before making the regulations.
	Regulations may be made by the Welsh Ministers in relation to the authority's devolved Welsh functions.
	The Welsh Ministers must consult a Minister of the Crown before making the regulations.
	Regulations may be made by the Scottish Ministers in relation to the authority's devolved Scottish functions.
	The Scottish Ministers must consult a Minister of the Crown before making the regulations.

Letter	Person by whom regulations may be made and procedural requirements
D	The regulations may be made by a Minister of the Crown.
	The Minister of the Crown must consult the Welsh Ministers before making the regulations.

(4) Before making regulations under subsection (2), the person making them must consult the Commission.

155   Power to impose specific duties: supplementary

(1) Regulations under section 153 or 154 may require a public authority to consider such matters as may be specified from time to time by –

    (a)   a Minister of the Crown, where the regulations are made by a Minister of the Crown;

    (b)   the Welsh Ministers, where the regulations are made by the Welsh Ministers;

    (c)   the Scottish Ministers, where the regulations are made by the Scottish Ministers.

(2) Regulations under section 153 or 154 may impose duties on a public authority that is a contracting authority within the meaning of the Public Sector Directive in connection with its public procurement functions.

(3) In subsection (2) –

'public procurement functions' means functions the exercise of which is regulated by the Public Sector Directive;

'the Public Sector Directive' means Directive 2004/18/EC of the European Parliament and of the Council of 31 March 2004 on the coordination of procedures for the award of public works contracts, public supply contracts and public service contracts, as amended from time to time.

(4) Subsections (1) and (2) do not affect the generality of section 153 or 154(2)(a).

(5) A duty imposed on a public authority under section 153 or 154 may be modified or removed by regulations made by –

    (a)   a Minister of the Crown, where the original duty was imposed by regulations made by a Minister of the Crown;

    (b)   the Welsh Ministers, where the original duty was imposed by regulations made by the Welsh Ministers;

    (c)   the Scottish Ministers, where the original duty was imposed by regulations made by the Scottish Ministers.

156   Enforcement

A failure in respect of a performance of a duty imposed by or under this Chapter does not confer a cause of action at private law.

157   Interpretation

(1) This section applies for the purposes of this Chapter.

(2) A relevant Welsh authority is a person (other than the Assembly Commission) whose functions –

    (a)   are exercisable only in or as regards Wales, and

    (b)   are wholly or mainly devolved Welsh functions.

(3) A cross-border Welsh authority is a person other than a relevant Welsh authority (or the Assembly Commission) who has any function that –

    (a)   is exercisable in or as regards Wales, and

    (b)   is a devolved Welsh function.

(4) The Assembly Commission has the same meaning as in the Government of Wales Act 2006.

(5) A function is a devolved Welsh function if it relates to –

    (a)   a matter in respect of which functions are exercisable by the Welsh Ministers, the First Minister for Wales or the Counsel General to the Welsh Assembly Government, or

    (b)   a matter within the legislative competence of the National Assembly for Wales.

(6) A relevant Scottish authority is a public body, public office or holder of a public office –

    (a)   which is not a cross-border Scottish authority or the Scottish Parliamentary Corporate Body,

    (b)   whose functions are exercisable only in or as regards Scotland, and

    (c)   at least some of whose functions do not relate to reserved matters.

(7) A cross-border Scottish authority is a cross-border public authority within the meaning given by section 88(5) of the Scotland Act 1998.

(8) A function is a devolved Scottish function if it –

    (a)   is exercisable in or as regards Scotland, and

    (b)   does not relate to reserved matters.

(9) Reserved matters has the same meaning as in the Scotland Act 1998.

CHAPTER 2   POSITIVE ACTION

158   Positive action: general

(1) This section applies if a person (P) reasonably thinks that –

    (a)   persons who share a protected characteristic suffer a disadvantage connected to the characteristic,

    (b)   persons who share a protected characteristic have needs that are different from the needs of persons who do not share it, or

    (c)   participation in an activity by persons who share a protected characteristic is disproportionately low.

(2) This Act does not prohibit P from taking any action which is a proportionate means of achieving the aim of –

    (a)   enabling or encouraging persons who share the protected characteristic to overcome or minimise that disadvantage,

    (b)   meeting those needs, or

    (c)   enabling or encouraging persons who share the protected characteristic to participate in that activity.

(3) Regulations may specify action, or descriptions of action, to which subsection (2) does not apply.

(4) This section does not apply to –

    (a)   action within section 159(3), or

    (b)   anything that is permitted by virtue of section 104.

(5) If section 104(7) is repealed by virtue of section 105, this section will not apply to anything that would have been so permitted but for the repeal.

(6) This section does not enable P to do anything that is prohibited by or under an enactment other than this Act.

159   Positive action: recruitment and promotion

(1) This section applies if a person (P) reasonably thinks that –

(a)   persons who share a protected characteristic suffer a disadvantage connected to the characteristic, or

(b)   participation in an activity by persons who share a protected characteristic is disproportionately low.

(2) Part 5 (work) does not prohibit P from taking action within subsection (3) with the aim of enabling or encouraging persons who share the protected characteristic to –

(a)   overcome or minimise that disadvantage, or

(b)   participate in that activity.

(3) That action is treating a person (A) more favourably in connection with recruitment or promotion than another person (B) because A has the protected characteristic but B does not.

(4) But subsection (2) applies only if –

(a)   A is as qualified as B to be recruited or promoted,

(b)   P does not have a policy of treating persons who share the protected characteristic more favourably in connection with recruitment or promotion than persons who do not share it, and

(c)   taking the action in question is a proportionate means of achieving the aim referred to in subsection (2).

(5) 'Recruitment' means a process for deciding whether to –

(a)   offer employment to a person,

(b)   make contract work available to a contract worker,

(c)   offer a person a position as a partner in a firm or proposed firm,

(d)   offer a person a position as a member of an LLP or proposed LLP,

(e)   offer a person a pupillage or tenancy in barristers' chambers,

(f)   take a person as an advocate's devil or offer a person membership of an advocate's stable,

(g)   offer a person an appointment to a personal office,

(h)   offer a person an appointment to a public office, recommend a person for such an appointment or approve a person's appointment to a public office, or

(i)   offer a person a service for finding employment.

(6) This section does not enable P to do anything that is prohibited by or under an enactment other than this Act.

PART 12   DISABLED PERSONS: TRANSPORT

CHAPTER 1   TAXIS, ETC.

160   Taxi accessibility regulations

(1) The Secretary of State may make regulations (in this Chapter referred to as 'taxi accessibility regulations') for securing that it is possible for disabled persons –

(a)   to get into and out of taxis in safety;

(b)   to do so while in wheelchairs;

(c)   to travel in taxis in safety and reasonable comfort;

(d)   to do so while in wheelchairs.

(2) The regulations may, in particular, require a regulated taxi to conform with provision as to –

(a)   the size of a door opening for the use of passengers;

(b)   the floor area of the passenger compartment;

(c)   the amount of headroom in the passenger compartment;

(d)   the fitting of restraining devices designed to ensure the stability of a wheelchair while the taxi is moving.

(3) The regulations may also –

(a)   require the driver of a regulated taxi which is plying for hire, or which has been hired, to comply with provisions as to the carrying of ramps or other devices designed to facilitate the loading and unloading of wheelchairs;

(b)   require the driver of a regulated taxi in which a disabled person is being carried while in a wheelchair to comply with provisions as to the position in which the wheelchair is to be secured.

(4) The driver of a regulated taxi which is plying for hire or has been hired commits an offence –

(a)   by failing to comply with a requirement of the regulations, or

(b)   if the taxi fails to conform with any provision of the regulations with which it is required to conform.

(5) A person guilty of an offence under subsection (4) is liable on summary conviction to a fine not exceeding level 3 on the standard scale.

(6) In this section –

'passenger compartment' has such meaning as is specified in taxi accessibility regulations;

'regulated taxi' means a taxi to which taxi accessibility regulations are expressed to apply.

161   Control of numbers of licensed taxis: exception

(1) This section applies if –

(a)   an application for a licence in respect of a vehicle is made under section 37 of the Town Police Clauses Act 1847,

(b)   it is possible for a disabled person –

(i)   to get into and out of the vehicle in safety,

(ii)   to travel in the vehicle in safety and reasonable comfort, and

(iii) to do the things mentioned in sub-paragraphs (i) and (ii) while in a wheelchair of a size prescribed by the Secretary of State, and

(c)   the proportion of taxis licensed in respect of the area to which the licence would (if granted) apply that conform to the requirement in paragraph (b) is less than the proportion that is prescribed by the Secretary of State.

(2) Section 16 of the Transport Act 1985 (which modifies the provisions of the Town Police Clauses Act 1847 about hackney carriages to allow a licence to ply for hire to be refused in order to limit the number of licensed carriages) does not apply in relation to the vehicle; and those provisions of the Town Police Clauses Act 1847 are to have effect subject to this section.

(3) In section 16 of the Transport Act 1985, after 'shall' insert '(subject to section 161 of the Equality Act 2010)'.

162   Designated transport facilities

(1) The appropriate authority may by regulations provide for the application of any taxi provision (with or without modification) to –

(a)   vehicles used for the provision of services under a franchise agreement, or

(b)   drivers of such vehicles.

(2) A franchise agreement is a contract entered into by the operator of a designated transport facility for the provision, by the other party to the contract, of hire car services –

(a)   for members of the public using any part of the facility, and
(b)   which involve vehicles entering any part of the facility.

(3) In this section –

'appropriate authority' means –

(a)   in relation to transport facilities in England and Wales, the Secretary of State;
(b)   in relation to transport facilities in Scotland, the Scottish Ministers;

'designated' means designated by order made by the appropriate authority;

'hire car' has such meaning as is prescribed by the appropriate authority;

'operator', in relation to a transport facility, means a person who is concerned with the management or operation of the facility;

'taxi provision' means a provision of –

(a)   this Chapter, or
(b)   regulations made in pursuance of section 20(2A) of the Civic Government (Scotland) Act 1982,

which applies in relation to taxis or drivers of taxis;

'transport facility' means premises which form part of a port, airport, railway station or bus station.

(4) For the purposes of section 2(2) of the European Communities Act 1972 (implementation of EU obligations), the Secretary of State may exercise a power conferred by this section on the Scottish Ministers.

163   Taxi licence conditional on compliance with taxi accessibility regulations

(1) A licence for a taxi to ply for hire must not be granted unless the vehicle conforms with the provisions of taxi accessibility regulations with which a vehicle is required to conform if it is licensed.
(2) Subsection (1) does not apply if a licence is in force in relation to the vehicle at any time during the period of 28 days immediately before the day on which the licence is granted.
(3) The Secretary of State may by order provide for subsection (2) to cease to have effect on a specified date.
(4) The power under subsection (3) may be exercised differently for different areas or localities.

164   Exemption from taxi accessibility regulations

(1) The Secretary of State may by regulations provide for a relevant licensing authority to apply for an order (an 'exemption order') exempting the authority from the requirements of section 163.
(2) Regulations under subsection (1) may, in particular, make provision requiring an authority proposing to apply for an exemption order –

(a)   to carry out such consultation as is specified;
(b)   to publish its proposals in the specified manner;
(c)   before applying for the order, to consider representations made about the proposal;
(d)   to make the application in the specified form.

In this subsection 'specified' means specified in the regulations.

(3) An authority may apply for an exemption order only if it is satisfied –

(a)   that, having regard to the circumstances in its area, it is inappropriate for section 163 to apply, and
(b)   that the application of that section would result in an unacceptable reduction in the number of taxis in its area.

(4) After consulting the Disabled Persons Transport Advisory Committee and such other persons as the Secretary of State thinks appropriate, the Secretary of State may –

    (a)   make an exemption order in the terms of the application for the order;

    (b)   make an exemption order in such other terms as the Secretary of State thinks appropriate;

    (c)   refuse to make an exemption order.

(5) The Secretary of State may by regulations make provision requiring a taxi plying for hire in an area in respect of which an exemption order is in force to conform with provisions of the regulations as to the fitting and use of swivel seats.

(6) Regulations under subsection (5) may make provision corresponding to section 163.

(7) In this section –

'relevant licensing authority' means an authority responsible for licensing taxis in any area of England and Wales other than the area to which the Metropolitan Public Carriage Act 1869 applies;

'swivel seats' has such meaning as is specified in regulations under subsection (5).

165   Passengers in wheelchairs

(1) This section imposes duties on the driver of a designated taxi which has been hired –

    (a)   by or for a disabled person who is in a wheelchair, or

    (b)   by another person who wishes to be accompanied by a disabled person who is in a wheelchair.

(2) This section also imposes duties on the driver of a designated private hire vehicle, if a person within paragraph (a) or (b) of subsection (1) has indicated to the driver that the person wishes to travel in the vehicle.

(3) For the purposes of this section –

    (a)   a taxi or private hire vehicle is 'designated' if it appears on a list maintained under section 167;

    (b)   'the passenger' means the disabled person concerned.

(4) The duties are –

    (a)   to carry the passenger while in the wheelchair;

    (b)   not to make any additional charge for doing so;

    (c)   if the passenger chooses to sit in a passenger seat, to carry the wheelchair;

    (d)   to take such steps as are necessary to ensure that the passenger is carried in safety and reasonable comfort;

    (e)   to give the passenger such mobility assistance as is reasonably required.

(5) Mobility assistance is assistance –

    (a)   to enable the passenger to get into or out of the vehicle;

    (b)   if the passenger wishes to remain in the wheelchair, to enable the passenger to get into and out of the vehicle while in the wheelchair;

    (c)   to load the passenger's luggage into or out of the vehicle;

    (d)   if the passenger does not wish to remain in the wheelchair, to load the wheelchair into or out of the vehicle.

(6) This section does not require the driver –

    (a)   unless the vehicle is of a description prescribed by the Secretary of State, to carry more than one person in a wheelchair, or more than one wheelchair, on any one journey;

    (b)   to carry a person in circumstances in which it would otherwise be lawful for the driver to refuse to carry the person.

(7) A driver of a designated taxi or designated private hire vehicle commits an offence by failing to comply with a duty imposed on the driver by this section.

(8) A person guilty of an offence under subsection (7) is liable on summary conviction to a fine not exceeding level 3 on the standard scale.

(9) It is a defence for a person charged with the offence to show that at the time of the alleged offence –

    (a)   the vehicle conformed to the accessibility requirements which applied to it, but

    (b)   it would not have been possible for the wheelchair to be carried safely in the vehicle.

(10) In this section and sections 166 and 167 'private hire vehicle' means –

    (a)   a vehicle licensed under section 48 of the Local Government (Miscellaneous Provisions) Act 1976;

    (b)   a vehicle licensed under section 7 of the Private Hire Vehicles (London) Act 1998;

    (c)   a vehicle licensed under an equivalent provision of a local enactment;

    (d)   a private hire car licensed under section 10 of the Civic Government (Scotland) Act 1982.

166   Passengers in wheelchairs: exemption certificates

(1) A licensing authority must issue a person with a certificate exempting the person from the duties imposed by section 165 (an 'exemption certificate') if satisfied that it is appropriate to do so –

    (a)   on medical grounds, or

    (b)   on the ground that the person's physical condition makes it impossible or unreasonably difficult for the person to comply with those duties.

(2) An exemption certificate is valid for such period as is specified in the certificate.

(3) The driver of a designated taxi is exempt from the duties imposed by section 165 if –

    (a)   an exemption certificate issued to the driver is in force, and

    (b)   the prescribed notice of the exemption is exhibited on the taxi in the prescribed manner.

(4) The driver of a designated private hire vehicle is exempt from the duties imposed by section 165 if –

    (a)   an exemption certificate issued to the driver is in force, and

    (b)   the prescribed notice of the exemption is exhibited on the vehicle in the prescribed manner.

(5) For the purposes of this section, a taxi or private hire vehicle is 'designated' if it appears on a list maintained under section 167.

(6) In this section and section 167 'licensing authority', in relation to any area, means the authority responsible for licensing taxis or, as the case may be, private hire vehicles in that area.

167   Lists of wheelchair-accessible vehicles

(1) For the purposes of section 165, a licensing authority may maintain a list of vehicles falling within subsection (2).

(2) A vehicle falls within this subsection if –

    (a)   it is either a taxi or a private hire vehicle, and

    (b)   it conforms to such accessibility requirements as the licensing authority thinks fit.

(3) A licensing authority may, if it thinks fit, decide that a vehicle may be included on a list

maintained under this section only if it is being used, or is to be used, by the holder of a special licence under that licence.

(4) In subsection (3) 'special licence' has the meaning given by section 12 of the Transport Act 1985 (use of taxis or hire cars in providing local services).

(5) 'Accessibility requirements' are requirements for securing that it is possible for disabled persons in wheelchairs –

   (a)   to get into and out of vehicles in safety, and
   (b)   to travel in vehicles in safety and reasonable comfort,

   either staying in their wheelchairs or not (depending on which they prefer).

(6) The Secretary of State may issue guidance to licensing authorities as to –

   (a)   the accessibility requirements which they should apply for the purposes of this section;
   (b)   any other aspect of their functions under or by virtue of this section.

(7) A licensing authority which maintains a list under subsection (1) must have regard to any guidance issued under subsection (6).

168   Assistance dogs in taxis

(1) This section imposes duties on the driver of a taxi which has been hired –

   (a)   by or for a disabled person who is accompanied by an assistance dog, or
   (b)   by another person who wishes to be accompanied by a disabled person with an assistance dog.

(2) The driver must –

   (a)   carry the disabled person's dog and allow it to remain with that person;
   (b)   not make any additional charge for doing so.

(3) The driver of a taxi commits an offence by failing to comply with a duty imposed by this section.

(4) A person guilty of an offence under this section is liable on summary conviction to a fine not exceeding level 3 on the standard scale.

169   Assistance dogs in taxis: exemption certificates

(1) A licensing authority must issue a person with a certificate exempting the person from the duties imposed by section 168 (an 'exemption certificate') if satisfied that it is appropriate to do so on medical grounds.

(2) In deciding whether to issue an exemption certificate the authority must have regard, in particular, to the physical characteristics of the taxi which the person drives or those of any kind of taxi in relation to which the person requires the certificate.

(3) An exemption certificate is valid –

   (a)   in respect of a specified taxi or a specified kind of taxi;
   (b)   for such period as is specified in the certificate.

(4) The driver of a taxi is exempt from the duties imposed by section 168 if –

   (a)   an exemption certificate issued to the driver is in force with respect to the taxi, and
   (b)   the prescribed notice of the exemption is exhibited on the taxi in the prescribed manner. The power to make regulations under paragraph (b) is exercisable by the Secretary of State.

(5) In this section 'licensing authority' means –

   (a)   in relation to the area to which the Metropolitan Public Carriage Act 1869 applies, Transport for London;

(b)   in relation to any other area in England and Wales, the authority responsible for licensing taxis in that area.

170   Assistance dogs in private hire vehicles

(1)   The operator of a private hire vehicle commits an offence by failing or refusing to accept a booking for the vehicle –

    (a)   if the booking is requested by or on behalf of a disabled person or a person who wishes to be accompanied by a disabled person, and

    (b)   the reason for the failure or refusal is that the disabled person will be accompanied by an assistance dog.

(2)   The operator commits an offence by making an additional charge for carrying an assistance dog which is accompanying a disabled person.

(3)   The driver of a private hire vehicle commits an offence by failing or refusing to carry out a booking accepted by the operator –

    (a)   if the booking is made by or on behalf of a disabled person or a person who wishes to be accompanied by a disabled person, and

    (b)   the reason for the failure or refusal is that the disabled person is accompanied by an assistance dog.

(4)   A person guilty of an offence under this section is liable on summary conviction to a fine not exceeding level 3 on the standard scale.

(5)   In this section –

'driver' means a person who holds a licence under –

    (a)   section 13 of the Private Hire Vehicles (London) Act 1998 ('the 1998 Act'),

    (b)   section 51 of the Local Government (Miscellaneous Provisions) Act 1976 ('the 1976 Act'), or

'licensing authority', in relation to any area in England and Wales, means the authority responsible for licensing private hire vehicles in that area;

'operator' means a person who holds a licence under –

    (a)   section 3 of the 1998 Act,

    (b)   section 55 of the 1976 Act, or

    (c)   an equivalent provision of a local enactment;

'private hire vehicle' means a vehicle licensed under –

    (a)   section 6 of the 1998 Act,

    (b)   section 48 of the 1976 Act, or

    (c)   an equivalent provision of a local enactment.

171   Assistance dogs in private hire vehicles: exemption certificates

(1)   A licensing authority must issue a driver with a certificate exempting the driver from the offence under section 170(3) (an 'exemption certificate') if satisfied that it is appropriate to do so on medical grounds.

(2)   In deciding whether to issue an exemption certificate the authority must have regard, in particular, to the physical characteristics of the private hire vehicle which the person drives or those of any kind of private hire vehicle in relation to which the person requires the certificate.

(3)   An exemption certificate is valid –

    (a)   in respect of a specified private hire vehicle or a specified kind of private hire vehicle;

    (b)   for such period as is specified in the certificate.

(4)   A driver does not commit an offence under section 170(3) if –

(a)   an exemption certificate issued to the driver is in force with respect to the private hire vehicle, and

(b)   the prescribed notice of the exemption is exhibited on the vehicle in the prescribed manner.

The power to make regulations under paragraph (b) is exercisable by the Secretary of State.

(5) In this section 'driver', 'licensing authority' and 'private hire vehicle' have the same meaning as in section 170.

172   Appeals

(1) A person who is aggrieved by the refusal of a licensing authority in England and Wales to issue an exemption certificate under section 166, 169 or 171 may appeal to a magistrates' court before the end of the period of 28 days beginning with the date of the refusal.

(2) A person who is aggrieved by the refusal of a licensing authority in Scotland to issue an exemption certificate under section 166 may appeal to the sheriff before the end of the period of 28 days beginning with the date of the refusal.

(3) On an appeal under subsection (1) or (2), the magistrates' court or sheriff may direct the licensing authority to issue the exemption certificate to have effect for such period as is specified in the direction.

(4) A person who is aggrieved by the decision of a licensing authority to include a vehicle on a list maintained under section 167 may appeal to a magistrates' court or, in Scotland, the sheriff before the end of the period of 28 days beginning with the date of the inclusion.

173   Interpretation

(1) In this Chapter –

'accessibility requirements' has the meaning given in section 167(5);

'assistance dog' means –

(a)   a dog which has been trained to guide a blind person;

(b)   a dog which has been trained to assist a deaf person;

(c)   a dog which has been trained by a prescribed charity to assist a disabled person who has a disability that consists of epilepsy or otherwise affects the person's mobility, manual dexterity, physical co-ordination or ability to lift, carry or otherwise move everyday objects;

(d)   a dog of a prescribed category which has been trained to assist a disabled person who has a disability (other than one falling within paragraph (c)) of a prescribed kind;

'taxi' –

(a)   means a vehicle which is licensed under section 37 of the Town Police Clauses Act 1847 or section 6 of the Metropolitan Public Carriage Act 1869, and

(b)   in sections 162 and 165 to 167, also includes a taxi licensed under section 10 of the Civic Government (Scotland) Act 1982,

but does not include a vehicle drawn by a horse or other animal;

'taxi accessibility regulations' has the meaning given by section 160(1).

(2) A power to make regulations under paragraph (c) or (d) of the definition of 'assistance dog' in subsection (1) is exercisable by the Secretary of State.

CHAPTER 2   PUBLIC SERVICE VEHICLES

174   PSV accessibility regulations

(1)   The Secretary of State may make regulations (in this Chapter referred to as 'PSV accessibility regulations') for securing that it is possible for disabled persons –

    (a)   to get on to and off regulated public service vehicles in safety and without unreasonable difficulty (and, in the case of disabled persons in wheelchairs, to do so while remaining in their wheelchairs), and

    (b)   to travel in such vehicles in safety and reasonable comfort.

(2)   The regulations may, in particular, make provision as to the construction, use and maintenance of regulated public service vehicles, including provision as to –

    (a)   the fitting of equipment to vehicles;

    (b)   equipment to be carried by vehicles;

    (c)   the design of equipment to be fitted to, or carried by, vehicles;

    (d)   the fitting and use of restraining devices designed to ensure the stability of wheelchairs while vehicles are moving;

    (e)   the position in which wheelchairs are to be secured while vehicles are moving.

(3)   In this section 'public service vehicle' means a vehicle which is –

    (a)   adapted to carry more than 8 passengers, and

    (b)   a public service vehicle for the purposes of the Public Passenger Vehicles Act 1981;

and in this Chapter 'regulated public service vehicle' means a public service vehicle to which PSV accessibility regulations are expressed to apply.

(4)   The regulations may make different provision –

    (a)   as respects different classes or descriptions of vehicle;

    (b)   as respects the same class or description of vehicle in different circumstances.

(5)   The Secretary of State must not make regulations under this section or section 176 or 177 without consulting –

    (a)   the Disabled Persons Transport Advisory Committee, and

    (b)   such other representative organisations as the Secretary of State thinks fit.

175   Offence of contravening PSV accessibility regulations

(1)   A person commits an offence by –

    (a)   contravening a provision of PSV accessibility regulations;

    (b)   using on a road a regulated public service vehicle which does not conform with a provision of the regulations with which it is required to conform;

    (c)   causing or permitting such a regulated public service vehicle to be used on a road.

(2)   A person guilty of an offence under this section is liable on summary conviction to a fine not exceeding level 4 on the standard scale.

(3)   If an offence under this section committed by a body corporate is committed with the consent or connivance of, or is attributable to neglect on the part of, a responsible person, the responsible person as well as the body corporate is guilty of the offence.

(4)   In subsection (3) a responsible person, in relation to a body corporate, is –

    (a)   a director, manager, secretary or similar officer;

    (b)   a person purporting to act in the capacity of a person mentioned in paragraph (a);

    (c)   in the case of a body corporate whose affairs are managed by its members, a member.

(5) If, in Scotland, an offence committed by a partnership or an unincorporated association is committed with the consent or connivance of, or is attributable to neglect on the part of, a partner or person concerned in the management of the association, the partner or person as well as the partnership or association is guilty of the offence.

176   Accessibility certificates

(1) A regulated public service vehicle must not be used on a road unless –

(a)   a vehicle examiner has issued a certificate (an 'accessibility certificate') that such provisions of PSV accessibility regulations as are prescribed are satisfied in respect of the vehicle, or

(b)   an approval certificate has been issued under section 177 in respect of the vehicle.

(2) Regulations may make provision –

(a)   with respect to applications for, and the issue of, accessibility certificates;

(b)   providing for the examination of vehicles in respect of which applications have been made;

(c)   with respect to the issue of copies of accessibility certificates which have been lost or destroyed.

(3) The operator of a regulated public service vehicle commits an offence if the vehicle is used in contravention of this section.

(4) A person guilty of an offence under this section is liable on summary conviction to a fine not exceeding level 4 on the standard scale.

(5) A power to make regulations under this section is exercisable by the Secretary of State.

(6) In this section 'operator' has the same meaning as in the Public Passenger Vehicles Act 1981.

177   Approval certificates

(1) The Secretary of State may approve a vehicle for the purposes of this section if satisfied that such provisions of PSV accessibility regulations as are prescribed for the purposes of section 176 are satisfied in respect of the vehicle.

(2) A vehicle which is so approved is referred to in this section as a 'type vehicle'.

(3) Subsection (4) applies if a declaration in the prescribed form is made by an authorised person that a particular vehicle conforms in design, construction and equipment with a type vehicle.

(4) A vehicle examiner may issue a certificate in the prescribed form (an 'approval certificate') that it conforms to the type vehicle.

(5) Regulations may make provision –

(a)   with respect to applications for, and grants of, approval under subsection (1);

(b)   with respect to applications for, and the issue of, approval certificates;

(c)   providing for the examination of vehicles in respect of which applications have been made;

(d)   with respect to the issue of copies of approval certificates in place of certificates which have been lost or destroyed.

(6) The Secretary of State may at any time withdraw approval of a type vehicle.

(7) If an approval is withdrawn –

(a)   no further approval certificates are to be issued by reference to the type vehicle; but

(b)   an approval certificate issued by reference to the type vehicle before the withdrawal continues to have effect for the purposes of section 176.

(8) A power to make regulations under this section is exercisable by the Secretary of State.

(9)   In subsection (3) 'authorised person' means a person authorised by the Secretary of State for the purposes of that subsection.

178   Special authorisations

(1)   The Secretary of State may by order authorise the use on roads of –

    (a)   a regulated public service vehicle of a class or description specified by the order, or

    (b)   a regulated public service vehicle which is so specified.

(2)   Nothing in sections 174 to 177 prevents the use of a vehicle in accordance with the order.

(3)   The Secretary of State may by order make provision for securing that provisions of PSV accessibility regulations apply to regulated public service vehicles of a description specified by the order, subject to any modifications or exceptions specified by the order.

(4)   An order under subsection (1) or (3) may make the authorisation or provision (as the case may be) subject to such restrictions and conditions as are specified by or under the order.

(5)   Section 207(2) does not require an order under this section that applies only to a specified vehicle, or to vehicles of a specified person, to be made by statutory instrument; but such an order is as capable of being amended or revoked as an order made by statutory instrument.

179   Reviews and appeals

(1)   Subsection (2) applies if the Secretary of State refuses an application for the approval of a vehicle under section 177(1) and, before the end of the prescribed period, the applicant –

    (a)   asks the Secretary of State to review the decision, and

    (b)   pays any fee fixed under section 180.

(2)   The Secretary of State must –

    (a)   review the decision, and

    (b)   in doing so, consider any representations made in writing by the applicant before the end of the prescribed period.

(3)   A person applying for an accessibility certificate or an approval certificate may appeal to the Secretary of State against the refusal of a vehicle examiner to issue the certificate.

(4)   An appeal must be made within the prescribed time and in the prescribed manner.

(5)   Regulations may make provision as to the procedure to be followed in connection with appeals.

(6)   On the determination of an appeal, the Secretary of State may –

    (a)   confirm, vary or reverse the decision appealed against;

    (b)   give directions to the vehicle examiner for giving effect to the Secretary of State's decision.

(7)   A power to make regulations under this section is exercisable by the Secretary of State.

180   Fees

(1)   The Secretary of State may charge such fees, payable at such times, as are prescribed in respect of –

    (a)   applications for, and grants of, approval under section 177(1);

    (b)   applications for, and the issue of, accessibility certificates and approval certificates;

    (c)   copies of such certificates;

    (d)   reviews and appeals under section 179.

(2) Fees received by the Secretary of State must be paid into the Consolidated Fund.

(3) The power to make regulations under subsection (1) is exercisable by the Secretary of State.

(4) The regulations may make provision for the repayment of fees, in whole or in part, in such circumstances as are prescribed.

(5) Before making the regulations the Secretary of State must consult such representative organisations as the Secretary of State thinks fit.

181   Interpretation

In this Chapter –

'accessibility certificate' has the meaning given in section 176(1);

'approval certificate' has the meaning given in section 177(4);

'PSV accessibility regulations' has the meaning given in section 174(1);

'regulated public service vehicle' has the meaning given in section 174(3).

CHAPTER 3   RAIL VEHICLES

182   Rail vehicle accessibility regulations

(1) The Secretary of State may make regulations (in this Chapter referred to as 'rail vehicle accessibility regulations') for securing that it is possible for disabled persons –

(a)   to get on to and off regulated rail vehicles in safety and without unreasonable difficulty;

(b)   to do so while in wheelchairs;

(c)   to travel in such vehicles in safety and reasonable comfort;

(d)   to do so while in wheelchairs.

(2) The regulations may, in particular, make provision as to the construction, use and maintenance of regulated rail vehicles including provision as to –

(a)   the fitting of equipment to vehicles;

(b)   equipment to be carried by vehicles;

(c)   the design of equipment to be fitted to, or carried by, vehicles;

(d)   the use of equipment fitted to, or carried by, vehicles;

(e)   the toilet facilities to be provided in vehicles;

(f)   the location and floor area of the wheelchair accommodation to be provided in vehicles;

(g)   assistance to be given to disabled persons.

(3) The regulations may contain different provision –

(a)   as respects different classes or descriptions of rail vehicle;

(b)   as respects the same class or description of rail vehicle in different circumstances;

(c)   as respects different networks.

(4) In this section –

'network' means any permanent way or other means of guiding or supporting rail vehicles, or any section of it;

'rail vehicle' means a vehicle constructed or adapted to carry passengers on a railway, tramway or prescribed system other than a vehicle used in the provision of a service for the carriage of passengers on the high-speed rail system or the conventional TEN rail system;

'regulated rail vehicle' means a rail vehicle to which provisions of rail vehicle accessibility regulations are expressed to apply.

(5) In subsection (4) –

'conventional TEN rail system' and 'high-speed rail system' have the meaning given in regulation 2(3) of the Railways (Interoperability) Regulations 2006 (S.I. 2006/ 397);

'prescribed system' means a system using a mode of guided transport ('guided transport' having the same meaning as in the Transport and Works Act 1992) that is specified in rail vehicle accessibility regulations;

'railway' and 'tramway' have the same meaning as in the Transport and Works Act 1992.

(6) The Secretary of State must exercise the power to make rail vehicle accessibility regulations so as to secure that on and after 1 January 2020 every rail vehicle is a regulated rail vehicle.

(7) Subsection (6) does not affect subsection (3), section 183(1) or section 207(4)(a).

(8) Before making regulations under subsection (1) or section 183, the Secretary of State must consult –

(a)   the Disabled Persons Transport Advisory Committee, and

(b)   such other representative organisations as the Secretary of State thinks fit.

183   Exemptions from rail vehicle accessibility regulations

(1) The Secretary of State may by order (an 'exemption order') –

(a)   authorise the use for carriage of a regulated rail vehicle even though the vehicle does not conform with the provisions of rail vehicle accessibility regulations with which it is required to conform;

(b)   authorise a regulated rail vehicle to be used for carriage otherwise than in conformity with the provisions of rail vehicle accessibility regulations with which use of the vehicle is required to conform.

(2) Authority under subsection (1)(a) or (b) may be for –

(a)   a regulated rail vehicle that is specified or of a specified description,

(b)   use in specified circumstances of a regulated rail vehicle, or

(c)   use in specified circumstances of a regulated rail vehicle that is specified or of a specified description.

(3) The Secretary of State may by regulations make provision as to exemption orders including, in particular, provision as to –

(a)   the persons by whom applications for exemption orders may be made;

(b)   the form in which applications are to be made;

(c)   information to be supplied in connection with applications;

(d)   the period for which exemption orders are to continue in force;

(e)   the revocation of exemption orders.

(4) After consulting the Disabled Persons Transport Advisory Committee and such other persons as the Secretary of State thinks appropriate, the Secretary of State may –

(a)   make an exemption order in the terms of the application for the order;

(b)   make an exemption order in such other terms as the Secretary of State thinks appropriate;

(c)   refuse to make an exemption order.

(5) The Secretary of State may make an exemption order subject to such conditions and restrictions as are specified.

(6) 'Specified' means specified in an exemption order.

184   Procedure for making exemption orders

(1) A statutory instrument that contains an order under section 183(1), if made without a

draft having been laid before and approved by a resolution of each House of Parliament, is subject to annulment in pursuance of a resolution of either House.

(2) The Secretary of State must consult the Disabled Persons Transport Advisory Committee before deciding which of the parliamentary procedures available under subsection (1) is to be adopted in connection with the making of any particular order under section 183(1).

(3) An order under section 183(1) may be made without a draft of the instrument that contains it having been laid before and approved by a resolution of each House of Parliament only if –

(a)   regulations under subsection (4) are in force; and

(b)   the making of the order without such laying and approval is in accordance with the regulations.

(4) The Secretary of State may by regulations set out the basis on which the Secretary of State, when making an order under section 183(1), will decide which of the parliamentary procedures available under subsection (1) is to be adopted in connection with the making of the order.

(5) Before making regulations under subsection (4), the Secretary of State must consult –

(a)   the Disabled Persons Transport Advisory Committee; and

(b)   such other persons as the Secretary of State considers appropriate.

185   Annual report on exemption orders

(1) After the end of each calendar year the Secretary of State must prepare a report on –

(a)   the exercise in that year of the power to make orders under section 183(1);

(b)   the exercise in that year of the discretion under section 184(1).

(2) A report under subsection (1) must (in particular) contain –

(a)   details of each order made under section 183(1) in the year in question;

(b)   details of consultation carried out under sections 183(4) and 184(2) in connection with orders made in that year under section 183(1).

(3) The Secretary of State must lay before Parliament each report prepared under this section.

186   Rail vehicle accessibility: compliance

(1) Schedule 20 (rail vehicle accessibility: compliance) has effect.

(2) This section and that Schedule are repealed at the end of 2010 if the Schedule is not brought into force (either fully or to any extent) before the end of that year.

187   Interpretation

(1) In this Chapter –

'rail vehicle' and 'regulated rail vehicle' have the meaning given in section 182(4);

'rail vehicle accessibility regulations' has the meaning given in section 182(1).

(2) For the purposes of this Chapter a vehicle is used 'for carriage' if it is used for the carriage of passengers.

CHAPTER 4   SUPPLEMENTARY

188   Forgery, etc.

(1) In this section 'relevant document' means –

(a)   an exemption certificate issued under section 166, 169 or 171;

(b)   a notice of a kind mentioned in section 166(3)(b), 169(4)(b) or 171(4)(b);

    (c)   an accessibility certificate (see section 176);

    (d)   an approval certificate (see section 177).

(2) A person commits an offence if, with intent to deceive, the person –

    (a)   forges, alters or uses a relevant document;

    (b)   lends a relevant document to another person;

    (c)   allows a relevant document to be used by another person;

    (d)   makes or has possession of a document which closely resembles a relevant document.

(3) A person guilty of an offence under subsection (2) is liable –

    (a)   on summary conviction, to a fine not exceeding the statutory maximum;

    (b)   on conviction on indictment, to imprisonment for a term not exceeding 2 years or to a fine or to both.

(4) A person commits an offence by knowingly making a false statement for the purpose of obtaining an accessibility certificate or an approval certificate.

(5) A person guilty of an offence under subsection (4) is liable on summary conviction to a fine not exceeding level 4 on the standard scale.

PART 13   DISABILITY: MISCELLANEOUS

189   Reasonable adjustments

Schedule 21 (reasonable adjustments: supplementary) has effect.

190   Improvements to let dwelling houses

(1) This section applies in relation to a lease of a dwelling house if each of the following applies –

    (a)   the tenancy is not a protected tenancy, a statutory tenancy or a secure tenancy;

    (b)   the tenant or another person occupying or intending to occupy the premises is a disabled person;

    (c)   the disabled person occupies or intends to occupy the premises as that person's only or main home;

    (d)   the tenant is entitled, with the consent of the landlord, to make improvements to the premises;

    (e)   the tenant applies to the landlord for consent to make a relevant improvement.

(2) Where the tenant applies in writing for the consent –

    (a)   if the landlord refuses to give consent, the landlord must give the tenant a written statement of the reason why the consent was withheld;

    (b)   if the landlord neither gives nor refuses to give consent within a reasonable time, consent must be taken to have been unreasonably withheld.

(3) If the landlord gives consent subject to a condition which is unreasonable, the consent must be taken to have been unreasonably withheld.

(4) If the landlord's consent is unreasonably withheld, it must be taken to have been given.

(5) On any question as to whether –

    (a)   consent was unreasonably withheld, or

    (b)   a condition imposed was unreasonable,

it is for the landlord to show that it was not.

(6) If the tenant fails to comply with a reasonable condition imposed by the landlord on the making of a relevant improvement, the failure is to be treated as a breach by the tenant of an obligation of the tenancy.

(7) An improvement to premises is a relevant improvement if, having regard to the disabled person's disability, it is likely to facilitate that person's enjoyment of the premises.

(8) Subsections (2) to (7) apply only in so far as provision of a like nature is not made by the lease.

(9) In this section –

'improvement' means an alteration in or addition to the premises and includes –

(a) an addition to or alteration in the landlord's fittings and fixtures;

(b) an addition or alteration connected with the provision of services to the premises;

(c) the erection of a wireless or television aerial;

(d) carrying out external decoration;

'lease' includes a sub-lease or other tenancy, and 'landlord' and 'tenant' are to be construed accordingly;

'protected tenancy' has the same meaning as in section 1 of the Rent Act 1977;

'statutory tenancy' is to be construed in accordance with section 2 of that Act;

'secure tenancy' has the same meaning as in section 79 of the Housing Act 1985.

PART 14   GENERAL EXCEPTIONS

191   Statutory provisions

Schedule 22 (statutory provisions) has effect.

192   National security

A person does not contravene this Act only by doing, for the purpose of safeguarding national security, anything it is proportionate to do for that purpose.

193   Charities

(1) A person does not contravene this Act only by restricting the provision of benefits to persons who share a protected characteristic if –

(a) the person acts in pursuance of a charitable instrument, and

(b) the provision of the benefits is within subsection (2).

(2) The provision of benefits is within this subsection if it is –

(a) a proportionate means of achieving a legitimate aim, or

(b) for the purpose of preventing or compensating for a disadvantage linked to the protected characteristic.

(3) It is not a contravention of this Act for –

(a) a person who provides supported employment to treat persons who have the same disability or a disability of a prescribed description more favourably than those who do not have that disability or a disability of such a description in providing such employment;

(b) a Minister of the Crown to agree to arrangements for the provision of supported employment which will, or may, have that effect.

(4) If a charitable instrument enables the provision of benefits to persons of a class defined by reference to colour, it has effect for all purposes as if it enabled the provision of such benefits –

(a) to persons of the class which results if the reference to colour is ignored, or

(b) if the original class is defined by reference only to colour, to persons generally.

(5) It is not a contravention of this Act for a charity to require members, or persons wishing

to become members, to make a statement which asserts or implies membership or acceptance of a religion or belief; and for this purpose restricting the access by members to a benefit, facility or service to those who make such a statement is to be treated as imposing such a requirement.

(6) Subsection (5) applies only if –

    (a)   the charity, or an organisation of which it is part, first imposed such a requirement before 18 May 2005, and

    (b)   the charity or organisation has not ceased since that date to impose such a requirement.

(7) It is not a contravention of section 29 for a person, in relation to an activity which is carried on for the purpose of promoting or supporting a charity, to restrict participation in the activity to persons of one sex.

(8) A charity regulator does not contravene this Act only by exercising a function in relation to a charity in a manner which the regulator thinks is expedient in the interests of the charity, having regard to the charitable instrument.

(9) Subsection (1) does not apply to a contravention of –

    (a)   section 39;
    (b)   section 40;
    (c)   section 41;
    (d)   section 55, so far as relating to the provision of vocational training.

(10) Subsection (9) does not apply in relation to disability.

194   Charities: supplementary

(1) This section applies for the purposes of section 193.

(2) That section does not apply to race, so far as relating to colour.

(3) 'Charity' –

    (a)   in relation to England and Wales, has the meaning given by section 1(1) of the Charities Act 2006;

    (b)   in relation to Scotland, means a body entered in the Scottish Charity Register.

(4) 'Charitable instrument' means an instrument establishing or governing a charity (including an instrument made or having effect before the commencement of this section).

(5) The charity regulators are –

    (a)   the Charity Commission for England and Wales;
    (b)   the Scottish Charity Regulator.

(6) Section 107(5) applies to references in subsection (5) of section 193 to members, or persons wishing to become members, of a charity.

(7) 'Supported employment' means facilities provided, or in respect of which payments are made, under section 15 of the Disabled Persons (Employment) Act 1944.

195   Sport

(1) A person does not contravene this Act, so far as relating to sex, only by doing anything in relation to the participation of another as a competitor in a gender-affected activity.

(2) A person does not contravene section 29, 33, 34 or 35, so far as relating to gender reassignment, only by doing anything in relation to the participation of a transsexual person as a competitor in a gender-affected activity if it is necessary to do so to secure in relation to the activity –

    (a)   fair competition, or
    (b)   the safety of competitors.

(3) A gender-affected activity is a sport, game or other activity of a competitive nature in

circumstances in which the physical strength, stamina or physique of average persons of one sex would put them at a disadvantage compared to average persons of the other sex as competitors in events involving the activity.

(4)   In considering whether a sport, game or other activity is gender-affected in relation to children, it is appropriate to take account of the age and stage of development of children who are likely to be competitors.

(5)   A person who does anything to which subsection (6) applies does not contravene this Act only because of the nationality or place of birth of another or because of the length of time the other has been resident in a particular area or place.

(6)   This subsection applies to –

(a)   selecting one or more persons to represent a country, place or area or a related association, in a sport or game or other activity of a competitive nature;

(b)   doing anything in pursuance of the rules of a competition so far as relating to eligibility to compete in a sport or game or other such activity.

196   General

Schedule 23 (general exceptions) has effect.

197   Age

(1)   A Minister of the Crown may by order amend this Act to provide that any of the following does not contravene this Act so far as relating to age –

(a)   specified conduct;

(b)   anything done for a specified purpose;

(c)   anything done in pursuance of arrangements of a specified description.

(2)   Specified conduct is conduct –

(a)   of a specified description,

(b)   carried out in specified circumstances, or

(c)   by or in relation to a person of a specified description.

(3)   An order under this section may –

(a)   confer on a Minister of the Crown or the Treasury a power to issue guidance about the operation of the order (including, in particular, guidance about the steps that may be taken by persons wishing to rely on an exception provided for by the order);

(b)   require the Minister or the Treasury to carry out consultation before issuing guidance under a power conferred by virtue of paragraph (a);

(c)   make provision (including provision to impose a requirement) that refers to guidance issued under a power conferred by virtue of paragraph (a).

(4)   Guidance given by a Minister of the Crown or the Treasury in anticipation of the making of an order under this section is, on the making of the order, to be treated as if it has been issued in accordance with the order.

(5)   For the purposes of satisfying a requirement imposed by virtue of subsection (3)(b), the Minister or the Treasury may rely on consultation carried out before the making of the order that imposes the requirement (including consultation carried out before the commencement of this section).

(6)   Provision by virtue of subsection (3)(c) may, in particular, refer to provisions of the guidance that themselves refer to a document specified in the guidance.

(7)   Guidance issued (or treated as issued) under a power conferred by virtue of subsection (3)(a) comes into force on such day as the person who issues the guidance may by order appoint; and an order under this subsection may include the text of the guidance or of extracts from it.

(8)   This section is not affected by any provision of this Act which makes special provision in relation to age.
(9)   The references to this Act in subsection (1) do not include references to –

    (a)   Part 5 (work);
    (b)   Chapter 2 of Part 6 (further and higher education).

PART 15   FAMILY PROPERTY

198   Abolition of husband's duty to maintain wife

The rule of common law that a husband must maintain his wife is abolished.

199   Abolition of presumption of advancement

(1)   The presumption of advancement (by which, for example, a husband is presumed to be making a gift to his wife if he transfers property to her, or purchases property in her name) is abolished.
(2)   The abolition by subsection (1) of the presumption of advancement does not have effect in relation to –

    (a)   anything done before the commencement of this section, or
    (b)   anything done pursuant to any obligation incurred before the commencement of this section.

200   Amendment of Married Women's Property Act 1964

(1)   In section 1 of the Married Women's Property Act 1964 (money and property derived from housekeeping allowance made by husband to be treated as belonging to husband and wife in equal shares) –

    (a)   for 'the husband for' substitute 'either of them for', and
    (b)   for 'the husband and the wife' substitute 'them'.

(2)   Accordingly, that Act may be cited as the Matrimonial Property Act 1964.
(3)   The amendments made by this section do not have effect in relation to any allowance made before the commencement of this section.

201   Civil partners: housekeeping allowance

(1)   After section 70 of the Civil Partnership Act 2004 insert –

'70A   Money and property derived from housekeeping allowance

Section 1 of the Matrimonial Property Act 1964 (money and property derived from housekeeping allowance to be treated as belonging to husband and wife in equal shares) applies in relation to –

    (a)   money derived from any allowance made by a civil partner for the expenses of the civil partnership home or for similar purposes, and
    (b)   any property acquired out of such money,

as it applies in relation to money derived from any allowance made by a husband or wife for the expenses of the matrimonial home or for similar purposes, and any property acquired out of such money.'

(2)   The amendment made by this section does not have effect in relation to any allowance made before the commencement of this section.

PART 16   GENERAL AND MISCELLANEOUS

Civil partnerships

202   Civil partnerships on religious premises

(1) The Civil Partnership Act 2004 is amended as follows.
(2) Omit section 6(1)(b) and (2) (prohibition on use of religious premises for registration of civil partnership).
(3) In section 6A (power to approve premises for registration of civil partnership), after subsection (2), insert –

'(2A) Regulations under this section may provide that premises approved for the registration of civil partnerships may differ from those premises approved for the registration of civil marriages.

(2B) Provision by virtue of subsection (2)(b) may, in particular, provide that applications for approval of premises may only be made with the consent (whether general or specific) of a person specified, or a person of a description specified, in the provision.

(2C) The power conferred by section 258(2), in its application to the power conferred by this section, includes in particular –

(a) power to make provision in relation to religious premises that differs from provision in relation to other premises;

(b) power to make different provision for different kinds of religious premises.'

(4) In that section, after subsection (3), insert –

'(3A) For the avoidance of doubt, nothing in this Act places an obligation on religious organisations to host civil partnerships if they do not wish to do so.

(3B) 'Civil marriage' means marriage solemnised otherwise than according to the rites of the Church of England or any other religious usages.

(3C) 'Religious premises' means premises which –

(a) are used solely or mainly for religious purposes, or

(b) have been so used and have not subsequently been used solely or mainly for other purposes.'

EU obligations

203   Harmonisation

(1) This section applies if –

(a) there is a Community obligation of the United Kingdom which a Minister of the Crown thinks relates to the subject matter of the Equality Acts,

(b) the obligation is to be implemented by the exercise of the power under section 2(2) of the European Communities Act 1972 (the implementing power), and

(c) the Minister thinks that it is appropriate to make harmonising provision in the Equality Acts.

(2) The Minister may by order make the harmonising provision.
(3) If the Minister proposes to make an order under this section, the Minister must consult persons and organisations the Minister thinks are likely to be affected by the harmonising provision.
(4) If, as a result of the consultation under subsection (3), the Minister thinks it appropriate to change the whole or part of the proposal, the Minister must carry out such further consultation with respect to the changes as the Minister thinks appropriate.
(5) The Equality Acts are the Equality Act 2006 and this Act.

(6) Harmonising provision is provision made in relation to relevant subject matter of the Equality Acts –

    (a)   which corresponds to the implementing provision, or
    (b)   which the Minister thinks is necessary or expedient in consequence of or related to provision made in pursuance of paragraph (a) or the implementing provision.

(7) The implementing provision is provision made or to be made in exercise of the implementing power in relation to so much of the subject matter of the Equality Acts as implements a Community obligation.

(8) Relevant subject matter of the Equality Acts is so much of the subject matter of those Acts as does not implement a Community obligation.

(9) A harmonising provision may amend a provision of the Equality Acts.

(10) The reference to this Act does not include a reference to this section or Schedule 24 or to a provision specified in that Schedule.

(11) A Minister of the Crown must report to Parliament on the exercise of the power under subsection (2) –

    (a)   at the end of the period of 2 years starting on the day this section comes into force;
    (b)   at the end of each succeeding period of 2 years.

204   Harmonisation: procedure

(1) If, after the conclusion of the consultation required under section 203, the Minister thinks it appropriate to proceed with the making of an order under that section, the Minister must lay before Parliament –

    (a)   a draft of a statutory instrument containing the order, together with
    (b)   an explanatory document.

(2) The explanatory document must –

    (a)   introduce and give reasons for the harmonising provision;
    (b)   explain why the Minister thinks that the conditions in subsection (1) of section 203 are satisfied;
    (c)   give details of the consultation carried out under that section;
    (d)   give details of the representations received as a result of the consultation;
    (e)   give details of such changes as were made as a result of the representations.

(3) Where a person making representations in response to the consultation has requested the Minister not to disclose them, the Minister must not disclose them under subsection (2)(d) if, or to the extent that, to do so would (disregarding any connection with proceedings in Parliament) constitute an actionable breach of confidence.

(4) If information in representations made by a person in response to consultation under section 203 relates to another person, the Minister need not disclose the information under subsection (2)(d) if or to the extent that –

    (a)   the Minister thinks that the disclosure of information could adversely affect the interests of that other person, and
    (b)   the Minister has been unable to obtain the consent of that other person to the disclosure.

(5) The Minister may not act under subsection (1) before the end of the period of 12 weeks beginning with the day on which the consultation under section 203(3) begins.

(6) Laying a draft of a statutory instrument in accordance with subsection (1) satisfies the condition as to laying imposed by subsection (8) of section 208, in so far as that subsection applies in relation to orders under section 203.

Application

205   Crown application

(1)   The following provisions of this Act bind the Crown –

  (a)   Part 1 (public sector duty regarding socio-economic inequalities);

  (b)   Part 3 (services and public functions), so far as relating to the exercise of public functions;

  (c)   Chapter 1 of Part 11 (public sector equality duty).

(2)   Part 5 (work) binds the Crown as provided for by that Part.

(3)   The remainder of this Act applies to Crown acts as it applies to acts done by a private person.

(4)   For the purposes of subsection (3), an act is a Crown act if (and only if) it is done –

  (a)   by or on behalf of a member of the executive,

  (b)   by a statutory body acting on behalf of the Crown, or

  (c)   by or on behalf of the holder of a statutory office acting on behalf of the Crown.

(5)   A statutory body or office is a body or office established by an enactment.

(6)   The provisions of Parts 2 to 4 of the Crown Proceedings Act 1947 apply to proceedings against the Crown under this Act as they apply to proceedings in England and Wales which, as a result of section 23 of that Act, are treated for the purposes of Part 2 of that Act as civil proceedings by or against the Crown.

(7)   The provisions of Part 5 of that Act apply to proceedings against the Crown under this Act as they apply to proceedings in Scotland which, as a result of that Part, are treated as civil proceedings by or against the Crown.

(8)   But the proviso to section 44 of that Act (removal of proceedings from the sheriff to the Court of Session) does not apply to proceedings under this Act.

206   Information society services

Schedule 25 (information society services) has effect.

Subordinate legislation

207   Exercise of power

(1)   A power to make an order or regulations under this Act is exercisable by a Minister of the Crown, unless there is express provision to the contrary.

(2)   Orders, regulations or rules under this Act must be made by statutory instrument.

(3)   Subsection (2) does not apply to –

  (a)   a transitional exemption order under Part 1 of Schedule 11,

  (b)   a transitional exemption order under Part 1 of Schedule 12, or

  (c)   an order under paragraph 1(3) of Schedule 14 that does not modify an enactment.

(4)   Orders or regulations under this Act –

  (a)   may make different provision for different purposes;

  (b)   may include consequential, incidental, supplementary, transitional, transitory or saving provision.

(5)   Nothing in section 163(4), 174(4) or 182(3) affects the generality of the power under subsection (4)(a).

(6)   The power under subsection (4)(b), in its application to section 37, 153, 154(2), 155(5), 197 or 216 or to paragraph 7(1) of Schedule 11 or paragraph 1(3) or 2(3) of Schedule 14, includes power to amend an enactment (including, in the case of section 197 or 216, this Act).

(7)   In the case of section 216 (commencement), provision by virtue of subsection (4)(b) may be included in a separate order from the order that provides for the commencement to which the provision relates; and, for that purpose, it does not matter –

    (a)   whether the order providing for the commencement includes provision by virtue of subsection (4)(b);

    (b)   whether the commencement has taken place.

(8)   A statutory instrument containing an Order in Council under section 82 (offshore work) is subject to annulment in pursuance of a resolution of either House of Parliament.

208   Ministers of the Crown, etc.

(1)   This section applies where the power to make an order or regulations under this Act is exercisable by a Minister of the Crown or the Treasury.

(2)   A statutory instrument containing (whether alone or with other provision) an order or regulations that amend this Act or another Act of Parliament, or an Act of the Scottish Parliament or an Act or Measure of the National Assembly for Wales, is subject to the affirmative procedure.

(3)   But a statutory instrument is not subject to the affirmative procedure by virtue of subsection (2) merely because it contains –

    (a)   an order under section 59 (local authority functions);

    (b)   an order under section 151 (power to amend list of public authorities for the purposes of the public sector equality duty) that provides for the omission of an entry where the authority concerned has ceased to exist or the variation of an entry where the authority concerned has changed its name;

    (c)   an order under paragraph 1(3) of Schedule 14 (educational charities and endowments) that modifies an enactment.

(4)   A statutory instrument containing (whether alone or with other provision) an order or regulations mentioned in subsection (5) is subject to the affirmative procedure.

(5)   The orders and regulations referred to in subsection (4) are –

    (a)   regulations under section 30 (services: ships and hovercraft);

    (b)   regulations under section 78 (gender pay gap information);

    (c)   regulations under section 81 (work: ships and hovercraft);

    (d)   an order under section 105 (election candidates: expiry of provision);

    (e)   regulations under section 106 (election candidates: diversity information);

    (f)   regulations under section 153 or 154(2) (public sector equality duty: powers to impose specific duties);

    (g)   regulations under section 184(4) (rail vehicle accessibility: procedure for exemption orders);

    (h)   an order under section 203 (EU obligations: harmonisation);

    (i)   regulations under paragraph 9(3) of Schedule 20 (rail vehicle accessibility: determination of turnover for purposes of penalties).

(6)   A statutory instrument that is not subject to the affirmative procedure by virtue of subsection (2) or (4) is subject to the negative procedure.

(7)   But a statutory instrument is not subject to the negative procedure by virtue of subsection (6) merely because it contains –

    (a)   an order under section 183(1) (rail vehicle accessibility: exemptions);

    (b)   an order under section 216 (commencement) that –

        (i)   does not amend an Act of Parliament, an Act of the Scottish Parliament or an Act or Measure of the National Assembly for Wales, and

        (ii)   is not made in reliance on section 207(7).

(8)   If a statutory instrument is subject to the affirmative procedure, the order or regulations

contained in it must not be made unless a draft of the instrument is laid before and approved by a resolution of each House of Parliament.

(9) If a statutory instrument is subject to the negative procedure, it is subject to annulment in pursuance of a resolution of either House of Parliament.

(10) If a draft of a statutory instrument containing an order or regulations under section 2, 151, 153, 154(2) or 155(5) would, apart from this subsection, be treated for the purposes of the Standing Orders of either House of Parliament as a hybrid instrument, it is to proceed in that House as if it were not a hybrid instrument.

209   The Welsh Ministers

(1) This section applies where the power to make an order or regulations under this Act is exercisable by the Welsh Ministers.

(2) A statutory instrument containing (whether alone or with other provision) an order or regulations mentioned in subsection (3) is subject to the affirmative procedure.

(3) The orders and regulations referred to in subsection (2) are –

    (a)   regulations under section 2 (socio-economic inequalities);

    (b)   an order under section 151 (power to amend list of public authorities for the purposes of the public sector equality duty);

    (c)   regulations under section 153 or 154(2) (public sector equality duty: powers to impose specific duties);

    (d)   regulations under section 155(5) that amend an Act of Parliament or an Act or Measure of the National Assembly for Wales (public sector equality duty: power to modify or remove specific duties).

(4) But a statutory instrument is not subject to the affirmative procedure by virtue of subsection (2) merely because it contains an order under section 151 that provides for –

    (a)   the omission of an entry where the authority concerned has ceased to exist, or

    (b)   the variation of an entry where the authority concerned has changed its name.

(5) A statutory instrument that is not subject to the affirmative procedure by virtue of subsection (2) is subject to the negative procedure.

(6) If a statutory instrument is subject to the affirmative procedure, the order or regulations contained in it must not be made unless a draft of the instrument is laid before and approved by a resolution of the National Assembly for Wales.

(7) If a statutory instrument is subject to the negative procedure, it is subject to annulment in pursuance of a resolution of the National Assembly for Wales.

210   The Scottish Ministers

(1) This section applies where the power to make an order, regulations or rules under this Act is exercisable by the Scottish Ministers.

(2) A statutory instrument containing (whether alone or with other provision) an order or regulations mentioned in subsection (3) is subject to the affirmative procedure.

(3) The orders and regulations referred to in subsection (2) are –

    (a)   regulations under section 2 (socio-economic inequalities);

    (b)   regulations under section 37 (power to make provision about adjustments to common parts in Scotland);

    (c)   an order under section 151 (power to amend list of public authorities for the purposes of the public sector equality duty);

    (d)   regulations under section 153 or 154(2) (public sector equality duty: powers to impose specific duties);

    (e)   regulations under section 155(5) that amend an Act of Parliament or an Act of the Scottish Parliament (public sector equality duty: power to modify or remove specific duties).

(4)   But a statutory instrument is not subject to the affirmative procedure by virtue of subsection (2) merely because it contains an order under section 151 that provides for –

(a)   the omission of an entry where the authority concerned has ceased to exist, or
(b)   the variation of an entry where the authority concerned has changed its name.

(5)   A statutory instrument that is not subject to the affirmative procedure by virtue of subsection (2) is subject to the negative procedure.

(6)   If a statutory instrument is subject to the affirmative procedure, the order or regulations contained in it must not be made unless a draft of the instrument is laid before and approved by a resolution of the Scottish Parliament.

(7)   If a statutory instrument is subject to the negative procedure, it is subject to annulment in pursuance of a resolution of the Scottish Parliament.

Amendments, etc.

211   Amendments, repeals and revocations

(1)   Schedule 26 (amendments) has effect.
(2)   Schedule 27 (repeals and revocations) has effect.

Interpretation

212   General interpretation

(1)   In this Act –

'armed forces' means any of the naval, military or air forces of the Crown;

'the Commission' means the Commission for Equality and Human Rights;

'detriment' does not, subject to subsection (5), include conduct which amounts to harassment;

'the Education Acts' has the meaning given in section 578 of the Education Act 1996;

'employment' and related expressions are (subject to subsection (11)) to be read with section 83;

'enactment' means an enactment contained in –

(a)   an Act of Parliament,
(b)   an Act of the Scottish Parliament,
(c)   an Act or Measure of the National Assembly for Wales, or
(d)   subordinate legislation;

'equality clause' means a sex equality clause or maternity equality clause;

'equality rule' means a sex equality rule or maternity equality rule;

'man' means a male of any age;

'maternity equality clause' has the meaning given in section 73;

'maternity equality rule' has the meaning given in section 75;

'non-discrimination rule' has the meaning given in section 61;

'occupational pension scheme' has the meaning given in section 1 of the Pension Schemes Act 1993;

'parent' has the same meaning as in –

(a)   the Education Act 1996 (in relation to England and Wales);
(b)   the Education (Scotland) Act 1980 (in relation to Scotland);

'prescribed' means prescribed by regulations;

'profession' includes a vocation or occupation;

'sex equality clause' has the meaning given in section 66;

'sex equality rule' has the meaning given in section 67;

'subordinate legislation' means –

(a)   subordinate legislation within the meaning of the Interpretation Act 1978, or

(b)   an instrument made under an Act of the Scottish Parliament or an Act or Measure of the National Assembly for Wales; 'substantial' means more than minor or trivial;

'trade' includes any business;

'woman' means a female of any age.

(2)   A reference (however expressed) to an act includes a reference to an omission.

(3)   A reference (however expressed) to an omission includes (unless there is express provision to the contrary) a reference to –

(a)   a deliberate omission to do something;

(b)   a refusal to do it;

(c)   a failure to do it.

(4)   A reference (however expressed) to providing or affording access to a benefit, facility or service includes a reference to facilitating access to the benefit, facility or service.

(5)   Where this Act disapplies a prohibition on harassment in relation to a specified protected characteristic, the disapplication does not prevent conduct relating to that characteristic from amounting to a detriment for the purposes of discrimination within section 13 because of that characteristic.

(6)   A reference to occupation, in relation to premises, is a reference to lawful occupation.

(7)   The following are members of the executive –

(a)   a Minister of the Crown;

(b)   a government department;

(c)   the Welsh Ministers, the First Minister for Wales or the Counsel General to the Welsh Assembly Government;

(d)   any part of the Scottish Administration.

(8)   A reference to a breach of an equality clause or rule is a reference to a breach of a term modified by, or included by virtue of, an equality clause or rule.

(9)   A reference to a contravention of this Act does not include a reference to a breach of an equality clause or rule, unless there is express provision to the contrary.

(10) 'Member', in relation to an occupational pension scheme, means an active member, a deferred member or a pensioner member (within the meaning, in each case, given by section 124 of the Pensions Act 1995).

(11) 'Employer', 'deferred member', 'pension credit member', 'pensionable service', 'pensioner member' and 'trustees or managers' each have, in relation to an occupational pension scheme, the meaning given by section 124 of the Pensions Act 1995.

(12) A reference to the accrual of rights under an occupational pension scheme is to be construed in accordance with that section.

(13) Nothing in section 28, 32, 84, 90, 95 or 100 is to be regarded as an express exception.

213   References to maternity leave, etc.

(1)   This section applies for the purposes of this Act.

(2)   A reference to a woman on maternity leave is a reference to a woman on –

(a)   compulsory maternity leave,

(b)   ordinary maternity leave, or

(c)   additional maternity leave.

(3)   A reference to a woman on compulsory maternity leave is a reference to a woman absent from work because she satisfies the conditions prescribed for the purposes of section 72(1) of the Employment Rights Act 1996.

(4) A reference to a woman on ordinary maternity leave is a reference to a woman absent from work because she is exercising the right to ordinary maternity leave.
(5) A reference to the right to ordinary maternity leave is a reference to the right conferred by section 71(1) of the Employment Rights Act 1996.
(6) A reference to a woman on additional maternity leave is a reference to a woman absent from work because she is exercising the right to additional maternity leave.
(7) A reference to the right to additional maternity leave is a reference to the right conferred by section 73(1) of the Employment Rights Act 1996.
(8) 'Additional maternity leave period' has the meaning given in section 73(2) of that Act.

214   Index of defined expressions

Schedule 28 lists the places where expressions used in this Act are defined or otherwise explained.

Final provisions

215   Money

There is to be paid out of money provided by Parliament any increase attributable to this Act in the expenses of a Minister of the Crown.

216   Commencement

(1) The following provisions come into force on the day on which this Act is passed –
     (a)   section 186(2) (rail vehicle accessibility: compliance);
     (b)   this Part (except sections 202 (civil partnerships on religious premises), 206 (information society services) and 211 (amendments, etc)).
(2) Part 15 (family property) comes into force on such day as the Lord Chancellor may by order appoint.
(3) The other provisions of this Act come into force on such day as a Minister of the Crown may by order appoint.

217   Extent

(1) This Act forms part of the law of England and Wales.
(2) This Act, apart from section 190 (improvements to let dwelling houses) and Part 15 (family property), forms part of the law of Scotland.
(3) Each of the following also forms part of the law of Northern Ireland –
     (a)   section 82 (offshore work);
     (b)   section 105(3) and (4) (expiry of Sex Discrimination (Election Candidates) Act 2002);
     (c)   section 199 (abolition of presumption of advancement).

218   Short title

This Act may be cited as the Equality Act 2010.

SCHEDULES

SCHEDULE 1   DISABILITY: SUPPLEMENTARY PROVISION

(Section 6)

PART 1   DETERMINATION OF DISABILITY

Impairment

1   Regulations may make provision for a condition of a prescribed description to be, or not to be, an impairment.

Long-term effects

2   (1)   The effect of an impairment is long-term if –

    (a)   it has lasted for at least 12 months,
    (b)   it is likely to last for at least 12 months, or
    (c)   it is likely to last for the rest of the life of the person affected.

  (2)   If an impairment ceases to have a substantial adverse effect on a person's ability to carry out normal day-to-day activities, it is to be treated as continuing to have that effect if that effect is likely to recur.

  (3)   For the purposes of sub-paragraph (2), the likelihood of an effect recurring is to be disregarded in such circumstances as may be prescribed.

  (4)   Regulations may prescribe circumstances in which, despite sub-paragraph (1), an effect is to be treated as being, or as not being, long-term.

Severe disfigurement

3   (1)   An impairment which consists of a severe disfigurement is to be treated as having a substantial adverse effect on the ability of the person concerned to carry out normal day-to-day activities.

  (2)   Regulations may provide that in prescribed circumstances a severe disfigurement is not to be treated as having that effect.

  (3)   The regulations may, in particular, make provision in relation to deliberately acquired disfigurement.

Substantial adverse effects

4   Regulations may make provision for an effect of a prescribed description on the ability of a person to carry out normal day-to-day activities to be treated as being, or as not being, a substantial adverse effect.

Effect of medical treatment

5   (1)   An impairment is to be treated as having a substantial adverse effect on the ability of the person concerned to carry out normal day-to-day activities if –

    (a)   measures are being taken to treat or correct it, and
    (b)   but for that, it would be likely to have that effect.

  (2)   'Measures' includes, in particular, medical treatment and the use of a prosthesis or other aid.

  (3)   Sub-paragraph (1) does not apply –

    (a)   in relation to the impairment of a person's sight, to the extent that the impairment is, in the person's case, correctable by spectacles or contact lenses or in such other ways as may be prescribed;

(b)   in relation to such other impairments as may be prescribed, in such circumstances as are prescribed.

Certain medical conditions

6   (1)   Cancer, HIV infection and multiple sclerosis are each a disability.
     (2)   HIV infection is infection by a virus capable of causing the Acquired Immune Deficiency Syndrome.

Deemed disability

7   (1)   Regulations may provide for persons of prescribed descriptions to be treated as having disabilities.
     (2)   The regulations may prescribe circumstances in which a person who has a disability is to be treated as no longer having the disability.
     (3)   This paragraph does not affect the other provisions of this Schedule.

Progressive conditions

8   (1)   This paragraph applies to a person (P) if –

(a)   P has a progressive condition,
(b)   as a result of that condition P has an impairment which has (or had) an effect on P's ability to carry out normal day-to-day activities, but
(c)   the effect is not (or was not) a substantial adverse effect.

     (2)   P is to be taken to have an impairment which has a substantial adverse effect if the condition is likely to result in P having such an impairment.
     (3)   Regulations may make provision for a condition of a prescribed description to be treated as being, or as not being, progressive.

Past disabilities

9   (1)   A question as to whether a person had a disability at a particular time ('the relevant time') is to be determined, for the purposes of section 6, as if the provisions of, or made under, this Act were in force when the act complained of was done had been in force at the relevant time.
     (2)   The relevant time may be a time before the coming into force of the provision of this Act to which the question relates.

PART 2   GUIDANCE

Preliminary

10   This Part of this Schedule applies in relation to guidance referred to in section 6(5).

Examples

11   The guidance may give examples of –

(a)   effects which it would, or would not, be reasonable, in relation to particular activities, to regard as substantial adverse effects;
(b)   substantial adverse effects which it would, or would not, be reasonable to regard as long-term.

Adjudicating bodies

12   (1)   In determining whether a person is a disabled person, an adjudicating body must take account of such guidance as it thinks is relevant.

(2)   An adjudicating body is –

    (a)   a court;

    (b)   a tribunal;

    (c)   a person (other than a court or tribunal) who may decide a claim relating to a contravention of Part 6 (education).

Representations

13   Before issuing the guidance, the Minister must –

    (a)   publish a draft of it;

    (b)   consider any representations made to the Minister about the draft;

    (c)   make such modifications as the Minister thinks appropriate in the light of the representations.

Parliamentary procedure

14   (1)   If the Minister decides to proceed with proposed guidance, a draft of it must be laid before Parliament.

    (2)   If, before the end of the 40-day period, either House resolves not to approve the draft, the Minister must take no further steps in relation to the proposed guidance.

    (3)   If no such resolution is made before the end of that period, the Minister must issue the guidance in the form of the draft.

    (4)   Sub-paragraph (2) does not prevent a new draft of proposed guidance being laid before Parliament.

    (5)   The 40-day period –

        (a)   begins on the date on which the draft is laid before both Houses (or, if laid before each House on a different date, on the later date);

        (b)   does not include a period during which Parliament is prorogued or dissolved;

        (c)   does not include a period during which both Houses are adjourned for more than 4 days.

Commencement

15   The guidance comes into force on the day appointed by order by the Minister.

Revision and revocation

16   (1)   The Minister may –

    (a)   revise the whole or part of guidance and re-issue it;

    (b)   by order revoke guidance.

    (2)   A reference to guidance includes a reference to guidance which has been revised and re-issued.

SCHEDULE 2   SERVICES AND PUBLIC FUNCTIONS: REASONABLE ADJUSTMENTS

(Section 31)

Preliminary

1   This Schedule applies where a duty to make reasonable adjustments is imposed on A by this Part.

The duty

2   (1)   A must comply with the first, second and third requirements.

(2)   For the purposes of this paragraph, the reference in section 20(3), (4) or (5) to a disabled person is to disabled persons generally.

(3)   Section 20 has effect as if, in subsection (4), for 'to avoid the disadvantage' there were substituted –

'(a)   to avoid the disadvantage, or

(b)   to adopt a reasonable alternative method of providing the service or exercising the function.'

(4)   In relation to each requirement, the relevant matter is the provision of the service, or the exercise of the function, by A.

(5)   Being placed at a substantial disadvantage in relation to the exercise of a function means –

(a)   if a benefit is or may be conferred in the exercise of the function, being placed at a substantial disadvantage in relation to the conferment of the benefit, or

(b)   if a person is or may be subjected to a detriment in the exercise of the function, suffering an unreasonably adverse experience when being subjected to the detriment.

(6)   In relation to the second requirement, a physical feature includes a physical feature brought by or on behalf of A, in the course of providing the service or exercising the function, on to premises other than those that A occupies (as well as including a physical feature in or on premises that A occupies).

(7)   If A is a service-provider, nothing in this paragraph requires A to take a step which would fundamentally alter –

(a)   the nature of the service, or

(b)   the nature of A's trade or profession.

(8)   If A exercises a public function, nothing in this paragraph requires A to take a step which A has no power to take.

Special provision about transport

3   (1)   This paragraph applies where A is concerned with the provision of a service which involves transporting people by land, air or water.

(2)   It is never reasonable for A to have to take a step which would –

(a)   involve the alteration or removal of a physical feature of a vehicle used in providing the service;

(b)   affect whether vehicles are provided;

(c)   affect what vehicles are provided;

(d)   affect what happens in the vehicle while someone is travelling in it.

(3)   But, for the purpose of complying with the first or third requirement, A may not rely on sub-paragraph (2)(b), (c) or (d) if the vehicle concerned is –

(a)   a hire-vehicle designed and constructed for the carriage of passengers, comprising more than 8 seats in addition to the driver's seat and having a maximum mass not exceeding 5 tonnes,

(b)   a hire-vehicle designed and constructed for the carriage of goods and having a maximum mass not exceeding 3.5 tonnes,

(c)   a vehicle licensed under section 48 of the Local Government (Miscellaneous Provisions) Act 1976 or section 7 of the Private Hire Vehicles (London) Act 1998 (or under a provision of a local Act corresponding to either of those provisions),

(d) a private hire car (within the meaning of section 23 of the Civic Government (Scotland) Act 1982),

(e) a public service vehicle (within the meaning given by section 1 of the Public Passenger Vehicles Act 1981),

(f) a vehicle built or adapted to carry passengers on a railway or tramway (within the meaning, in each case, of the Transport and Works Act 1992),

(g) a taxi,

(h) a vehicle deployed to transport the driver and passengers of a vehicle that has broken down or is involved in an accident, or

(i) a vehicle deployed on a system using a mode of guided transport (within the meaning of the Transport and Works Act 1992).

(4) In so far as the second requirement requires A to adopt a reasonable alternative method of providing the service to disabled persons, A may not, for the purpose of complying with the requirement, rely on sub-paragraph (2)(b), (c) or (d) if the vehicle is within sub-paragraph (3)(h).

(5) A may not, for the purpose of complying with the first, second or third requirement rely on sub-paragraph (2) of this paragraph if A provides the service by way of a hire-vehicle built to carry no more than 8 passengers.

(6) For the purposes of sub-paragraph (5) in its application to the second requirement, a part of a vehicle is to be regarded as a physical feature if it requires alteration in order to facilitate the provision of –

(a) hand controls to enable a disabled person to operate braking and accelerator systems in the vehicle, or

(b) facilities for the stowage of a wheelchair.

(7) For the purposes of sub-paragraph (6)(a), fixed seating and in-built electrical systems are not physical features; and for the purposes of sub-paragraph (6)(b), fixed seating is not a physical feature.

(8) In the case of a vehicle within sub-paragraph (3), a relevant device is not an auxiliary aid for the purposes of the third requirement.

(9) A relevant device is a device or structure, or equipment, the installation, operation or maintenance of which would necessitate making a permanent alteration to, or which would have a permanent effect on, the internal or external fabric of the vehicle.

(10) Regulations may amend this paragraph so as to provide for sub-paragraph (2) not to apply, or to apply only so far as is prescribed, in relation to vehicles of a prescribed description.

Interpretation

4 (1) This paragraph applies for the purposes of paragraph 3.

(2) A 'hire-vehicle' is a vehicle hired (by way of a trade) under a hiring agreement to which section 66 of the Road Traffic Offenders Act 1988 applies.

(3) A 'taxi', in England and Wales, is a vehicle –

(a) licensed under section 37 of the Town Police Clauses Act 1847,

(b) licensed under section 6 of the Metropolitan Public Carriage Act 1869, or

(c) drawn by one or more persons or animals.

(4) A 'taxi', in Scotland, is –

(a) a hire car engaged, by arrangements made in a public place between the person to be transported (or a person acting on that person's behalf) and the driver, for a journey starting there and then, or

(b) a vehicle drawn by one or more persons or animals.

SCHEDULE 3   SERVICES AND PUBLIC FUNCTIONS: EXCEPTIONS

(Section 31)

PART 1   CONSTITUTIONAL MATTERS

Parliament

1   (1)   Section 29 does not apply to the exercise of –

(a)   a function of Parliament;
(b)   a function exercisable in connection with proceedings in Parliament.

(2)   Sub-paragraph (1) does not permit anything to be done to or in relation to an individual unless it is done by or in pursuance of a resolution or other deliberation of either House or of a Committee of either House.

Legislation

2   (1)   Section 29 does not apply to preparing, making or considering –

(a)   an Act of Parliament;
(b)   a Bill for an Act of Parliament;
(c)   an Act of the Scottish Parliament;
(d)   a Bill for an Act of the Scottish Parliament;
(e)   an Act of the National Assembly for Wales;
(f)   a Bill for an Act of the National Assembly for Wales.

(2)   Section 29 does not apply to preparing, making, approving or considering –

(a)   a Measure of the National Assembly for Wales;
(b)   a proposed Measure of the National Assembly for Wales.

(3)   Section 29 does not apply to preparing, making, confirming, approving or considering an instrument which is made under an enactment by –

(a)   a Minister of the Crown;
(b)   the Scottish Ministers or a member of the Scottish Executive;
(c)   the Welsh Ministers, the First Minister for Wales or the Counsel General to the Welsh Assembly Government.

(4)   Section 29 does not apply to preparing, making, confirming, approving or considering an instrument to which paragraph 6(a) of Schedule 2 to the Synodical Government Measure 1969 (1969 No. 2) (Measures, Canons, Acts of Synod, orders, etc.) applies.

(5)   Section 29 does not apply to anything done in connection with the preparation, making, consideration, approval or confirmation of an instrument made by –

(a)   Her Majesty in Council;
(b)   the Privy Council.

(6)   Section 29 does not apply to anything done in connection with the imposition of a requirement or condition which comes within Schedule 22 (statutory provisions).

Judicial functions

3   (1)   Section 29 does not apply to –

(a)   a judicial function;
(b)   anything done on behalf of, or on the instructions of, a person exercising a judicial function;

(c)   a decision not to commence or continue criminal proceedings;

(d)   anything done for the purpose of reaching, or in pursuance of, a decision not to commence or continue criminal proceedings.

(2)   A reference in sub-paragraph (1) to a judicial function includes a reference to a judicial function conferred on a person other than a court or tribunal.

Armed forces

4   (1)   Section 29(6), so far as relating to relevant discrimination, does not apply to anything done for the purpose of ensuring the combat effectiveness of the armed forces.

(2)   'Relevant discrimination' is –

(a)   age discrimination;

(b)   disability discrimination;

(c)   gender reassignment discrimination;

(d)   sex discrimination.

Security services, etc.

5   Section 29 does not apply to –

(a)   the Security Service;

(b)   the Secret Intelligence Service;

(c)   the Government Communications Headquarters;

(d)   a part of the armed forces which is, in accordance with a requirement of the Secretary of State, assisting the Government Communications Headquarters.

PART 2   EDUCATION

6   In its application to a local authority in England and Wales, section 29, so far as relating to age discrimination or religious or belief-related discrimination, does not apply to –

(a)   the exercise of the authority's functions under section 14 of the Education Act 1996 (provision of schools);

(b)   the exercise of its function under section 13 of that Act in so far as it relates to a function of its under section 14 of that Act.

7   In its application to an education authority, section 29, so far as relating to age discrimination or religious or belief-related discrimination, does not apply to –

(a)   the exercise of the authority's functions under section 17 of the Education (Scotland) Act 1980 (provision of schools);

(b)   the exercise of its functions under section 1 of that Act, section 2 of the Standards in Scotland's Schools etc. Act 2000 (asp 6) or section 4 or 5 of the Education (Additional Support for Learning) (Scotland) Act 2004 (asp 4) (general responsibility for education) in so far as it relates to a matter specified in paragraph (a);

(c)   the exercise of its functions under subsection (1) of section 50 of the Education (Scotland) Act 1980 (education of pupils in exceptional circumstances) in so far as it consists of making arrangements of the description referred to in subsection (2) of that section.

8   (1)   In its application to a local authority in England and Wales or an education authority, section 29, so far as relating to sex discrimination, does not apply to the exercise of the authority's functions in relation to the establishment of a school.

(2)   But nothing in sub-paragraph (1) is to be taken as disapplying section 29 in

relation to the exercise of the authority's functions under section 14 of the Education Act 1996 or section 17 of the Education (Scotland) Act 1982.

9   Section 29, so far as relating to age discrimination, does not apply in relation to anything done in connection with –

(a)   the curriculum of a school,
(b)   admission to a school,
(c)   transport to or from a school, or
(d)   the establishment, alteration or closure of schools.

10   (1)   Section 29, so far as relating to disability discrimination, does not require a local authority in England or Wales exercising functions under the Education Acts or an education authority exercising relevant functions to remove or alter a physical feature.

(2)   Relevant functions are functions under –

(a)   the Education (Scotland) Act 1980,
(b)   the Education (Scotland) Act 1996,
(c)   the Standards in Scotland's Schools etc. Act 2000, or
(d)   the Education (Additional Support for Learning) (Scotland) Act 2004.

11   Section 29, so far as relating to religious or belief-related discrimination, does not apply in relation to anything done in connection with –

(a)   the curriculum of a school;
(b)   admission to a school which has a religious ethos;
(c)   acts of worship or other religious observance organised by or on behalf of a school (whether or not forming part of the curriculum);
(d)   the responsible body of a school which has a religious ethos;
(e)   transport to or from a school;
(f)   the establishment, alteration or closure of schools.

12   This Part of this Schedule is to be construed in accordance with Chapter 1 of Part 6.

PART 3   HEALTH AND CARE

Blood services

13   (1)   A person operating a blood service does not contravene section 29 only by refusing to accept a donation of an individual's blood if –

(a)   the refusal is because of an assessment of the risk to the public, or to the individual, based on clinical, epidemiological or other data obtained from a source on which it is reasonable to rely, and
(b)   the refusal is reasonable.

(2)   A blood service is a service for the collection and distribution of human blood for the purposes of medical services.

(3)   'Blood' includes blood components.

Health and safety

14   (1)   A service-provider (A) who refuses to provide the service to a pregnant woman does not discriminate against her in contravention of section 29 because she is pregnant if –

(a)   A reasonably believes that providing her with the service would, because she is pregnant, create a risk to her health or safety,
(b)   A refuses to provide the service to persons with other physical conditions, and

(c)   the reason for that refusal is that A reasonably believes that providing the service to such persons would create a risk to their health or safety.

(2)   A service-provider (A) who provides, or offers to provide, the service to a pregnant woman on conditions does not discriminate against her in contravention of section 29 because she is pregnant if –

(a)   the conditions are intended to remove or reduce a risk to her health or safety,

(b)   A reasonably believes that the provision of the service without the conditions would create a risk to her health or safety,

(c)   A imposes conditions on the provision of the service to persons with other physical conditions, and

(d)   the reason for the imposition of those conditions is that A reasonably believes that the provision of the service to such persons without those conditions would create a risk to their health or safety.

Care within the family

15   A person (A) does not contravene section 29 only by participating in arrangements under which (whether or not for reward) A takes into A's home, and treats as members of A's family, persons requiring particular care and attention.

PART 4   IMMIGRATION

Disability

16   (1)   This paragraph applies in relation to disability discrimination.

(2)   Section 29 does not apply to –

(a)   a decision within sub-paragraph (3);

(b)   anything done for the purposes of or in pursuance of a decision within that sub-paragraph.

(3)   A decision is within this sub-paragraph if it is a decision (whether or not taken in accordance with immigration rules) to do any of the following on the ground that doing so is necessary for the public good –

(a)   to refuse entry clearance;

(b)   to refuse leave to enter or remain in the United Kingdom;

(c)   to cancel leave to enter or remain in the United Kingdom;

(d)   to vary leave to enter or remain in the United Kingdom;

(e)   to refuse an application to vary leave to enter or remain in the United Kingdom.

(4)   Section 29 does not apply to –

(a)   a decision taken, or guidance given, by the Secretary of State in connection with a decision within sub-paragraph (3);

(b)   a decision taken in accordance with guidance given by the Secretary of State in connection with a decision within that sub-paragraph.

Nationality and ethnic or national origins

17   (1)   This paragraph applies in relation to race discrimination so far as relating to –

(a)   nationality, or

(b)   ethnic or national origins.

(2)   Section 29 does not apply to anything done by a relevant person in the exercise of functions exercisable by virtue of a relevant enactment.

(3)   A relevant person is –

    (a)   a Minister of the Crown acting personally, or

    (b)   a person acting in accordance with a relevant authorisation.

(4)   A relevant authorisation is a requirement imposed or express authorisation given –

    (a)   with respect to a particular case or class of case, by a Minister of the Crown acting personally;

    (b)   with respect to a particular class of case, by a relevant enactment or by an instrument made under or by virtue of a relevant enactment.

(5)   The relevant enactments are –

    (a)   the Immigration Acts,

    (b)   the Special Immigration Appeals Commission Act 1997,

    (c)   a provision made under section 2(2) of the European Communities Act 1972 which relates to immigration or asylum, and

    (d)   a provision of Community law which relates to immigration or asylum.

(6)   The reference in sub-paragraph (5)(a) to the Immigration Acts does not include a reference to –

    (a)   sections 28A to 28K of the Immigration Act 1971 (powers of arrest, entry and search, etc.), or

    (b)   section 14 of the Asylum and Immigration (Treatment of Claimants, etc.) Act 2004 (power of arrest).

Religion or belief

18   (1)   This paragraph applies in relation to religious or belief-related discrimination.

    (2)   Section 29 does not apply to a decision within sub-paragraph (3) or anything done for the purposes of or in pursuance of a decision within that sub-paragraph.

    (3)   A decision is within this sub-paragraph if it is a decision taken in accordance with immigration rules –

        (a)   to refuse entry clearance or leave to enter the United Kingdom, or to cancel leave to enter or remain in the United Kingdom, on the grounds that the exclusion of the person from the United Kingdom is conducive to the public good, or

        (b)   to vary leave to enter or remain in the United Kingdom, or to refuse an application to vary leave to enter or remain in the United Kingdom, on the grounds that it is undesirable to permit the person to remain in the United Kingdom.

    (4)   Section 29 does not apply to a decision within sub-paragraph (5), or anything done for the purposes of or in pursuance of a decision within that sub-paragraph, if the decision is taken on grounds mentioned in sub-paragraph (6).

    (5)   A decision is within this sub-paragraph if it is a decision (whether or not taken in accordance with immigration rules) in connection with an application for entry clearance or for leave to enter or remain in the United Kingdom.

    (6)   The grounds referred to in sub-paragraph (4) are –

        (a)   the grounds that a person holds an office or post in connection with a religion or belief or provides a service in connection with a religion or belief,

        (b)   the grounds that a religion or belief is not to be treated in the same way as certain other religions or beliefs, or

        (c)   the grounds that the exclusion from the United Kingdom of a person to whom paragraph (a) applies is conducive to the public good.

(7)   Section 29 does not apply to –

        (a)   a decision taken, or guidance given, by the Secretary of State in connection with a decision within sub-paragraph (3) or (5);

        (b)   a decision taken in accordance with guidance given by the Secretary of State in connection with a decision within either of those sub-paragraphs.

Interpretation

19   A reference to entry clearance, leave to enter or remain or immigration rules is to be construed in accordance with the Immigration Act 1971.

PART 5   INSURANCE, ETC.

Services arranged by employer

20 (1)   Section 29 does not apply to the provision of a relevant financial service if the provision is in pursuance of arrangements made by an employer for the service-provider to provide the service to the employer's employees, and other persons, as a consequence of the employment.

    (2)   'Relevant financial service' means –

        (a)   insurance or a related financial service, or

        (b)   a service relating to membership of or benefits under a personal pension scheme (within the meaning given by section 1 of the Pension Schemes Act 1993).

Disability

21 (1)   It is not a contravention of section 29, so far as relating to disability discrimination, to do anything in connection with insurance business if –

        (a)   that thing is done by reference to information that is both relevant to the assessment of the risk to be insured and from a source on which it is reasonable to rely, and

        (b)   it is reasonable to do that thing.

    (2)   'Insurance business' means business which consists of effecting or carrying out contracts of insurance; and that definition is to be read with –

        (a)   section 22 of the Financial Services and Markets Act 2000,

        (b)   any relevant order under that Act, and

        (c)   Schedule 2 to that Act.

Sex, gender reassignment, pregnancy and maternity

22 (1)   It is not a contravention of section 29, so far as relating to relevant discrimination, to do anything in relation to an annuity, life insurance policy, accident insurance policy or similar matter involving the assessment of risk if –

        (a)   that thing is done by reference to actuarial or other data from a source on which it is reasonable to rely, and

        (b)   it is reasonable to do that thing.

    (2)   In the case of a contract of insurance, or a contract for related financial services,

entered into before 6 April 2008, sub-paragraph (1) applies only in relation to differences in premiums and benefits that are applicable to a person under the contract.

(3)   In the case of a contract of insurance, or a contract for related financial services, entered into on or after 6 April 2008, sub-paragraph (1) applies only in relation to differences in premiums and benefits if –

   (a)   the use of sex as a factor in the assessment of risk is based on relevant and accurate actuarial and statistical data,
   (b)   the data are compiled, published (whether in full or in summary form) and regularly updated in accordance with guidance issued by the Treasury,
   (c)   the differences are proportionate having regard to the data, and
   (d)   the differences do not result from costs related to pregnancy or to a woman's having given birth in the period of 26 weeks ending on the day on which the thing in question is done.

(4)   'Relevant discrimination' is –

   (a)   gender reassignment discrimination;
   (b)   pregnancy and maternity discrimination;
   (c)   sex discrimination.

(5)   For the purposes of the application of sub-paragraph (3) to gender reassignment discrimination by virtue of section 13, that section has effect as if in subsection (1), after 'others' there were inserted 'of B's sex'.

(6)   In the application of sub-paragraph (3) to a contract entered into before 22 December 2008, paragraph (d) is to be ignored.

Existing insurance policies

23 (1)   It is not a contravention of section 29, so far as relating to relevant discrimination, to do anything in connection with insurance business in relation to an existing insurance policy.

(2)   'Relevant discrimination' is –

   (a)   age discrimination;
   (b)   disability discrimination;
   (c)   gender reassignment discrimination;
   (d)   pregnancy and maternity discrimination;
   (e)   race discrimination;
   (f)   religious or belief-related discrimination;
   (g)   sex discrimination;
   (h)   sexual orientation discrimination.

(3)   An existing insurance policy is a policy of insurance entered into before the date on which this paragraph comes into force.

(4)   Sub-paragraph (1) does not apply where an existing insurance policy was renewed, or the terms of such a policy were reviewed, on or after the date on which this paragraph comes into force.

(5)   A review of an existing insurance policy which was part of, or incidental to, a general reassessment by the service-provider of the pricing structure for a group of policies is not a review for the purposes of sub-paragraph (4).

(6)   'Insurance business' has the meaning given in paragraph 21.

PART 6   MARRIAGE

Gender reassignment: England and Wales

24   (1)   A person does not contravene section 29, so far as relating to gender reassignment discrimination, only because of anything done in reliance on section 5B of the Marriage Act 1949 (solemnisation of marriages involving person of acquired gender).

(2)   A person (A) whose consent to the solemnisation of the marriage of a person (B) is required under section 44(1) of the Marriage Act 1949 (solemnisation in registered building) does not contravene section 29, so far as relating to gender reassignment discrimination, by refusing to consent if A reasonably believes that B's gender has become the acquired gender under the Gender Recognition Act 2004.

(3)   Sub-paragraph (4) applies to a person (A) who may, in a case that comes within the Marriage Act 1949 (other than the case mentioned in sub-paragraph (1)), solemnise marriages according to a form, rite or ceremony of a body of persons who meet for religious worship.

(4)   A does not contravene section 29, so far as relating to gender reassignment discrimination, by refusing to solemnise, in accordance with a form, rite or ceremony as described in sub-paragraph (3), the marriage of a person (B) if A reasonably believes that B's gender has become the acquired gender under the Gender Recognition Act 2004.

Gender reassignment: Scotland

25   (1)   An approved celebrant (A) does not contravene section 29, so far as relating to gender reassignment discrimination, only by refusing to solemnise the marriage of a person (B) if A reasonably believes that B's gender has become the acquired gender under the Gender Recognition Act 2004.

(2)   In sub-paragraph (1) 'approved celebrant' has the meaning given in section 8(2)(a) of the Marriage (Scotland) Act 1977 (persons who may solemnise marriage).

PART 7   SEPARATE AND SINGLE SERVICES

Separate services for the sexes

26   (1)   A person does not contravene section 29, so far as relating to sex discrimination, by providing separate services for persons of each sex if –

(a)   a joint service for persons of both sexes would be less effective, and
(b)   the limited provision is a proportionate means of achieving a legitimate aim.

(2)   A person does not contravene section 29, so far as relating to sex discrimination, by providing separate services differently for persons of each sex if –

(a)   a joint service for persons of both sexes would be less effective,
(b)   the extent to which the service is required by one sex makes it not reasonably practicable to provide the service otherwise than as a separate service provided differently for each sex, and
(c)   the limited provision is a proportionate means of achieving a legitimate aim.

(3)   This paragraph applies to a person exercising a public function in relation to the provision of a service as it applies to the person providing the service.

Single-sex services

27   (1)   A person does not contravene section 29, so far as relating to sex discrimination, by providing a service only to persons of one sex if –

(a)   any of the conditions in sub-paragraphs (2) to (7) is satisfied, and
(b)   the limited provision is a proportionate means of achieving a legitimate aim.

(2)   The condition is that only persons of that sex have need of the service.

(3)   The condition is that –

(a)   the service is also provided jointly for persons of both sexes, and
(b)   the service would be insufficiently effective were it only to be provided jointly.

(4)   The condition is that –

(a)   a joint service for persons of both sexes would be less effective, and
(b)   the extent to which the service is required by persons of each sex makes it not reasonably practicable to provide separate services.

(5)   The condition is that the service is provided at a place which is, or is part of –

(a)   a hospital, or
(b)   another establishment for persons requiring special care, supervision or attention.

(6)   The condition is that –

(a)   the service is provided for, or is likely to be used by, two or more persons at the same time, and
(b)   the circumstances are such that a person of one sex might reasonably object to the presence of a person of the opposite sex.

(7)   The condition is that –

(a)   there is likely to be physical contact between a person (A) to whom the service is provided and another person (B), and
(b)   B might reasonably object if A were not of the same sex as B.

(8)   This paragraph applies to a person exercising a public function in relation to the provision of a service as it applies to the person providing the service.

Gender reassignment

28   (1)   A person does not contravene section 29, so far as relating to gender reassignment discrimination, only because of anything done in relation to a matter within sub-paragraph (2) if the conduct in question is a proportionate means of achieving a legitimate aim.

(2)   The matters are –

(a)   the provision of separate services for persons of each sex;
(b)   the provision of separate services differently for persons of each sex;
(c)   the provision of a service only to persons of one sex.

Services relating to religion

29   (1)   A minister does not contravene section 29, so far as relating to sex discrimination, by providing a service only to persons of one sex or separate services for persons of each sex, if –

(a)   the service is provided for the purposes of an organised religion,

      (b)   it is provided at a place which is (permanently or for the time being) occupied or used for those purposes, and

      (c)   the limited provision of the service is necessary in order to comply with the doctrines of the religion or is for the purpose of avoiding conflict with the strongly held religious convictions of a significant number of the religion's followers.

(2)   The reference to a minister is a reference to a minister of religion, or other person, who –

      (a)   performs functions in connection with the religion, and

      (b)   holds an office or appointment in, or is accredited, approved or recognised for purposes of, a relevant organisation in relation to the religion.

(3)   An organisation is a relevant organisation in relation to a religion if its purpose is –

      (a)   to practise the religion,

      (b)   to advance the religion,

      (c)   to teach the practice or principles of the religion,

      (d)   to enable persons of the religion to receive benefits, or to engage in activities, within the framework of that religion, or

      (e)   to foster or maintain good relations between persons of different religions.

(4)   But an organisation is not a relevant organisation in relation to a religion if its sole or main purpose is commercial.

Services generally provided only for persons who share a protected characteristic

30   If a service is generally provided only for persons who share a protected characteristic, a person (A) who normally provides the service for persons who share that characteristic does not contravene section 29(1) or (2) –

      (a)   by insisting on providing the service in the way A normally provides it, or

      (b)   if A reasonably thinks it is impracticable to provide the service to persons who do not share that characteristic, by refusing to provide the service.

PART 8   TELEVISION, RADIO AND ON-LINE BROADCASTING AND DISTRIBUTION

31 (1)   Section 29 does not apply to the provision of a content service (within the meaning given by section 32(7) of the Communications Act 2003).

    (2)   Sub-paragraph (1) does not apply to the provision of an electronic communications network, electronic communications service or associated facility (each of which has the same meaning as in that Act).

PART 9   TRANSPORT

Application to disability

32   This Part of this Schedule applies in relation to disability discrimination.

Transport by air

33 (1)   Section 29 does not apply to –

      (a)   transporting people by air;

      (b)   a service provided on a vehicle for transporting people by air.

(2)   Section 29 does not apply to anything governed by Regulation (EC) No 1107/2006 of the European Parliament and of the Council of 5 July 2006 concerning the rights of disabled persons and persons with reduced mobility when travelling by air.

Transport by land

34   (1)   Section 29 does not apply to transporting people by land, unless the vehicle concerned is –

(a)   a hire-vehicle designed and constructed for the carriage of passengers and comprising no more than 8 seats in addition to the driver's seat,

(b)   a hire-vehicle designed and constructed for the carriage of passengers, comprising more than 8 seats in addition to the driver's seat and having a maximum mass not exceeding 5 tonnes,

(c)   a hire-vehicle designed and constructed for the carriage of goods and having a maximum mass not exceeding 3.5 tonnes,

(d)   a vehicle licensed under section 48 of the Local Government (Miscellaneous Provisions) Act 1976 or section 7 of the Private Hire Vehicles (London) Act 1998 (or under a provision of a local Act corresponding to either of those provisions),

(e)   a private hire car (within the meaning of section 23 of the Civic Government (Scotland) Act 1982),

(f)   a public service vehicle (within the meaning given by section 1 of the Public Passenger Vehicles Act 1981),

(g)   a vehicle built or adapted to carry passengers on a railway or tramway (within the meaning, in each case, of the Transport and Works Act 1992),

(h)   a taxi,

(i)   a vehicle deployed to transport the driver and passengers of a vehicle that has broken down or is involved in an accident, or

(j)   a vehicle deployed on a system using a mode of guided transport (within the meaning of the Transport and Works Act 1992).

(2)   Paragraph 4 of Schedule 2 applies for the purposes of this paragraph as it applies for the purposes of paragraph 3 of that Schedule.

Power to amend

PART 10   SUPPLEMENTARY

35   (1)   A Minister of the Crown may by order amend this Schedule –

(a)   so as to add, vary or omit an exception to section 29, so far as relating to disability, religion or belief or sexual orientation;

(b)   so as to add, vary or omit an exception to section 29(6), so far as relating to gender reassignment, pregnancy and maternity, race or sex.

(2)   But provision by virtue of sub-paragraph (1) may not amend this Schedule –

(a)   so as to omit an exception in paragraph 1, 2 or 3;

(b)   so as to reduce the extent to which an exception in paragraph 1, 2 or 3 applies.

(3)   For the purposes of an order under sub-paragraph (1)(a), so far as relating to disability, which makes provision in relation to transport by air, it does not matter whether the transport is within or outside the United Kingdom.

(4)   Before making an order under this paragraph the Minister must consult the Commission.

(5)   Nothing in this paragraph affects the application of any other provision of this Act to conduct outside England and Wales or Scotland.

SCHEDULE 4   PREMISES: REASONABLE ADJUSTMENTS

(Section 38)

Preliminary

1   This Schedule applies where a duty to make reasonable adjustments is imposed on A by this Part.

The duty in relation to let premises

2   (1)   This paragraph applies where A is a controller of let premises.
(2)   A must comply with the first and third requirements.
(3)   For the purposes of this paragraph, the reference in section 20(3) to a provision, criterion or practice of A's includes a reference to a term of the letting.
(4)   For those purposes, the reference in section 20(3) or (5) to a disabled person is a reference to a disabled person who –

(a)   is a tenant of the premises, or
(b)   is otherwise entitled to occupy them.

(5)   In relation to each requirement, the relevant matters are –

(a)   the enjoyment of the premises;
(b)   the use of a benefit or facility, entitlement to which arises as a result of the letting.

(6)   Sub-paragraph (2) applies only if A receives a request from or on behalf of the tenant or a person entitled to occupy the premises to take steps to avoid the disadvantage or provide the auxiliary aid.
(7)   If a term of the letting that prohibits the tenant from making alterations puts the disabled person at the disadvantage referred to in the first requirement, A is required to change the term only so far as is necessary to enable the tenant to make alterations to the let premises so as to avoid the disadvantage.
(8)   It is never reasonable for A to have to take a step which would involve the removal or alteration of a physical feature.
(9)   For the purposes of this paragraph, physical features do not include furniture, furnishings, materials, equipment or other chattels in or on the premises; and none of the following is an alteration of a physical feature –

(a)   the replacement or provision of a sign or notice;
(b)   the replacement of a tap or door handle;
(c)   the replacement, provision or adaptation of a door bell or door entry system;
(d)   changes to the colour of a wall, door or any other surface.

(10)   The terms of a letting include the terms of an agreement relating to it.

The duty in relation to premises to let

3   (1)   This paragraph applies where A is a controller of premises to let.
(2)   A must comply with the first and third requirements.
(3)   For the purposes of this paragraph, the reference in section 20(3) or (5) to a disabled person is a reference to a disabled person who is considering taking a letting of the premises.
(4)   In relation to each requirement, the relevant matter is becoming a tenant of the premises.

(5)   Sub-paragraph (2) applies only if A receives a request by or on behalf of a disabled person within sub-paragraph (3) for A to take steps to avoid the disadvantage or provide the auxiliary aid.

(6)   Nothing in this paragraph requires A to take a step which would involve the removal or alteration of a physical feature.

(7)   Sub-paragraph (9) of paragraph 2 applies for the purposes of this paragraph as it applies for the purposes of that paragraph.

The duty in relation to commonhold units

4   (1)   This paragraph applies where A is a commonhold association; and the reference to a commonhold association is a reference to the association in its capacity as the person who manages a commonhold unit.

(2)   A must comply with the first and third requirements.

(3)   For the purposes of this paragraph, the reference in section 20(3) to a provision, criterion or practice of A's includes a reference to –

(a)   a term of the commonhold community statement, or

(b)   any other term applicable by virtue of the transfer of the unit to the unit-holder.

(4)   For those purposes, the reference in section 20(3) or (5) to a disabled person is a reference to a disabled person who –

(a)   is the unit-holder, or

(b)   is otherwise entitled to occupy the unit.

(5)   In relation to each requirement, the relevant matters are –

(a)   the enjoyment of the unit;

(b)   the use of a benefit or facility, entitlement to which arises as a result of a term within sub-paragraph (3)(a) or (b).

(6)   Sub-paragraph (2) applies only if A receives a request from or on behalf of the unit-holder or a person entitled to occupy the unit to take steps to avoid the disadvantage or provide the auxiliary aid.

(7)   If a term within sub-paragraph (3)(a) or (b) that prohibits the unit-holder from making alterations puts the disabled person at the disadvantage referred to in the first requirement, A is required to change the term only so far as is necessary to enable the unit-holder to make alterations to the unit so as to avoid the disadvantage.

(8)   It is never reasonable for A to have to take a step which would involve the removal or alteration of a physical feature; and sub-paragraph (9) of paragraph 2 applies in relation to a commonhold unit as it applies in relation to let premises.

The duty in relation to common parts

5   (1)   This paragraph applies where A is a responsible person in relation to common parts.

(2)   A must comply with the second requirement.

(3)   For the purposes of this paragraph, the reference in section 20(4) to a physical feature is a reference to a physical feature of the common parts.

(4)   For those purposes, the reference in section 20(4) to a disabled person is a reference to a disabled person who –

(a)   is a tenant of the premises,

(b)   is a unit-holder, or

(c)   is otherwise entitled to occupy the premises, and uses or intends to use the premises as the person's only or main home.

(5)   In relation to the second requirement, the relevant matter is the use of the common parts.

(6)   Sub-paragraph (2) applies only if –

(a)   A receives a request by or on behalf of a disabled person within sub-paragraph (4) for A to take steps to avoid the disadvantage, and

(b)   the steps requested are likely to avoid or reduce the disadvantage.

Consultation on adjustments relating to common parts

6   (1)   In deciding whether it is reasonable to take a step for the purposes of paragraph 5, A must consult all persons A thinks would be affected by the step.

(2)   The consultation must be carried out within a reasonable period of the request being made.

(3)   A is not required to have regard to a view expressed against taking a step in so far as A reasonably believes that the view is expressed because of the disabled person's disability.

(4)   Nothing in this paragraph affects anything a commonhold association is required to do pursuant to Part 1 of the Commonhold and Leasehold Reform Act 2002.

Agreement on adjustments relating to common parts

7   (1)   If A decides that it is reasonable to take a step for the purposes of paragraph 5, A and the disabled person must agree in writing the rights and responsibilities of each of them in relation to the step.

(2)   An agreement under this paragraph must, in particular, make provision as to the responsibilities of the parties in relation to –

(a)   the costs of any work to be undertaken;

(b)   other costs arising from the work;

(c)   the restoration of the common parts to their former condition if the relevant disabled person stops living in the premises.

(3)   It is always reasonable before the agreement is made for A to insist that the agreement should require the disabled person to pay –

(a)   the costs referred to in paragraphs (a) and (b) of sub-paragraph (2), and

(b)   the costs of the restoration referred to in paragraph (c) of that sub-paragraph.

(4)   If an agreement under this paragraph is made, A's obligations under the agreement become part of A's interest in the common parts and pass on subsequent disposals accordingly.

(5)   Regulations may require a party to an agreement under this paragraph to provide, in prescribed circumstances, prescribed information about the agreement to persons of a prescribed description.

(6)   The regulations may require the information to be provided in a prescribed form.

(7)   Regulations may make provision as to circumstances in which an agreement under this paragraph is to cease to have effect, in so far as the agreement does not itself make provision for termination.

Victimisation

8   (1)   This paragraph applies where the relevant disabled person comes within paragraph 2(4)(b), 4(4)(b) or 5(4)(c).

(2)   A must not, because of costs incurred in connection with taking steps to comply with a requirement imposed for the purposes of paragraph 2, 4 or 5, subject to a detriment –

    (a)   a tenant of the premises, or

    (b)   the unit-holder.

Regulations

9 (1)   This paragraph applies for the purposes of section 36 and this Schedule.

   (2)   Regulations may make provision as to –

    (a)   circumstances in which premises are to be treated as let, or as not let, to a person;

    (b)   circumstances in which premises are to be treated as being, or as not being, to let;

    (c)   who is to be treated as being, or as not being, a person entitled to occupy premises otherwise than as tenant or unit-holder;

    (d)   who is to be treated as being, or as not being, a person by whom premises are let;

    (e)   who is to be treated as having, or as not having, premises to let;

    (f)   who is to be treated as being, or as not being, a manager of premises.

   (3)   Provision made by virtue of this paragraph may amend this Schedule.

SCHEDULE 5   PREMISES: EXCEPTIONS

(Section 38)

Owner-occupier

1 (1)   This paragraph applies to the private disposal of premises by an owner-occupier.

   (2)   A disposal is a private disposal only if the owner-occupier does not –

    (a)   use the services of an estate agent for the purpose of disposing of the premises, or

    (b)   publish (or cause to be published) an advertisement in connection with their disposal.

   (3)   Section 33(1) applies only in so far as it relates to race.

   (4)   Section 34(1) does not apply in so far as it relates to –

    (a)   religion or belief, or

    (b)   sexual orientation.

   (5)   In this paragraph –

'estate agent' means a person who, by way of profession or trade, provides services for the purpose of –

    (a)   finding premises for persons seeking them, or

    (b)   assisting in the disposal of premises;

'owner-occupier' means a person who –

    (a)   owns an estate or interest in premises, and

    (b)   occupies the whole of them.

2 (1)   Section 36(1)(a) does not apply if –

    (a)   the premises are, or have been, the only or main home of a person by whom they are let, and

    (b)   since entering into the letting, neither that person nor any other by whom they are let has used a manager for managing the premises.

(2)   A manager is a person who, by profession or trade, manages let premises.

(3)   Section 36(1)(b) does not apply if –

    (a)   the premises are, or have been, the only or main home of a person who has them to let, and

    (b)   neither that person nor any other who has the premises to let uses the services of an estate agent for letting the premises.

(4)   'Estate agent' has the meaning given in paragraph 1.

Small premises

3   (1)   This paragraph applies to anything done by a person in relation to the disposal, occupation or management of part of small premises if –

    (a)   the person or a relative of that person resides, and intends to continue to reside, in another part of the premises, and

    (b)   the premises include parts (other than storage areas and means of access) shared with residents of the premises who are not members of the same household as the resident mentioned in paragraph (a).

(2)   Sections 33(1), 34(1) and 35(1) apply only in so far as they relate to race.

(3)   Premises are small if –

    (a)   the only other persons occupying the accommodation occupied by the resident mentioned in sub-paragraph (1)(a) are members of the same household,

    (b)   the premises also include accommodation for at least one other household,

    (c)   the accommodation for each of those other households is let, or available for letting, on a separate tenancy or similar agreement, and

    (d)   the premises are not normally sufficient to accommodate more than two other households.

(4)   Premises are also small if they are not normally sufficient to provide residential accommodation for more than six persons (in addition to the resident mentioned in sub-paragraph (1)(a) and members of the same household).

(5)   In this paragraph, 'relative' means –

    (a)   spouse or civil partner,

    (b)   unmarried partner,

    (c)   parent or grandparent,

    (d)   child or grandchild (whether or not legitimate),

    (e)   the spouse, civil partner or unmarried partner of a child or grandchild,

    (f)   brother or sister (whether of full blood or half-blood), or

    (g)   a relative within paragraph (c), (d), (e) or (f) whose relationship arises as a result of marriage or civil partnership.

(6)   In sub-paragraph (5), a reference to an unmarried partner is a reference to the other member of a couple consisting of –

    (a)   a man and a woman who are not married to each other but are living together as husband and wife, or

    (b)   two people of the same sex who are not civil partners of each other but are living together as if they were.

4   (1)   Section 36(1) does not apply if –

    (a)   the premises in question are small premises,

(b)   the relevant person or a relative of that person resides, and intends to continue to reside, in another part of the premises, and

(c)   the premises include parts (other than storage areas and means of access) shared with residents of the premises who are not members of the same household as the resident mentioned in paragraph (b).

(2)   The relevant person is the person who, for the purposes of section 36(1), is –

(a)   the controller of the premises, or

(b)   the responsible person in relation to the common parts to which the premises relate.

(3)   'Small premises' and 'relative' have the same meaning as in paragraph 3.

5   A Minister of the Crown may by order amend paragraph 3 or 4.

SCHEDULE 6   OFFICE-HOLDERS: EXCLUDED OFFICES

(Section 52)

Work to which other provisions apply

1   (1)   An office or post is not a personal or public office in so far as one or more of the provisions mentioned in sub-paragraph (2) –

(a)   applies in relation to the office or post, or

(b)   would apply in relation to the office or post but for the operation of some other provision of this Act.

(2)   Those provisions are –

(a)   section 39 (employment);

(b)   section 41 (contract work);

(c)   section 44 (partnerships).

(d)   section 45 (LLPs);

(e)   section 47 (barristers);

(f)   section 48 (advocates);

(g)   section 55 (employment services) so far as applying to the provision of work experience within section 56(2)(a) or arrangements within section 56(2)(c) for such provision.

Political offices

2   (1)   An office or post is not a personal or public office if it is a political office.

(2)   A political office is an office or post set out in the second column of the following Table –

Political setting	Office or post
Houses of Parliament	An office of the House of Commons held by a member of that House
	An office of the House of Lords held by a member of that House
	A Ministerial office within the meaning of section 2 of the House of Commons Disqualification Act 1975

Political setting	Office or post
	The office of the Leader of the Opposition within the meaning of the Ministerial and other Salaries Act 1975
	The office of the Chief Opposition Whip, or of an Assistant Opposition Whip, within the meaning of that Act
Scottish Parliament	An office of the Scottish Parliament held by a member of the Parliament
	The office of a member of the Scottish Executive
	The office of a junior Scottish Minister
National Assembly for Wales	An office of the National Assembly for Wales held by a member of the Assembly
	The office of a member of the Welsh Assembly Government
Local government in England (outside London)	An office of a county council, district council or parish council in England held by a member of the council
	An office of the Council of the Isles of Scilly held by a member of the Council
Local government in London	An office of the Greater London Authority held by the Mayor of London or a member of the London Assembly
	An office of a London borough council held by a member of the council
	An office of the Common Council of the City of London held by a member of the Council
Local government in Wales	An office of a county council, county borough council or community council in Wales held by a member of the council
Local government in Scotland	An office of a council constituted under section 2 of the Local Government etc. (Scotland) Act 1994 held by a member of the council
	An office of a council established under section 51 of the Local Government (Scotland) Act 1973 held by a member of the council
Political parties	An office of a registered political party

(3)   The reference to a registered political party is a reference to a party registered in the Great Britain register under Part 2 of the Political Parties, Elections and Referendums Act 2000.

Honours etc.

3   A life peerage (within the meaning of the Life Peerages Act 1958), or any other dignity or honour conferred by the Crown, is not a personal or public office.

SCHEDULE 7   EQUALITY OF TERMS: EXCEPTIONS

(Section 80)

PART 1   TERMS OF WORK

Compliance with laws regulating employment of women, etc.

1   Neither a sex equality clause nor a maternity equality clause has effect in relation to terms of work affected by compliance with laws regulating –

(a)   the employment of women;
(b)   the appointment of women to personal or public offices.

Pregnancy, etc.

2   A sex equality clause does not have effect in relation to terms of work affording special treatment to women in connection with pregnancy or childbirth.

PART 2   OCCUPATIONAL PENSION SCHEMES

Preliminary

3   (1)   A sex equality rule does not have effect in relation to a difference as between men and women in the effect of a relevant matter if the difference is permitted by or by virtue of this Part of this Schedule.

(2)   'Relevant matter' has the meaning given in section 67.

State retirement pensions

4   (1)   This paragraph applies where a man and a woman are eligible, in such circumstances as may be prescribed, to receive different amounts by way of pension.

(2)   The difference is permitted if, in prescribed circumstances, it is attributable only to differences between men and women in the retirement benefits to which, in prescribed circumstances, the man and woman are or would be entitled.

(3)   'Retirement benefits' are benefits under sections 43 to 55 of the Social Security Contributions and Benefits Act 1992 (state retirement pensions).

Actuarial factors

5   (1)   A difference as between men and women is permitted if it consists of applying to the calculation of the employer's contributions to an occupational pension scheme actuarial factors which –

(a)   differ for men and women, and
(b)   are of such description as may be prescribed.

(2)   A difference as between men and women is permitted if it consists of applying to the determination of benefits of such description as may be prescribed actuarial factors which differ for men and women.

Power to amend

6   (1)   Regulations may amend this Part of this Schedule so as to add, vary or omit provision about cases where a difference as between men and women in the effect of a relevant matter is permitted.

    (2)   The regulations may make provision about pensionable service before the date on which they come into force (but not about pensionable service before 17 May 1990).

SCHEDULE 8   WORK: REASONABLE ADJUSTMENTS

(Section 83)

PART 1   INTRODUCTORY

Preliminary

1   This Schedule applies where a duty to make reasonable adjustments is imposed on A by this Part of this Act.

The duty

2   (1)   A must comply with the first, second and third requirements.

    (2)   For the purposes of this paragraph –

       (a)   the reference in section 20(3) to a provision, criterion or practice is a reference to a provision, criterion or practice applied by or on behalf of A;

       (b)   the reference in section 20(4) to a physical feature is a reference to a physical feature of premises occupied by A;

       (c)   the reference in section 20(3), (4) or (5) to a disabled person is to an interested disabled person.

    (3)   In relation to the first and third requirements, a relevant matter is any matter specified in the first column of the applicable table in Part 2 of this Schedule.

    (4)   In relation to the second requirement, a relevant matter is –

       (a)   a matter specified in the second entry of the first column of the applicable table in Part 2 of this Schedule, or

       (b)   where there is only one entry in a column, a matter specified there.

    (5)   If two or more persons are subject to a duty to make reasonable adjustments in relation to the same interested disabled person, each of them must comply with the duty so far as it is reasonable for each of them to do so.

3   (1)   This paragraph applies if a duty to make reasonable adjustments is imposed on A by section 55 (except where the employment service which A provides is the provision of vocational training within the meaning given by section 56(6)(b)).

    (2)   The reference in section 20(3), (4) and (5) to a disabled person is a reference to an interested disabled person.

    (3)   In relation to each requirement, the relevant matter is the employment service which A provides.

    (4)   Sub-paragraph (5) of paragraph 2 applies for the purposes of this paragraph as it applies for the purposes of that paragraph.

PART 2   INTERESTED DISABLED PERSON

Preliminary

4   An interested disabled person is a disabled person who, in relation to a relevant matter, is of a description specified in the second column of the applicable table in this Part of this Schedule.

Employers (see section 39)

5   (1)   This paragraph applies where A is an employer.

Relevant matter	Description of disabled person
Deciding to whom to offer employment.	A person who is, or has notified A that the person may be, an applicant for the employment.
Employment by A.	An applicant for employment by A.
	An employee of A's.

(2)   Where A is the employer of a disabled contract worker (B), A must comply with the first, second and third requirements on each occasion when B is supplied to a principal to do contract work.

(3)   In relation to the first requirement (as it applies for the purposes of sub-paragraph (2)) –

(a)   the reference in section 20(3) to a provision, criterion or practice is a reference to a provision, criterion or practice applied by or on behalf of all or most of the principals to whom B is or might be supplied,

(b)   the reference to being put at a substantial disadvantage is a reference to being likely to be put at a substantial disadvantage that is the same or similar in the case of each of the principals referred to in paragraph (a), and

(c)   the requirement imposed on A is a requirement to take such steps as it would be reasonable for A to have to take if the provision, criterion or practice were applied by or on behalf of A.

(4)   In relation to the second requirement (as it applies for the purposes of sub-paragraph (2)) –

(a)   the reference in section 20(4) to a physical feature is a reference to a physical feature of premises occupied by each of the principals referred to in sub-paragraph (3)(a),

(b)   the reference to being put at a substantial disadvantage is a reference to being likely to be put at a substantial disadvantage that is the same or similar in the case of each of those principals, and

(c)   the requirement imposed on A is a requirement to take such steps as it would be reasonable for A to have to take if the premises were occupied by A.

(5)   In relation to the third requirement (as it applies for the purposes of sub-paragraph (2)) –

(a)   the reference in section 20(5) to being put at a substantial disadvantage is a reference to being likely to be put at a substantial disadvantage that is the same or similar in the case of each of the principals referred to in sub-paragraph (3)(a), and

(b)   the requirement imposed on A is a requirement to take such steps as it would be reasonable for A to have to take if A were the person to whom B was supplied.

Principals in contract work (see section 41)

6   (1)   This paragraph applies where A is a principal.

Relevant matter	Description of disabled person
Contract work that A may make available.	A person who is, or has notified A that the person may be, an applicant to do the work.
Contract work that A makes available.	A person who is supplied to do the work.

(2)   A is not required to do anything that a disabled person's employer is required to do by virtue of paragraph 5.

Partnerships (see section 44)

7   (1)   This paragraph applies where A is a firm or a proposed firm.

Relevant matter	Description of disabled person
Deciding to whom to offer a position as a partner.	A person who is, or has notified A that the person may be, a candidate for the position.
A position as a partner.	A candidate for the position.
	The partner who holds the position.

(2)   Where a firm or proposed firm (A) is required by this Schedule to take a step in relation to an interested disabled person (B) –

(a)   the cost of taking the step is to be treated as an expense of A;

(b)   the extent to which B should (if B is or becomes a partner) bear the cost is not to exceed such amount as is reasonable (having regard in particular to B's entitlement to share in A's profits).

LLPs (see section 45)

8   (1)   This paragraph applies where A is an LLP or a proposed LLP.

Relevant matter	Description of disabled person
Deciding to whom to offer a position as a member.	A person who is, or has notified A that the person may be, a candidate for the position.
A position as a member.	A candidate for the position.
	The member who holds the position.

(2)   Where an LLP or proposed LLP (A) is required by this Schedule to take a step in relation to an interested disabled person (B) –

(a)   the cost of taking the step is to be treated as an expense of A;

(b)   the extent to which B should (if B is or becomes a member) bear the cost is not to exceed such amount as is reasonable (having regard in particular to B's entitlement to share in A's profits).

Barristers and their clerks (see section 47)

9   This paragraph applies where A is a barrister or barrister's clerk.

Relevant matter	Description of disabled person
Deciding to whom to offer a pupillage or tenancy.	A person who is, or has notified A that the person may be, an applicant for the pupillage or tenancy.
A pupillage or tenancy.	An applicant for the pupillage or tenancy.
	The pupil or tenant.

Advocates and their clerks (see section 48)

10   This paragraph applies where A is an advocate or advocate's clerk.

Relevant matter	Description of disabled person
Deciding who to offer to take as a devil or to offer membership of a stable.	A person who applies, or has notified A that the person may apply, to be taken as a devil or to become a member of the stable.
The relationship with a devil or membership of a stable.	An applicant to be taken as a devil or to become a member of the stable.
	The devil or member.

Persons making appointments to offices etc. (see sections 49 to 51)

11   This paragraph applies where A is a person who has the power to make an appointment to a personal or public office.

Relevant matter	Description of disabled person
Deciding to whom to offer the appointment.	A person who is, or has notified A that the person may be, seeking the appointment.
	A person who is being considered for the appointment.
Appointment to the office.	A person who is seeking, or being considered for, appointment to the office.

12   This paragraph applies where A is a relevant person in relation to a personal or public office.

Relevant matter	Description of disabled person
Appointment to the office.	A person appointed to the office.

13   This paragraph applies where A is a person who has the power to make a recommendation for, or give approval to, an appointment to a public office.

Relevant matter	Description of disabled person
Deciding who to recommend or approve for appointment to the office.	A person who is, or has notified A that the person may be, seeking recommendation or approval for appointment to the office.
	A person who is being considered for recommendation or approval for appointment to the office.
An appointment to the office.	A person who is seeking, or being considered for, appointment to the office in question.

14   In relation to the second requirement in a case within paragraph 11, 12 or 13, the reference in paragraph 2(2)(b) to premises occupied by A is to be read as a reference to premises –

    (a)   under the control of A, and
    (b)   at or from which the functions of the office concerned are performed.

Qualifications bodies (see section 53)

15   (1)   This paragraph applies where A is a qualifications body.

Relevant matter	Description of disabled person
Deciding upon whom to confer a relevant qualification.	A person who is, or has notified A that the person may be, an applicant for the conferment of the qualification.
Conferment by the body of a relevant qualification.	An applicant for the conferment of the qualification.
	A person who holds the qualification.

    (2)   A provision, criterion or practice does not include the application of a competence standard.

Employment service-providers (see section 55)

16   This paragraph applies where –

    (a)   A is an employment service-provider, and

(b)   the employment service which A provides is vocational training within the meaning given by section 56(6)(b).

Relevant matter	Description of disabled person
Deciding to whom to offer to provide the service.	A person who is, or has notified A that the person may be, an applicant for the provision of the service.
Provision by A of the service.	A person who applies to A for the provision of the service.
	A person to whom A provides the service.

Trade organisations (see section 57)

17   This paragraph applies where A is a trade organisation.

Relevant matter	Description of disabled person
Deciding to whom to offer membership of the organisation.	A person who is, or has notified A that the person may be, an applicant for membership.
Membership of the organisation.	An applicant for membership.
	A member.

Local authorities (see section 58)

18   (1)   This paragraph applies where A is a local authority.

Relevant matter	Description of disabled person
A member's carrying-out of official business.	The member.

(2)   Regulations may, for the purposes of a case within this paragraph, make provision –

(a)   as to circumstances in which a provision, criterion or practice is, or is not, to be taken to put a disabled person at the disadvantage referred to in the first requirement;

(b)   as to circumstances in which a physical feature is, or is not, to be taken to put a disabled person at the disadvantage referred to in the second requirement;

(c)   as to circumstances in which it is, or in which it is not, reasonable for a local authority to be required to take steps of a prescribed description;

(d)   as to steps which it is always, or which it is never, reasonable for a local authority to take.

Occupational pensions (see section 61)

19   This paragraph applies where A is, in relation to an occupational pension scheme, a responsible person within the meaning of section 61.

Relevant matter	Description of disabled person
Carrying out A's functions in relation to the scheme.	A person who is or may be a member of the scheme.

PART 3   LIMITATIONS ON THE DUTY

Lack of knowledge of disability, etc.

20   (1)   A is not subject to a duty to make reasonable adjustments if A does not know, and could not reasonably be expected to know –

(a)   in the case of an applicant or potential applicant, that an interested disabled person is or may be an applicant for the work in question;

(b)   in any other case referred to in this Part of this Schedule, that an interested disabled person has a disability and is likely to be placed at the disadvantage referred to in the first, second or third requirement.

(2)   An applicant is, in relation to the description of A specified in the first column of the table, a person of a description specified in the second column (and the reference to a potential applicant is to be construed accordingly).

Description of A	Applicant
An employer	An applicant for employment
A firm or proposed firm	A candidate for a position as a partner
An LLP or proposed LLP	A candidate for a position as a member
A barrister or barrister's clerk	An applicant for a pupillage or tenancy
An advocate or advocate's clerk	An applicant for being taken as an advocate's devil or for becoming a member of a stable
A relevant person in relation to a personal or public office	A person who is seeking appointment to, or recommendation or approval for appointment to, the office
A qualifications body	An applicant for the conferment of a relevant qualification
An employment service-provider	An applicant for the provision of an employment service
A trade organisation	An applicant for membership

(3)   If the duty to make reasonable adjustments is imposed on A by section 55, this paragraph applies only in so far as the employment service which A provides is vocational training within the meaning given by section 56(6)(b).

SCHEDULE 9   WORK: EXCEPTIONS

(Section 83)

PART 1   OCCUPATIONAL REQUIREMENTS

General

1 (1)   A person (A) does not contravene a provision mentioned in sub-paragraph (2) by applying in relation to work a requirement to have a particular protected characteristic, if A shows that, having regard to the nature or context of the work –

   (a)   it is an occupational requirement,
   (b)   the application of the requirement is a proportionate means of achieving a legitimate aim, and
   (c)   the person to whom A applies the requirement does not meet it (or A has reasonable grounds for not being satisfied that the person meets it).

   (2)   The provisions are –

   (a)   section 39(1)(a) or (c) or (2)(b) or (c);
   (b)   section 41(1)(b);
   (c)   section 44(1)(a) or (c) or (2)(b) or (c);
   (d)   section 45(1)(a) or (c) or (2)(b) or (c);
   (e)   section 49(3)(a) or (c) or (6)(b) or (c);
   (f)   section 50(3)(a) or (c) or (6)(b) or (c);
   (g)   section 51(1).

   (3)   The references in sub-paragraph (1) to a requirement to have a protected characteristic are to be read –

   (a)   in the case of gender reassignment, as references to a requirement not to be a transsexual person (and section 7(3) is accordingly to be ignored);
   (b)   in the case of marriage and civil partnership, as references to a requirement not to be married or a civil partner (and section 8(2) is accordingly to be ignored).

   (4)   In the case of a requirement to be of a particular sex, sub-paragraph (1) has effect as if in paragraph (c), the words from '(or' to the end were omitted.

Religious requirements relating to sex, marriage etc., sexual orientation

2 (1)   A person (A) does not contravene a provision mentioned in sub-paragraph (2) by applying in relation to employment a requirement to which sub-paragraph (4) applies if A shows that –

   (a)   the employment is for the purposes of an organised religion,
   (b)   the application of the requirement engages the compliance or non-conflict principle, and
   (c)   the person to whom A applies the requirement does not meet it (or A has reasonable grounds for not being satisfied that the person meets it).

   (2)   The provisions are –

   (a)   section 39(1)(a) or (c) or (2)(b) or (c);
   (b)   section 49(3)(a) or (c) or (6)(b) or (c);
   (c)   section 50(3)(a) or (c) or (6)(b) or (c);
   (d)   section 51(1).

(3)   A person does not contravene section 53(1) or (2)(a) or (b) by applying in relation to a relevant qualification (within the meaning of that section) a requirement to which sub-paragraph (4) applies if the person shows that –

(a)   the qualification is for the purposes of employment mentioned in sub-paragraph (1)(a), and

(b)   the application of the requirement engages the compliance or non-conflict principle.

(4)   This sub-paragraph applies to –

(a)   a requirement to be of a particular sex;

(b)   a requirement not to be a transsexual person;

(c)   a requirement not to be married or a civil partner;

(d)   a requirement not to be married to, or the civil partner of, a person who has a living former spouse or civil partner;

(e)   a requirement relating to circumstances in which a marriage or civil partnership came to an end;

(f)   a requirement related to sexual orientation.

(5)   The application of a requirement engages the compliance principle if the requirement is applied so as to comply with the doctrines of the religion.

(6)   The application of a requirement engages the non-conflict principle if, because of the nature or context of the employment, the requirement is applied so as to avoid conflicting with the strongly held religious convictions of a significant number of the religion's followers.

(7)   A reference to employment includes a reference to an appointment to a personal or public office.

(8)   In the case of a requirement within sub-paragraph (4)(a), sub-paragraph (1) has effect as if in paragraph (c) the words from '(or' to the end were omitted.

Other requirements relating to religion or belief

3   A person (A) with an ethos based on religion or belief does not contravene a provision mentioned in paragraph 1(2) by applying in relation to work a requirement to be of a particular religion or belief if A shows that, having regard to that ethos and to the nature or context of the work –

(a)   it is an occupational requirement,

(b)   the application of the requirement is a proportionate means of achieving a legitimate aim, and

(c)   the person to whom A applies the requirement does not meet it (or A has reasonable grounds for not being satisfied that the person meets it).

Armed forces

4   (1)   A person does not contravene section 39(1)(a) or (c) or (2)(b) by applying in relation to service in the armed forces a relevant requirement if the person shows that the application is a proportionate means of ensuring the combat effectiveness of the armed forces.

(2)   A relevant requirement is –

(a)   a requirement to be a man;

(b)   a requirement not to be a transsexual person.

(3)   This Part of this Act, so far as relating to age or disability, does not apply to service in the armed forces; and section 55, so far as relating to disability, does not apply to work experience in the armed forces.

Employment services

5   (1)   A person (A) does not contravene section 55(1) or (2) if A shows that A's treatment of another person relates only to work the offer of which could be refused to that other person in reliance on paragraph 1, 2, 3 or 4.

    (2)   A person (A) does not contravene section 55(1) or (2) if A shows that A's treatment of another person relates only to training for work of a description mentioned in sub-paragraph (1).

    (3)   A person (A) does not contravene section 55(1) or (2) if A shows that –

        (a)   A acted in reliance on a statement made to A by a person with the power to offer the work in question to the effect that, by virtue of sub-paragraph (1) or (2), A's action would be lawful, and

        (b)   it was reasonable for A to rely on the statement.

    (4)   A person commits an offence by knowingly or recklessly making a statement such as is mentioned in sub-paragraph (3)(a) which in a material respect is false or misleading.

    (5)   A person guilty of an offence under sub-paragraph (4) is liable on summary conviction to a fine not exceeding level 5 on the standard scale.

Interpretation

6   (1)   This paragraph applies for the purposes of this Part of this Schedule.

    (2)   A reference to contravening a provision of this Act is a reference to contravening that provision by virtue of section 13.

    (3)   A reference to work is a reference to employment, contract work, a position as a partner or as a member of an LLP, or an appointment to a personal or public office.

    (4)   A reference to a person includes a reference to an organisation.

    (5)   A reference to section 39(2)(b), 44(2)(b), 45(2)(b), 49(6)(b) or 50(6)(b) is to be read as a reference to that provision with the omission of the words 'or for receiving any other benefit, facility or service'.

    (6)   A reference to section 39(2)(c), 44(2)(c), 45(2)(c), 49(6)(c), 50(6)(c), 53(2)(a) or 55(2)(c) (dismissal, etc.) does not include a reference to that provision so far as relating to sex.

    (7)   The reference to paragraph (b) of section 41(1), so far as relating to sex, is to be read as if that paragraph read –

        '(b)   by not allowing the worker to do the work.'

PART 2   EXCEPTIONS RELATING TO AGE

Preliminary

7   For the purposes of this Part of this Schedule, a reference to an age contravention is a reference to a contravention of this Part of this Act, so far as relating to age.

Retirement

8   (1)   It is not an age contravention to dismiss a relevant worker at or over the age of 65 if the reason for the dismissal is retirement.

    (2)   Each of the following is a relevant worker –

        (a)   an employee within the meaning of section 230(1) of the Employment Rights Act 1996;

        (b)   a person in Crown employment;

        (c)   a relevant member of the House of Commons staff;

       (d)   a relevant member of the House of Lords staff.

(3)   Retirement is a reason for dismissal only if it is a reason for dismissal by virtue of Part 10 of the Employment Rights Act 1996.

Applicants at or approaching retirement age

9   (1)   A person does not contravene section 39(1)(a) or (c), so far as relating to age, in a case where the other person –

       (a)   has attained the age limit, or would have attained it before the end of six months beginning with the date on which the application for the employment had to be made, and

       (b)   would, if recruited for the employment, be a relevant worker within the meaning of paragraph 8.

    (2)   The age limit is whichever is the greater of –

       (a)   the age of 65, and

       (b)   the normal retirement age in the case of the employment concerned.

    (3)   The reference to the normal retirement age is to be construed in accordance with section 98ZH of the Employment Rights Act 1996.

Benefits based on length of service

10   (1)   It is not an age contravention for a person (A) to put a person (B) at a disadvantage when compared with another (C), in relation to the provision of a benefit, facility or service in so far as the disadvantage is because B has a shorter period of service than C.

    (2)   If B's period of service exceeds 5 years, A may rely on sub-paragraph (1) only if A reasonably believes that doing so fulfils a business need.

    (3)   A person's period of service is whichever of the following A chooses –

       (a)   the period for which the person has been working for A at or above a level (assessed by reference to the demands made on the person) that A reasonably regards as appropriate for the purposes of this paragraph, or

       (b)   the period for which the person has been working for A at any level.

    (4)   The period for which a person has been working for A must be based on the number of weeks during the whole or part of which the person has worked for A.

    (5)   But for that purpose A may, so far as is reasonable, discount –

       (a)   periods of absence;

       (b)   periods that A reasonably regards as related to periods of absence.

    (6)   For the purposes of sub-paragraph (3)(b), a person is to be treated as having worked for A during any period in which the person worked for a person other than A if –

       (a)   that period counts as a period of employment with A as a result of section 218 of the Employment Rights Act 1996, or

       (b)   if sub-paragraph (a) does not apply, that period is treated as a period of employment by an enactment pursuant to which the person's employment was transferred to A.

    (7)   For the purposes of this paragraph, the reference to a benefit, facility or service does not include a reference to a benefit, facility or service which may be provided only by virtue of a person's ceasing to work.

The national minimum wage: young workers

11 (1)   It is not an age contravention for a person to pay a young worker (A) at a lower rate than that at which the person pays an older worker (B) if –

(a)   the hourly rate for the national minimum wage for a person of A's age is lower than that for a person of B's age, and

(b)   the rate at which A is paid is below the single hourly rate.

(2)   A young worker is a person who qualifies for the national minimum wage at a lower rate than the single hourly rate; and an older worker is a person who qualifies for the national minimum wage at a higher rate than that at which the young worker qualifies for it.

(3)   The single hourly rate is the rate prescribed under section 1(3) of the National Minimum Wage Act 1998.

The national minimum wage: apprentices

12 (1)   It is not an age contravention for a person to pay an apprentice who does not qualify for the national minimum wage at a lower rate than the person pays an apprentice who does.

(2)   An apprentice is a person who –

(a)   is employed under a contract of apprenticeship, or

(b)   as a result of provision made by virtue of section 3(2)(a) of the National Minimum Wage Act 1998 (persons not qualifying), is treated as employed under a contract of apprenticeship.

Redundancy

13 (1)   It is not an age contravention for a person to give a qualifying employee an enhanced redundancy payment of an amount less than that of an enhanced redundancy payment which the person gives to another qualifying employee, if each amount is calculated on the same basis.

(2)   It is not an age contravention to give enhanced redundancy payments only to those who are qualifying employees by virtue of sub-paragraph (3)(a) or (b).

(3)   A person is a qualifying employee if the person –

(a)   is entitled to a redundancy payment as a result of section 135 of the Employment Rights Act 1996,

(b)   agrees to the termination of the employment in circumstances where the person would, if dismissed, have been so entitled,

(c)   would have been so entitled but for section 155 of that Act (requirement for two years' continuous employment), or

(d)   agrees to the termination of the employment in circumstances where the person would, if dismissed, have been so entitled but for that section.

(4)   An enhanced redundancy payment is a payment the amount of which is, subject to sub-paragraphs (5) and (6), calculated in accordance with section 162(1) to (3) of the Employment Rights Act 1996.

(5)   A person making a calculation for the purposes of sub-paragraph (4) –

(a)   may treat a week's pay as not being subject to a maximum amount;

(b)   may treat a week's pay as being subject to a maximum amount above that for the time being specified in section 227(1) of the Employment Rights Act 1996;

(c)   may multiply the appropriate amount for each year of employment by a figure of more than one.

(6)   Having made a calculation for the purposes of sub-paragraph (4) (whether or

not in reliance on sub-paragraph (5)), a person may multiply the amount calculated by a figure of more than one.

(7)   In sub-paragraph (5), 'the appropriate amount' has the meaning given in section 162 of the Employment Rights Act 1996, and 'a week's pay' is to be read with Chapter 2 of Part 14 of that Act.

(8)   For the purposes of sub-paragraphs (4) to (6), the reference to 'the relevant date' in subsection (1)(a) of section 162 of that Act is, in the case of a person who is a qualifying employee by virtue of sub-paragraph (3)(b) or (d), to be read as reference to the date of the termination of the employment.

Life assurance

14 (1)   This paragraph applies if a person (A) takes early retirement because of ill health.

(2)   It is not an age contravention to provide A with life assurance cover for the period starting when A retires and ending –

(a)   if there is a normal retirement age, when A attains the normal retirement age;

(b)   in any other case, when A attains the age of 65.

(3)   The normal retirement age in relation to A is the age at which, when A retires, persons holding comparable positions in the same undertaking are normally required to retire.

Child care

15 (1)   A person does not contravene a relevant provision, so far as relating to age, only by providing, or making arrangements for or facilitating the provision of, care for children of a particular age group.

(2)   The relevant provisions are –

(a)   section 39(2)(b);
(b)   section 41(1)(c);
(c)   section 44(2)(b);
(d)   section 45(2)(b);
(e)   section 47(2)(b);
(f)   section 48(2)(b);
(g)   section 49(6)(b);
(h)   section 50(6)(b);
(i)   section 57(2)(a);
(j)   section 58(3)(a).

(3)   Facilitating the provision of care for a child includes –

(a)   paying for some or all of the cost of the provision;
(b)   helping a parent of the child to find a suitable person to provide care for the child;
(c)   enabling a parent of the child to spend more time providing care for the child or otherwise assisting the parent with respect to the care that the parent provides for the child.

(4)   A child is a person who has not attained the age of 17.
(5)   A reference to care includes a reference to supervision.

Contributions to personal pension schemes

16 (1)   A Minister of the Crown may by order provide that it is not an age contravention for an employer to maintain or use, with respect to contributions to personal

pension schemes, practices, actions or decisions relating to age which are of a specified description.

(2)   An order authorising the use of practices, actions or decisions which are not in use before the order comes into force must not be made unless the Minister consults such persons as the Minister thinks appropriate.

(3)   'Personal pension scheme' has the meaning given in section 1 of the Pension Schemes Act 1993; and 'employer', in relation to a personal pension scheme, has the meaning given in section 318(1) of the Pensions Act 2004.

PART 3   OTHER EXCEPTIONS

Non-contractual payments to women on maternity leave

17 (1)   A person does not contravene section 39(1)(b) or (2), so far as relating to pregnancy and maternity, by depriving a woman who is on maternity leave of any benefit from the terms of her employment relating to pay.

(2)   The reference in sub-paragraph (1) to benefit from the terms of a woman's employment relating to pay does not include a reference to –

   (a)   maternity-related pay (including maternity-related pay that is increase-related),

   (b)   pay (including increase-related pay) in respect of times when she is not on maternity leave, or

   (c)   pay by way of bonus in respect of times when she is on compulsory maternity leave.

(3)   For the purposes of sub-paragraph (2), pay is increase-related in so far as it is to be calculated by reference to increases in pay that the woman would have received had she not been on maternity leave.

(4)   A reference to terms of her employment is a reference to terms of her employment that are not in her contract of employment, her contract of apprenticeship or her contract to do work personally.

(5)   'Pay' means benefits –

   (a)   that consist of the payment of money to an employee by way of wages or salary, and

   (b)   that are not benefits whose provision is regulated by the contract referred to in sub-paragraph (4).

(6)   'Maternity-related pay' means pay to which a woman is entitled –

   (a)   as a result of being pregnant, or

   (b)   in respect of times when she is on maternity leave.

Benefits dependent on marital status, etc.

18 (1)   A person does not contravene this Part of this Act, so far as relating to sexual orientation, by doing anything which prevents or restricts a person who is not married from having access to a benefit, facility or service –

   (a)   the right to which accrued before 5 December 2005 (the day on which section 1 of the Civil Partnership Act 2004 came into force), or

   (b)   which is payable in respect of periods of service before that date.

(2)   A person does not contravene this Part of this Act, so far as relating to sexual orientation, by providing married persons and civil partners (to the exclusion of all other persons) with access to a benefit, facility or service.

Provision of services etc. to the public

19 (1)   A does not contravene a provision mentioned in sub-paragraph (2) in relation to the provision of a benefit, facility or service to B if A is concerned with the provision (for payment or not) of a benefit, facility or service of the same description to the public.

   (2)   The provisions are –

           (a)   section 39(2) and (4);
           (b)   section 41(1) and (3);
           (c)   sections 44(2) and (6) and 45(2) and (6);
           (d)   sections 49(6) and (8) and 50(6), (7), (9) and (10).

   (3)   Sub-paragraph (1) does not apply if –

           (a)   the provision by A to the public differs in a material respect from the provision by A to comparable persons,
           (b)   the provision to B is regulated by B's terms, or
           (c)   the benefit, facility or service relates to training.

   (4)   'Comparable persons' means –

           (a)   in relation to section 39(2) or (4), the other employees;
           (b)   in relation to section 41(1) or (3), the other contract workers supplied to the principal;
           (c)   in relation to section 44(2) or (6), the other partners of the firm;
           (d)   in relation to section 45(2) or (6), the other members of the LLP;
           (e)   in relation to section 49(6) or (8) or 50(6), (7), (9) or (10), persons holding offices or posts not materially different from that held by B.

   (5)   'B's terms' means –

           (a)   the terms of B's employment,
           (b)   the terms on which the principal allows B to do the contract work,
           (c)   the terms on which B has the position as a partner or member, or
           (d)   the terms of B's appointment to the office.

   (6)   A reference to the public includes a reference to a section of the public which includes B.

Insurance contracts, etc.

20 (1)   It is not a contravention of this Part of this Act, so far as relating to relevant discrimination, to do anything in relation to an annuity, life insurance policy, accident insurance policy or similar matter involving the assessment of risk if –

           (a)   that thing is done by reference to actuarial or other data from a source on which it is reasonable to rely, and
           (b)   it is reasonable to do it.

   (2)   'Relevant discrimination' is –

           (a)   gender reassignment discrimination;
           (b)   marriage and civil partnership discrimination;
           (c)   pregnancy and maternity discrimination;
           (d)   sex discrimination.

SCHEDULE 10   ACCESSIBILITY FOR DISABLED PUPILS

(Section 88)

Accessibility strategies

1   (1)   A local authority in England and Wales must, in relation to schools for which it is the responsible body, prepare –

     (a)   an accessibility strategy;
     (b)   further such strategies at such times as may be prescribed.

  (2)   An accessibility strategy is a strategy for, over a prescribed period –

     (a)   increasing the extent to which disabled pupils can participate in the schools' curriculums;
     (b)   improving the physical environment of the schools for the purpose of increasing the extent to which disabled pupils are able to take advantage of education and benefits, facilities or services provided or offered by the schools;
     (c)   improving the delivery to disabled pupils of information which is readily accessible to pupils who are not disabled.

  (3)   The delivery in sub-paragraph (2)(c) must be –

     (a)   within a reasonable time;
     (b)   in ways which are determined after taking account of the pupils' disabilities and any preferences expressed by them or their parents.

  (4)   An accessibility strategy must be in writing.
  (5)   A local authority must keep its accessibility strategy under review during the period to which it relates and, if necessary, revise it.
  (6)   A local authority must implement its accessibility strategy.

2   (1)   In preparing its accessibility strategy, a local authority must have regard to –

     (a)   the need to allocate adequate resources for implementing the strategy;
     (b)   guidance as to the matters mentioned in sub-paragraph (3).

  (2)   The authority must also have regard to guidance as to compliance with paragraph 1(5).
  (3)   The matters are –

     (a)   the content of an accessibility strategy;
     (b)   the form in which it is to be produced;
     (c)   persons to be consulted in its preparation.

  (4)   Guidance may be issued –

     (a)   for England, by a Minister of the Crown;
     (b)   for Wales, by the Welsh Ministers.

  (5)   A local authority must, if asked, make a copy of its accessibility strategy available for inspection at such reasonable times as it decides.
  (6)   A local authority in England must, if asked by a Minister of the Crown, give the Minister a copy of its accessibility strategy.
  (7)   A local authority in Wales must, if asked by the Welsh Ministers, give them a copy of its accessibility strategy.

Accessibility plans

3   (1)   The responsible body of a school in England and Wales must prepare –

     (a)   an accessibility plan;

(b)   further such plans at such times as may be prescribed.

(2)   An accessibility plan is a plan for, over a prescribed period –

(a)   increasing the extent to which disabled pupils can participate in the school's curriculum,

(b)   improving the physical environment of the school for the purpose of increasing the extent to which disabled pupils are able to take advantage of education and benefits, facilities or services provided or offered by the school, and

(c)   improving the delivery to disabled pupils of information which is readily accessible to pupils who are not disabled.

(3)   The delivery in sub-paragraph (2)(c) must be –

(a)   within a reasonable time;

(b)   in ways which are determined after taking account of the pupils' disabilities and any preferences expressed by them or their parents.

(4)   An accessibility plan must be in writing.

(5)   The responsible body must keep its accessibility plan under review during the period to which it relates and, if necessary, revise it.

(6)   The responsible body must implement its accessibility plan.

(7)   A relevant inspection may extend to the performance by the responsible body of its functions in relation to the preparation, publication, review, revision and implementation of its accessibility plan.

(8)   A relevant inspection is an inspection under –

(a)   Part 1 of the Education Act 2005, or

(b)   Chapter 1 of Part 4 of the Education and Skills Act 2008 (regulation and inspection of independent education provision in England).

4   (1)   In preparing an accessibility plan, the responsible body must have regard to the need to allocate adequate resources for implementing the plan.

(2)   The proprietor of an independent educational institution (other than an Academy) must, if asked, make a copy of the school's accessibility plan available for inspection at such reasonable times as the proprietor decides.

(3)   The proprietor of an independent educational institution in England (other than an Academy) must, if asked by a Minister of the Crown, give the Minister a copy of the school's accessibility plan.

(4)   The proprietor of an independent school in Wales (other than an Academy) must, if asked by the Welsh Ministers, give them a copy of the school's accessibility plan.

Power of direction

5   (1)   This sub-paragraph applies if the appropriate authority is satisfied (whether or not on a complaint) that a responsible body –

(a)   has acted or is proposing to act unreasonably in the discharge of a duty under this Schedule, or

(b)   has failed to discharge such a duty.

(2)   This sub-paragraph applies if the appropriate authority is satisfied (whether or not on a complaint) that a responsible body of a school specified in sub-paragraph (3) –

(a)   has acted or is proposing to act unreasonably in the discharge of a duty the body has in relation to the provision to the authority of copies of the body's accessibility plan or the inspection of that plan, or

(b)   has failed to discharge the duty.

(3)   The schools are –

    (a)   schools approved under section 342 of the Education Act 1996 (non-maintained special schools);

    (b)   Academies.

(4)   This sub-paragraph applies if a Tribunal has made an order under paragraph 5 of Schedule 17 and the appropriate authority is satisfied (whether or not on a complaint) that the responsible body concerned –

    (a)   has acted or is proposing to act unreasonably in complying with the order, or

    (b)   has failed to comply with the order.

(5)   If sub-paragraph (1), (2) or (4) applies, the appropriate authority may give a responsible body such directions as the authority thinks expedient as to –

    (a)   the discharge by the body of the duty, or

    (b)   compliance by the body with the order.

(6)   A direction may be given in relation to sub-paragraph (1) or (2) even if the performance of the duty is contingent on the opinion of the responsible body.

(7)   A direction may not, unless sub-paragraph (8) applies, be given to the responsible body of a school in England in respect of a matter –

    (a)   that has been complained about to a Local Commissioner in accordance with Chapter 2 of Part 10 of the Apprenticeships, Skills, Children and Learning Act 2009 (parental complaints against governing bodies etc.), or

    (b)   that the appropriate authority thinks could have been so complained about.

(8)   This sub-paragraph applies if –

    (a)   the Local Commissioner has made a recommendation to the responsible body under section 211(4) of the Apprenticeships, Skills, Children and Learning Act 2009 (statement following investigation) in respect of the matter, and

    (b)   the responsible body has not complied with the recommendation.

(9)   A direction –

    (a)   may be varied or revoked by the appropriate authority;

    (b)   may be enforced, on the application of the appropriate authority, by a mandatory order obtained in accordance with section 31 of the Senior Courts Act 1981.

(10)   The appropriate authority is –

    (a)   in relation to the responsible body of a school in England, the Secretary of State;

    (b)   in relation to the responsible body of a school in Wales, the Welsh Ministers.

Supplementary

6   (1)   This paragraph applies for the purposes of this Schedule.

    (2)   Regulations may prescribe services which are, or are not, to be regarded as being –

    (a)   education;

    (b)   a benefit, facility or service.

(3)   The power to make regulations is exercisable by –

> (a)   in relation to England, a Minister of the Crown;
> (b)   in relation to Wales, the Welsh Ministers.

(4) 'Disabled pupil' includes a disabled person who may be admitted to the school as a pupil.

(5) 'Responsible body' means –

> (a)   in relation to a maintained school or a maintained nursery school, the local authority or governing body;
> (b)   in relation to a pupil referral unit, the local authority;
> (c)   in relation to an independent educational institution, the proprietor;
> (d)   in relation to a special school not maintained by a local authority, the proprietor.

(6) 'Governing body', in relation to a maintained school, means the body corporate (constituted in accordance with regulations under section 19 of the Education Act 2002) which the school has as a result of that section.

(7) 'Maintained school' has the meaning given in section 20 of the School Standards and Framework Act 1998; and 'maintained nursery school' has the meaning given in section 22 of that Act.

SCHEDULE 11   SCHOOLS: EXCEPTIONS

(Section 89)

PART 1   SEX DISCRIMINATION

Admission to single-sex schools

1   (1)   Section 85(1), so far as relating to sex, does not apply in relation to a single-sex school.

> (2)   A single-sex school is a school which –

> > (a)   admits pupils of one sex only, or
> > (b)   on the basis of the assumption in sub-paragraph (3), would be taken to admit pupils of one sex only.

> (3)   That assumption is that pupils of the opposite sex are to be disregarded if –

> > (a)   their admission to the school is exceptional, or
> > (b)   their numbers are comparatively small and their admission is confined to particular courses or classes.

> (4)   In the case of a school which is a single-sex school by virtue of sub-paragraph (3)(b), section 85 (2)(a) to (d), so far as relating to sex, does not prohibit confining pupils of the same sex to particular courses or classes.

Single-sex boarding at schools

2   (1)   Section 85(1), so far as relating to sex, does not apply in relation to admission as a boarder to a school to which this paragraph applies.

> (2)   Section 85(2)(a) to (d), so far as relating to sex, does not apply in relation to boarding facilities at a school to which this paragraph applies.

> (3)   This paragraph applies to a school (other than a single-sex school) which has some pupils as boarders and others as non-boarders and which –

> > (a)   admits as boarders pupils of one sex only, or
> > (b)   on the basis of the assumption in sub-paragraph (4), would be taken to admit as boarders pupils of one sex only.

> (4)   That assumption is that pupils of the opposite sex admitted as boarders are to be disregarded if their numbers are small compared to the numbers of other pupils admitted as boarders.

Single-sex schools turning co-educational

3   (1)   If the responsible body of a single-sex school decides to alter its admissions arrangements so that the school will cease to be a single-sex school, the body may apply for a transitional exemption order in relation to the school.

       (2)   If the responsible body of a school to which paragraph 2 applies decides to alter its admissions arrangements so that the school will cease to be one to which that paragraph applies, the body may apply for a transitional exemption order in relation to the school.

       (3)   A transitional exemption order in relation to a school is an order which, during the period specified in the order as the transitional period, authorises –

            (a)   sex discrimination by the responsible body of the school in the arrangements it makes for deciding who is offered admission as a pupil;

            (b)   the responsible body, in the circumstances specified in the order, not to admit a person as a pupil because of the person's sex.

       (4)   Paragraph 4 applies in relation to the making of transitional exemption orders.

       (5)   The responsible body of a school does not contravene this Act, so far as relating to sex discrimination, if –

            (a)   in accordance with a transitional exemption order, or

            (b)   pending the determination of an application for a transitional exemption order in relation to the school,

       it does not admit a person as a pupil because of the person's sex.

4   (1)   In the case of a maintained school within the meaning given by section 32 of the Education and Inspections Act 2006, a transitional exemption order may be made in accordance with such provision as is made in regulations under section 21 of that Act (orders made by local authority or adjudicator in relation to schools in England).

       (2)   In the case of a school in Wales maintained by a local authority, a transitional exemption order may be made in accordance with paragraph 22 of Schedule 6, or paragraph 17 of Schedule 7, to the School Standards and Framework Act 1998 (orders made by Welsh Ministers).

       (3)   In the case of a school in Scotland managed by an education authority or in respect of which the managers are for the time being receiving grants under section 73(c) or (d) of the Education (Scotland) Act 1980 –

            (a)   the responsible body may submit to the Scottish Ministers an application for the making of a transitional exemption order, and

            (b)   the Scottish Ministers may make the order.

       (4)   Where, under section 113A of the Learning and Skills Act 2000, the Learning and Skills Council for England make proposals to the Secretary of State for an alteration in the admissions arrangements of a single-sex school or a school to which paragraph 2 applies –

            (a)   the making of the proposals is to be treated as an application to the Secretary of State for the making of a transitional exemption order, and

            (b)   the Secretary of State may make the order.

       (5)   Where proposals are made to the Welsh Ministers under section 113A of the Learning and Skills Act 2000 for an alteration in the admissions arrangements of a single-sex school or a school to which paragraph 2 applies –

            (a)   the making of the proposals is to be treated as an application to the Welsh Ministers for the making of a transitional exemption order, and

            (b)   the Welsh Ministers may make the order.

(6)   In the case of a school in England or Wales not coming within sub-paragraph (1), (2), (4) or (5) or an independent school in Scotland –

    (a)   the responsible body may submit to the Commission an application for the making of a transitional exemption order, and

    (b)   the Commission may make the order.

(7)   An application under sub-paragraph (6) must specify –

    (a)   the period proposed by the responsible body as the transitional period to be specified in the order,

    (b)   the stages within that period by which the body proposes to move to the position where section 85(1)(a) and (c), so far as relating to sex, is complied with, and

    (c)   any other matters relevant to the terms and operation of the order applied for.

(8)   The Commission must not make an order on an application under sub-paragraph (6) unless satisfied that the terms of the application are reasonable, having regard to –

    (a)   the nature of the school's premises,

    (b)   the accommodation, equipment and facilities available, and

    (c)   the responsible body's financial resources.

PART 2   RELIGIOUS OR BELIEF-RELATED DISCRIMINATION

School with religious character etc.

5   Section 85(1) and (2)(a) to (d), so far as relating to religion or belief, does not apply in relation to –

    (a)   a school designated under section 69(3) of the School Standards and Framework Act 1998 (foundation or voluntary school with religious character);

    (b)   a school listed in the register of independent schools for England or for Wales, if the school's entry in the register records that the school has a religious ethos;

    (c)   a school transferred to an education authority under section 16 of the Education (Scotland) Act 1980 (transfer of certain schools to education authorities) which is conducted in the interest of a church or denominational body;

    (d)   a school provided by an education authority under section 17(2) of that Act (denominational schools);

    (e)   a grant-aided school (within the meaning of that Act) which is conducted in the interest of a church or denominational body;

    (f)   a school registered in the register of independent schools for Scotland if the school admits only pupils who belong, or whose parents belong, to one or more particular denominations;

    (g)   a school registered in that register if the school is conducted in the interest of a church or denominational body.

Curriculum, worship, etc.

6   Section 85(2)(a) to (d), so far as relating to religion or belief, does not apply in relation to anything done in connection with acts of worship or other religious observance organised by or on behalf of a school (whether or not forming part of the curriculum).

Power to amend

7   (1)   A Minister of the Crown may by order amend this Part of this Schedule –

    (a)   so as to add, vary or omit an exception to section 85;

(b) so as to make provision about the construction or application of section 19(2)(d) in relation to section 85.

(2) The power under sub-paragraph (1) is exercisable only in relation to religious or belief-related discrimination.

(3) Before making an order under this paragraph the Minister must consult –

(a) the Welsh Ministers,
(b) the Scottish Ministers, and
(c) such other persons as the Minister thinks appropriate.

PART 3   DISABILITY DISCRIMINATION

Permitted form of selection

8   (1) A person does not contravene section 85(1), so far as relating to disability, only by applying a permitted form of selection.

(2) In relation to England and Wales, a permitted form of selection is –

(a) in the case of a maintained school which is not designated as a grammar school under section 104 of the School Standards and Framework Act 1998, a form of selection mentioned in section 99(2) or (4) of that Act;
(b) in the case of a maintained school which is so designated, its selective admission arrangements (within the meaning of section 104 of that Act);
(c) in the case of an independent educational institution, arrangements which provide for some or all of its pupils to be selected by reference to general or special ability or aptitude, with a view to admitting only pupils of high ability or aptitude.

(3) In relation to Scotland, a permitted form of selection is –

(a) in the case of a school managed by an education authority, arrangements approved by the Scottish Ministers for the selection of pupils for admission;
(b) in the case of an independent school, arrangements which provide for some or all of its pupils to be selected by reference to general or special ability or aptitude, with a view to admitting only pupils of high ability or aptitude.

(4) 'Maintained school' has the meaning given in section 22 of the School Standards and Framework Act 1998.

SCHEDULE 12   FURTHER AND HIGHER EDUCATION EXCEPTIONS

(Section 94)

PART 1   SINGLE-SEX INSTITUTIONS, ETC.

Admission to single-sex institutions

1   (1) Section 91(1), so far as relating to sex, does not apply in relation to a single-sex institution.

(2) A single-sex institution is an institution to which section 91 applies, which –

(a) admits students of one sex only, or
(b) on the basis of the assumption in sub-paragraph (3), would be taken to admit students of one sex only.

(3) That assumption is that students of the opposite sex are to be disregarded if –

(a)   their admission to the institution is exceptional, or

(b)   their numbers are comparatively small and their admission is confined to particular courses or classes.

(4)   In the case of an institution which is a single-sex institution by virtue of sub-paragraph (3)(b), section 91(2)(a) to (d), so far as relating to sex, does not prohibit confining students of the same sex to particular courses or classes.

Single-sex institutions turning co-educational

2   (1)   If the responsible body of a single-sex institution decides to alter its admissions arrangements so that the institution will cease to be a single-sex institution, the body may apply for a transitional exemption order in relation to the institution.

(2)   A transitional exemption order relating to an institution is an order which, during the period specified in the order as the transitional period, authorises –

(a)   sex discrimination by the responsible body of the institution in the arrangements it makes for deciding who is offered admission as a student;

(b)   the responsible body, in the circumstances specified in the order, not to admit a person as a student because of the person's sex.

(3)   Paragraph 3 applies in relation to the making of a transitional exemption order.

(4)   The responsible body of an institution does not contravene this Act, so far as relating to sex discrimination, if –

(a)   in accordance with a transitional exemption order, or

(b)   pending the determination of an application for a transitional exemption order in relation to the institution,

it does not admit a person as a student because of the person's sex.

(5)   The responsible body of an institution does not contravene this Act, so far as relating to sex discrimination, if –

(a)   in accordance with a transitional exemption order, or

(b)   pending the determination of an application for a transitional exemption order in relation to the institution,

it discriminates in the arrangements it makes for deciding who is offered admission as a student.

3   (1)   In the case of a single-sex institution –

(a)   its responsible body may submit to the Commission an application for the making of a transitional exemption order, and

(b)   the Commission may make the order.

(2)   An application under sub-paragraph (1) must specify –

(a)   the period proposed by the responsible body as the transitional period to be specified in the order,

(b)   the stages, within that period, by which the body proposes to move to the position where section 91(1)(a) and (c), so far as relating to sex, is complied with, and

(c)   any other matters relevant to the terms and operation of the order applied for.

(3)   The Commission must not make an order on an application under sub-paragraph (1) unless satisfied that the terms of the application are reasonable, having regard to –

(a)   the nature of the institution's premises,

(b)   the accommodation, equipment and facilities available, and

(c)   the responsible body's financial resources.

PART 2   OTHER EXCEPTIONS

Occupational requirements

4   A person (P) does not contravene section 91(1) or (2) if P shows that P's treatment of another person relates only to training that would help fit that other person for work the offer of which the other person could be refused in reliance on Part 1 of Schedule 9.

Institutions with a religious ethos

5   (1)   The responsible body of an institution which is designated for the purposes of this paragraph does not contravene section 91(1), so far as relating to religion or belief, if, in the admission of students to a course at the institution –

(a)   it gives preference to persons of a particular religion or belief,
(b)   it does so to preserve the institution's religious ethos, and
(c)   the course is not a course of vocational training.

(2)   A Minister of the Crown may by order designate an institution if satisfied that the institution has a religious ethos.

Benefits dependent on marital status, etc.

6   A person does not contravene section 91, so far as relating to sexual orientation, by providing married persons and civil partners (to the exclusion of all other persons) with access to a benefit, facility or service.

Child care

7   (1)   A person does not contravene section 91(2)(b) or (d), so far as relating to age, only by providing, or making arrangements for or facilitating the provision of, care for children of a particular age group.

(2)   Facilitating the provision of care for a child includes –

(a)   paying for some or all of the cost of the provision;
(b)   helping a parent of the child to find a suitable person to provide care for the child;
(c)   enabling a parent of the child to spend more time providing care for the child or otherwise assisting the parent with respect to the care that the parent provides for the child.

(3)   A child is a person who has not attained the age of 17.
(4)   A reference to care includes a reference to supervision.

SCHEDULE 13   EDUCATION: REASONABLE ADJUSTMENTS

(Section 98)

Preliminary

1   This Schedule applies where a duty to make reasonable adjustments is imposed on A by this Part.

The duty for schools

2   (1)   This paragraph applies where A is the responsible body of a school to which section 85 applies.

(2)   A must comply with the first and third requirements.
(3)   For the purposes of this paragraph –

(a)   the reference in section 20(3) to a provision, criterion or practice is a reference to a provision, criterion or practice applied by or on behalf of A;

(b)   the reference in section 20(3) or (5) to a disabled person is –

    (i)   in relation to a relevant matter within sub-paragraph (4)(a), a reference to disabled persons generally;

    (ii)   in relation to a relevant matter within sub-paragraph (4)(b), a reference to disabled pupils generally.

(4)   In relation to each requirement, the relevant matters are –

(a)   deciding who is offered admission as a pupil;

(b)   provision of education or access to a benefit, facility or service.

The duty for further or higher education institutions

3   (1)   This paragraph applies where A is the responsible body of an institution to which section 91 applies.

    (2)   A must comply with the first, second and third requirements.

    (3)   For the purposes of this paragraph –

(a)   the reference in section 20(3) to a provision, criterion or practice is a reference to a provision, criterion or practice applied by or on behalf of A;

(b)   the reference in section 20(4) to a physical feature is a reference to a physical feature of premises occupied by A;

(c)   the reference in section 20(3), (4) or (5) to a disabled person is –

    (i)   in relation to a relevant matter within sub-paragraph (4)(a), a reference to disabled persons generally;

    (ii)   in relation to a relevant matter within sub-paragraph (4)(b) or (c), a reference to disabled students generally;

    (iii)   in relation to a relevant matter within sub-paragraph (4)(d) or (e) below, a reference to an interested disabled person.

(4)   In relation to each requirement, the relevant matters are –

(a)   deciding who is offered admission as a student;

(b)   provision of education;

(c)   access to a benefit, facility or service;

(d)   deciding on whom a qualification is conferred;

(e)   a qualification that A confers.

4   (1)   An interested disabled person is a disabled person who, in relation to a relevant matter specified in the first column of the table, is of a description specified in the second column.

Case	Description of disabled person
Deciding upon whom to confer a qualification.	A person who is, or has notified A that the person may be, an applicant for the conferment of the qualification.
A qualification that A confers.	An applicant for the conferment by A of the qualification.
	A person on whom A confers the qualification.

(2)   A provision, criterion or practice does not include the application of a competence standard.

(3)   A competence standard is an academic, medical or other standard applied for the purpose of determining whether or not a person has a particular level of competence or ability.

The duty relating to certain other further or higher education courses

5   (1)   This paragraph applies where A is the responsible body in relation to a course to which section 92 applies.

(2)   A must comply with the first, second and third requirements; but if A is the governing body of a maintained school (within the meaning given by that section), A is not required to comply with the second requirement.

(3)   For the purposes of this paragraph –

(a)   the reference in section 20(3) to a provision, criterion or practice is a reference to a provision, criterion or practice applied by or on behalf of A;

(b)   the reference in section 20(4) to a physical feature is a reference to a physical feature of premises occupied by A;

(c)   the reference in section 20(3), (4) or (5) to a disabled person is –

(i)   in relation to a relevant matter within sub-paragraph (4)(a), a reference to disabled persons generally;

(ii)   in relation to a relevant matter within sub-paragraph (4)(b), a reference to disabled persons generally who are enrolled on the course.

(4)   In relation to each requirement, the relevant matters are –

(a)   arrangements for enrolling persons on a course of further or higher education secured by A;

(b)   services provided by A for persons enrolled on the course.

The duty relating to recreational or training facilities

6   (1)   This paragraph applies where A is the responsible body in relation to facilities to which section 93 applies.

(2)   A must comply with the first, second and third requirements.

(3)   For the purposes of this paragraph –

(a)   the reference in section 20(3) to a provision, criterion or practice is a reference to a provision, criterion or practice applied by or on behalf of A;

(b)   the reference in section 20(4) to a physical feature is a reference to a physical feature of premises occupied by A;

(c)   the reference in section 20(3), (4) or (5) to a disabled person is a reference to disabled persons generally.

(4)   In relation to each requirement, the relevant matter is A's arrangements for providing the recreational or training facilities.

Code of practice

7   In deciding whether it is reasonable for A to have to take a step for the purpose of complying with the first, second or third requirement, A must have regard to relevant provisions of a code of practice issued under section 14 of the Equality Act 2006.

Confidentiality requests

8   (1)   This paragraph applies if a person has made a confidentiality request of which A is aware.

(2)   In deciding whether it is reasonable for A to have to take a step in relation to that person so as to comply with the first, second or third requirement, A must have regard to the extent to which taking the step is consistent with the request.

(3)   In a case within paragraph 2, a 'confidentiality request' is a request –

(a)   that the nature or existence of a disabled person's disability be treated as confidential, and

(b)   which satisfies either of the following conditions.

(4)   The first condition is that the request is made by the person's parent.

(5)   The second condition is that –

(a)   it is made by the person, and

(b)   A reasonably believes that the person has sufficient understanding of the nature and effect of the request.

(6)   In a case within paragraph 3, a 'confidentiality request' is a request by a disabled person that the nature or existence of the person's disability be treated as confidential.

The duty for general qualifications bodies

9   (1)   This paragraph applies where A is a qualifications body for the purposes of section 96.

(2)   Paragraphs 3 and 4(1), so far as relating to qualifications, apply to a qualifications body as they apply to a responsible body.

(3)   This paragraph is subject to section 96(7).

SCHEDULE 14   EDUCATIONAL CHARITIES AND ENDOWMENTS

(Section 99)

Educational charities

1   (1)   This paragraph applies to a trust deed or other instrument –

(a)   which concerns property applicable for or in connection with the provision of education in an establishment in England and Wales to which section 85 or 91 applies, and

(b)   which in any way restricts the benefits available under the instrument to persons of one sex.

(2)   Sub-paragraph (3) applies if, on the application of the trustees or the responsible body (within the meaning of that section), a Minister of the Crown is satisfied that the removal or modification of the restriction would be conducive to the advancement of education without sex discrimination.

(3)   The Minister may by order make such modifications of the instrument as appear to the Minister expedient for removing or modifying the restriction.

(4)   If the trust was created by a gift or bequest, an order must not be made until the end of the period of 25 years after the date when the gift or bequest took effect.

(5)   Sub-paragraph (4) does not apply if the donor or the personal representatives of the donor or testator consent in writing to making the application for the order.

(6)   The Minister must require the applicant to publish a notice –

(a)   containing particulars of the proposed order;

(b)   stating that representations may be made to the Minister within a period specified in the notice.

(7)   The period must be not less than one month beginning with the day after the date of the notice.

(8)   The applicant must publish the notice in the manner specified by the Minister.

(9)   The cost of publication may be paid out of the property of the trust.

(10)   Before making the order, the Minister must take account of representations made in accordance with the notice.

Educational endowments

2   (1)   This paragraph applies to an educational endowment –

(a)   to which section 104 of the Education (Scotland) Act 1980 applies, and

(b)   which in any way restricts the benefit of the endowment to persons of one sex.

(2)   Sub-paragraph (3) applies if, on the application of the governing body of an educational endowment, the Scottish Ministers are satisfied that the removal or modification of the provision which restricts the benefit of the endowment to persons of one sex would be conducive to the advancement of education without sex discrimination.

(3)   The Scottish Ministers may by order make such provision as they think expedient for removing or modifying the restriction.

(4)   If the Scottish Ministers propose to make such an order they must publish a notice in such manner as they think sufficient for giving information to persons they think may be interested in the endowment –

(a)   containing particulars of the proposed order;

(b)   stating that representations may be made with respect to the proposal within such period as is specified in the notice.

(5)   The period must be not less than one month beginning with the day after the date of publication of the notice.

(6)   The cost of publication is to be paid out of the funds of the endowment to which the notice relates.

(7)   Before making an order, the Scottish Ministers –

(a)   must consider representations made in accordance with the notice;

(b)   may cause a local inquiry to be held into the representations under section 67 of the Education (Scotland) Act 1980.

(8)   A reference to an educational endowment includes a reference to –

(a)   a scheme made or approved for the endowment under Part 6 of the Education (Scotland) Act 1980;

(b)   in the case of an endowment the governing body of which is entered in the Scottish Charity Register, a scheme approved for the endowment under section 39 or 40 of the Charities and Trustee Investment (Scotland) Act 2005 (asp 10);

(c)   an endowment which is, by virtue of section 108(1) of the Education (Scotland) Act 1980, treated as if it were an educational endowment (or which would, but for the disapplication of that section by section 122(4) of that Act, be so treated);

(d)   a university endowment, the Carnegie Trust, a theological endowment and a new endowment.

(9)   Expressions used in this paragraph and in Part 6 of the Education (Scotland) Act 1980 have the same meaning in this paragraph as in that Part.

SCHEDULE 15   ASSOCIATIONS: REASONABLE ADJUSTMENTS

(Section 107)

Preliminary

1   This Schedule applies where a duty to make reasonable adjustments is imposed on an association (A) by this Part.

The duty

2   (1)   A must comply with the first, second and third requirements.

(2)   For the purposes of this paragraph, the reference in section 20(3), (4) or (5) to a disabled person is a reference to disabled persons who –

(a)   are, or are seeking to become or might wish to become, members,

(b)   are associates, or

(c)   are, or are likely to become, guests.

(3)   Section 20 has effect as if, in subsection (4), for 'to avoid the disadvantage' there were substituted –

'(a)   to avoid the disadvantage, or

(b)   to adopt a reasonable alternative method of affording access to the benefit, facility or service or of admitting persons to membership or inviting persons as guests.'

(4)   In relation to the first and third requirements, the relevant matters are –

(a)   access to a benefit, facility or service;

(b)   members' or associates' retaining their rights as such or avoiding having them varied;

(c)   being admitted to membership or invited as a guest.

(5)   In relation to the second requirement, the relevant matters are –

(a)   access to a benefit, facility or service;

(b)   being admitted to membership or invited as a guest.

(6)   In relation to the second requirement, a physical feature includes a physical feature brought by or on behalf of A, in the course of or for the purpose of providing a benefit, facility or service, on to premises other than those that A occupies (as well as including a physical feature in or on premises that A occupies).

(7)   Nothing in this paragraph requires A to take a step which would fundamentally alter –

(a)   the nature of the benefit, facility or service concerned, or

(b)   the nature of the association.

(8)   Nor does anything in this paragraph require a member or associate in whose house meetings of the association take place to make adjustments to a physical feature of the house.

SCHEDULE 16   ASSOCIATIONS: EXCEPTIONS

(Section 107)

Single characteristic associations

1   (1)   An association does not contravene section 101(1) by restricting membership to persons who share a protected characteristic.

(2)   An association that restricts membership to persons who share a protected characteristic does not breach section 101(3) by restricting the access by associates to a benefit, facility or service to such persons as share the characteristic.

(3)   An association that restricts membership to persons who share a protected characteristic does not breach section 102(1) by inviting as guests, or by permitting to be invited as guests, only such persons as share the characteristic.

(4)   Sub-paragraphs (1) to (3), so far as relating to race, do not apply in relation to colour.

(5)   This paragraph does not apply to an association that is a registered political party.

Health and safety

2   (1)   An association (A) does not discriminate against a pregnant woman in contravention of section 101(1)(b) because she is pregnant if –

(a)   the terms on which A is prepared to admit her to membership include a term intended to remove or reduce a risk to her health or safety,

(b)   A reasonably believes that admitting her to membership on terms which do not include that term would create a risk to her health or safety,

(c)   the terms on which A is prepared to admit persons with other physical conditions to membership include a term intended to remove or reduce a risk to their health or safety, and

(d)   A reasonably believes that admitting them to membership on terms which do not include that term would create a risk to their health or safety.

(2)   Sub-paragraph (1) applies to section 102(1)(b) as it applies to section 101(1)(b); and for that purpose a reference to admitting a person to membership is to be read as a reference to inviting the person as a guest or permitting the person to be invited as a guest.

(3)   An association (A) does not discriminate against a pregnant woman in contravention of section 101(2)(a) or (3)(a) or 102(2)(a) because she is pregnant if –

(a)   the way in which A affords her access to a benefit, facility or service is intended to remove or reduce a risk to her health or safety,

(b)   A reasonably believes that affording her access to the benefit, facility or service otherwise than in that way would create a risk to her health or safety,

(c)   A affords persons with other physical conditions access to the benefit, facility or service in a way that is intended to remove or reduce a risk to their health or safety, and

(d)   A reasonably believes that affording them access to the benefit, facility or service otherwise than in that way would create a risk to their health or safety.

(4)   An association (A) which does not afford a pregnant woman access to a benefit, facility or service does not discriminate against her in contravention of section 101(2)(a) or (3)(a) or 102(2) (a) because she is pregnant if –

(a)   A reasonably believes that affording her access to the benefit, facility or service would, because she is pregnant, create a risk to her health or safety,

(b)   A does not afford persons with other physical conditions access to the benefit, facility or service, and

(c)   the reason for not doing so is that A reasonably believes that affording them access to the benefit, facility or service would create a risk to their health or safety.

(5)   An association (A) does not discriminate against a pregnant woman under section 101(2)(c) or (3)(c) because she is pregnant if –

(a)   the variation of A's terms of membership, or rights as an associate, is intended to remove or reduce a risk to her health or safety,

(b)   A reasonably believes that not making the variation to A's terms or rights would create a risk to her health or safety,

(c)   A varies the terms of membership, or rights as an associate, of persons with other physical conditions,

(d)   the variation of their terms or rights is intended to remove or reduce a risk to their health or safety, and

(e)   A reasonably believes that not making the variation to their terms or rights would create a risk to their health or safety.

SCHEDULE 17   DISABLED PUPILS: ENFORCEMENT

(Section 116)

PART 1   INTRODUCTORY

1   In this Schedule –

'the Tribunal' means –

(a)   in relation to a school in England, the First-tier Tribunal;

(b)   in relation to a school in Wales, the Special Educational Needs Tribunal for Wales;

(c)   in relation to a school in Scotland, an Additional Support Needs Tribunal for Scotland; 'the English Tribunal' means the First-tier Tribunal; 'the Welsh Tribunal' means the Special Educational Needs Tribunal for Wales;

'the Scottish Tribunal' means an Additional Support Needs Tribunal for Scotland;

'responsible body' is to be construed in accordance with section 85.

PART 2   TRIBUNALS IN ENGLAND AND WALES

Introductory

2   This Part of this Schedule applies in relation to the English Tribunal and the Welsh Tribunal.

Jurisdiction

3   A claim that a responsible body has contravened Chapter 1 of Part 6 because of a person's disability may be made to the Tribunal by the person's parent.

Time for bringing proceedings

4   (1)   Proceedings on a claim may not be brought after the end of the period of 6 months starting with the date when the conduct complained of occurred.

(2)   If, in relation to proceedings or prospective proceedings under section 27 of the Equality Act 2006, the dispute is referred for conciliation in pursuance of arrangements under that section before the end of that period, the period is extended by 3 months.

(3)   The Tribunal may consider a claim which is out of time.

(4)   Sub-paragraph (3) does not apply if the Tribunal has previously decided under that sub-paragraph not to consider a claim.

(5)   For the purposes of sub-paragraph (1) –

(a)   if the contravention is attributable to a term in a contract, the conduct is to be treated as extending throughout the duration of the contract;

(b)   conduct extending over a period is to be treated as occurring at the end of the period;

(c)   failure to do something is to be treated as occurring when the person in question decided on it.

(6)   In the absence of evidence to the contrary, a person (P) is to be taken to decide on failure to do something –

(a)   when P acts inconsistently with doing it, or

(b)   if P does not act inconsistently, on the expiry of the period in which P might reasonably have been expected to do it.

Powers

5   (1)   This paragraph applies if the Tribunal finds that the contravention has occurred.

(2)   The Tribunal may make such order as it thinks fit.

(3)   The power under sub-paragraph (2) –

(a)   may, in particular, be exercised with a view to obviating or reducing the adverse effect on the person of any matter to which the claim relates;

(b)   does not include power to order the payment of compensation.

Procedure

6   (1)   This paragraph applies in relation to the Welsh Tribunal.

(2)   The Welsh Ministers may by regulations make provision as to –

(a)   the proceedings on a claim under paragraph 3;

(b)   the making of a claim.

(3)   The regulations may, in particular, include provision –

(a)   as to the manner in which a claim must be made;

(b)   for enabling functions relating to preliminary or incidental matters (including in particular a decision under paragraph 4(3) to be performed by the President or by the person occupying the chair);

(c)   enabling hearings to be conducted in the absence of a member other than the person occupying the chair;

(d)   as to persons who may appear on behalf of the parties;

(e)   for granting such rights to disclosure or inspection of documents or to further particulars as may be granted by the county court;

(f)   requiring persons to attend to give evidence and produce documents;

(g)   for authorising the administration of oaths to witnesses;

(h)   for deciding claims without a hearing in prescribed circumstances;

(i)   as to the withdrawal of claims;

(j)   for enabling the Tribunal to stay proceedings;

(k)   for the award of costs or expenses;

(l)   for settling costs or expenses (and, in particular, for enabling costs to be assessed in the county court);

(m)   for the registration and proof of decisions and orders;

(n)   for enabling prescribed decisions to be reviewed, or prescribed orders to be varied or revoked, in such circumstances as may be decided in accordance with the regulations.

(4)   Proceedings must be held in private, except in prescribed circumstances.

(5)   The Welsh Ministers may pay such allowances for the purpose of or in connection with the attendance of persons at the Tribunal as they may decide.

(6)   Part 1 of the Arbitration Act 1996 does not apply to the proceedings, but regulations may make provision in relation to such proceedings that corresponds of that Part.

(7)   The regulations may make provision for a claim to be heard, in prescribed circumstances, with an appeal under Part 4 of the Education Act 1996 (special educational needs).

(8)   A person commits an offence by failing to comply with –

(a)   a requirement in respect of the disclosure or inspection of documents imposed by virtue of sub-paragraph (3)(e), or

(b)   a requirement imposed by virtue of sub-paragraph (3)(f).

(9)   A person guilty of the offence is liable on summary conviction to a fine not exceeding level 3 on the standard scale.

PART 3   TRIBUNALS IN SCOTLAND

Introductory

7   This Part of this Schedule applies in relation to the Scottish Tribunal.

Jurisdiction

8   A claim that a responsible body has contravened Chapter 1 of Part 6 because of a person's disability may be made to the Tribunal by –

(a)   the person's parent;
(b)   where the person has capacity to make the claim, the person.

Powers

9   (1)   This paragraph applies if the Tribunal finds the contravention has occurred.
(2)   The Tribunal may make such order as it thinks fit.
(3)   The power under sub-paragraph (2) –

(a)   may, in particular, be exercised with a view to obviating or reducing the adverse effect on the person of any matter to which the claim relates;
(b)   does not include power to order the payment of compensation.

Procedure etc.

10   (1)   The Scottish Ministers may make rules as to –

(a)   the proceedings on a claim under paragraph 8;
(b)   the making of a claim.

(2)   The rules may, in particular, include provision for or in connection with –

(a)   the form and manner in which a claim must be made;
(b)   the time within which a claim is to be made;
(c)   the withdrawal of claims;
(d)   the recovery and inspection of documents;
(e)   the persons who may appear on behalf of the parties;
(f)   the persons who may be present at proceedings alongside any party or witness to support the party or witness;
(g)   enabling specified persons other than the parties to appear or be represented in specified circumstances;
(h)   requiring specified persons to give notice to other specified persons of specified matters;
(i)   the time within which any such notice must be given;
(j)   enabling Tribunal proceedings to be conducted in the absence of any member of a Tribunal other than the convener;
(k)   enabling any matters that are preliminary or incidental to the determination of proceedings to be determined by the convenor of a Tribunal alone or with such other members of the Tribunal as may be specified;
(l)   enabling Tribunals to be held in private;
(m)   enabling a Tribunal to exclude any person from attending all or part of Tribunal proceedings;
(n)   enabling a Tribunal to impose reporting restrictions in relation to all or part of Tribunal proceedings;

(o)   enabling a Tribunal to determine specified matters without holding a hearing;

(p)   the recording and publication of decisions and orders of a Tribunal;

(q)   enabling a Tribunal to commission medical and other reports in specified circumstances;

(r)   requiring a Tribunal to take specified actions, or to determine specified proceedings, within specified periods;

(s)   enabling a Tribunal to make an award of expenses;

(t)   the taxation or assessment of such expenses;

(u)   enabling a Tribunal, in specified circumstances, to review, or to vary or revoke, any of its decisions, orders or awards;

(v)   enabling a Tribunal, in specified circumstances, to review the decisions, orders or awards of another Tribunal and take such action (including variation and revocation) in respect of those decisions, orders or awards as it thinks fit.

Appeals

11   (1)   Either of the persons specified in sub-paragraph (2) may appeal on a point of law to the Court of Session against a decision of a Tribunal relating to a claim under this Schedule.

(2)   Those persons are –

(a)   the person who made the claim;

(b)   the responsible body.

(3)   Where the Court of Session allows an appeal under sub-paragraph (1) it may –

(a)   remit the reference back to the Tribunal or to a differently constituted Tribunal to be considered again and give the Tribunal such directions about the consideration of the case as the Court thinks fit;

(b)   make such ancillary orders as it considers necessary or appropriate.

Amendment of Education (Additional Support for Learning) (Scotland) Act 2004

12   The Education (Additional Support for Learning) (Scotland) Act 2004 (asp 4) is amended as follows –

(a)   in section 17(1), omit 'to exercise the functions which are conferred on a Tribunal by virtue of this Act';

(b)   after section 17(1), insert –

'(1A) Tribunals are to exercise the functions which are conferred on them by virtue of –

(a)   this Act, and

(b)   the Equality Act 2010';

(c)   in the definition of 'Tribunal functions' in paragraph 1 of Schedule 1, after 'Act' insert 'or the Equality Act 2010'.

PART 4   ADMISSIONS AND EXCLUSIONS

Admissions

13   (1)   This paragraph applies if appeal arrangements have been made in relation to admissions decisions.

(2)   A claim that a responsible body has, because of a person's disability, contravened Chapter 1 of Part 6 in respect of an admissions decision must be made under the appeal arrangements.

(3)   The body hearing the claim has the powers it has in relation to an appeal under the appeal arrangements.

(4)   Appeal arrangements are arrangements under –

(a)   section 94 of the School Standards and Framework Act 1998, or

(b)   an agreement between the responsible body for an Academy and the Secretary of State under section 482 of the Education Act 1996,

enabling an appeal to be made by the person's parent against the decision.

(5)   An admissions decision is –

(a)   a decision of a kind mentioned in section 94(1) or (2) of the School Standards and Framework Act 1998;

(b)   a decision as to the admission of a person to an Academy taken by the responsible body or on its behalf.

Exclusions

14   (1)   This paragraph applies if appeal arrangements have been made in relation to exclusion decisions.

(2)   A claim that a responsible body has, because of a person's disability, contravened Chapter 1 of Part 6 in respect of an exclusion decision must be made under the appeal arrangements.

(3)   The body hearing the claim has the powers it has in relation to an appeal under the appeal arrangements.

(4)   Appeal arrangements are arrangements under –

(a)   section 52(3) of the Education Act 2002, or

(b)   an agreement between the responsible body for an Academy and the Secretary of State under section 482 of the Education Act 1996,

enabling an appeal to be made by the person's parent against the decision.

(5)   An exclusion decision is –

(a)   a decision of a kind mentioned in 52(3) of the Education Act 2002;

(b)   a decision taken by the responsible body or on its behalf not to reinstate a pupil who has been permanently excluded from an Academy by its head teacher.

(6)   'Responsible body', in relation to a maintained school, includes the discipline committee of the governing body if that committee is required to be established as a result of regulations made under section 19 of the Education Act 2002.

(7)   'Maintained school' has the meaning given in section 20(7) of the School Standards and Framework Act 1998.

SCHEDULE 18   PUBLIC SECTOR EQUALITY DUTY: EXCEPTIONS

(Section 149)

Children

1   (1)   Section 149, so far as relating to age, does not apply to the exercise of a function relating to –

(a)   the provision of education to pupils in schools;

(b)   the provision of benefits, facilities or services to pupils in schools;

       (c)   the provision of accommodation, benefits, facilities or services in community homes pursuant to section 53(1) of the Children Act 1989;

       (d)   the provision of accommodation, benefits, facilities or services pursuant to arrangements under section 82(5) of that Act (arrangements by the Secretary of State relating to the accommodation of children);

       (e)   the provision of accommodation, benefits, facilities or services in residential establishments pursuant to section 26(1)(b) of the Children (Scotland) Act 1995.

(2)   'Pupil' and 'school' each have the same meaning as in Chapter 1 of Part 6.

Immigration

2   (1)   In relation to the exercise of immigration and nationality functions, section 149 has effect as if subsection (1)(b) did not apply to the protected characteristics of age, race or religion or belief; but for that purpose 'race' means race so far as relating to –

       (a)   nationality, or

       (b)   ethnic or national origins.

(2)   'Immigration and nationality functions' means functions exercisable by virtue of –

       (a)   the Immigration Acts (excluding sections 28A to 28K of the Immigration Act 1971 so far as they relate to criminal offences),

       (b)   the British Nationality Act 1981,

       (c)   the British Nationality (Falkland Islands) Act 1983,

       (d)   the British Nationality (Hong Kong) Act 1990,

       (e)   the Hong Kong (War Wives and Widows) Act 1996,

       (f)   the British Nationality (Hong Kong) Act 1997,

       (g)   the Special Immigration Appeals Commission Act 1997, or

       (h)   a provision made under section 2(2) of the European Communities Act 1972, or of Community law, which relates to the subject matter of an enactment within paragraphs (a) to (g).

Judicial functions, etc.

3   (1)   Section 149 does not apply to the exercise of –

       (a)   a judicial function;

       (b)   a function exercised on behalf of, or on the instructions of, a person exercising a judicial function.

(2)   The references to a judicial function include a reference to a judicial function conferred on a person other than a court or tribunal.

Exceptions that are specific to section 149(2)

4   (1)   Section 149(2) (application of section 149(1) to persons who are not public authorities but by whom public functions are exercisable) does not apply to –

       (a)   a person listed in sub-paragraph (2);

       (b)   the exercise of a function listed in sub-paragraph (3).

(2)   Those persons are –

       (a)   the House of Commons;

       (b)   the House of Lords;

       (c)   the Scottish Parliament;

       (d)   the National Assembly for Wales;

       (e)   the General Synod of the Church of England;

(f)   the Security Service;
(g)   the Secret Intelligence Service;
(h)   the Government Communications Headquarters;
(i)   a part of the armed forces which is, in accordance with a requirement of
        the Secretary of State, assisting the Government Communications Head-
        quarters.

(3)   Those functions are –

(a)   a function in connection with proceedings in the House of Commons or
        the House of Lords;
(b)   a function in connection with proceedings in the Scottish Parliament
        (other than a function of the Scottish Parliamentary Corporate Body);
(c)   a function in connection with proceedings in the National Assembly for
        Wales (other than a function of the Assembly Commission).

Power to amend Schedule

5   (1)   A Minister of the Crown may by order amend this Schedule so as to add, vary or
            omit an exception to section 149.
    (2)   But provision by virtue of sub-paragraph (1) may not amend this Schedule –

(a)   so as to omit an exception in paragraph 3;
(b)   so as to omit an exception in paragraph 4(1) so far as applying for the
        purposes of paragraph 4(2)(a) to (e) or (3);
(c)   so as to reduce the extent to which an exception referred to in paragraph
        (a) or (b) applies.

SCHEDULE 19   PUBLIC AUTHORITIES

(Section 150)

PART 1   PUBLIC AUTHORITIES: GENERAL

Ministers of the Crown and government departments

A Minister of the Crown.

A government department other than the Security Service, the Secret Intelligence Service or
the Government Communications Headquarters.

Armed forces

Any of the armed forces other than any part of the armed forces which is, in accordance with a
requirement of the Secretary of State, assisting the Government Communications Headquarters.

National Health Service

A Strategic Health Authority established under section 13 of the National Health Service Act
2006, or continued in existence by virtue of that section.

A Primary Care Trust established under section 18 of that Act, or continued in existence by
virtue of that section.

An NHS trust established under section 25 of that Act.

A Special Health Authority established under section 28 of that Act other than NHS Blood
and Transplant and the NHS Business Services Authority.

An NHS foundation trust within the meaning given by section 30 of that Act.

Local government

A county council, district council or parish council in England.

A parish meeting constituted under section 13 of the Local Government Act 1972.

Charter trustees constituted under section 246 of that Act for an area in England.

The Greater London Authority.

A London borough council.

The Common Council of the City of London in its capacity as a local authority or port health authority.

The Sub-Treasurer of the Inner Temple or the Under-Treasurer of the Middle Temple, in that person's capacity as a local authority.

The London Development Agency.

The London Fire and Emergency Planning Authority.

Transport for London.

The Council of the Isles of Scilly.

The Broads Authority established by section 1 of the Norfolk and Suffolk Broads Act 1988.

A regional development agency established by the Regional Development Agencies Act 1998 (other than the London Development Agency).

A fire and rescue authority constituted by a scheme under section 2 of the Fire and Rescue Services Act 2004, or a scheme to which section 4 of that Act applies, for an area in England.

An internal drainage board which is continued in being by virtue of section 1 of the Land Drainage Act 1991 for an area in England.

A National Park authority established by an order under section 63 of the Environment Act 1995 for an area in England.

A Passenger Transport Executive for an integrated transport area in England (within the meaning of Part 2 of the Transport Act 1968).

A port health authority constituted by an order under section 2 of the Public Health (Control of Disease) Act 1984 for an area in England.

A waste disposal authority established by virtue of an order under section 10(1) of the Local Government Act 1985.

A joint authority established under Part 4 of that Act for an area in England (including, by virtue of section 77(9) of the Local Transport Act 2008, an Integrated Transport Authority established under Part 5 of that Act of 2008).

A body corporate established pursuant to an order under section 67 of the Local Government Act 1985.

A joint committee constituted in accordance with section 102(1)(b) of the Local Government Act 1972 for an area in England.

A joint board which is continued in being by virtue of section 263(1) of that Act for an area in England.

Other educational bodies

The governing body of an educational establishment maintained by an English local authority (within the meaning of section 162 of the Education and Inspections Act 2006).

The governing body of an institution in England within the further education sector (within the meaning of section 91(3) of the Further and Higher Education Act 1992).

The governing body of an institution in England within the higher education sector (within the meaning of section 91(5) of that Act).

Police

A police authority established under section 3 of the Police Act 1996.

The Metropolitan Police Authority established under section 5B of that Act.

The Common Council of the City of London in its capacity as a police authority.

PART 2   PUBLIC AUTHORITIES: RELEVANT WELSH AUTHORITIES

Welsh Assembly Government, etc.

The Welsh Ministers.

The First Minister for Wales.

The Counsel General to the Welsh Assembly Government.

A subsidiary of the Welsh Ministers (within the meaning given by section 134(4) of the Government of Wales Act 2006).

National Health Service

A Local Health Board established under section 11 of the National Health Service (Wales) Act 2006.

An NHS trust established under section 18 of that Act. A Special Health Authority established under section 22 of that Act other than NHS Blood and Transplant and the NHS Business Services Authority.

A Community Health Council in Wales.

Local government

A county council, county borough council or community council in Wales.

Charter trustees constituted under section 246 of the Local Government Act 1972 for an area in Wales.

A fire and rescue authority constituted by a scheme under section 2 of the Fire and Rescue Services Act 2004, or a scheme to which section 4 of that Act applies, for an area in Wales.

An internal drainage board which is continued in being by virtue of section 1 of the Land Drainage Act 1991 for an area in Wales.

A National Park authority established by an order under section 63 of the Environment Act 1995 for an area in Wales.

A port health authority constituted by an order under section 2 of the Public Health (Control of Disease) Act 1984 for an area in Wales.

A joint authority established under Part 4 of the Local Government Act 1985 for an area in Wales.

A joint committee constituted in accordance with section 102(1)(b) of the Local Government Act 1972 for an area in Wales.

A joint board which is continued in being by virtue of section 263(1) of that Act for an area in Wales.

Other educational bodies

The governing body of an educational establishment maintained by a Welsh local authority (within the meaning of section 162 of the Education and Inspections Act 2006).

The governing body of an institution in Wales within the further education sector (within the meaning of section 91(3) of the Further and Higher Education Act 1992).

The governing body of an institution in Wales within the higher education sector (within the meaning of section 91(5) of that Act).

PART 3   PUBLIC AUTHORITIES: RELEVANT SCOTTISH AUTHORITIES

Scottish Administration

An office-holder in the Scottish Administration (within the meaning given by section 126(7)(a) of the Scotland Act 1998).

National Health Service

A Health Board constituted under section 2 of the National Health Service (Scotland) Act 1978.

A Special Health Board constituted under that section.

Local government

A council constituted under section 2 of the Local Government etc. (Scotland) Act 1994.

A community council established under section 51 of the Local Government (Scotland) Act 1973.

A joint board within the meaning of section 235(1) of that Act.

A joint fire and rescue board constituted by a scheme under section 2(1) of the Fire (Scotland) Act 2005.

A licensing board established under section 5 of the Licensing (Scotland) Act 2005, or continued in being by virtue of that section.

A National Park authority established by a designation order made under section 6 of the National Parks (Scotland) Act 2000.

Scottish Enterprise and Highlands and Islands Enterprise, established under the Enterprise and New Towns (Scotland) Act 1990.

Other educational bodies

An education authority in Scotland (within the meaning of section 135(1) of the Education (Scotland) Act 1980).

The managers of a grant-aided school (within the meaning of that section).

The board of management of a college of further education (within the meaning of section 36(1) of the Further and Higher Education (Scotland) Act 1992).

In the case of such a college of further education not under the management of a board of management, the board of governors of the college or any person responsible for the management of the college, whether or not formally constituted as a governing body or board of governors.

The governing body of an institution within the higher education sector (within the meaning of Part 2 of the Further and Higher Education (Scotland) Act 1992).

Police

A police authority established under section 2 of the Police (Scotland) Act 1967.

SCHEDULE 20   RAIL VEHICLE ACCESSIBILITY: COMPLIANCE

(Section 186)

Rail vehicle accessibility compliance certificates

1   (1)   A regulated rail vehicle which is prescribed, or is of a prescribed class or description, must not be used for carriage unless a compliance certificate is in force for the vehicle.

(2)   A 'compliance certificate' is a certificate that the Secretary of State is satisfied that the regulated rail vehicle conforms with the provisions of rail vehicle accessibility regulations with which it is required to conform.

(3)   A compliance certificate is subject to such conditions as are specified in it.

(4)   A compliance certificate may not be issued for a rail vehicle unless the Secretary of State has been provided with a report of a compliance assessment of the vehicle.

(5)   A 'compliance assessment' is an assessment of a rail vehicle against provisions of rail vehicle accessibility regulations with which the vehicle is required to conform.

(6)   If a regulated rail vehicle is used for carriage in contravention of sub-paragraph (1), the Secretary of State may require the operator of the vehicle to pay a penalty.

(7)   The Secretary of State must review a decision not to issue a compliance certificate if before the end of the prescribed period the applicant –

(a)   asks the Secretary of State to review the decision, and
(b)   pays any fee fixed under paragraph 4.

(8)   For the purposes of the review, the Secretary of State must consider any representations made by the applicant in writing before the end of the pre-scribed period.

Regulations as to compliance certificates

2   (1)   Regulations may make provision as to compliance certificates.
    (2)   The regulations may (in particular) include provision –

(a)   as to applications for and issue of certificates;
(b)   specifying conditions to which certificates are subject;
(c)   as to the period for which a certificate is in force;
(d)   as to circumstances in which a certificate ceases to be in force;
(e)   dealing with failure to comply with a specified condition;
(f)   for the examination of rail vehicles in respect of which applications have been made;
(g)   with respect to the issue of copies of certificates in place of those which have been lost or destroyed.

Regulations as to compliance assessments

3   (1)   Regulations may make provision as to compliance assessments.
    (2)   The regulations –

(a)   may make provision as to the person who has to have carried out the assessment;
(b)   may (in particular) require that the assessment be one carried out by a

person who has been appointed by the Secretary of State to carry out compliance assessments (an 'appointed assessor').

(3)   For the purposes of any provisions in the regulations made by virtue of sub-paragraph (2)(b), the regulations –

(a)   may make provision about appointments of appointed assessors, including (in particular) –

(i)   provision for an appointment to be on application or otherwise than on application;
(ii)   provision as to who may be appointed;
(iii)   provision as to the form of applications for appointment;
(iv)   provision as to information to be supplied with applications for appointment;
(v)   provision as to terms and conditions, or the period or termination, of an appointment;
(vi)   provision for terms and conditions of an appointment, including any as to its period or termination, to be as agreed by the Secretary of State when making the appointment;

(b)   may make provision authorising an appointed assessor to charge fees in connection with, or incidental to, the carrying out of a compliance assessment, including (in particular) –

(i)   provision restricting the amount of a fee;
(ii)   provision authorising fees that contain a profit element;
(iii)   provision for advance payment of fees;

(c)   may make provision requiring an appointed assessor to carry out a compliance assessment, and to do so in accordance with any procedures that may be prescribed, if prescribed conditions (which may include conditions as to the payment of fees to the assessor) are satisfied;

(d)   must make provision for the referral to the Secretary of State of disputes between –

(i)   an appointed assessor carrying out a compliance assessment, and
(ii)   the person who requested the assessment,

relating to which provisions of rail vehicle accessibility regulations the vehicle is to be assessed against or to what amounts to conformity with any of those provisions.

(4)   For the purposes of sub-paragraph (3)(b) to (d) a compliance assessment includes pre-assessment activities (for example, a consideration of how the outcome of a compliance assessment would be affected by the carrying out of particular proposed work).

Fees in respect of compliance certificates

4   (1)   The Secretary of State may charge such fees, payable at such times, as are prescribed in respect of –

(a)   applications for, and the issue of, compliance certificates;
(b)   copies of compliance certificates;
(c)   reviews under paragraph 1(7);
(d)   referrals of disputes under provision made by virtue of paragraph 3(3)(d).

(2)   Fees received by the Secretary of State must be paid into the Consolidated Fund.
(3)   Regulations under this paragraph may make provision for the repayment of fees, in whole or in part, in such circumstances as are prescribed.

(4)   Before making regulations under this paragraph the Secretary of State must consult such representative organisations as the Secretary of State thinks fit.

Penalty for using rail vehicle that does not conform with accessibility regulations

5   (1)   If the Secretary of State thinks that a regulated rail vehicle does not conform with a provision of rail vehicle accessibility regulations with which it is required to conform, the Secretary of State may give the operator of the vehicle a notice –

(a)   identifying the vehicle, the provision and how the vehicle fails to conform;
(b)   specifying the improvement deadline.

(2)   The improvement deadline may not be earlier than the end of the prescribed period beginning with the day the notice is given.

(3)   Sub-paragraph (4) applies if –

(a)   the Secretary of State has given a notice under sub-paragraph (1),
(b)   the improvement deadline specified in the notice has passed, and
(c)   the Secretary of State thinks that the vehicle still does not conform with the provision identified in the notice.

(4)   The Secretary of State may give the operator a further notice –

(a)   identifying the vehicle, the provision and how the vehicle fails to conform;
(b)   specifying the final deadline.

(5)   The final deadline may not be earlier than the end of the prescribed period beginning with the day the further notice is given.

(6)   The Secretary of State may require the operator to pay a penalty if –

(a)   the Secretary of State has given notice under sub-paragraph (4), and
(b)   the vehicle is used for carriage at a time after the final deadline when the vehicle does not conform with the provision identified in the notice.

Penalty for using rail vehicle otherwise than in conformity with accessibility regulations

6   (1)   If the Secretary of State thinks that a regulated rail vehicle has been used for carriage otherwise than in conformity with a provision of rail vehicle accessibility regulations with which the use of the vehicle is required to conform, the Secretary of State may give the operator of the vehicle a notice –

(a)   identifying the provision and how it was breached;
(b)   identifying each vehicle operated by the operator that is covered by the notice;
(c)   specifying the improvement deadline.

(2)   The improvement deadline may not be earlier than the end of the prescribed period beginning with the day the notice is given.

(3)   Sub-paragraph (4) applies if –

(a)   the Secretary of State has given a notice under sub-paragraph (1),
(b)   the improvement deadline specified in the notice has passed, and
(c)   the Secretary of State thinks that a vehicle covered by the notice has after that deadline been used for carriage otherwise than in conformity with the provision identified in the notice.

(4)   The Secretary of State may give the operator a further notice –

(a)   identifying the provision and how it was breached;

(b)   identifying each vehicle operated by the operator that is covered by the further notice;

(c)   specifying the final deadline.

(5)   The final deadline may not be earlier than the end of the prescribed period beginning with the day the further notice is given.

(6)   The Secretary of State may require the operator to pay a penalty if –

(a)   the Secretary of State has given notice under sub-paragraph (4), and

(b)   a vehicle covered by the notice is at a time after the final deadline used for carriage otherwise than in conformity with the provision identified in the notice.

Inspection of rail vehicles

7   (1)   If the condition in sub-paragraph (2) is satisfied, a person authorised by the Secretary of State (an 'inspector') may inspect a regulated rail vehicle for conformity with provisions of the accessibility regulations with which it is required to conform.

(2)   The condition is that the Secretary of State –

(a)   has reasonable grounds for suspecting that the vehicle does not conform with such provisions, or

(b)   has given a notice under paragraph 5(1) or (4) relating to the vehicle.

(3)   For the purpose of exercising the power under sub-paragraph (1) an inspector may –

(a)   enter premises if the inspector has reasonable grounds for suspecting that the vehicle is at the premises;

(b)   enter the vehicle;

(c)   require any person to afford such facilities and assistance with respect to matters under the person's control as are necessary to enable the inspector to exercise the power.

(4)   An inspector must, if required to do so, produce evidence of the Secretary of State's authorisation.

(5)   For the purposes of paragraph 5(1) the Secretary of State may draw such inferences as appear proper from any obstruction of the exercise of the power under sub-paragraph (1).

(6)   Sub-paragraphs (7) and (8) apply if the power under sub-paragraph (1) is exercisable by virtue of sub-paragraph (2)(b).

(7)   The Secretary of State may treat paragraph 5(3)(c) as satisfied in relation to a vehicle if –

(a)   the inspector takes steps to exercise the power after a notice is given under paragraph 5(1) but before a notice is given under paragraph 5(4), and

(b)   a person obstructs the exercise of the power.

(8)   The Secretary of State may require the operator of a vehicle to pay a penalty if –

(a)   the operator, or a person acting on the operator's behalf, intentionally obstructs the exercise of the power, and

(b)   the obstruction occurs after a notice has been given under paragraph 5(4) in respect of the vehicle.

(9)   In this paragraph 'inspect' includes test.

Supplementary powers

8   (1)   For the purposes of paragraph 5 the Secretary of State may give notice to a person requiring the person to supply the Secretary of State by a time specified in the notice with a vehicle number or other identifier for a rail vehicle –

(a)   of which the person is the operator, and
(b)   which is specified in the notice.

(2)   The time specified may not be earlier than the end of the period of 14 days beginning with the day the notice is given.

(3)   If the person does not comply with the notice, the Secretary of State may require the person to pay a penalty.

(4)   If the Secretary of State has given a notice to a person under paragraph 5(1) or 6(1), the Secretary of State may request the person to supply the Secretary of State, by a time specified in the request, with a statement detailing the steps taken in response to the notice.

(5)   The time specified may not be earlier than the improvement deadline.

(6)   The Secretary of State may treat paragraph 5(3)(c) or (as the case may be) paragraph 6(3)(c) as being satisfied in relation to a vehicle if a request under sub-paragraph (4) is not complied with by the time specified.

Penalties: amount, due date and recovery

9   (1)   In this paragraph and paragraphs 10 to 12 'penalty' means a penalty under this Schedule.

(2)   The amount of a penalty must not exceed whichever is the lesser of –

(a)   the maximum prescribed for the purposes of this sub-paragraph;
(b)   10% of the turnover of the person on whom it is imposed.

(3)   Turnover is to be determined by such means as are prescribed.

(4)   A penalty must be paid to the Secretary of State before the end of the prescribed period.

(5)   A sum payable as a penalty may be recovered as a debt due to the Secretary of State.

(6)   In proceedings for recovery of a penalty no question may be raised as to –

(a)   liability to the penalty;
(b)   its amount.

(7)   Sums paid to the Secretary of State as a penalty must be paid into the Consolidated Fund.

Penalties: code of practice

10 (1)   The Secretary of State must issue a code of practice specifying matters to be considered in determining the amount of a penalty.

(2)   The Secretary of State may –

(a)   revise the whole or part of the code;
(b)   issue the code as revised.

(3)   Before issuing the code the Secretary of State must lay a draft of it before Parliament.

(4)   After laying the draft before Parliament, the Secretary of State may bring the code into operation by order.

(5)   The Secretary of State must have regard to the code and any other relevant matter –

(a)   when imposing a penalty;
(b)   when considering an objection under paragraph 11.

(6)   In sub-paragraphs (3) to (5) a reference to the code includes a reference to the code as revised.

Penalties: procedure

11 (1)   If the Secretary of State decides that a person is liable to a penalty the Secretary of State must notify the person.

(2)   The notification must –

(a)   state the Secretary of State's reasons for the decision;
(b)   state the amount of the penalty;
(c)   specify the date by which and manner in which the penalty must be paid;
(d)   explain how the person may object to the penalty.

(3)   The person may give the Secretary of State notice of objection to the penalty on the ground that –

(a)   the person is not liable to the penalty, or
(b)   the amount of the penalty is too high.

(4)   A notice of objection must –

(a)   be in writing;
(b)   give the reasons for the objection;
(c)   be given before the end of the period prescribed for the purposes of this sub-paragraph.

(5)   On considering a notice of objection the Secretary of State may –

(a)   cancel the penalty;
(b)   reduce the amount of the penalty;
(c)   do neither of those things.

(6)   The Secretary of State must inform the objector of the decision under sub-paragraph (5) before the end of the period prescribed for the purposes of this sub-paragraph (or such longer period as is agreed with the objector).

Penalties: appeals

12 (1)   A person may appeal to the court against a penalty on the ground that –

(a)   the person is not liable to the penalty;
(b)   the amount of the penalty is too high.

(2)   The court may –

(a)   allow the appeal and cancel the penalty;
(b)   allow the appeal and reduce the amount of the penalty;
(c)   dismiss the appeal.

(3)   An appeal under this section is a re-hearing of the Secretary of State's decision and is to be determined having regard to –

(a)   any code of practice under paragraph 10 which has effect at the time of the appeal;
(b)   any other matter which the court thinks is relevant (whether or not the Secretary of State was aware of it).

(4)   An appeal may be brought under this section whether or not –

(a)   the person has given notice of objection under paragraph 11(3);
(b)   the penalty has been reduced under paragraph 11(5).

(5)   In this section 'the court' is –

(a)   in England and Wales, a county court;

(b)   in Scotland, the sheriff.

(6)   The sheriff may transfer the proceedings to the Court of Session.

(7)   If the sheriff makes a determination under sub-paragraph (2), a party to the proceedings may appeal against the determination on a point of law to –

(a)   the Sheriff Principal, or

(b)   the Court of Session.

Forgery, etc.

13   (1)   Section 188 has effect –

(a)   as if a compliance certificate were a 'relevant document ;

(b)   as if subsection (4) included a reference to a compliance certificate.

(2)   A person commits an offence by pretending, with intent to deceive, to be a person authorised to exercise a power under paragraph 7.

(3)   A person guilty of an offence under sub-paragraph (2) is liable on summary conviction to a fine not exceeding level 4 on the standard scale.

Regulations

14   A power to make regulations under this Schedule is exercisable by the Secretary of State.

Interpretation

15   (1)   In this Schedule –

'compliance assessment' has the meaning given in paragraph 1(5);

'compliance certificate' has the meaning given in paragraph 1(2);

'operator', in relation to a rail vehicle, means the person having the management of the vehicle.

(2)   If an exemption order under section 183 authorises the use of a rail vehicle even though the vehicle does not conform with a provision of rail vehicle accessibility regulations, a reference in this Schedule to provisions of rail vehicle accessibility regulations with which the vehicle is required to conform does not, in relation to the vehicle, include a reference to that provision.

SCHEDULE 21   REASONABLE ADJUSTMENTS: SUPPLEMENTARY

(Section 189)

Preliminary

1   This Schedule applies for the purposes of Schedules 2, 4, 8, 13 and 15.

Binding obligations, etc.

2   (1)   This paragraph applies if –

(a)   a binding obligation requires A to obtain the consent of another person to an alteration of premises which A occupies,

(b)   where A is a controller of let premises, a binding obligation requires A to obtain the consent of another person to a variation of a term of the tenancy, or

(c)   where A is a responsible person in relation to common parts, a binding obligation requires A to obtain the consent of another person to an alteration of the common parts.

(2)   For the purpose of discharging a duty to make reasonable adjustments –

      (a)   it is always reasonable for A to have to take steps to obtain the consent, but

      (b)   it is never reasonable for A to have to make the alteration before the consent is obtained.

(3)   In this Schedule, a binding obligation is a legally binding obligation in relation to premises, however arising; but the reference to a binding obligation in sub-paragraph (1)(a) or (c) does not include a reference to an obligation imposed by a tenancy.

(4)   The steps referred to in sub-paragraph (2)(a) do not include applying to a court or tribunal.

Landlord's consent

3   (1)   This paragraph applies if –

      (a)   A occupies premises under a tenancy,

      (b)   A is proposing to make an alteration to the premises so as to comply with a duty to make reasonable adjustments, and

      (c)   but for this paragraph, A would not be entitled to make the alteration.

(2)   This paragraph also applies if –

      (a)   A is a responsible person in relation to common parts,

      (b)   A is proposing to make an alteration to the common parts so as to comply with a duty to make reasonable adjustments,

      (c)   A is the tenant of property which includes the common parts, and

      (d)   but for this paragraph, A would not be entitled to make the alteration.

(3)   The tenancy has effect as if it provided –

      (a)   for A to be entitled to make the alteration with the written consent of the landlord,

      (b)   for A to have to make a written application for that consent,

      (c)   for the landlord not to withhold the consent unreasonably, and

      (d)   for the landlord to be able to give the consent subject to reasonable conditions.

(4)   If a question arises as to whether A has made the alteration (and, accordingly, complied with a duty to make reasonable adjustments), any constraint attributable to the tenancy must be ignored unless A has applied to the landlord in writing for consent to the alteration.

(5)   For the purposes of sub-paragraph (1) or (2), A must be treated as not entitled to make the alteration if the tenancy –

      (a)   imposes conditions which are to apply if A makes an alteration, or

      (b)   entitles the landlord to attach conditions to a consent to the alteration.

Proceedings before county court or sheriff

4   (1)   This paragraph applies if, in a case within Part 3, 4, 6 or 7 of this Act –

      (a)   A has applied in writing to the landlord for consent to the alteration, and

      (b)   the landlord has refused to give consent or has given consent subject to a condition.

(2)   A (or a disabled person with an interest in the alteration being made) may refer the matter to a county court or, in Scotland, the sheriff.

(3)   The county court or sheriff must determine whether the refusal or condition is unreasonable.

(4)   If the county court or sheriff finds that the refusal or condition is unreasonable, the county court or sheriff –

(a)   may make such declaration as it thinks appropriate;
(b)   may make an order authorising A to make the alteration specified in the order (and requiring A to comply with such conditions as are so specified).

Joining landlord as party to proceedings

5   (1)   This paragraph applies to proceedings relating to a contravention of this Act by virtue of section 20.
(2)   A party to the proceedings may request the employment tribunal, county court or sheriff ('the judicial authority') to direct that the landlord is joined or sisted as a party to the proceedings.
(3)   The judicial authority –

(a)   must grant the request if it is made before the hearing of the complaint or claim begins;
(b)   may refuse the request if it is made after the hearing begins;
(c)   must refuse the request if it is made after the complaint or claim has been determined.

(4)   If the landlord is joined or sisted as a party to the proceedings, the judicial authority may determine whether –

(a)   the landlord has refused to consent to the alteration;
(b)   the landlord has consented subject to a condition;
(c)   the refusal or condition was unreasonable.

(5)   If the judicial authority finds that the refusal or condition was unreasonable, it –

(a)   may make such declaration as it thinks appropriate;
(b)   may make an order authorising A to make the alteration specified in the order (and requiring A to comply with such conditions as are so specified);
(c)   may order the landlord to pay compensation to the complainant or claimant.

(6)   An employment tribunal may act in reliance on sub-paragraph (5)(c) instead of, or in addition to, acting in reliance on section 124(2); but if it orders the landlord to pay compensation it must not do so in reliance on section 124(2).
(7)   If a county court or the sheriff orders the landlord to pay compensation, it may not order A to do so.

Regulations

6   (1)   Regulations may make provision as to circumstances in which a landlord is taken for the purposes of this Schedule to have –

(a)   withheld consent;
(b)   withheld consent reasonably;
(c)   withheld consent unreasonably.

(2)   Regulations may make provision as to circumstances in which a condition subject to which a landlord gives consent is taken –

(a)   to be reasonable;
(b)   to be unreasonable.

(3)   Regulations may make provision supplementing or modifying the preceding paragraphs of this Schedule, or provision made under this paragraph, in relation to a case where A's tenancy is a sub-tenancy.
(4)   Provision made by virtue of this paragraph may amend the preceding paragraphs of this Schedule.

Interpretation

7   An expression used in this Schedule and in Schedule 2, 4, 8, 13 or 15 has the same meaning in this Schedule as in that Schedule.

SCHEDULE 22   STATUTORY PROVISIONS

(Section 191)

Statutory authority

1   (1)   A person (P) does not contravene a provision specified in the first column of the table, so far as relating to the protected characteristic specified in the second column in respect of that provision, if P does anything P must do pursuant to a requirement specified in the third column.

Specified provision	Protected characteristic	Requirement
Parts 3 to 7	Age	A requirement of an enactment
Parts 3 to 7 and 12	Disability	A requirement of an enactment
		A relevant requirement or condition imposed by virtue of an enactment
Parts 3 to 7	Religion or belief	A requirement of an enactment
		A relevant requirement or condition imposed by virtue of an enactment
Section 29(6) and Parts 6 and 7	Sex	A requirement of an enactment
Parts 3, 4, 6 and 7	Sexual orientation	A requirement of an enactment
		A relevant requirement or condition imposed by virtue of an enactment

(2)   A reference in the table to Part 6 does not include a reference to that Part so far as relating to vocational training.

(3)   In this paragraph a reference to an enactment includes a reference to –

(a)   a Measure of the General Synod of the Church of England;

(b)   an enactment passed or made on or after the date on which this Act is passed.

(4)   In the table, a relevant requirement or condition is a requirement or condition imposed (whether before or after the passing of this Act) by –

(a)   a Minister of the Crown;

(b)   a member of the Scottish Executive;

(c)   the National Assembly for Wales (constituted by the Government of Wales Act 1998);

(d)   the Welsh Ministers, the First Minister for Wales or the Counsel General to the Welsh Assembly Government.

Protection of women

2   (1)   A person (P) does not contravene a specified provision only by doing in relation to a woman (W) anything P is required to do to comply with –

(a)   a pre-1975 Act enactment concerning the protection of women;

(b)   a relevant statutory provision (within the meaning of Part 1 of the Health and Safety at Work etc. Act 1974) if it is done for the purpose of the protection of W (or a description of women which includes W);

(c)   a requirement of a provision specified in Schedule 1 to the Employment Act 1989 (provisions concerned with protection of women at work).

(2)   The references to the protection of women are references to protecting women in relation to –

(a)   pregnancy or maternity, or

(b)   any other circumstances giving rise to risks specifically affecting women.

(3)   It does not matter whether the protection is restricted to women.

(4)   These are the specified provisions –

(a)   Part 5 (work);

(b)   Part 6 (education), so far as relating to vocational training.

(5)   A pre-1975 Act enactment is an enactment contained in –

(a)   an Act passed before the Sex Discrimination Act 1975;

(b)   an instrument approved or made by or under such an Act (including one approved or made after the passing of the 1975 Act).

(6)   If an Act repeals and re-enacts (with or without modification) a pre-1975 enactment then the provision re-enacted must be treated as being in a pre-1975 enactment.

(7)   For the purposes of sub-paragraph (1)(c), a reference to a provision in Schedule 1 to the Employment Act 1989 includes a reference to a provision for the time being having effect in place of it.

(8)   This paragraph applies only to the following protected characteristics –

(a)   pregnancy and maternity;

(b)   sex.

Educational appointments, etc: religious belief

3   (1)   A person does not contravene Part 5 (work) only by doing a relevant act in connection with the employment of another in a relevant position.

(2)   A relevant position is –

(a)   the head teacher or principal of an educational establishment;

(b)   the head, a fellow or other member of the academic staff of a college, or institution in the nature of a college, in a university;

(c)   a professorship of a university which is a canon professorship or one to which a canonry is annexed.

(3)   A relevant act is anything it is necessary to do to comply with –

(a)   a requirement of an instrument relating to the establishment that the head teacher or principal must be a member of a particular religious order;

(b)   a requirement of an instrument relating to the college or institution that the holder of the position must be a woman;

(c)   an Act or instrument in accordance with which the professorship is a canon professorship or one to which a canonry is annexed.

(4)   Sub-paragraph (3)(b) does not apply to an instrument taking effect on or after 16 January 1990 (the day on which section 5(3) of the Employment Act 1989 came into force).

(5)   A Minister of the Crown may by order provide that anything in sub-paragraphs (1) to (3) does not have effect in relation to –

(a)   a specified educational establishment or university;

(b)   a specified description of educational establishments.

(6)   An educational establishment is –

(a)   a school within the meaning of the Education Act 1996 or the Education (Scotland) Act 1980;

(b)   a college, or institution in the nature of a college, in a university;

(c)   an institution designated by order made, or having effect as if made, under section 129 of the Education Reform Act 1988;

(d)   a college of further education within the meaning of section 36 of the Further and Higher Education (Scotland) Act 1992;

(e)   a university in Scotland;

(f)   an institution designated by order under section 28 of the Further and Higher Education Act 1992 or section 44 of the Further and Higher Education (Scotland) Act 1992.

(7)   This paragraph does not affect paragraph 2 of Schedule 9.

4   A person does not contravene this Act only by doing anything which is permitted for the purposes of –

(a)   section 58(6) or (7) of the School Standards and Framework Act 1998 (dismissal of teachers because of failure to give religious education efficiently);

(b)   section 60(4) and (5) of that Act (religious considerations relating to certain appointments);

(c)   section 124A of that Act (preference for certain teachers at independent schools of a religious character).

Crown employment, etc.

5   (1)   A person does not contravene this Act –

(a)   by making or continuing in force rules mentioned in sub-paragraph (2);

(b)   by publishing, displaying or implementing such rules;

(c)   by publishing the gist of such rules.

(2)   The rules are rules restricting to persons of particular birth, nationality, descent or residence –

(a)   employment in the service of the Crown;

(b)   employment by a prescribed public body;

(c)   holding a public office (within the meaning of section 50).

(3)   The power to make regulations for the purpose of sub-paragraph (2)(b) is exercisable by the Minister for the Civil Service.

(4)   In this paragraph 'public body' means a body (whether corporate or unincorporated) exercising public functions (within the meaning given by section 31(4)).

SCHEDULE 23   GENERAL EXCEPTIONS

(Section 196)

Acts authorised by statute or the executive

1   (1)   This paragraph applies to anything done –

    (a)   in pursuance of an enactment;

    (b)   in pursuance of an instrument made by a member of the executive under an enactment;

    (c)   to comply with a requirement imposed (whether before or after the passing of this Act) by a member of the executive by virtue of an enactment;

    (d)   in pursuance of arrangements made (whether before or after the passing of this Act) by or with the approval of, or for the time being approved by, a Minister of the Crown;

    (e)   to comply with a condition imposed (whether before or after the passing of this Act) by a Minister of the Crown.

(2)   A person does not contravene Part 3, 4, 5 or 6 by doing anything to which this paragraph applies which discriminates against another because of the other's nationality.

(3)   A person (A) does not contravene Part 3, 4, 5 or 6 if, by doing anything to which this paragraph applies, A discriminates against another (B) by applying to B a provision, criterion or practice which relates to –

    (a)   B's place of ordinary residence;

    (b)   the length of time B has been present or resident in or outside the United Kingdom or an area within it.

Organisations relating to religion or belief

2   (1)   This paragraph applies to an organisation the purpose of which is –

    (a)   to practise a religion or belief,

    (b)   to advance a religion or belief,

    (c)   to teach the practice or principles of a religion or belief,

    (d)   to enable persons of a religion or belief to receive any benefit, or to engage in any activity, within the framework of that religion or belief, or

    (e)   to foster or maintain good relations between persons of different religions or beliefs.

(2)   This paragraph does not apply to an organisation whose sole or main purpose is commercial.

(3)   The organisation does not contravene Part 3, 4 or 7, so far as relating to religion or belief or sexual orientation, only by restricting –

    (a)   membership of the organisation;

    (b)   participation in activities undertaken by the organisation or on its behalf or under its auspices;

    (c)   the provision of goods, facilities or services in the course of activities undertaken by the organisation or on its behalf or under its auspices;

    (d)   the use or disposal of premises owned or controlled by the organisation.

(4)   A person does not contravene Part 3, 4 or 7, so far as relating to religion or belief or sexual orientation, only by doing anything mentioned in sub-paragraph (3) on behalf of or under the auspices of the organisation.

(5)   A minister does not contravene Part 3, 4 or 7, so far as relating to religion or belief or sexual orientation, only by restricting –

(a)   participation in activities carried on in the performance of the minister's functions in connection with or in respect of the organisation;

(b)   the provision of goods, facilities or services in the course of activities carried on in the performance of the minister's functions in connection with or in respect of the organisation.

(6)   Sub-paragraphs (3) to (5) permit a restriction relating to religion or belief only if it is imposed –

(a)   because of the purpose of the organisation, or

(b)   to avoid causing offence, on grounds of the religion or belief to which the organisation relates, to persons of that religion or belief.

(7)   Sub-paragraphs (3) to (5) permit a restriction relating to sexual orientation only if it is imposed –

(a)   because it is necessary to comply with the doctrine of the organisation, or

(b)   to avoid conflict with strongly held convictions within sub-paragraph (9).

(8)   In sub-paragraph (5), the reference to a minister is a reference to a minister of religion, or other person, who –

(a)   performs functions in connection with a religion or belief to which the organisation relates, and

(b)   holds an office or appointment in, or is accredited, approved or recognised for the purposes of the organisation.

(9)   The strongly held convictions are –

(a)   in the case of a religion, the strongly held religious convictions of a significant number of the religion's followers;

(b)   in the case of a belief, the strongly held convictions relating to the belief of a significant number of the belief's followers.

(10)   This paragraph does not permit anything which is prohibited by section 29, so far as relating to sexual orientation, if it is done –

(a)   on behalf of a public authority, and

(b)   under the terms of a contract between the organisation and the public authority.

(11)   In the application of this paragraph in relation to sexual orientation, sub-paragraph (1)(e) must be ignored.

(12)   In the application of this paragraph in relation to sexual orientation, in sub-paragraph (3)(d), 'disposal' does not include disposal of an interest in premises by way of sale if the interest being disposed of is –

(a)   the entirety of the organisation's interest in the premises, or

(b)   the entirety of the interest in respect of which the organisation has power of disposal.

(13)   In this paragraph –

(a)   'disposal' is to be construed in accordance with section 38;

(b)   'public authority' has the meaning given in section 150(1).

(c)   residential accommodation all or part of which should be used only by persons of the same sex because of the nature of the sanitary facilities serving the accommodation.

(7)   A benefit, facility or service is linked to communal accommodation if –

(a)   it cannot properly and effectively be provided except for those using the accommodation, and

(b)   a person could be refused use of the accommodation in reliance on sub-paragraph (1) (a).

(8)   This paragraph does not apply for the purposes of Part 5 (work) unless such arrangements as are reasonably practicable are made to compensate for –

(a)   in a case where sub-paragraph (1)(a) applies, the refusal of use of the accommodation;

(b)   in a case where sub-paragraph (1)(b) applies, the refusal of provision of the benefit, facility or service.

Communal accommodation

3   (1)   A person does not contravene this Act, so far as relating to sex discrimination or gender reassignment discrimination, only because of anything done in relation to –

(a)   the admission of persons to communal accommodation;

(b)   the provision of a benefit, facility or service linked to the accommodation.

(2)   Sub-paragraph (1)(a) does not apply unless the accommodation is managed in a way which is as fair as possible to both men and women.

(3)   In applying sub-paragraph (1)(a), account must be taken of –

(a)   whether and how far it is reasonable to expect that the accommodation should be altered or extended or that further accommodation should be provided, and

(b)   the frequency of the demand or need for use of the accommodation by persons of one sex as compared with those of the other.

(4)   In applying sub-paragraph (1)(a) in relation to gender reassignment, account must also be taken of whether and how far the conduct in question is a proportionate means of achieving a legitimate aim.

(5)   Communal accommodation is residential accommodation which includes dormitories or other shared sleeping accommodation which for reasons of privacy should be used only by persons of the same sex.

(6)   Communal accommodation may include –

(a)   shared sleeping accommodation for men and for women;

(b)   ordinary sleeping accommodation;

(c)   residential accommodation all or part of which should be used only by persons of the same sex because of the nature of the sanitary facilities serving the accommodation.

(7)   A benefit, facility or service is linked to communal accommodation if –

(a)   it cannot properly and effectively be provided except for those using the accommodation, and

(b)   a person could be refused use of the accommodation in reliance on sub-paragraph (1)(a).

(8)   This paragraph does not apply for the purposes of Part 5 (work) unless such arrangements as are reasonably practicable are made to compensate for –

(a)   in a case where sub-paragraph (1)(a) applies, the refusal of use of the accommodation;

(b)   in a case where sub-paragraph (1)(b) applies, the refusal of provision of the benefit, facility or service.

Training provided to non-EEA residents, etc.

4   (1)   A person (A) does not contravene this Act, so far as relating to nationality, only by providing a non-resident (B) with training, if A thinks that B does not intend to exercise in Great Britain skills B obtains as a result.

(2)   A non-resident is a person who is not ordinarily resident in an EEA state.

(3)   The reference to providing B with training is –

(a)   if A employs B in relevant employment, a reference to doing anything in or in connection with the employment;

(b)   if A as a principal allows B to do relevant contract work, a reference to doing anything in or in connection with allowing B to do the work;

(c)   in a case within paragraph (a) or (b) or any other case, a reference to affording B access to facilities for education or training or ancillary benefits.

(4)   Employment or contract work is relevant if its sole or main purpose is the provision of training in skills.

(5)   In the case of training provided by the armed forces or Secretary of State for purposes relating to defence, sub-paragraph (1) has effect as if –

(a)   the reference in sub-paragraph (2) to an EEA state were a reference to Great Britain, and

(b)   in sub-paragraph (4), for 'its sole or main purpose is' there were substituted 'it is for purposes including'.

(6)   'Contract work' and 'principal' each have the meaning given in section 41.

SCHEDULE 24   HARMONISATION: EXCEPTIONS

(Section 203)

Part 1 (public sector duty regarding socio-economic inequalities)

Chapter 2 of Part 5 (occupational pensions)

Section 78 (gender pay gap)

Section 106 (election candidates: diversity information)

Chapters 1 to 3 and 5 of Part 9 (enforcement), except section 136

Sections 142 and 146 (unenforceable terms, declaration in respect of void terms)

Chapter 1 of Part 11 (public sector equality duty)

Part 12 (disabled persons: transport)

Part 13 (disability: miscellaneous)

Section 197 (power to specify age exceptions)

Part 15 (family property)

Part 16 (general and miscellaneous)

Schedule 1 (disability: supplementary provision)

In Schedule 3 (services and public functions: exceptions) –

(a)   in Part 3 (health and care), paragraphs 13 and 14;

(b)   Part 4 (immigration);

(c)   Part 5 (insurance);

(d)   Part 6 (marriage);

(e)   Part 7 (separate and single services), except paragraph 30;

(f)   Part 8 (television, radio and on-line broadcasting and distribution);

(g)   Part 9 (transport);
(h)   Part 10 (supplementary)

Schedule 4 (premises: reasonable adjustments)

Schedule 5 (premises: exceptions), except paragraph 1

Schedule 6 (office-holders: excluded offices), except so far as relating to colour or nationality or marriage and civil partnership

Schedule 8 (work: reasonable adjustments)

In Schedule 9 (work: exceptions) –
(a)   Part 1 (general), except so far as relating to colour or nationality;
(b)   Part 2 (exceptions relating to age);
(c)   Part 3 (other exceptions), except paragraph 19 so far as relating to colour or nationality

Schedule 10 (education: accessibility for disabled pupils)

Schedule 13 (education: reasonable adjustments), except paragraphs 2, 5, 5 and 9

Schedule 17 (education: disabled pupils: enforcement)

Schedule 18 (public sector equality duty: exceptions)

Schedule 19 (list of public authorities)

Schedule 20 (rail vehicle accessibility: compliance)

Schedule 21 (reasonable adjustments: supplementary)

In Schedule 22 (exceptions: statutory provisions), paragraphs 2 and 5

Schedule 23 (general exceptions), except paragraph 2

Schedule 25 (information society services)

SCHEDULE 25   INFORMATION SOCIETY SERVICES

(Section 206)

Service providers

1   (1)   This paragraph applies where a person concerned with the provision of an information society service (an 'information society service provider') is established in Great Britain.
     (2)   This Act applies to anything done by the person in an EEA state (other than the United Kingdom) in providing the service as this Act would apply if the act in question were done by the person in Great Britain.

2   (1)   This paragraph applies where an information society service provider is established in an EEA state (other than the United Kingdom).
     (2)   This Act does not apply to anything done by the person in providing the service.

Exceptions for mere conduits

3   (1)   An information society service provider does not contravene this Act only by providing so much of an information society service as consists in –

     (a)   the provision of access to a communication network, or
     (b)   the transmission in a communication network of information provided by the recipient of the service.

     (2)   But sub-paragraph (1) applies only if the service provider does not –

(a)   initiate the transmission,
(b)   select the recipient of the transmission, or
(c)   select or modify the information contained in the transmission.

(3)   For the purposes of sub-paragraph (1), the provision of access to a communication network, and the transmission of information in a communication network, includes the automatic, intermediate and transient storage of the information transmitted so far as the storage is solely for the purpose of carrying out the transmission in the network.

(4)   Sub-paragraph (3) does not apply if the information is stored for longer than is reasonably necessary for the transmission.

Exception for caching

4   (1)   This paragraph applies where an information society service consists in the transmission in a communication network of information provided by a recipient of the service.

(2)   The information society service provider does not contravene this Act only by doing anything in connection with the automatic, intermediate and temporary storage of information so provided if –

(a)   the storage of the information is solely for the purpose of making more efficient the onward transmission of the information to other recipients of the service at their request, and
(b)   the condition in sub-paragraph (3) is satisfied.

(3)   The condition is that the service-provider –

(a)   does not modify the information,
(b)   complies with such conditions as are attached to having access to the information, and
(c)   (where sub-paragraph (4) applies) expeditiously removes the information or disables access to it.

(4)   This sub-paragraph applies if the service-provider obtains actual knowledge that –

(a)   the information at the initial source of the transmission has been removed from the network,
(b)   access to it has been disabled, or
(c)   a court or administrative authority has required the removal from the network of, or the disablement of access to, the information.

Exception for hosting

5   (1)   An information society service provider does not contravene this Act only by doing anything in providing so much of an information society service as consists in the storage of information provided by a recipient of the service, if –

(a)   the service provider had no actual knowledge when the information was provided that its provision amounted to a contravention of this Act, or
(b)   on obtaining actual knowledge that the provision of the information amounted to a contravention of that section, the service provider expeditiously removed the information or disabled access to it.

(2)   Sub-paragraph (1) does not apply if the recipient of the service is acting under the authority of the control of the service provider.

Monitoring obligations

6   An injunction or interdict under Part 1 of the Equality Act 2006 may not impose on a person concerned with the provision of a service of a description given in paragraph 3(1), 4(1) or 5(1) –

    (a)   a liability the imposition of which would contravene Article 12, 13 or 14 of the E-Commerce Directive;

    (b)   a general obligation of the description given in Article 15 of that Directive.

Interpretation

7   (1)   This paragraph applies for the purposes of this Schedule.

    (2)   'Information society service' –

        (a)   has the meaning given in Article 2(a) of the E-Commerce Directive (which refers to Article 1(2) of Directive 98/34/EC of the European Parliament and of the Council of 22 June 1998 laying down a procedure for the provision of information in the field of technical standards and regulations), and

        (b)   is summarised in recital 17 of the E-Commerce Directive as covering 'any service normally provided for remuneration, at a distance, by means of electronic equipment for the processing (including digital compression) and storage of data, and at the individual request of a recipient of a service'.

    (3)   'The E-Commerce Directive' means Directive 2000/31/EC of the European Parliament and of the Council of 8 June 2000 on certain legal aspects of information society services, in particular electronic commerce, in the Internal Market (Directive on electronic commerce).

    (4)   'Recipient' means a person who (whether for professional purposes or not) uses an information society service, in particular for seeking information or making it accessible.

    (5)   An information society service-provider is 'established' in a country or territory if the service-provider –

        (a)   effectively pursues an economic activity using a fixed establishment in that country or territory for an indefinite period, and

        (b)   is a national of an EEA state or a body mentioned in Article 48 of the EEC treaty.

    (6)   The presence or use in a particular place of equipment or other technical means of providing an information society service is not itself sufficient to constitute the establishment of a service-provider.

    (7)   Where it cannot be decided from which of a number of establishments an information society service is provided, the service is to be regarded as provided from the establishment at the centre of the information society service provider's activities relating to that service.

    (8)   Section 212(4) does not apply to references to providing a service.

SCHEDULE 26   AMENDMENTS

(Section 211)

Local Government Act 1988

1   Part 2 of the Local Government Act 1988 (public supply or works contracts) is amended as follows.

2   In section 17 (local and other public authority contracts: exclusion of non-commercial considerations) –

(a)   omit subsection (9), and
(b)   after that subsection insert –

'(10)   This section does not prevent a public authority to which it applies from exercising any function regulated by this section with reference to a non-commercial matter to the extent that the authority considers it necessary or expedient to do so to enable or facilitate compliance with –

(a)   the duty imposed on it by section 149 of the Equality Act 2010 (public sector equality duty), or
(b)   any duty imposed on it by regulations under section 153 or 154 of that Act (powers to impose specific duties).'

3   Omit section 18 (exceptions to section 17 relating to race relations matters).
4   In section 19 (provisions supplementary to or consequential on section 17) omit subsection (10).

Employment Act 1989

5   (1)   Section 12 of the Employment Act 1989 (Sikhs: requirements as to safety helmets) is amended as follows.
(2)   In subsection (1), for 'requirement or condition', in the first three places, substitute 'provision, criterion or practice'.
(3)   In that subsection, for the words from 'section 1(1)(b)' to the end substitute 'section 19 of the Equality Act 2010 (indirect discrimination), the provision, criterion or practice is to be taken as one in relation to which the condition in subsection (2)(d) of that section (proportionate means of achieving a legitimate aim) is satisfied'.
(4)   In subsection (2), for the words from 'the Race Relations Act' to the end substitute 'section 13 of the Equality Act 2010 as giving rise to discrimination against any other person'.

Equality Act 2006

6   The Equality Act 2006 is amended as follows.

7   (1)   Section 8 (equality and diversity) is amended as follows.
(2)   In subsection (1) –

(a)   in paragraph (d) for 'equality enactments' substitute 'Equality Act 2010', and
(b)   in paragraph (e) for 'the equality enactments' substitute 'that Act'.

(3)   In subsection (4) for 'Disability Discrimination Act 1995 (c. 50)' substitute 'Equality Act 2010'.

8   In section 10(2) (meaning of group) for paragraph (d) substitute –

'(d)   gender reassignment (within the meaning of section 7 of the Equality Act 2010),'.

9   For section 11(3)(c) (interpretation) substitute –

'(c)   a reference to the equality and human rights enactments is a reference to the Human Rights Act 1998, this Act and the Equality Act 2010.'

10   (1)   Section 14 (codes of practice) is amended as follows.
(2)   For subsection (1) substitute –

'(1)   The Commission may issue a code of practice in connection with any matter addressed by the Equality Act 2010.'

(3)   In subsection (2)(a) for 'a provision or enactment listed in subsection (1)' substitute 'the Equality Act 2010 or an enactment made under that Act'.

(4)   In subsection (3) –

    (a)   in paragraph (a) for 'section 49G(7) of the Disability Discrimination Act 1995 (c. 50)' substitute 'section 190(7) of the Equality Act 2010', and

    (b)   for paragraph (c)(iv) substitute –

    '(iv)   section 190 of the Equality Act 2010.'

(5)   In subsection (5)(a) for 'listed in subsection (1)' substitute 'a matter addressed by the Equality Act 2010'.

(6)   In subsection (9) for 'section 76A' to 'duties)' substitute 'section 149, 153 or 154 of the Equality Act 2010 (public sector equality duty)'.

11   In section 16(4) (inquiries: matters which the Commission may consider and report on) for 'equality enactments' substitute 'Equality Act 2010'.

12   In section 21(2)(b) (unlawful act notice: specification of legislative provision) for 'equality enactments' substitute 'Equality Act 2010'.

13   After section 24 insert –

'24A   Enforcement powers: supplemental

    (1)   This section has effect in relation to –

        (a)   an act which is unlawful because, by virtue of any of sections 13 to 18 of the Equality Act 2010, it amounts to a contravention of any of Parts 3, 4, 5, 6 or 7 of that Act,

        (b)   an act which is unlawful because it amounts to a contravention of section 60(1) of that Act (or to a contravention of section 111 or 112 of that Act that relates to a contravention of section 60(1) of that Act) (enquiries about disability and health),

        (c)   an act which is unlawful because it amounts to a contravention of section 106 of that Act (information about diversity in range of election candidates etc.),

        (d)   an act which is unlawful because, by virtue of section 108(1) of that Act, it amounts to a contravention of any of Parts 3, 4, 5, 6 or 7 of that Act, or

        (e)   the application of a provision, criterion or practice which, by virtue of section 19 of that Act, amounts to a contravention of that Act.

    (2)   For the purposes of sections 20 to 24 of this Act, it is immaterial whether the Commission knows or suspects that a person has been or may be affected by the unlawful act or application.

    (3)   For those purposes, an unlawful act includes making arrangements to act in a particular way which would, if applied to an individual, amount to a contravention mentioned in subsection (1)(a).

    (4)   Nothing in this Act affects the entitlement of a person to bring proceedings under the Equality Act 2010 in respect of a contravention mentioned in subsection (1).'

14   Omit section 25 (restraint of unlawful advertising etc.).

15   Omit section 26 (supplemental).

16   (1)   Section 27 (conciliation) is amended as follows.

    (2)   For subsection (1) (disputes in relation to which the Commission may make arrangements for the provision of conciliation services) substitute –

'(1)   The Commission may make arrangements for the provision of conciliation services for disputes in respect of which proceedings have been or could be determined by virtue of section 114 of the Equality Act 2010.'

17 (1)   Section 28 (legal assistance) is amended as follows.

    (2)   In subsection (1) –

        (a)   in paragraph (a) for 'equality enactments' substitute 'Equality Act 2010', and

        (b)   in paragraph (b) for 'the equality enactments' substitute 'that Act'.

    (3)   In subsection (5) for 'Part V of the Disability Discrimination Act 1995 (c. 50) (public' substitute 'Part 12 of the Equality Act 2010 (disabled persons:'.

    (4)   In subsection (6) –

        (a)   for 'the equality enactments', on the first occasion it appears, substitute 'the Equality Act 2010', and

        (b)   for 'the equality enactments', on each other occasion it appears, substitute 'that Act'.

    (5)   In subsection (7) –

        (a)   in paragraph (a) for 'equality enactments' substitute 'Equality Act 2010', and

        (b)   in paragraph (b) for 'the equality enactments' substitute 'that Act'.

    (6)   In subsection (8) for 'Part V of the Disability Discrimination Act 1995 (c. 50)' substitute 'Part 12 of the Equality Act 2010'.

    (7)   In subsection (9) for 'equality enactments' substitute 'Equality Act 2010'.

    (8)   In subsection (12) –

        (a)   for 'A reference in' to 'includes a reference' substitute 'This section applies', and

        (b)   after paragraph (b) add 'as it applies to the Equality Act 2010.'

18 For section 31(1) (duties in respect of which Commission may assess compliance) substitute –

    '(1)   The Commission may assess the extent to which or the manner in which a person has complied with a duty under or by virtue of section 149, 153 or 154 of the Equality Act 2010 (public sector equality duty).'

19 (1)   Section 32 (public sector duties: compliance notice) is amended as follows.

    (2)   For subsection (1) substitute –

    '(1)   This section applies where the Commission thinks that a person has failed to comply with a duty under or by virtue of section 149, 153 or 154 of the Equality Act 2010 (public sector equality duty).'

    (3)   In subsection (4) for 'section 76A' to 'Disability Discrimination Act 1995' substitute 'section 149 of the Equality Act 2010'.

    (4)   In subsection (9)(a) for 'section 76A' to 'Disability Discrimination Act 1995 (c. 50)' substitute 'section 149 of the Equality Act 2010'.

    (5)   In subsection (9)(b) for 'in any other case' substitute 'where the notice related to a duty by virtue of section 153 or 154 of that Act'.

    (6)   In subsection (11) for 'section 76B' to 'Disability Discrimination Act 1995' substitute 'section 153 or 154 of the Equality Act 2010'.

20 Omit section 33 (equality and human rights enactments).

21 (1)   Section 34 (meaning of unlawful) is amended as follows.

    (2)   In subsection (1) for 'equality enactments' substitute 'Equality Act 2010'.

    (3)   In subsection (2) –

      (a)   after 'virtue of' insert 'any of the following provisions of the Equality Act 2010', and

      (b)   for paragraphs (a) to (c) substitute –

           '(a)   section 1 (public sector duty regarding socio-economic inequalities),

           (b)   section 149, 153 or 154 (public sector equality duty),

           (c)   Part 12 (disabled persons: transport), or

           (d)   section 190 (disability: improvements to let dwelling houses).'

22   (1)   Section 35 (general: definitions) is amended as follows.

      (2)   In the definition of 'religion or belief', for 'Part 2 (as defined by section 44)' substitute 'section 10 of the Equality Act 2010'.

      (3)   For the definition of 'sexual orientation' substitute –

           '"sexual orientation" has the same meaning as in section 12 of the Equality Act 2010.'

23   In section 39(4) (orders subject to affirmative resolution procedure) for ', 27(10) or 33(3)' substitute 'or 27(10)'.

24   Omit section 43 (transitional: rented housing in Scotland).

25   Omit Part 2 (discrimination on grounds of religion or belief).

26   Omit section 81 (regulations).

27   Omit Part 4 (public functions).

28   In section 94(3) (extent: Northern Ireland) –

      (a)   omit 'and 41 to 56', and

      (b)   omit 'and the Disability Discrimination Act 1995 (c. 50)'.

29   (1)   Schedule 1 (the Commission: constitution, etc.) is amended as follows.

      (2)   In paragraph 52(3)(a) for 'Parts 1, 3, 4, 5 and 5B of the Disability Discrimination Act 1995 (c. 50)' substitute 'Parts 2, 3, 4, 6, 7, 12 and 13 of the Equality Act 2010, in so far as they relate to disability'.

      (3)   In paragraph 53 for 'Part 2 of the Disability Discrimination Act 1995 (c. 50)' substitute 'Part 5 of the Equality Act 2010'.

      (4)   In paragraph 54 for 'Part 2 of the Disability Discrimination Act 1995' substitute 'Part 5 of the Equality Act 2010'.

30   In Schedule 3 (consequential amendments), omit paragraphs 6 to 35 and 41 to 56.

SCHEDULE 27   REPEALS AND REVOCATIONS

(Section 211)

PART 1   REPEALS

Short title	Extent of repeal
Equal Pay Act 1970	The whole Act.
Sex Discrimination Act 1975	The whole Act.
Race Relations Act 1976	The whole Act.
Sex Discrimination Act 1986	The whole Act.

Short title	Extent of repeal
Local Government Act 1988	Section 17(9).
	Section 18.
	Section 19(10).
Employment Act 1989	Sections 1 to 7.
	Section 9.
Social Security Act 1989	In Schedule 5, paragraph 5.
Disability Discrimination Act 1995	The whole Act.
Pensions Act 1995	Sections 62 to 65.
Greater London Authority Act 1999	Section 404.
Sex Discrimination (Election Candidates) Act 2002	Section 1.
Civil Partnership Act 2004	Section 6(1)(b) and (2).
Education (Additional Support for Learning) (Scotland) Act 2004	In section 17(1) 'to exercise the functions which are conferred on a Tribunal by virtue of this Act'.
Equality Act 2006	Section 25.
	Section 26.
	Section 33.
	Section 43.
	Part 2.
	Section 81.
	Part 4.
	In section 94(3) 'and 41 to 56' and 'and the Disability Discrimination Act 1995 (c. 50)'.
	In Schedule 3 – (a) paragraphs 6 to 35; (b) paragraphs 41 to 56.

PART 2   REVOCATIONS

Title	Extent of revocation
Occupational Pension Schemes (Equal Treatment) Regulations 1995 (S.I. 1995/3183)	The whole Regulations.

Title	Extent of revocation
Employment Equality (Religion or Belief) Regulations 2003 (S.I. 2003/1660)	The whole Regulations.
Employment Equality (Sexual Orientation) Regulations 2003 (S.I. 2003/1661)	The whole Regulations.
Disability Discrimination Act 1995 (Pensions) Regulations 2003 (S.I. 2003/2770)	The whole Regulations.
Occupational Pension Schemes (Equal Treatment) (Amendment) Regulations 2005 (S.I. 2005/1923)	The whole Regulations.
Employment Equality (Age) Regulations 2006 (S.I. 2006/1031)	The whole Regulations (other than Schedules 6 and 8).
Equality Act (Sexual Orientation) Regulations 2007 (S.I. 2007/1263)	The whole Regulations.
Sex Discrimination (Amendment of Legislation) Regulations 2008 (S.I. 2008/963)	The whole Regulations.

SCHEDULE 28   INDEX OF DEFINED EXPRESSIONS

(Section 214)

Expression	Provision
Accrual of rights, in relation to an occupational pension scheme	Section 212(12)
Additional maternity leave	Section 213(6) and (7)
Additional maternity leave period	Section 213(8)
Age discrimination	Section 25(1)
Age group	Section 5(2)
Armed forces	Section 212(1)
Association	Section 107(2)
Auxiliary aid	Section 20(11)
Belief	Section 10(2)
Breach of an equality clause or rule	Section 212(8)
The Commission	Section 212(1)
Commonhold	Section 38(7)

Expression	Provision
Compulsory maternity leave	Section 213(3)
Contract work	Section 41(6)
Contract worker	Section 41(7)
Contravention of this Act	Section 212(9)
Crown employment	Section 83(9)
Detriment	Section 212(1) and (5)
Disability	Section 6(1)
Disability discrimination	Section 25(2)
Disabled person	Section 6(2) and (4)
Discrimination	Sections 13 to 19, 21 and 108
Disposal, in relation to premises	Section 38(3) to (5)
Education Acts	Section 212(1)
Employer, in relation to an occupational pension scheme	Section 212(11)
Employment	Section 212(1)
Enactment	Section 212(1)
Equality clause	Section 212(1)
Equality rule	Section 212(1)
Firm	Section 46(2)
Gender reassignment	Section 7(1)
Gender reassignment discrimination	Section 25(3)
Harassment	Section 26(1)
Independent educational institution	Section 89(7)
LLP	Section 46(4)
Man	Section 212(1)
Marriage and civil partnership	Section 8
Marriage and civil partnership discrimination	Section 25(4)
Maternity equality clause	Section 212(1)
Maternity equality rule	Section 212(1)
Maternity leave	Section 213(2)
Member, in relation to an occupational pension scheme	Section 212(10)

Expression	Provision
Member of the executive	Section 212(7)
Non-discrimination rule	Section 212(1)
Occupation, in relation to premises	Section 212(6)
Occupational pension scheme	Section 212(1)
Offshore work	Section 82(3)
Ordinary maternity leave	Section 213(4) and (5)
Parent	Section 212(1)
Pension credit member	Section 212(11)
Pensionable service	Section 212(11)
Pensioner member	Section 212(11)
Personal office	Section 49(2)
Physical feature	Section 20(10)
Pregnancy and maternity discrimination	Section 25(5)
Premises	Section 38(2)
Prescribed	Section 212(1)
Profession	Section 212(1)
Proposed firm	Section 46(3)
Proposed LLP	Section 46(5)
Proprietor, in relation to a school	Section 89(4)
Protected characteristics	Section 4
Protected period, in relation to pregnancy	Section 18(6)
Provision of a service	Sections 31 and 212(4)
Public function	Sections 31(4) and 150(5)
Public office	Sections 50(2) and 52(4)
Pupil	Section 89(3)
Race	Section 9(1)
Race discrimination	Section 25(6)
Reasonable adjustments, duty to make	Section 20
Relevant member of the House of Commons staff	Section 83(5)
Relevant member of the House of Lords staff	Section 83(6)

Expression	Provision
Relevant person, in relation to a personal or public office	Section 52(6)
Religion	Section 10(1)
Religious or belief-related discrimination	Section 25(7)
Requirement, the first, second or third	Section 20
Responsible body, in relation to a further or higher education institution	Section 91(12)
Responsible body, in relation to a school	Section 85(9)
School	Section 89(5) and (6)
Service-provider	Section 29(1)
Sex	Section 11
Sex discrimination	Section 25(8)
Sex equality clause	Section 212(1)
Sex equality rule	Section 212(1)
Sexual orientation	Section 12(1)
Sexual orientation discrimination	Section 25(9)
Student	Section 94(3)
Subordinate legislation	Section 212(1)
Substantial	Section 212(1)
Taxi, for the purposes of Part 3 (services and public functions)	Schedule 2, paragraph 4
Taxi, for the purposes of Chapter 1 of Part 12 (disabled persons: transport)	Section 173(1)
Tenancy	Section 38(6)
Trade	Section 212(1)
Transsexual person	Section 7(2)
Trustees or managers, in relation to an occupational pension scheme	Section 212(11)
University	Section 94(4)
Victimisation	Section 27(1)
Vocational training	Section 56(6)
Woman	Section 212(1)

INDEX